THE CAMBRIDGE COMPANION TO
ALLEGORY

Allegory is a vast subject, and its history can be daunting to students and even advanced scholars venturing outside their own historical specializations. This *Companion* will present, lucidly, systematically, and expertly, the various threads that comprise the allegorical tradition over its entire chronological range. Beginning with Greek antiquity, the volume shows how the earliest systems of allegory arose in poetry dealing with philosophy, mystery religions, and hermeneutics. Once the earliest histories and themes of the allegorical tradition have been presented, the volume turns to literary, intellectual, and cultural manifestations of allegory through the Middle Ages and the Renaissance. The essays in the last section address literary and theoretical approaches to allegory in the modern era, from reactions to allegory in the eighteenth and nineteenth centuries to reevaluations of its power in the thought of the twentieth century and beyond.

A complete list of books in the series is at the back of this book.

D1593604

THE CAMBRIDGE
COMPANION TO
ALLEGORY

EDITED BY
RITA COPELAND
University of Pennsylvania

and

PETER T. STRUCK
University of Pennsylvania

CAMBRIDGE
UNIVERSITY PRESS

CAMBRIDGE UNIVERSITY PRESS
Cambridge, New York, Melbourne, Madrid, Cape Town, Singapore,
São Paulo, Delhi, Dubai, Tokyo

Cambridge University Press
The Edinburgh Building, Cambridge CB2 8RU, UK

Published in the United States of America by Cambridge University Press, New York

www.cambridge.org
Information on this title: www.cambridge.org/9780521680820

© Cambridge University Press 2010

First published 2010

Printed in the United Kingdom at the University Press, Cambridge

A catalog record for this publication is available from the British Library

Library of Congress Cataloguing in Publication data
The Cambridge companion to allegory / edited by Rita Copeland and Peter Struck.
p.   cm. – (Cambridge companions to literature)
Includes index.
ISBN 978-0-521-86229-5 (hardback)
1. Allegory.   I. Copeland, Rita.   II. Struck, Peter T., 1954–   III. Title.   IV. Series.
PN56.A5C35   2010
809′.915 – dc22   2009048601

ISBN 978-0-521-86229-5 Hardback
ISBN 978-0-521-68082-0 Paperback

CONTENTS

List of illustrations   *page* vii
Contributors   viii
Chronology   ix

Introduction   1
RITA COPELAND AND PETER T. STRUCK

PART I   ANCIENT FOUNDATIONS

1 Early Greek allegory   15
   DIRK OBBINK

2 Hellenistic allegory and early imperial rhetoric   26
   GLENN W. MOST

3 Origen as theorist of allegory: Alexandrian contexts   39
   DANIEL BOYARIN

PART II   PHILOSOPHY, THEOLOGY, AND POETRY 200 TO 1200

4 Allegory and ascent in Neoplatonism   57
   PETER T. STRUCK

5 Allegory in Christian late antiquity   71
   DENYS TURNER

6 Allegory in Islamic literatures   83
   PETER HEATH

7 Twelfth-century allegory: philosophy and imagination   101
   JON WHITMAN

CONTENTS

PART III   LITERARY ALLEGORY: PHILOSOPHY AND FIGURATION

8   Allegory in the *Roman de la Rose*   119
    KEVIN BROWNLEE

9   Dante and allegory   128
    ALBERT R. ASCOLI

10 Medieval secular allegory: French and English   136
    STEPHANIE GIBBS KAMATH AND RITA COPELAND

11 Medieval religious allegory: French and English   148
    NICOLETTE ZEEMAN

12 Renaissance allegory from Petrarch to Spenser   162
    MICHAEL MURRIN

13 Protestant allegory   177
    BRIAN CUMMINGS

14 Allegorical drama   191
    BLAIR HOXBY

PART IV   THE FALL AND RISE OF ALLEGORY

15 Romanticism's errant allegory   211
    THERESA M. KELLEY

16 American allegory to 1900   229
    DEBORAH L. MADSEN

17 Walter Benjamin's concept of allegory   241
    HOWARD CAYGILL

18 Hermeneutics, deconstruction, allegory   254
    STEVEN MAILLOUX

19 Allegory happens: allegory and the arts post-1960   266
    LYNETTE HUNTER

    Further reading   281
    Index   286

ILLUSTRATIONS

Figures 14.1 and 14.2 Two of several allegorical figures danced in the *Ballet de Monseigneur le Duc de Vendosme* (1610), Bibliothèque nationale de France. *page* 198–99

Figure 14.3 The first *intermedio* of 1589, Florence. By permission of the Folger Shakespeare Library. 202

Figure 14.4 Diagram for a performance of *The Castle of Perseverance* (c. 1400–25). The Metropolitan Museum of Art, Harris Brisbane Dick Fund, 1926 [26.70.4(32)] Image © Metropolitan Museum of Art. 204

Figure 15.1 J. M. W. Turner, *The Slave Ship*, or *Slavers throwing overboard the Dead and Dying – Typhoon coming on*, 1840, Oil on canvas, 90.8 × 122.6 cm, Museum of Fine Arts, Boston, Henry Lillie Pierce Fund, 99.22 Photograph © 2010 Museum of Fine Arts, Boston. 226

CONTRIBUTORS

ALBERT R. ASCOLI University of California, Berkeley

DANIEL BOYARIN University of California, Berkeley

KEVIN BROWNLEE University of Pennsylvania

HOWARD CAYGILL Goldsmiths College, University of London

RITA COPELAND University of Pennsylvania

BRIAN CUMMINGS University of Sussex

PETER HEATH American University of Sharjah

BLAIR HOXBY Stanford University

LYNETTE HUNTER University of California, Davis

STEPHANIE GIBBS KAMATH University of Massachusetts, Boston

THERESA M. KELLEY University of Wisconsin

DEBORAH MADSEN Université de Genève

STEVEN MAILLOUX Loyola Marymount University

GLENN W. MOST Scuola Normale Superiore di Pisa and University of Chicago

MICHAEL MURRIN University of Chicago

DIRK OBBINK Oxford University

PETER T. STRUCK University of Pennsylvania

DENYS TURNER Yale Divinity School

JON WHITMAN Hebrew University of Jerusalem

NICOLETTE ZEEMAN King's College, Cambridge

CHRONOLOGY

For practical reasons of space, this chronology focuses on the fields of literature, philosophy, and theology, and does not extend to the important fields of music and the visual arts, with the exception of works in those fields discussed in this volume. A chronology such as this is necessarily selective, and is intended to give readers a general map of the history and development of allegory and allegorical theory.

BCE

8th c.	Homer (Greek epic poet)
8th c.	Hesiod (Greek epic poet)
7th c.	Archilochus (Greek iambic and elegiac poet)
born 625–620	Alcaeus (Greek lyric poet)
fl. 544	Pherecydes of Syros (earliest Greek prose writer)
fl. 537	Xenophanes (Greek poet, theologian, and natural philosopher)
fl. c. 525	Theagenes of Rhegium (Greek commentator on Homer)
fl. c. 500	Heraclitus (Greek philosopher)
fl. early 5th c.	Parmenides (Greek philosopher)
fl. mid 5th c.	Anaxagoras (Greek philosopher)
5th c.	Metrodorus of Lampsacus (Greek commentator on Homer)
c. 485–c. 380	Gorgias of Leontini (Greek sophist)

born 460	Democritus (Greek philosopher)
c. 460–c. 386	Aristophanes (Greek comic poet)
c. 429–347	Plato (Greek philosopher)
c. 430–before 350	Xenophon (Greek philosopher)
4th c.	Derveni Papyrus (earliest preserved commentary on Homer)
4th c.	Alcidamas (Greek rhetorician and sophist)
384–322	Aristotle (Greek philosopher)
335–263	Zeno of Citium (Greek founder of Stoic philosophy)
331–232	Cleanthes (Greek Stoic philosopher)
c. 280–207	Chrysippus (Greek Stoic philosopher)
fl. mid 3rd c.	Apollonius Rhodius (Greek epic poet)
c. 216–144	Aristarchus (Greek grammarian and commentator on poetry)
fl. early 2nd c.	Crates of Mallus (Greek commentator on poetry)
116–27	Varro (Roman scholar, grammarian, poet, and statesman)
c. 110–c. 40/35	Philodemus (Greek poet, philosopher, and literary commentator)
106–43	Cicero (Roman statesman, rhetorician, and philosopher)
c. 86–82	*Rhetorica ad Herennium* (rhetorical handbook)
70–19	Virgil (Roman epic poet)

CE

fl. early 1st c.	Philo (Alexandrian-Jewish philosopher, commentator, and statesman)
1st c.	Cornutus (Stoic philosopher, commentator, and rhetorician)

1st c.?	*On Style* (rhetorical handbook attributed to Demetrius)
d. *c.* 64–65	Paul (Christian apostle and interpreter of Christ's teachings)
c. 35–90s	Quintilian (Roman lawyer and rhetorician)
before 50–after 120	Plutarch (Greek philosopher, moralist, and biographer)
c. 50–*c.* 135	Akiva ben Joseph (Palestinian rabbinic sage)
2nd c.	Numenius of Apamea (Greek Platonist philosopher)
fl. early 2nd c.?	Heraclitus the Allegorist (Greek commentator on Homer)
mid–late 2nd c.	Artemidorus of Daldis (Greek authority on dreams)
late 2nd c.?	*Life of Homer* (Greek commentary on Homer attributed to Plutarch)
184/5–254/5	Origen (Christian church father schooled in Platonism)
late 2nd or early 3rd c.	*Chaldean Oracles* (Platonist-inspired oracular text)
205–69/70	Plotinus (philosopher and founding figure of Neoplatonism)
234–*c.* 305	Porphyry (Neoplatonist philosopher and Homeric commentator)
c. 245–*c.* 325	Lactantius (rhetorician and Christian apologist; *Divine Institutions*)
c. 245–*c.* 325	Iamblichus (Neoplatonist philosopher and theurgist)
4th c.	Servius (Roman grammarian and commentator)
4th c.	Calcidius (Latin translator and interpreter of Plato's *Timaeus*)
c. 347–420	Jerome (Christian church father)

348–after 405	Prudentius (Christian Latin poet; *Psychomachia*)
354–430	Augustine (Christian church father)
c. 360–c. 435	John Cassian (*Conferences*, earliest formulation of fourfold method of scriptural interpretation)
fl. early 5th c.	Macrobius (Roman scholar and literary commentator)
410/12–85	Proclus (Neoplatonic philosopher and commentator)
fl. late 5th c.	Martianus Capella (Roman scholar and poet; *The Marriage of Philology and Mercury*)
fl. late 5th or early 6th c.	Pseudo-Dionysius the Areopagite (Christian Neoplatonist)
fl. late 5th or early 6th c.	Fulgentius (*Mythologies*; *Expositions of the Content of Virgil*)
c. 480–524/5	Boethius (*Consolation of Philosophy*)
540–604	Gregory the Great (scriptural commentator)
c. 560–636	Isidore of Seville (*Etymologies*)
673–735	Bede (*On Schemes and Tropes*; scriptural commentary)
d. 750	Ibn al-Muqaffa' (beast fables/mirror for princes)
c. 730–804	Alcuin of York (scriptural commentary)
c. 810–77	John Scotus Eriugena (*Periphyseon*)
c. 841–908	Remigius of Auxerre (commentaries on Boethius, Martianus Capella)
870–950	Al-Fārābī (Islamic philosopher, commentaries on Plato and Aristotle)
c. 900?	Vatican Mythographer I (allegorical readings of classical myth)
before 950?	Vatican Mythographer II

c. 950?	*Epistles of the Brethren of Purity* (Islamic allegorical texts)
c. 952–1022	Notker the German (Notker Labeo) of St. Gall (German glosses on Martianus Capella)
980–1037	Avicenna (Ibn Sīna) (philosopher, commentator on Plato and Aristotle)
1021–58/70	Solomon ibn Gabirol (Avicebron) (Jewish philosopher; *Fountain of Life*)
1058–1111	Al-Ghazālī (Islamic philosopher and scientist)
c. 1075–*c.* 1140	Judah ha-Levi (Jewish allegorical poet)
c. 1075–1131	Sanā'ī (*The Garden of Reality; The Law of the Path*)
c. 1090?–1139	Avempace (Ibn Bājja) (Islamic philosopher)
1090/91–1153	Bernard of Clairvaux (sermons on the Song of Songs)
c. 1090–*c.* 1154	William of Conches (Christian Neoplatonist)
1092/3–1164	Abraham ben Ezra (Ibn Ezra) (Jewish philosopher and scriptural exegete)
c. 1095–*c.* 1156	Thierry of Chartres (Christian Neoplatonist)
1096–1141	Hugh of St. Victor (scriptural commentary; exegetical theory)
1098–1179	Hildegard of Bingen (*Scivias* and other visionary writings)
c. 1110–85	Ibn Ṭufail (Islamic philosophical allegorist)
fl. 1136–50	Bernardus Silvestris (*Cosmographia;* commentaries on Virgil, Martianus Capella)
c. 1116–1202/3	Alan of Lille (*Plaint of Nature, Anticlaudianus*)
1126–98	Averroes (Ibn Rushd) (Islamic philosopher and commentator)
c. 1135–*c.* 90	Chrétien de Troyes (courtly romances)

1135–1204	Maimonides (Jewish philosopher; *Guide of the Perplexed*)
1150?–1220	Farīd al-Dīn ʿAṭṭār (Persian mystical allegorist)
c. 1150–c. 1200	Jean d'Hanville (*Architrenius*)
1154–91	Suhrawardī (Persian philosopher)
c. 1150–90?	Vatican Mythographer III
fl. c. 1150?	Arnulf of Orléans (commentaries on Ovid)
c. 1150	Nivardus (*Ysengrimus* [Latin beast fable])
c. 1160–1230	Samuel ibn Tibbon (translator of Maimonides' *Guide* into Hebrew; biblical commentator)
1165–1240	Ibn ʿArabī (Arabic mystical allegorist)
c. 1170–c. 1220	Wolfram von Eschenbach (*Parzifal*)
c. 1190?–after 1250?	Gonzalo de Berceo (lives of saints and Marian miracles in Castilian)
1194–1270	Moses Nahmanides (kabbalist and biblical commentator)
1200–46	Thomas Gallus (mystical Neoplatonist)
c. 1207–82?	Mechthild von Magdeburg (German mystic; *Flowing Light of the Godhead*)
fl. 1225/30	Guillaume de Lorris (*Roman de la Rose*)
1207–73	Jalāl al-Dīn Rūmī (Persian mystical allegorist)
1217/21–74	Bonaventure (works of spirituality and biblical commentary)
c. 1220–30	*Queste del saint graal*
c. 1224–74	Thomas Aquinas (theories of literal and allegorical senses of Scripture)
1232–1316	Ramón Llull (Spanish philosopher and mystic)
1240–c. 1291	Abraham Abulafia (kabbalistic scholar)
c. 1240–1305	Moses de Leon (*Zohar* [Book of Splendor], kabbalistic work)

fl. *c.* 1270	Jean de Meun (*Roman de la Rose*)
c. 1286	*Il Fiore* (Italian imitation of *Roman de la Rose*, sometimes attributed to Dante)
c. 1260–*c.* 1327	Meister Eckhart (Latin and German mystical writings)
1265–1321	Dante Alighieri (*Commedia*, *Epistle to Can Grande*)
c. 1270–1349	Nicholas of Lyra (literal expositions of Scripture)
c. 1283–*c.* 1350	Juan Ruiz (*Libro de buen amor* [Book of Good Love])
1288–1344	Gersonides (rabbinical authority, rationalist critic of allegorical interpretations)
c. 1295–after 1358	Guillaume de Deguileville (*Pelerinage de la vie humaine*)
c. 1295–1366	Heinrich Suso (Latin and German mystical writings)
before 1300	*Der Minne Lehre* (allegorical love poem)
c. 1300–49	Richard Rolle (Latin and English mystical writings)
c. 1300–77	Guillaume de Machaut (allegorical love poetry)
1304–74	Francis Petrarch (Latin and Italian poetry and criticism)
after 1309	*Ovide moralisé*
d. 1310	Marguerite Porete (*Mirror of Simple Souls*)
1313–75	Giovanni Boccaccio (*Genealogies of the Gentile Gods*)
c. 1330–*c.* 1387	William Langland (*Piers Plowman*)
c. 1330–1405	Évrart de Conty (*Echecs amoureux*)
c. 1330–1408	John Gower (*Confessio amantis*, *Mirroir de l'homme*)

c. 1330–84	John Wyclif (reformist English theologian and exegete)
1337–1404	Jean Froissart (allegorical love poetry)
c. 1340–1400	Geoffrey Chaucer (dream visions)
c. 1346–1406	Eustache Deschamps (allegorical love poetry)
c. 1350–1414	Johannes von Tepl (*Der Ackermann aus Böhmen*, debate between a Plowman and Death)
c. 1364–1430	Christine de Pizan (dream visions; didactic allegories)
1401–2	*Querelle du Roman de la Rose* (exchanges among Christine de Pizan, Jean Gerson, Jean de Montreuil, Pierre Col)
c. 1365–1458	Hermann von Sachsenheim (allegorical love poetry)
c. 1366–1426	Thomas Hoccleve (*Male Regle*; *Regiment of Princes*)
c. 1370–*c.* 1451	John Lydgate (allegorical narratives)
1380–1459	Poggio Bracciolini (Florentine humanist)
1384–1434	Enrique de Villena (*Doze trabajos de Hércules* [allegorical interpretations of thc labors of Hercules, in Catalan and Castilian versions]; prose translation of Dante's *Commedia*)
c. 1385/95–1430	Alain Chartier (French allegorical love poetry)
1394–1465	Charles d'Orléans (French and English allegorical poetry)
1398–1458	Iñigo López de Mendoza, marqués de Santillana (*Triumphete de amor*)
c. 1400	British Library MS Cotton Nero A.x (contains the poems *Pearl*, *Sir Gawain and the Green Knight*, *Cleanness*, *Patience*)

c. 1400?	*Dezir a las siete virtudes* (Spanish allegorical poem [once attributed to Francisco Imperial], of Dantean inspiration)
c. 1400–25	*Castle of Perseverance*
c. 1400?–*c.* 1460?	Alfonse de la Torre (*Visión deleitable*, encyclopedic allegory)
1402/3–71	Denys the Carthusian (mystical theologian; scriptural commentary)
c. 1407–57	Lorenzo Valla (Italian humanist)
1411–56	Juan de Mena (*Laberinto de Fortuna*, Spanish political allegory)
1414–92	'Abd al-Raḥmān Jāmī (Arabic philosophical allegorist)
1415/24–92	William Caxton (English printer and translator)
1424–98	Cristoforo Landino (Florentine humanist and classical scholar)
1433–99	Marsilio Ficino (Florentine humanist, commentary on Plato's *Phaedrus*)
1433–1527	Francesco Colonna (*Hypnerotomachia Poliphili* [Dream of Poliphilo], Italian dream allegory)
c. 1437–*c.* 1498	Diego de San Pedro (*Cárcel de Amor* [Prison of Love], allegorical romance)
1439	*Bien-Avisé, Mal-Avisé*
c. 1441–94	Matteo Maria Boiardo (*Orlando innamorato*)
c. 1450–1500	*Wisdom*
1454–94	Angelo Poliziano (Florentine classical scholar and poet)
1455–1522	Johannes Reuchlin (German humanist)
c. 1460–1529	John Skelton (*Bowge of Court, Magnyfycence*)
1463–94	Giovanni Pico della Mirandola (*Heptaplus*)

c. 1469–1536	Desiderius Erasmus (*Enchiridion militis christiani*; *De copia rerum ac verborum*)
c. 1474–1523	Stephen Hawes (*Pastime of Pleasure*)
1474–1533	Ludovico Ariosto (*Orlando Furioso*)
1476	*L'Homme juste et l'homme mondain*
1478–1535	Thomas More (*Utopia*)
c. 1480–1556	Fuzūlī (Turkish allegorical poet)
1483–1546	Martin Luther (Protestant hermeneutics)
c. 1484–*c.* 1542	Johannes Susenbrotus (*Epitome troporum*)
1492–1550	Andrea Alciati (*Emblematum liber*)
1494–1576	Hans Sachs (German poet and dramatist)
c. 1495–1520	*Everyman*
1497–1560	Philipp Melanchthon (rhetorician; *Elementa rhetorices*)
1501–36	Garcilaso de la Vega (Spanish poet)
1515–82	Teresa of Avila (Spanish visionary writer)
1520–82	Natale Conti (Italian mythographer)
1524/5–80	Luís Vaz de Camões (*Os Lusíadas*, Portuguese epic)
1524–85	Pierre de Ronsard (*Pléiade* poet)
c. 1525–60	Joachim du Bellay (*Pléiade* poet)
1529–90	George Puttenham (*Art of English Poesie*)
1534–1612	Giovanni Bardi (creator of the *intermedio* or allegorical interlude with music and dance)
1544–95	Torquato Tasso (*Gerusalemme liberata*; *Gerusalemme conquistata*)
1546–1634	Henry Peacham (the Elder) (*Garden of Eloquence*)
c. 1550–1602	Emilio de Cavalieri (*La rappresentazione di Anima e di Corpo*, opera)

1552–99	Edmund Spenser (*Fairie Queene*)
1552–1630	Agrippa d'Aubigné (*Les Tragiques*)
1554–86	Sir Philip Sidney (English poet and literary theorist)
c. 1555–1622	Cesare Ripa (*Iconologia*)
1561–1627	Luis de Góngora (Spanish poet, *Soledades*)
1564–93	Christopher Marlowe (*Dr. Faustus*)
1564–1616	William Shakespeare (thematic links with tradition of allegorical drama)
1572/3–1637	Ben Jonson (*Hymenaei* and other masques)
1578–1639	Jakob Bidermann (*Cenodoxus*)
1581	*Balet comique de la Royne*
1587–1679	Joost van den Vondel (Dutch baroque dramatist)
1588–1679	Thomas Hobbes (English rationalist philosopher)
1597–1639	Martin Opitz (German baroque dramatist and theorist)
1600–81	Pedro Calderón de la Barca (allegorical drama; *autos sacramentales*)
1606–81	Jakob Masen (German Jesuit dramatist and theorist)
1606–84	Pierre Corneille (French dramatist)
1607–58	Georg Philipp Harsdörffer (German baroque poet)
1608–74	John Milton (*Comus, Paradise Lost*)
1616–64	Andreas Gryphius (German baroque dramatist)
1628–88	John Bunyan (*Pilgrim's Progress*)
1631–1700	John Dryden (*Absalom and Achitophel*; political satire; fables)

1632–1704	John Locke (English rationalist philosopher)
1635–83	Daniel Caspar von Lohenstein (German baroque dramatist)
c. 1640–c. 1704	Johann Christian Hallmann (German baroque dramatist)
1667–1745	Jonathan Swift (*Tale of a Tub* and other political satire)
1668–1744	Giambattista Vico (rhetoric and poetics; *The New Science*)
1688–1772	Emanuel Swedenborg (Swedish philosopher and mystic)
1709–84	Samuel Johnson (*Rasselas*)
1712–78	Jean-Jacques Rousseau (*Julie, ou la Nouvelle Héloïse*)
1714	*Le Tableau allégorique des moeurs*
1724–1804	Immanuel Kant (aesthetic theory, *Critique of Judgment*)
1749–1832	J. W. Goethe (*Faust*; "Über Laokoon," "Symbolik")
1752–1832	Philip Freneau (American poet)
1757–99	Şeyh Galip (Ottoman allegorical poet; *Story of Beauty and Love*)
1757–1827	William Blake (English Romantic poet and illustrator)
1759–1805	Friedrich von Schiller (German Neoclassical dramatist, philosopher, poet; *On the Aesthetic Education of Man*)
1767–1845	A. W. Schlegel (German Romantic poet and critic)
1770–1831	G. W. F. Hegel (*Aesthetics* [*Lectures on Fine Arts*])
1770–1850	William Wordsworth (*The Prelude*)

1772–1801	Novalis (German Romantic poet and critic)
1772–1829	K. W. F. Schlegel (German Romantic poet and critic)
1772–1834	Samuel Taylor Coleridge (*Biographia literaria*, literary criticism)
1775–1851	J. M. W. Turner (English Romantic painter, promoted by John Ruskin)
1778–1830	William Hazlitt (essayist and poet)
1792–1822	Percy Bysshe Shelley (Romantic poet)
1795–1821	John Keats (Romantic poet)
1797–1851	Mary Shelley (*Frankenstein*)
1797–1856	Heinrich Heine (German Romantic poet)
1803–82	Ralph Waldo Emerson (American essayist, Transcendentalist)
1804–64	Nathaniel Hawthorne (American novelist)
1809–49	Edgar Allan Poe (American poet, short story writer, essayist)
1817–62	Henry David Thoreau (American essayist, Transcendentalist)
1819–91	Herman Melville (American novelist)
1819–92	Walt Whitman (American poet)
1819–1900	John Ruskin (art critic and essayist; *Modern Painters*)
1821–67	Charles Baudelaire (French Symbolist poet)
1856–1939	Sigmund Freud (*The Interpretation of Dreams*)
1874–1929	Hugo von Hoffmansthal (German librettist; festival plays)
1875–1926	Rainer Maria Rilke (German poet and essayist)
1883–1924	Franz Kafka (German novelist)

1889–1976	Martin Heidegger (German philosopher, phenomenologist)
1892–1940	Walter Benjamin (German essayist and literary critic; *The Origin of German Tragic Drama*)
1895–1975	Mikhail Bakhtin (Russian semiotician and literary theorist)
1898–1956	Bertolt Brecht (German dramatist and theorist)
1899–1977	Vladimir Nabokov (Russian and American novelist)
1900–2002	Hans-Georg Gadamer (German philosopher; *Truth and Method*)
1903–50	George Orwell (British novelist; *Animal Farm, Nineteen Eighty Four*)
1905–80	Jean-Paul Sartre (French philosopher and novelist; *Nausée*)
1906–89	Samuel Beckett (Irish dramatist)
1911–93	William Golding (British novelist)
1912–91	Northrop Frye (literary critic; *Anatomy of Criticism*)
1913–60	Albert Camus (French novelist)
1913–2005	Paul Ricoeur (philosopher of language and hermeneutics; *The Rule of Metaphor*)
1917–93	Anthony Burgess (British novelist)
1919–83	Paul de Man (literary theorist; "The Rhetoric of Temporality," "Semiology and Rhetoric")
1922–2008	Alain Robbe-Grillet (French novelist and dramatist)
1927–	Gabriel García Márquez (Colombian novelist)
1930–2004	Jacques Derrida (French philosopher and poststructuralist theorist; *Of Grammatology*)
1930–	John Barth (American novelist)

1937–   Thomas Pynchon (American novelist)

1939–   Margaret Atwood (Canadian novelist)

1940–92   Angela Carter (British novelist)

1943–   Nicole Brossard (French-Canadian novelist)

1944–2001   W. G. Sebald (German novelist)

1946–   Philip Pullman (British fantasy writer)

1951–   Bill Viola (American video artist)

1952–   Orhan Pamuk (Turkish novelist)

1954–   Cindy Sherman (American photographer)

1959–   Ben Okri (Nigerian novelist)

RITA COPELAND AND PETER T. STRUCK

Introduction

The definition of allegory is found in understanding its history. The subject of allegory is vast, comprising many different practices of writing, interpreting, and representing. It is bound up with developments not only in literature and art, but also in mythology, religion, rhetoric, and intellectual culture over the centuries. Thus any theoretical statement about allegory that seeks to capture its essence can only be as good as the historical understanding on which it is founded.

This volume seeks to provide that historical perspective. It traces the development of allegory in the European tradition from antiquity to the modern era, emphasizing its progress through literary culture. The essays assembled here traverse the fields that inform allegorical thought and practice in literature and in textual interpretation. Within the broad scope of the European tradition we incorporate the emergence of allegory in ancient Greece and Rome, Judaism, Christianity, and Islam. We begin with Greek antiquity, showing how the earliest systems of allegory arose in poetry in relation to philosophy, mystery religions, and hermeneutics or interpretation. By proceeding chronologically, this volume accounts for how allegory came to be understood, by late antiquity and the early Middle Ages, as both a theological problem and a literary device, or how sacred and secular conceptions of allegory could be seen to co-exist in the same text. Once the Greek and Roman, Jewish, and early Christian histories have been laid out and the various threads of the allegorical tradition have been considered separately, the volume turns to literary, intellectual, and cultural manifestations of allegory through the Middle Ages and the Early Modern period. The essays in the last section address literary and theoretical approaches to allegory in the modern era, from reactions to allegory in the eighteenth and nineteenth centuries through reevaluations of its power in the thought of the twentieth century and beyond.

Definitions, background, and overview

Post-classical criticism has applied the term "allegory" to denote a range of practices and habits of thought. The term itself has Greek origins: *allos* (other) and *agoreuein* (to speak in public), produce the sense of "other-speaking." In its most common usage it refers to two related procedures, a manner of composing and a method of interpreting. To compose allegorically is usually understood as writing with a double meaning: what appears on the surface and another meaning to which the apparent sense points. Allegorical interpretation (allegoresis) is understood as explaining a work, or a figure in myth, or any created entity, as if there were another sense to which it referred, that is, presuming the work or figure to be encoded with meaning intended by the author or a higher spiritual authority. Literary allegory has been treated by turns as a genre, a mode, a technique, or a rhetorical device or trope, related to metaphor and sometimes defined as "extended (or continued) metaphor."[1] As every critic who has attempted a definition is forced to acknowledge, the nature of allegorical writing is elusive, its surface by turns mimetic and anti-mimetic, its procedures intricate and at times seemingly inconsistent, and its meaning or "other" sense – how it is encoded, or what it refers to extrinsically – often indeterminate. But much of the difficulty associated with allegorical writing, how to define it, how to explicate it, and even how to identify it as such, derives from its intimate relationship with its historical complement, allegorical interpretation.

Allegorical interpretation is in fact the older of these two procedures, or at least the first to leave observable traces of itself as a systematic practice. The Greek noun *allēgoria* did not come into use until the Roman period. At the end of the first century CE, Plutarch is still calling it a new term. But the mode of thinking to which the term was attached has deep classical roots. The central concepts of ancient allegorical reading are represented in a cluster of terms: "symbol" (*symbolon*), *hyponoia* ("under-meaning"), and "enigma" (*aenigma*).[2] In one of the earliest extensive testimonies to allegorical interpretation, the work of the Derveni commentator (fourth century BCE), the key term is "enigma": this commentary presents a cosmological and religious explanation of an Orphic poem, often by bringing etymological pressure to bear on individual names and terms, and finds

1 Defining allegory as "extended metaphor" occurs in antiquity: see Quintilian, *Institutio oratoria*, 8.6.44. Among well-known modern uses of it, see Rosemond Tuve, *Elizabethan and Metaphysical Imagery: Renaissance Poetic and Twentieth-Century Critics* (Chicago: University of Chicago Press, 1947), pp. 105–6.
2 Peter Struck, *Birth of the Symbol: Ancient Readers at the Limits of Their Texts* (Princeton: Princeton University Press, 2004), p. 23.

mystical truths and cultic significance embedded in the poetic language and the figures of myth. At its most fundamental, such allegorizing is a search for esoteric truths, for meaning that is concealed but ultimately interpretable. The later term *allêgoria* was thus nearly synonymous with *symbolon*, the encoded expression of a mystical or philosophical truth, a manifestation of transcendental meaning that is at once immediate and remote. This is the model of allegorical thought that Plato found problematic because not all readers of poetry would be intellectually equipped to discover its immanent truths (although Plato himself was famously to construct some of the most enduring philosophical allegories, notably the Allegory of the Cave and the Myth of Er in the *Republic*). This remained the model pursued by Stoic philosophers in their theology, physics, and metaphysics, and which they in turn bequeathed to Greek commentators on Homer during the Hellenistic period. It also informed a strong tradition of later Latin mythographical commentary which focused its attention on Virgil: the commentator Fulgentius (fifth or sixth century) elevated Virgil's poetry to philosophical status by extracting latent cosmographical truths from the poetic narrative, and the massive commentary on the *Aeneid* by the grammarian Servius (fourth century) often engages allegorical perspectives.[3]

Jewish and early Christian thinkers would build their edifices of exegesis and scriptural allegory on the ancient foundation of esoteric reading. Theirs too was a hermeneutic aimed at the transcendent truths which are concealed in language. In rabbinic exegesis as well as in the thought of such early Christian figures as Paul and Origen, the indeterminacy of the scriptural text is held in tension with the guaranteed and complete truth of the inner *logos*. The vast metaphysical elaborations of Greek Neoplatonism were also to emerge, in late antiquity, out of this early system of allegorical hermeneutics. Neoplatonist commentators turned their attention to the transcendent meanings that they saw hidden in poetic and philosophical myth, for example, Porphyry's commentary on the Cave of the Nymphs episode in the *Odyssey* and Proclus' commentary on Plato's Myth of Er. Neoplatonist allegorism cast a powerful influence forward on medieval and humanist reading habits. Certain strains in the early Islamic allegorical tradition also reflect Platonic thought about the different parts of the soul and the layering of the cosmos. The Platonist influence was mediated to the Western Middle Ages through the writings of a few Neoplatonists who wrote in Latin,

---

3 These traditions are collected and surveyed in Jan Ziolkowski and Michael C. J. Putnam, eds. and trans., *The Virgilian Tradition: The First Fifteen Hundred Years* (New Haven: Yale University Press, 2008). See also Christopher Baswell, *Virgil in Medieval England: Figuring the Aeneid from the Twelfth Century to Chaucer* (Cambridge: Cambridge University Press, 1995).

notably Macrobius, and by the all-important Latin commentary-translation of Plato's *Timaeus* by Calcidius (fourth century CE). This hermeneutical influence also extended into the Latin Middle Ages through the Christian Neoplatonist known as the Pseudo-Dionysius, whose mystical writings in Greek were translated into Latin by John Scotus Eriugena in the ninth century. Of course the recovery of classical Greek by Humanist scholars, starting in the fifteenth century, ushered in a new era of enthusiasm for Neoplatonist allegory.

In Roman times, the Greek term *allêgoria* came to substitute for the term *hyponoia*, that is, "other-speaking" for "under-meaning." In this usage, the term denoted the fruit of interpretive quests, a meaning that would be enshrined in Neoplatonist commentaries on Plato and Homer, along with the term *symbolon*. But the conceptual shift from "meaning" (*hyponoia*) to "speaking" (*allêgoria*) also paved the way for the reception of the Greek term in Latin, where its emphasis on the text as "speaking" rather than merely "meaning" allowed the Latin term *allegoria* to gravitate into the orbit of the rhetoricians. The Latin rhetoricians treated it as a trope akin either to metaphor or to irony. Thus it was that allegory, which had begun in philosophy, moved into poetics. *Allegoria* came to denote a form of writing as well as a form of reading. As a compositional technique, it became a property of rhetoric. In the rhetorical handbooks (such as Quintilian's *Institutio oratoria*) it acquired a rather narrow sense as an ornamental device involving a double meaning (saying one thing and meaning another; *Institutio oratoria* 8.6.44).

This layering of terminology, where the Latin term took on a different valence from the same word in Greek, is one of the reasons why the history of allegory in the post-classical West is extremely tricky. "Allegory" became a rhetorical term relatively late in its history. Because the word was the same from Greek to Latin, the force of the earlier meaning could certainly accompany the term in its new linguistic environment; but in that new environment it had another contextual value, as a simple rhetorical trope. This was a source of some ambiguity for many centuries in both sacred and secular writing. When Christian theologians in the Latin West adopted the terminology of earlier Greek Christian writers, the Greek word *allêgoria* found its obvious counterpart in Latin *allegoria*, but the transference across linguistic contexts created confusion about whether the word "allegory" referred to a verbal trope or something more profound. The word *allegoria* as we find it used by the Latin church fathers would typically refer to a spiritual sense of Scripture, either the whole of the spiritual meaning that is latent in the literal sense, or one division of a tripartite spiritual sense. In the early fifth century, John Cassian gave a formal stamp to the notion of a multi-valent spiritual sense, in his outline of the four-fold system of scriptural interpretation: he spoke of a literal or historical sense, and of three spiritual senses, tropology (which concerns the soul), allegory (which concerns the revelation of mysteries prefigured in history), and anagogy (which concerns the divine secrets of heaven). But in the same era as Cassian, Augustine could treat theological allegory, or the spiritual sense of Scripture, as another dimension of the rhetorical trope, as a special aspect of the trope found in the spiritual realities of Scripture rather than in its words (*De trinitate* 15.9.15). It appears that for Augustine, the rhetorical trope was the standard from which a specialized scriptural form had to be distinguished.

Thus we see that there was some ambiguity of terms: how can a verbal trope, which is rather restricted in its value, share a term (and a category) with a profound form of hidden spiritual meaning? How can "allegory" be a fact or event in Scripture that is imbued with sacred mystery beyond itself, as well as an ornamental device of language? Across the Middle Ages, from Bede in the eighth century to Aquinas in the thirteenth, there were attempts to solve this dilemma. But where medieval Christian thinkers apprehended this difficulty, they did not express it as a semantic problem (Greek term versus Latin term, an overlapping of two cultural meanings at the site of one word). Rather, medieval thinkers tended to see it as a distinction between sacred meaning and human language, or sometimes between sacred and secular texts. For example, in the twelfth century, Bernardus Silvestris would try to resolve this by distinguishing between the allegory that is proper to Scripture, in which a historical truth points to a spiritual truth, and the "integument" or fictional covering that is appropriate for secular philosophy, which may use myths or fables that have no meaning in themselves but which refer to a latent philosophical truth. But medieval vernacular authors, notably Guillaume de Lorris and Jean de Meun (authors of the *Roman de la Rose*), and spectacularly Dante, found that they could play with accepted distinctions between allegory as verbal trope and allegory as theological or cosmological truth, in order to lay claim to much greater authority than traditionally accorded secular poetry.

A crucial outgrowth of the newer literary dimension of allegory was the transference of the reading process into the compositional process, a passage from reading narratives allegorically to writing narrative allegories. Jane K. Brown defines allegory as "a mode of representation which renders the supernatural visible."[4] This definition is valuable because it can

---

4 Jane K. Brown, *The Persistence of Allegory: Drama and Neoclassicism from Shakespeare to Wagner* (Philadelphia: University of Philadelphia Press, 2007), p. 5.

describe both the interpretive process, which moves from what is already visible to transcendent referents, and the compositional process, which seeks to express imagistically what is otherwise abstract or invisible. The device of personification is bound up with both of these processes of rendering the abstract visible. In allegorical interpretation of myth, mythical deities or other figures were understood to represent cosmological forces or abstract values. This is an underlying assumption of the influential theory of allegorical interpretation that we find in Macrobius' *Commentary on the Dream of Scipio* (*c.* 400 CE), in which the *fabula* or "fabulous narration" (a mythical narrative or a dream narrative) is understood to contain a philosophical truth.[5] Personification is also an ancient device of poetry; in the rhetorical handbooks of antiquity it was treated under the term *prosopopoeia*, in which an imaginary character speaks.[6] In various forms, personification was always a central component of allegorical procedures. Thus it is not surprising that it became the most prominent form of allegorical composition from late antiquity through the late Renaissance. Personification played a large role in the development of mythological poetry in the Middle Ages and the Renaissance: for example, in the Latin philosophical allegories of the twelfth century, such as the *Cosmographia* of Bernardus Silvestris and the *De planctu Naturae* (Plaint of Nature) by Alan of Lille, where philosophical and scientific ideas are personified as speakers and actors in a dramatic narrative; the thirteenth-century *Roman de la Rose*; Chaucer's dream visions, which contain a few mythological personifications; the moral and mythological figures of Spenser's *Fairie Queene*; and masques such as Milton's *Comus*.

The archetype of personification allegory is the *Psychomachia* (early fifth century CE) by the Christian Latin poet Prudentius. This influential narrative can be read most simply as an allegory of virtues and vices, depicting a battle (*machê*) in cosmic, eternal terms for the human soul (*psychê*). Its main, quasi-epic action is the great struggle between personified virtues and vices (Faith and Idolatry, Chastity and Lust, Patience and Anger, and other pairs) in which the virtues prevail. In its concluding lines the poem glosses its own meaning: the narrative has represented the moral vicissitudes of the human soul on the difficult path towards salvation. The *Psychomachia* illustrates how personification allegory inverts allegorical interpretation. Here we encounter a transcendent truth directly through a set of abstractions

---

5 Macrobius, *Commentary on the Dream of Scipio*, trans. William Harris Stahl (New York: Columbia University Press, 1952).
6 On this topic, see James Paxson, *Poetics of Personification* (Cambridge: Cambridge University Press, 1994).

which have been given concrete form at the narrative level, but which operate as universal, not particular values. What the characters represent is clear from their names, but the usefulness of the moral lesson depends on translating it out of its universal terms and back into a human, temporal perspective.[7] But the poem also adopts the terms of the figural allegorization that was applied to Scripture, in which the events in one historical frame prefigure and are fulfilled by the events in a future time or outside of human temporality. In his prologue, Prudentius recounts the events in the life of the patriarch Abraham, which he tells us serve as a paradigm (*figura*) for the eternal truths of salvation after the incarnation of Christ. In different degrees, personification allegory also structures two of the most influential didactic texts of late antiquity. *The Marriage of Mercury and Philology* by Martianus Capella (fifth or sixth century) is an encyclopedic survey of knowledge given dramatic form as a celestial marriage of intellect (Mercury) and learning (Philology); here each of the Seven Liberal Arts (grammar, dialectic, rhetoric, geometry, arithmetic, astronomy, music) is personified as a female figure who comes before the celestial assembly to deliver an account of her art. Boethius' *Consolation of Philosophy* (524 CE) was a wellspring not only for a long tradition of literary imitators but also, in turn, of philosophical allegorists; in this work Lady Philosophy appears to the distraught Boethius, and through a series of careful, dialectical arguments persuades him of the superiority of a philosophical perspective on worldly suffering.

The ideological orders of post-classical allegory – until the period after the Counter-Reformation – are religious or mystical on the one hand, and philosophical or ethical on the other hand. This is the case not only for western European allegory, but also for Islamic allegory, in which mystical and philosophical superstructures dominate. Under the category of ethical we can place the erotic allegories of the Middle Ages (the *Roman de la Rose* and its secular tradition) because these refer to the immanent "law" of love, which constrains and coerces, but also refines the sensibilities of the lover who obeys its rule. In the medieval and early modern European tradition, personification narrative came to be an important element of literary allegory, often in the classic form of personified abstractions, but also in the form of mythological figures, as in Agrippa d'Aubigné's apocalyptic religious poem *Les Tragiques* (1616 CE), as well as historical figures who dynamically embody a moral condition, as in parts of Dante's *Commedia*. Some of the most complex narratives, among them the *Commedia*, Langland's *Piers Plowman*, and Spenser's *Fairie Queene*, combine and test these forms to reveal the

---

7 See Gordon Teskey, *Allegory and Violence* (Ithaca: Cornell University Press, 1996), p. 18.

interconnection among several ideological orders: moral, political or historical, and theological. For example, in the *Fairie Queene* the events of recent English political history are mapped onto the economies of salvation (the triumph of Protestantism) and of private virtue, and all of these orders are figured through the intricacies of characterization in a romance narrative. Angus Fletcher famously argued that a cosmic world view of a guaranteed reality, a single hierarchical order, was necessary for the meaningful workings of literary allegory.[8] In this way, allegory as literary production sustained its intimate connection with the oldest form of allegorism, ascent to the ideal through its visible manifestations.

It should be noted that personification in a strict sense, that is, abstractions that are materially instantiated, was not necessary to the mechanics of allegory, even though it could have an important function in allegorical imagery. One of its most secure places was in allegorical drama, as in the religious morality plays of the later Middle Ages, or the *autos sacramentales* (sacramental acts in dramatic form) of the Counter-Reformation period in Spain, of which Calderón's plays are prominent examples, and in the political and philosophical allegories of court entertainments that persisted into the eighteenth century. But in terms of the consequences for the later history of allegory, perhaps the most important genre to define itself through allegorical personification was the German Baroque *Trauerspiel* or "mourning play," which came to be despised by Romantic critics and which was given a profound theoretical rehabilitation by Walter Benjamin in the 1920s. While the mourning play adopts the mechanics of allegory, its outlook already suggests a loss of faith in the capacity of the allegorical image to lead to an apprehension of eschatological reality.

The notion of an external, hierarchical order which could imbue allegory with an assured, transcendent meaning, began to break down with the failure of the Counter-Reformation and the rise of new philosophical and scientific empiricisms. Under these newer ideological conditions, literary and visual allegory persisted, but its scope as a form of spiritual empowerment was diminished. Apart from the question of a single religious outlook and the anti-sacramental character of Protestantism, even the certainties of a Neoplatonic philosophical order were unfixed.[9] Neoclassical aesthetics did not reject allegory, but imposed on it a much stricter formal limitation of a clear, symmetrical, and fixed correspondence between

8 Angus Fletcher, *Allegory: The Theory of a Symbolic Mode* (Ithaca: Cornell University Press, 1964), chapter 2.
9 On the inner conflicts of Protestant allegory, see Thomas H. Luxon, *Literal Figures: Puritan Allegory and the Reformation Crisis in Representation* (Chicago: University of Chicago Press, 1995).

a figure and the abstraction it represents. Neoclassical criticism isolated personification as the principal mark of allegory. Indeed it was Neoclassical criticism that bestowed the name "allegory" on personification fiction. Such critical prescriptions constrained the parameters within which allegory was seen to function. In Neoclassical literary cultures allegory still played an important role, but its terms were more limited. For example, political, religious, and topical satires, such as Jonathan Swift's *Tale of a Tub*, deployed personifications to great and comic effect, barely disguising the objects of the satire (and allegory has long been a refuge of political satirists, as many modern examples attest). Enlightenment philosophers (for example, John Locke) tended to take a dim view of rhetorical ornamentation in general, and relegated allegory to a rather debased position among rhetorical ornaments.

Under these diminished conditions, what was left for allegory? Goethe could dismiss it for its instrumentality, that its function is simply to yield up meaning: "The allegorical differs from the symbolic in that what the latter designates indirectly, the former designates directly."[10] But in fact the drama of allegory was not over, and there were further acts to be played out. The first of these was within Romanticism itself. Coleridge, like Goethe, distinguished allegory from symbol in terms of the difference between a mechanical "translation" and an organic "translucence." But in one of the great historical paradoxes, what Romantic aesthetic theory embraced in the concept of the "symbol" was nothing less than Neoplatonic allegorical thought: in other words, in extruding what they conceived as mere "allegory" from the precincts of their aesthetics, they were doing nothing less than recuperating the oldest model of allegorical immanence under the aegis of what they called "symbol," a term which they resuscitated from the Greek Neoplatonic tracts they read. The symbol was now the site in which the highest imaginative realities were embodied. Nineteenth-century American literary and intellectual culture also made a significant contribution to the latter-day history of allegory. The American Transcendentalists were beneficiaries of European Romantic thought and aesthetics, and were also avid readers of Neoplatonist philosophical writings. From these influences Ralph Waldo Emerson generated a model of the individual mind partaking of a universal divine intelligence, and of the poet as inspired individual who can interpret human reality in allegorical relation to the realm of the spirit. This also offered a new purchase for a theological dimension of allegory which had persisted (although often challenged) through the Protestant Reformation.

10 Quoted in Tzvetan Todorov, *Theories of the Symbol*, trans. Catherine Porter (Ithaca: Cornell University Press, 1982), p. 199.

The fortunes of the allegorical took another turn with the work of Walter Benjamin. Benjamin found in the *Trauerspiel* or mourning play of the German Baroque a critical turning point in the early modern world. According to Benjamin, these allegorical dramas, with their unfathomably strange imagery, provide no interpretive passage between the material sign and a theological ideal. The possibilities of meaningful representation are called into question: the signs are dead weight (like corpses of the dead), dissolving the link that enables a hermeneutical movement between figures and their meaning, between human life and abstract truth. On Benjamin's view, Renaissance allegory maintained the fiction that an assured meaning was accessible through and immanent in visible signs, but it was the Baroque *Trauerspiel* that presaged modernity by exposing the chasm separating human life from a transcendent ideal.[11] Here allegory entails alienation from meaning, and is suggestive of the very condition of history and human temporality.

For later theorists, Benjamin's reading offered a powerful vindication of allegory for modernity. Twentieth-century critical thought has embraced allegory in ways that are indebted to Benjamin's revisionist reading. Poststructuralist theory, and Paul de Man's work in particular, has turned to allegory as the paradigmatic instance of rhetoric and rhetorical language, of the sign whose meaning cannot be fixed but is continually deferred, both calling for and resisting interpretation. As a sign of a deferred or absent meaning, allegory has also been incorporated into psychoanalytic thought about desire and sublimation.[12] In the charged theoretical debates of the later twentieth century, allegory has once again occupied a critical position, this time as the trope of tropes, by its very name ("other-speaking") announcing itself as the definitive mark of the contingency of language and its referential claims. And conversely, as de Man famously argued, all reading, all critical practice, is allegoresis, that is, allegorical interpretation. Such revisionist understandings of the otherness of allegory within critical theory have had their counterparts in contemporary literary, artistic, and performance cultures, in linguistic or visual or narrative forms that focus attention on their own enigmatic and impenetrable surface, or that make conspicuous and disingenuous claims to represent a traumatic truth that can never be apprehended in its terrible wholeness.

Like no other property of poetics, allegory has a long, complex, and traceable history. Like metaphor, metonymy, and synecdoche, allegory is a

---

11 Teskey, *Allegory and Violence*, pp. 12–14.

12 See, for example, Julia Kristeva, *Black Sun: Depression and Melancholia*, trans. Leon S. Roudiez (New York: Columbia University Press, 1989), p. 111.

trope, but unlike these, it is also the name for what lies behind and beyond language. Wherever we encounter it, it is trailing its entire cultural history behind it. In its transformations from era to era, it is a gauge of ideological shifts. It has its beginnings as a hallmark of theological certainty, but in its postmodern arrival it signals the retreat of such certainty. The essays in this volume examine the key cultural and formal instantiations of allegory at the most important junctures of its history, and together they present a coherent account of its development over time.

PART I

Ancient foundations

I

DIRK OBBINK

Early Greek allegory

Where and when the impulse to read poems allegorically emerged is impossible to say.[1] It is surely the case that among the Greeks evidence for reading allegorically, that is, reading with the expectation that a poem's surface overlays hidden registers of meaning, is as old as any evidence we have for reading poetry. In contrast, the formalist approach that Aristotle develops, in which a reader of poetry sets out to appreciate how poems in general produce the effects they do, within parameters of genre and taking into account levels of style, modes of diction, types of plot structures and characters, and appropriate methods of moving the emotions of the audience, are a comparatively late development. Rather than try to figure out *how* poems in general produce their meanings, the allegorical reader sets out to find *what* a particular poem means. These readers exhibit an approach to poetry that sees it primarily as a repository of hidden insight.

Several ideas are not a part of this early picture of allegorical reading, and it will be useful to disambiguate them first. The idea that allegory is one trope among others, for example, a kind of extended metaphor, is a later

---

[1] Many materials relating to criticism of mythic poetry and religion survive as fragments, often in the form of quotations in later authors. These include quotations from Protagoras, Prodicus, Gorgias, Alcidamas, and the treatise known as *Dissoi Logoi*. They are most accessible in Hermann Diels and Walther Kranz, eds., *Die Fragmente der Vorsokratiker* (abbreviated here as "Diels-Kranz"), 3 vols., 6th edition (Berlin: Weidmann, 1951–2), II, especially nos. 80, 82, and 90; translation by Rosamond K. Sprague, *The Older Sophists* (Columbia, SC: University of South Carolina Press, 1972), pp. 3–28, 30–67, 279–93. Seminal treatments of these and other texts discussed in this chapter include: Rudolf Pfeiffer, *History of Classical Scholarship from the Beginnings to the End of the Hellenistic Age* (Oxford: Clarendon, 1968), chapter 2, pp. 16–56; Nicholas James Richardson, "Aristotle's Reading of Homer and Its Background," in Robert Lamberton and John J. Keaney, eds., *Homer's Ancient Readers* (Princeton: Princeton University Press, 1992), pp. 30–40; Paul Decharme, *La Critique des traditions religieuses chez les grecs* (Paris: Picard, 1904), chapter 1. References to Plato's works use the "Stephanus" numbers, the universal system for citing Plato, based on the page numbers of a 1578 edition by Henri Estienne.

tradition. This development, which will inform a notion of allegory that is more domesticated and functional than we find in the classical period, will await the rhetorical critics of the late Hellenistic period. Nor do we find in this earliest period an idea of allegory as a self-conscious or distinct literary procedure of composing personification fictions, in which characters are correlated to abstract ideas in a one-to-one correspondence. Prudentius and Martianus Capella leave behind flourishing examples of this, but not until one thousand years after the period considered here. Also missing during this period is, strictly speaking, the notion of "allegory" (*allêgoria*) itself. We find readers using other terms to anchor their discussions of the nuggets of wisdom which they supposed great poets had tucked away in their poetry, including the terms *hyponoia* (under-sense) and *symbolon* (symbol), but with central position occupied by the notion of the *aenigma* (enigma). Readers of enigmas and undermeanings in this period are not rare, though some broad treatments of literary criticism treat allegory as though it were an exotic overgrowth of later periods. In fact, quite a number of examples of allegorical reading can be found during this early period, with differences of approach to be sure, but always with an interest in locating some hidden, other meaning under the surface of the poet's words. This essay will proceed by attempting to locate from where the inclination to read this way may have come, and to look at a few particularly rich examples of such reading.

Inspiration

Allegorical reading is of course a separate issue from purposefully composing poetry to contain undermeanings and hidden senses. But poets could and did use what has come to be commonly recognized as allegory: Zeus's jars in Homer's *Iliad* (24.527–33), the Hawk and the Nightingale in Hesiod's *Works and Days* (204–12), and the "Ship of State" image in the lyric fragments of Alcaeus (seventh to sixth century BCE),[2] together with widespread personification of abstractions in art, were all well-known examples by the fifth century BCE. Recognition of them as having signification that extended beyond their literal senses may have led naturally to a non-literal way of reading. But one finds no inclination in the poets to produce a theory of allegorical interpretation, whether of works of art or of the physical world.

2 Fragments 6 and 326. The fragments of Alcaeus are conveniently found in David A. Campbell, ed. and trans., *Greek Lyric*, I: *Sappho and Alcaeus*, Loeb Classical Library (Cambridge, MA: Harvard University Press, 1982).

The work of the Presocratic philosopher Democritus (b. 460–457 BCE), however, presents some clues for such a theory. He conceived of a close link (perhaps analogical) between a cosmos of words in a literary work (Homer's *Iliad*) and a cosmos of elements in the universe (*stoicheia*): he said that "Homer, having an inspired nature, fashioned an order (or, 'world,' *kosmos*) of all sorts of words" (or, perhaps "verses," *epê*; 68 B 21 Diels-Kranz).[3] Looking further in what survives of Democritus' work, we find an interest in Homer that seems to have focused on words and expressions: he wrote, for example, "On Homer or: On Orthoepeia and Glosses" (68 A 33.11, B 21–25 Diels-Kranz). This seems to be an early attempt to foist a type of fictionality on Homer, inspired (as he claimed to be) by the Muses. Such a theory would have gone a long way to make a world in many ways not corresponding to our own explicable and acceptable to readers of a literal or traditionally minded cast, and may have arisen to meet such a purpose. As such it seems to speak to the early requirement of "propriety" in all types of cultural discourse (*to prepon*) as can be seen, for example, from Xenophanes' censure of the practice of singing about battles of Titans, Giants, or about violent dissent at a symposium.[4]

Knowledge and *sophia*, Interpretation

Allegoresis is a kind of reading that looks for knowledge. Other readers of poems may be after a pleasing communion with a supposed ancestral past, the delight of aesthetic appreciation, or even a more transformative emotional experience. But the allegorical reader is uniquely attuned to the poem as a rich and powerful source of insight into the gods, the world, and the place of humans in it. Various kinds of speculation are preserved on just where this knowledge is supposed to have come from. Plato (*Protagoras* 316D, *Theaetetus* 180CD) retails the theories of certain sophists that historical poets deliberately concealed wisdom by using poetry as a kind of screening device. Sometimes we get the explanation (as in Plato's *Ion*, Xenophon's *Symposium* 3.5–6, 4.6–7, or Aristophanes' *Frogs* 1030ff) that Orpheus, Musaeus, Hesiod, and Homer were educators who originally taught men fundamental arts. Homer teaches all things, even the art of war and shipbuilding. This seems to have been intended to meet the early demand that poetry be useful, or even make one an excellent man. Plato at *Protagoras* 338Eff gives a famous discussion of Simonides' poem on virtue

---

3 Cf. Lucretius, *On the Nature of Things*, 1.196–8, 2.686–94, and see Democritus, Diels-Kranz, B 18 and B 112.

4 Xenophanes, fragment 1, in Martin L. West, ed., *Iambi et Elegi Graeci* (Oxford: Oxford University Press, 1972).

(*aretê*) that suggests as much: Protagoras begins by claiming that the "principal part of education" is to be expert in discussions of poetry (*peri epôn*). Protagoras, according to other sources, gave similar explications of passages in Homer that demonstrate concern for grammar and other attempts to systematize human knowledge (80 A 1 no. 53, A28–29 Diels-Kranz). Aristophanes at *Clouds* 658ff parodies discussions by "Socrates" of grammatical gender; and Plato at *Phaedrus* 267C (= 80 A 26 Diels-Kranz, cf. 24) attests Protagoras' concern for *orthoepeia* (proper diction). His contemporary Prodicus wrote *Peri onomatôn orthotêtos* (*On the Correctness of Words*; 84 A 11 Diels-Kranz) and had an interest in synonyms, which indicates an interest in Homer as a repository of data about language, and not just as a teller of tall tales about battles and misbehaving gods.[5] Plato's *Cratylus* shows followers of "Heraclitus," renowned for his dark ambiguity, finding ultimate reality in an exploration of names for things.[6]

But sometimes we get a more nuanced picture: a hunt for *hyponoiai*, "hidden ideas." Theagenes of Rhegium (8 Diels-Kranz) was something of an innovator in this direction from about 525 BCE and thus as early as the sixth century. Later reports tell us that he defended Homer's account of the battle of the gods in *Iliad* 20 as an allegory of the "strife" of the natural elements. Metrodorus of Lampsacus (61 Diels-Kranz), in the fifth century, subscribed to an extreme form of systematic allegory which suggests that we should see the gods each as different parts of the human body, with the heroes as parts of the universe.[7] The model for allegory here is the biological organism, with its target being to relate parts to the whole, microcosm to macrocosm, although exactly what Metrodorus was trying to explain, whether about the text of Homer or the nature of the world (or both) is far from transparent, as is almost the rule in allegory.[8] This aspect of allegory is a function of its being one step toward abstraction, from concrete example to an abstract or, at any rate, a general idea.

Thus it is clear that from early on in the Greek tradition there existed different types of allegory, and not only allegory but also etymology (the practice of finding meaning in the supposed derivations of words),

---

5 Robert Lamberton, *Homer the Theologian* (Berkeley: University of California Press, 1986); Jean Pépin, *Mythe et allégorie. Les origines grecques et les contestations judéo-chrétiennes*, 2nd edn. (Paris: Études Augustiniennes, 1976).

6 The tradition becomes especially important for Hellenistic readers and later criticism: James J. O'Hara, *True Names: Vergil and the Alexandrian Tradition of Etymological Word-Play* (Ann Arbor: University of Michigan Press, 1996).

7 Cf. Nicholas James Richardson, "Homeric Professors in the Age of the Sophists," *Proceedings of the Cambridge Philological Society* 201 (1975), 65–81.

8 Cf. Richardson, "Homeric Professors," 69–70.

metaphor, simile, polyonymy (multiple names for the same thing), and analogy.[9] There is a desire for recourse to extended forms of metonymical explanation involving multiple correspondence as early as the early fifth century, that is to say *hyponoia* and allegory in the specific and restricted sense of hidden meanings, rather than the later rhetorical sense of a trope among others.

Metrodorus, a "pupil" or follower of Anaxagoras, seems to have developed Anaxagoras' view "that Homer's poetry was about virtue and justice" (59 A 1 § 11 Diels-Kranz). Here we have allegory on the moral level. Metrodorus is evincing a desire to make Homer's poetry acceptable by seeking in it a coherent, self-consistent, and ethically acceptable view of the world, which would in some way be true as well. It is rare for any literary critic in antiquity to generalize in this way about a work. Plato portrays Socrates as familiar with such a view of allegory (e.g., *Phaedrus* 229C–30A on Boreas and Oreithyia; *Republic* 378B–E), and even as attracted by it in his youth; but later he abandons it as laborious and inefficient, in favor of a more general dismissal of the value of the interpretation of poetry (by poets or anyone else).[10] One could further compare his view of inspiration as irrational, for example, in the *Ion* and in the *Phaedrus*.[11]

An early and unique proponent of vigorous allegorical reading comes in the form of *P.Derveni* (our earliest surviving Greek papyrus: 4th c. BCE), an extreme allegorical interpretation of an Orphic poem on the origins of the gods, by an unknown sophist.[12] Being closer to the Presocratics, the Derveni commentator seems to be developing interests in causes and the soul similar to those that flourished in Plato's work. As is typical of the allegory of the Sophists, the commentator shows the application of the latest scientific theories of the day in order to derive an extension of meaning from the text, drawing it into the sphere of the author's own interests, namely religion and cult. As the commentator understands it, the Orphic poem as a whole is "enigmatic" (*ainigmatôdês*). There are said to be enigmatic references to

9 See David Dawson, *Allegorical Readers and Cultural Revision in Ancient Alexandria* (Berkeley: University of California Press, 1992).

10 *Protagoras* 347Cff, *Hippias Minor* 365CD, *Apology* 22BC, *Meno* 99CD.

11 See J. Tate, "Plato and Allegorical Interpretation," *Classical Quarterly* 23 (1929), 142–54.

12 For critical text and translation, see T. Kouremenos, et al., *The Derveni Papyrus* (Florence: Olschki, 2006); cf. Gábor Betegh, *The Derveni Papyrus: Cosmology, Theology, and Interpretation* (Cambridge: Cambridge University Press, 2004); the first edition appeared in *Zeitschrift für Papyrologie und Epigraphik* 47 (1982), p. 300ff. Discussion and alternative views in the essays in André Laks and Glenn W. Most, eds., *Studies on the Derveni Papyrus* (Oxford: Clarendon, 1997); Richard Janko, "The Derveni Papyrus: An Interim Text," *Zeitschrift für Papyrologie und Epigraphik* 141 (2000), 1–62.

cosmological elements: Zeus is interpreted as air (col. 13,5), Moira as a kind of breath (*to pneuma*; 14,3), Okeanos is said to be air (13,5). The sun is said to be a generative element:
Col. 16.1–11:

> It has been made clear that he called the sun a genital organ (or "reverend": *aidoion*). And he says that the things that now exist have come to be from existing things:

> Of the first-born king, the revered one. And onto him all the immortals grew, blessed gods and goddesses And rivers and lovely springs and everything else That had been born then; and he himself was alone.

> In these verses he indicates that the things that exist always existed and that the things that exist now have come to be out of existing things. The phrase, 'and he himself was alone': in saying this he makes clear that Mind itself being alone is worth everything, just as if everything else were nothing. For it is not possible for these things to be . . .

Here the author begins with asserting equivalences, but branches out into a more fulsome observation on the nature of the cosmos. Everything comes to be out of preexisting things and the mind has some sort of ontological priority to the whole – and then the text breaks off. The prominence of mind here may be a hint of an Anaxagorean dimension at work, since Anaxagoras thought that mind was the governing agency of the cosmos. Also noteworthy is the Derveni commentator's use of *lemmata* (short segments of text) interspersed with commentary on them, a commentary form that was to become standard in later centuries.

The commentator further suggests a specifically linguistic dimension to his equivalences. Demeter, Hera, Rhea are said to be Earth (19,3):
Col. 22:

> Therefore he (sc. Orpheus) named (i.e. in his poem) everything likewise in the noblest possible way, knowing the nature of mankind, that not all of them have the same nature nor do they all want the same things. When they are in a position of power they say what they desire, whatever they happen to be wishing, never the same things, sometimes through greed, sometimes through ignorance. Ge, Meter, Rhea, and Hera: they are all the same she. She was called Ge by custom; Meter because everything comes from her. Ge and Gaia according to each people's dialect. She was named Demeter just as if she is Ge-meter: one name from both. For it was the same thing. And it was also said in the *Hymns*:

> Demeter Rhea Ge Meter Hestia Deio.

For she is called Deio too because she was cut asunder (i.e. ravaged) in the mixture (or: 'in sexual intercourse'). And he will make clear that, according to the (verses? epic poems?)... And Rea because many and... creatures were born... from her. Rhea (was called?)...

The commentator gives a theory of naming that authorizes exuberant interpretive leaps. The poet Orpheus has designated the various pieces of the cosmos, not according to the view that names correspond to things on a one-to-one basis, but rather with the idea that names accommodate their audiences in some fashion, so that a single entity might have multiple designations. His synthetic view of cosmology here finds an etymological counterpart. Just as the multiplicity of things that exist is traceable back to a prior unity, so also names multiply, but their referents are in some sense "the same." This view sets up a hidden reality beneath language and invites a reader to interpretive action.

But it is not only the mystic text that carries a hidden meaning. The actions of cultic practice are equally invitations to interpret. The Eumenides, to whom the initiated (*mustai*) sacrifice, are in fact souls (2,6–10). People are overcome by pleasure and remain ignorant of what is of concern in the next world (col. 1). One passage in particular shows the author appearing to criticize traditional ritual and religious practice:
Col. 20:

[About all those (i) who] after performing a public rite in the cities have seen the holy things (i.e. have been initiated), I wonder less that they fail to attain knowledge, since it is impossible to listen to what is being said and learn it simultaneously. But all those (ii) who have learned (i.e. been initiated) from one who makes a craft of the holy rites deserve to be wondered at and pitied. They deserve (iia) to be wondered at because, thinking before the ceremony that they will attain knowledge, they go away after being initiated before they have understood, without even asking additional questions, as though because they understood (i.e. thinking that they have understood) something of what they have seen or heard or learned. And they (iib) must be pitied because it is not enough that their money is spent, but they go off deprived even of their judgement.

Hoping before performing the holy rites to gain knowledge, nevertheless they go away after being initiated deprived even of their expectation...

The author draws a distinction between those who have seen sacred things (*ta hiera*) after performing a public rite in the cities and those who do so after going to a private professional priest. He is not surprised to hear about the first, but the second group evokes pity from him because these people intend to gain knowledge before the ceremony but go away without asking additional questions and without understanding what they have seen or heard or learned. They have spent their money too soon, and as a result have lost their judgment (*gnômê*). This seems to assert both an epistemological and an ethical need for some kind of allegorical interpretation. Unlike those who go away without understanding what they have seen or heard or learned, the Derveni commentator asks questions about the Orphic poem, engaging in procedures of interpretation that use instruction in cosmology and mythology as a form of initiation, that is, by engaging in a re-mythologizing of the Orphic poet's originally conceptual insights.[13] The author thus invokes contemporary scientific research on causes and particle theory (in particular that of Diogenes of Apollonia) to make his target text seem modern and up to date, while exercising his real concern for deep-level understanding of private mysteries and social moralizing. So also Euthyphro in Plato's dialogue boasts the ability to interpret (perhaps oracularly), for the benefit of the Athenian assembly, the myth in Hesiod about Zeus killing his father, Cronus. These readings suggest a cluster of interpretive practices, using inspired poetry and cultic practices as prooftexts that promise profound insight into the divine, the cosmos, and the human place in it.

Effects of poetry on the emotions

In looking for sources of inspiration for such extravagant non-literal readings, several further veins of study hold promise. Gorgias in his *Defense of Helen* (82 B 11 Diels-Kranz) praises the power of discourse (*logos*) and persuasion (8–14), in poetry (9), incantations (10), other forms of speeches (including those of orators and even *meteôrologoi*, i.e., cosmologists), compared with the effect of drugs. He identified terror, pity, and longing as effects of poetry (9); he saw sorrow, pleasure, fear, and confidence as effects of speeches (14).[14] This seems to go to a generalizing tendency in the interpretation of discourse, over and against a literal and specific understanding of it. So Gorgias (82 B 23 Diels-Kranz) famously pronounced on the paradoxical, illusory nature of tragedy. He claimed that by means of stories and emotions, tragedy creates a deception in which the deceiver is more honest than the deceived, and the deceived is wiser than one who is not deceived.

---

13 For the idea, see Walter Burkert, "Orpheus und die Vorsokratiker. Bemerkungen zum Derveni-Papyrus und zur pythagoreischen Zahlenlehre," *Antike und Abendland* 14 (1968), 93–114, developed further in Dirk Obbink, "Allegory and Exegesis in the Derveni Papyrus: The Origin of Greek Scholarship," in G. R. Boys-Stones, ed., *Metaphor, Allegory and the Classical Tradition* (Oxford: Oxford University Press, 2003), pp. 177–88.

14 Cf. Douglas M. MacDowell, *Gorgias, Encomium of Helen* (Bristol: Bristol Classical Press, 1982).

This entails one of the most basic moves in allegory: here a tragedy is not literally what it appears to be (a pathetically sad story), but rather a vehicle for expressing general truths through the ideas that lie beneath the surface of the text. So in Plato's *Ion*, the professional performer Ion says that he experiences tears and terror when he recites Homer's poetry and evokes similar emotional reactions in his audience (*Ion* 535B), but also claims to be able to give exegetical explanations of passages in Homer. However, he does not have the same powers of explanation for other poets who leave him unmoved (531A). The dubious credibility of Ion's claim here, that the emotional appeal of the poetry helps him "understand" Homer, may offer a further context for Plato's focus in the *Republic* on the emotions in his discussions of poetry and its epistemological dimension. In *Republic* 387B–89A he was deeply suspicious of the power of tears and laments, excess laughter, and pleasure derived from laments (605Cff) to instruct with sufficient rigor; hence his objections to the effect of poetry on the moral character of the young.[15]

Morality and mimesis

We have already alluded to an early view that poetry could instruct: in Aristophanes' *Frogs* 1034–36, Aeschylus is portrayed as representative of the old order (Homer taught useful things, *chrêst' edidaxen*), against the Sophistic approach of Euripides. Alcidamas held that such general knowledge, as opposed to a hard-headedly literal understanding of narrative, could emerge from the discursive arts through imitation (*mimêsis*).[16] A rival of Plato and fellow follower (with Isocrates) of Gorgias, he made such a claim in his *Mouseion*: the *Odyssey* is a "splendid mirror of human life" (*kalon anthrôpinou biou katoptron*).[17] The metaphor appears already in Pindar (*Nemean Odes* 7.14): song is a "mirror for splendid deeds" (*ergois kalois esoptron*). So honors could be paid to Homer (and other poets) as an *historikos*, as a scientific researcher of human nature.[18] Lycurgus of Athens (fourth century BCE) pays such honor to poets in his oration *Against Leocrates* 102: poets, "when they imitate human life, by picking out the most beautiful deeds,

15 See also Robert Wardy, *The Birth of Rhetoric: Gorgias, Plato and their Successors* (London: Routledge, 1996).

16 For text and commentary, see John V. Muir, *Alcidamas, Works and Fragments* (London: Bristol Classical Press, 2001); Neil O'Sullivan, *Alcidamas, Aristophanes, and the Beginnings of Greek Stylistic Theory*, Hermes Einzelschrift 60 (Stuttgart: Steiner, 1992).

17 Cited at Aristotle, *Rhetoric* 1406b12f.

18 Nicholas James Richardson, "The Contest of Homer and Hesiod and Alcidamas' *Mouseion*," *Classical Quarterly* 31 (1981), 1–10.

win people over by persuasion through discourse and demonstration."[19] (Again, Plato provides a useful contrast. At *Republic* book 10, 596D, he uses the image of the mirror rather differently, claiming that painting and poetry are "at a third remove from reality.") Such comments attest to the possibility that poetic imitation provides generalizable instruction in what is to be admired, rather than a straightforward tale of human adventure. In the classical period and fifth century we find the use of themes, episodes, and characters from Homer and other poets for moral allegory or illustration. This can be seen in the treatises of the sophist Antisthenes, a Cynic philosopher who used the *Iliad* and *Odyssey* as traditional material to illustrate his own moral views.[20] Significantly, Alcidamas' *Mouseion* included a version of the *Contest of Homer and Hesiod* where Homer and Hesiod are judged on literary and ethical grounds (Hesiod wins, because he praised farming in peacetime!), as part of an account (partly fictionalized) of the two poets' lives and deaths, honors, and achievements, including generalized contributions to human knowledge. Wouldn't we call this allegory? Even Plato himself makes such moves. In the *Hippias Minor* Achilles and Odysseus are seen as having had to make paradigmatic moral choices, and in the *Symposium* (208E–09E) poets are linked with lawgivers as potential benefactors of society, though again it is true that by the time of *Republic* book 10 (599B–600B) this view is roundly dismissed. The Plato of the *Republic* may even be echoing and answering Alcidamas specifically.[21]

Writing and allegory

A neglected aspect in the development of allegory in the Greek tradition is the advent of writing, and the consequent tension in written versus oral, or prepared versus improvised discourse. Alcidamas attacks the value of prepared speeches and the written word in *On Sophists*,[22] so also Isocrates' *Panegyricus* 11. And Plato's *Phaedrus* ends with discussion over the relative value of the two, with Socrates deciding in favor of the oral over Lysias' prepared speech (*Phaedrus* 274Cff.). The introduction of books, writing,

19 For fuller context see also the text in *Minor Attic Orators* 2, trans. J. O. Burtt, Loeb Classical Library (Cambridge, MA: Harvard University Press; London: William Heinemann, 1962).
20 Cf. Richardson, "Homeric Professors," 77–81.
21 Cf. Richardson, "Contest," 8 (in the affirmative), but see O'Sullivan, *Alcidamas*, chapter 3, pp. 64–66 for doubts.
22 Ludwig Radermacher, *Artium scriptores. Reste der voraristotelischen Rhetorik*, Österreichische Akademie der Wissenschaften, Philosophisch-Historische Klasse, 227.3 (Vienna 1951), B22. 15, pp. 135–41.

and literacy in the fifth and early fourth centuries brought about changes in practice and thought.[23] By the end of the fifth century, allegory was becoming associated with the book, as the Derveni Papyrus shows. But there must have existed an earlier stage of predominantly oral allegorical exegesis, represented by Plato's dialogue *Ion*. So also Isocrates in his *Panathenaicus* (342–39 BCE) speaks (18) of the common herd of sophists, some of whom sit in the Lyceum discussing poets, especially Homer and Hesiod, "saying nothing original but just reciting their verses and repeating by memory the cleverest thing said by others about them in the past."[24]

One of the things that is produced by early allegory is commentary, another is myth. The former entailed a view that all literature is other literature, that every utterance demands its own gloss; the latter re-introduced the sense of wonder associated with understanding something that goes beyond oneself and beyond the literal and into literary appreciation.

23 See the essays in Harvey Yunis, ed., *Written Texts and the Rise of Literate Culture in Ancient Greece* (Cambridge: Cambridge University Press, 2003).
24 For fuller context see the text in *Isocrates 2*, trans. George Norlin, Loeb Classical Library, 3 vols. (Cambridge, MA: Harvard University Press; London: Heinemann, 1980)

2

GLENN W. MOST

Hellenistic allegory and early imperial rhetoric

The philosophical heritage

In their explicit doctrines, Plato and Aristotle express distrust and disdain for allegorical interpretation; but they do not manage to slam the door upon it altogether. Plato explicitly repudiates the allegories (*hyponoiai*) with which traditional tales of divine violence and immorality might be rescued for children (*Republic* 2.378D) and makes fun of attempts to make sense of myths by rationalizing them (*Phaedrus* 229C–30A). And yet the same Plato takes pains to introduce into crucial moments of various dialogues extended mythic narratives, often transparently allegorical in character, which seem designed to supply the philosophically correct forms of myth from which students will be able to learn acceptable views, once the incorrect forms transmitted to them by their traditional culture have been discarded. His independent-minded student Aristotle shares his teacher's anti-allegorical tastes: in his view of the development of human thought he disregards claims for the poets' philosophical seriousness and instead consigns their alleged cosmological views to the period before genuine philosophy began, while in his work on poetry he entirely ignores allegorical interpretations of epic,[1] substituting for them the view that what makes Homer and other poets philosophically interesting are not any covert philosophical doctrines but the structures of human thought and action they explicitly portray. And yet the same Aristotle derives from Plato's view (*Timaeus* 21D–25D) that human history has been punctuated by periodically recurring cataclysms the notion that at least some myths contain a kernel of philosophical truth from before the deluge (*Metaphysics* 12.8 1074b1–14, *De philosophia* Fragment 13, ed. Rose). Evidently the pro-allegorical pressure that came from such sources as natural philosophy, the poets' advocates, and the mystery religions was simply too strong to be ignored altogether: thrown out

---

1 We find a single apparent exception, surely a doxographical report: Fragment 175 in Valentin Rose, *Aristotelis qui ferebantur librorum fragmenta* (Leipzig: Teubner, 1886).

the front door, it slips back in through the window, in various kinds of accommodation.

Nonetheless, until the beginning of the Hellenistic period, allegory was philosophically marginal – and indeed it remained so for generations, at least in the schools that Plato and Aristotle had founded and that continued to bear their founders' imprint. Plato's first successors in the Academy, Speusippus and Xenocrates, sought their gods not in traditional poetry, which they entirely neglected, but in (quasi-)mathematical objects and other entities; whereas Aristotle's students in the Lyceum did indeed investigate earlier Greek poetry – so especially Heracleides Ponticus, Chamaeleon, Praxiphanes, and later Satyrus – but their studies were devoted exclusively to the poets' biographies, the genres of their works, difficult passages explained non-allegorically, and lexicographical questions, and not to any underlying allegorical meanings.

However, the partition of philosophy in the Hellenistic period into various competing schools and the ensuing doctrinal polarization among them meant that what Academics and Peripatetics neglected could come to seem irresistibly attractive to their professional rivals (and vice versa). Epicurus, to be sure, seems to have had little patience with traditional Greek poetry, though his interpretation of the gods as moral paradigms useful for human beings could well have opened the door to allegorical recuperation of the myths, and though a passage in Lucretius' *De rerum natura*, in which the terrors of the underworld are interpreted as the emotional suffering of miscreants in the present life (3.978–1023), shows how a psychological allegoresis of some traditional myths could be thought compatible with the rational standards of Epicureanism. Yet there are no traces of any systematic effort at allegorization among Epicureans.

Where Epicurus feared to tread, the Stoics did not hesitate to rush in. It was the first generations of Stoics (perhaps developing here, as in other fields, ideas put forward by Antisthenes and other earlier thinkers) who brought allegorical interpretation from the margins of the philosophical enterprise to its center, and it was the dominance of later Stoicism during the first centuries of the Roman Empire that – even more than Neoplatonism, important though its own contribution was – bequeathed allegory to Western culture as a respectable, indeed virtually indispensable way to save both the poets' myths and the philosophers' doctrines. Not that this was a self-evident choice – Cicero's *On the Nature of the Gods* and Philodemus' *On Piety* demonstrate how easily the Stoics' allegory could become a target for nasty polemics on the part of their Academic and Epicurean rivals, who had no trouble making fun of Stoic claims for allegorical meanings in ancient poems and cult practices. Why, then, did the Stoics expose themselves to professional ridicule by adopting allegory? They must have thought they had very good reasons to do so.

And indeed, they did: not only the larger cultural context but also more narrow philosophical considerations would have made their choice seem entirely reasonable to them. Culturally, the Mediterranean world after Alexander's death was no longer quite the one Plato and Aristotle had known: its horizons were broader and its structures vaster, it was filled with newly discovered cultures and newly available information, the small Greek polis which had once provided the limit of intelligibility for human virtue and action had now become somewhat less dominant. Texts and practices that had always been adequately validated simply by being anchored in highly specific micro-cultural contexts could now come to seem trivial or meaningless once they were repositioned within this turbulently cosmopolitan new world. Allegory was a way of decontextualizing them out of the determinate local situations and traditions from which they had originally arisen and for which they had once been intended, and of recontextualizing them within conceptual systems that were universally valid and comprehensible – and thereby it supplied a meaning to them which one did not need to have special local knowledge or to be a member of a specific political community in order to understand and appreciate. In this way, a broad cultural heritage could be rescued, if not from immediate extinction, then from gradual irrelevance; and on the one hand, disoriented Greeks could thereby manage to maintain their traditional allegiances, while, on the other hand, the rescued prestige of their traditions could benefit their rescuers too, shedding the corroborative light of an ancient wisdom upon the new Stoic doctrines.

So in pragmatic terms the Stoics' adoption of allegory was a shrewd tactic. But given that the Stoics were not cultural entrepreneurs but philosophers, they also devised philosophical systems which, whatever else they did, also provided a broad rationale for allegorical interpretation. The Stoic convictions that the foundation for both the being and the intelligibility of the world was a universal *logos* developing gradually towards fulfillment and perfection, and that the whole cosmos was organized as the truest polis in which both gods and humans were citizens, meant that no moment of history, nor any part of the world, could be totally devoid of the at least partial presence of this *logos*. Allegorical interpretation made manifest that portion of the universal *logos* which had always been contained, sometimes scarcely visible, in even the most apparently absurd practices and recalcitrant myths – and thereby made its own modest contribution to the eventual supremacy of that *logos*. A tripartite theology attributed by Augustine (*The City of*

God 6.12) to Varro (Fragments 6 and 7),[2] which goes back certainly to Hellenistic sources, and presumably to Stoic philosophy (cf. SVF 2.1009),[3] distinguishes three kinds of discourses about the gods, mythical, physical, and political, assigning the first to the poets, the second to the philosophers, and the third to the people. On this view, the philosophers' demonstration that the words of the poets or the cults of the cities contain allegorically veiled tenets of natural philosophy does not falsify either traditional poetry or popular religion, but restores to them their full meaning and is entirely harmonious with them. Stoic allegorical interpretation of the poets, then, is not a purely literary exercise: together with the exegesis of statues and cult practices and with the etymology of names and epithets, it restores a theological system for which the poetic texts, whatever the intentions of their actual human authors, provide evidence that is ancient and authoritative but not *sui generis*.

Interpreting old poems for a new world

Nonetheless, the ancient poets possessed an undeniable prestige and ubiquity, and the first generations of Stoics did their best to deploy allegory and etymology in order to bring them into their own philosophical fold. Zeno of Citium, the founder of Stoicism, wrote five books of *Homeric Problems* (SVF 1.41) and commentaries on the *Iliad*, the *Odyssey*, and the *Margites* ascribed to Homer (SVF 1.274); he also interpreted Hesiod's *Theogony* (SVF 1.167) and may well have written a commentary on it (SVF 1.100, 103–05). He identified Hera with the air, Zeus with the aether, Poseidon with the sea, Hephaistos with fire, and so forth (SVF 1.169) – neither surprisingly, given that according to the Stoics the particular gods are contained within the natural world as manifestations of the single dominant god (hence Stoic theology forms a part of Stoic physics), nor innovatively (most of these identifications can be traced back for centuries, some of them back to Homer himself). His student Cleanthes continued the work of reconciling with the tenets of Stoicism the traditions deriving from Orpheus and Musaeus and the poems of Homer, Hesiod, Euripides, and other poets (SVF 1.539), corroborating his teacher's identification of the traditional gods with natural phenomena, focusing perhaps especially upon Zeus as the supreme aether (SVF 1.535–37) and upon Apollo as the sun (SVF 1.540–43); our sources report some of his attempts to import Stoic doctrines into the poems of

---

2 In Varro, *Antiquitates rerum divinarum*, ed. Burkhart Cardauns, 2 vols. (Wiesbaden: Steiner, 1976), 1: 18–19.

3 SVF = J. von Arnim, ed., *Stoicorum Veterum Fragmenta*, 4 vols. (Leipzig: Teubner, 1905–24).

Homer and Euripides by means of bizarre textual conjectures (SVF 1.535, 549, 562). Cleanthes' student, Chrysippus, then went on to systematize and refine the theological doctrines and allegorical and etymological practices of his predecessors; and in numerous treatises, especially *On the Gods* in three books – the first one explained the physical nature of the gods one by one, the second harmonized the poetic texts of Orpheus, Musaeus, Hesiod, and Homer to these explanations (SVF 2.1077–78), the third was devoted to Zeus – he formulated a comprehensive exposition of the subject which remained authoritative for centuries. He probably systematized the heterogeneous hodgepodge of the Greek pantheon, dividing the gods into seven categories and assigning the inventions of the poets to the sixth one;[4] as far as we can tell from the fragments, he seems to have continued along much the same lines as Zeno and Cleanthes, equating the traditional gods with natural phenomena, etymologizing their names and epithets, and never intervening into the poetic texts except when this was absolutely convenient. His allegorical justification of a notorious cult statue (or painting) which apparently showed Hera engaging in oral sex with Zeus (SVF 2.1071–74) was particularly controversial; a number of fragments of his (sometimes seemingly quite capricious) interpretations and emendations of passages in Homer's *Iliad* and Hesiod's *Theogony* are preserved in the scholia to these poems, in various lexica, and in other philosophical and compilatory works.

But it is only in fragments that the first Stoics' work on Greek poetry has reached us, despite its volume, intensity, and breadth. Of course, given the shipwreck of so much of Hellenistic Greek philosophy, this need not surprise us – works of original philosophy, authoritative but sometimes rebarbatively obscure, were all too easily replaced by later user-friendlier compilations (such as, for Stoic allegories of the gods, Cornutus' first century CE *Compendium of Greek Theology*), and the decline of Stoicism in the later Roman Empire meant that the texts of its founders came eventually to lack the institutional support and passionate defenders which protected those of Plato and Aristotle (Epicurus' remains were saved largely by Diogenes Laertius' enthusiasm). But in the case of the Stoics' allegorical interpretations, another factor intervened to restrict their survival.

For the most important channel for the transmission and interpretation of the older Greek poets to later ages passed through Alexandria. Here a group of philologists, gathered together during the third and second centuries BCE by the first Ptolemies, helped consolidate their patrons' claim to be the legitimate successors of the glories of Classical Greece. In this way they

---

4 SVF 2.1009, but the attribution to Chrysippus is uncertain.

laid the foundations for a different kind of literary scholarship from what contemporary Stoics were practicing. Some later Latin sources report that a dispute pitted the Alexandrian philologists Aristophanes of Byzantium and Aristarchus,[5] who followed the principle of analogy in grammatical questions, against other linguists, apparently Stoics (like, perhaps, Crates of Mallus, a Stoic contemporary of Aristarchus, working at the rival royal center of Pergamum), who preferred to adopt the opposing rule of anomaly; and though it is unlikely that the terms of the controversy were precisely those our sources indicate, it seems highly probable that Alexandrians and Stoics parted ways in linguistic theory – and not only there: for Aristarchus' guiding principle in his literary exegesis (whoever actually formulated it in these terms) was *Homêron ex Homêrou saphênizein* ("to elucidate Homer from Homer"), and it is hard to see any point to such a precept except to defend one mode of interpretation which remained resolutely within the poet's own words and conceptions, against an allegorical strategy which did not hesitate to posit explanatory equivalences between elements within the poem and doctrines of a later and foreign philosophy. So too, Aristarchus' notion of a heroic age in world history whose customs were mirrored in the archaic Greek epic poems seems to have been designed to insulate Homer and the other early Greek poets from the kind of anachronism to which allegorical interpretations like the Stoics' were all too susceptible.

While we must remain skeptical about any simplistic or monolithic opposition between the Stoic allegories of Pergamum (essentially the product of Crates and a couple of disciples) and the historical and critical philology of Alexandria (the fruit of five generations of scholarly discipline), there can be little doubt that some such opposition did help shape the development of literary scholarship during the Hellenistic period; and given that it is to the Alexandrian philologists that the most important strands of our textual transmission and ancient commentaries on Greek poetry go back, it is easy to see why Stoic allegories are cited in them fragmentarily, infrequently, more in the less scholarly scholia, and for the most part disparagingly. Nonetheless, enough remains of the most important figures of the generations after Chrysippus for us to be able to form some idea of what happened when Stoic allegorical techniques were combined with Hellenistic literary scholarship and applied to the interpretation of older Greek poetry.

Both of the most important Stoic literary scholars of this period came to philology from philosophy: Crates was a practicing Stoic philosopher in

---

5 Varro, *On the Latin Language*, trans. Roland G. Kent, Loeb Classical Library, 2 vols. (Cambridge, MA: Harvard University Press, 1938), 9.12, 10.68; Charisius, *Artis grammaticae libri V*, ed. Karl Barwick (Leipzig: Teubner, 1925 [reprint 1964]), p. 149.26.

Cilicia when he was called to the court of Pergamum, and Apollodorus of Athens studied in Athens with Chrysippus' student Diogenes of Babylon before leaving for Alexandria and thence to Pergamum. Crates probably wrote two monographs on Homer (it is debated whether he wrote commentaries and doubtful whether he prepared critical editions), in which he combined detailed discussion of textual problems (Aristarchus and he disagreed frequently) with interpretations of passages and episodes in terms of physical allegory (especially cosmology and astronomy) and etymology. Thus the scene in which Hephaestus manufactures the shield of Achilles, which the Alexandrian philologist Zenodotus had rejected, was defended by Crates as an allegory of the ten circles of the heavens – Achilles' shield, just like Agamemnon's, he called "an imitation of the cosmos;"[6] his cosmological interests led him to work also on other texts, such as Hesiod's *Theogony*, the *Rhesus* attributed to Euripides, and Aratus' *Phaenomena*.

If Crates is best seen as a Stoic philosopher applying physical doctrines to poems so as to reach an accommodation with them, Apollodorus' work demonstrates that by now, only about one generation later, the Alexandrian model of philology has become an inescapable criterion of seriousness: many of his questions resemble familiar Stoic ones, but the answers he seeks for them are usually couched in terms that the school of Aristarchus too would have recognized. Besides important works on world chronology from the fall of Troy until his own times, on Homeric geography in terms of the Catalogue of Ships (he seems to have followed Aristarchus in interpreting the Homeric epics as representations of the heroic age), as well as lesser studies on comedy, Apollodorus also wrote *On the Gods*, a monumental treatise in 24 books on Homeric religion in which, at least according to Philodemus (though he may have been oversimplifying matters), he was combating "in some way" (*pou*) against the "allegorizers"[7] (Fragment 103) – and who else could these have been if not the Stoics? In this work he sought to explain the names and epithets of the gods by deriving them not from Stoic philosophy (even though, as was only natural, a number of his etymologies coincided with the Stoics') and "not from their places of cult... but from the capacities of their souls or... the features of their bodies" (Fragment 353.11): thus Zeus is called *Dôdônaios* not because of his oracle at Dodona

---

6 Fragment 23a, d, f in Hans Joachim Mette, *Sphairopoiia. Untersuchungen zur Kosmologie des Krates von Pergamon* (Munich: C. H. Beck, 1936).

7 *Sunoikeountes*. For the fragments of Apollodorus of Athens, see Felix Jacoby, ed., *Die Fragmente der griechischen Historiker*, Zweiter Teil: Zeitgeschichte, B. Spezialgeschichte, Autobiographien und Memoiren, Zeittafeln (Berlin: Weidmann, 1929), pp. 1022–128.

but because he gives (*didômi*: Fragment 88), and Apollo's epithet *Dêlios* derives not from the island of Delos but from the fact that he renders all things clear (*dêla*: Fragment 95.32). Apollodorus' investigation of the gods' attributes, as assigned to them by Homer (in Varro's terms, "mythical theology"), is neither not the tenets of a modern philosophy ("physical theology"), nor the specificities of attested cult practice ("political theology"), but rather their fundamental natures as individual divine persons. With Apollodorus, creative Stoic literary scholarship is reaccommodated once and for all with the mainstream of Alexandrian philology – allegorical treatises are still produced in the following centuries, but at least the ones that survive are either not literary[8] or not really philosophical[9] or not Stoic (the Neoplatonists).

The poetics and rhetoric of allegory

One way to provide readers with philosophically unexceptionable poetry was to apply allegorical interpretation to the ancient masterpieces of Greek literature; another was to create new poems already satisfactorily equipped with an intentionally produced allegorical subtext. After all, the line between the one theoretical concept, a wise poem containing permanently valid truths, however limited its human author's knowledge, and the other, a wise poet enabled by divine enthusiasm or philosophical insight to devise such truths consciously and communicate them to his audience, had always been thin and sometimes evanescent; and no one could deny that there were cases throughout Greek literature, indeed as early as the *Iliad* itself, in which passages of an evidently allegorical intent were inserted into larger heroic narratives.

So in one sense there had long been a tradition that made possible the intentional composition of poetic texts with philosophical subtexts. Nonetheless, Cleanthes' "Hymn to Zeus" (SVF 1.537) seems to have been a genuine novelty in Greek cultural history. Plato had shown Socrates praying to the god Pan (*Phaedrus* 279B–C) – but this Pan was a highly specific local deity, present at the very spot on the Ilissus where Socrates was praying (cf. 230B–C, 263D), and while the content of Socrates' prayer was perhaps somewhat unusual in its modesty and morality, its form was thoroughly conventional. Aristotle had composed a hymn to *Aretê* ("Virtue") in honor of Hermias,[10] but this had been an encomium of an abstract concept (one

---

8 E.g., Cornutus, *Compendium of Greek Theology*.

9 E.g., Heraclitus, *Homeric Allegories*; Pseudo-Plutarch, *On the Life and Poetry of Homer*.

10 Fragment 842 in Denys L. Page, ed., *Poetae melici Graeci* (Oxford: Clarendon Press, 1962) = Aristotle, Fragment 675 in Rose, ed., *Aristotelis ... fragmenta* (note above).

to which he devotes much attention in his philosophical writings), for the sake of which heroes ancient and modern had toiled mightily.

Cleanthes seems to have been the first Greek philosopher to compose an allegorical hymn, one which was directed to a single anthropomorphic god of the traditional pantheon but reinterpreted this god systematically in terms of an elaborate philosophical doctrine. Cleanthes' Hymn begins mightily:

> Most glorious of the immortals, many-named, all-powerful always,
> Zeus, first cause of nature, steering all things with law,
> Hail! It is right for all mortals to call upon you.
> For from you is our origin, we who have received by lot the image of your
> voice,
> we alone of all mortal creatures that live and move upon the earth.
> Accordingly, I will hymn you and will always sing of your power.
>
> (1–6)[11]

And it goes on to explain the role of this supreme god in guiding the universe, in directing "the universal *logos* which moves through all things" (12–13), and in ensuring the rule of order and goodness. It concludes,

> But Zeus, all-giving, dark-clouded, bright-lightninged,
> rescue humans from baleful ignorance,
> scatter it from their soul, let them encounter
> the wisdom on which you rely as you steer all things with justice,
> so that we may be honored and honor you in return,
> hymning your deeds continuously, as befits
> one who is mortal; for there is no greater glory for mortals
> nor for gods than to hymn in justice the universal eternal law.
>
> (32–39)

Cleanthes' Hymn already accomplishes in its very composition the duty of hymning Zeus it assigns to all human beings, and it need not – indeed it could not – have been sung in any normal temple of Zeus as part of his traditional cult worship (though there is no reason we cannot suppose that it might have been performed, or have been intended to be performed, in the Stoic classroom): the fit Stoic reader will recognize in every word a clearly marked tenet of the school's philosophy and will be confirmed in his doctrinal and moral choices; any outsider into whose hands the text might fall will not be done positive harm by it and might even be guided through it to a deeper wisdom.

---

11 Cleanthes' Hymn can be found in SVF 1.537. For a full translation, see Johan C. Thom, ed., *Cleanthes' Hymn to Zeus: Text, Translation, and Commentary* (Tübingen: Mohr Siebeck, 2005).

As philosophers go, Cleanthes is not a bad poet (among moderns, Nietzsche and Heidegger at least were far worse ones). But once allegory had become a philosophically legitimate instrument of poetic composition, genuinely talented poets could make use of it strategically in order to add an appearance of depth and sophistication to their works, to advertise their own learning, and sometimes to achieve effects of irony and wit – all the more as the texts of the ancient poets they read in school were equipped with commentaries into which, despite the best efforts of Aristarchus and his like, bits of allegorical interpretation had already started to infiltrate. Two brief examples from some of the best poets of this period will serve to illustrate some of the purposes to which poetic allegory could be put.

At the beginning of book 3 of Apollonius Rhodius' *Argonautica*, Aphrodite offers a bribe to her unruly son Eros to get him to make Medea fall in love with Jason. She asks:

> Will you be good, and do me a favor I am going to ask of you? Then I will
> give you one of Zeus's lovely toys, the one that his fond nurse Adrasteia made
> for him in the Idaean cave when he was still a child and liked to play. It is
> a perfect ball; Hephaestus himself could not make you a better toy. Its zones
> are golden, and two circular joins curve around each of them; the seams are
> concealed, as a twisting dark blue pattern plays over them. When you throw
> it up, it will leave a fiery trail behind it like a meteor in the sky.
>
> $(3.131-41)^{12}$

The scene of a petulant mother and her rambunctious child could have come straight out of comedy – were these characters not divine, and were the outcome of this farcical exchange not so tragic: adult passion, suffering, and death, and all for a child's toy. But what a toy! Zeus' infancy brings us back to the earliest days of world history (no longer does he like to play); Adrasteia is associated with primordial forces of cosmic retribution like Nemesis and Ananke (her name means "she who cannot be outrun"); and the ball is an unmistakable symbol of the universe, with its golden zones (the celestial zones), the two circular joins (the celestial equator and the ecliptic), its twisting dark blue band (perhaps the zodiac), and its fiery path through the heavens – and just in case any readers might miss the unhidden meaning, Apollonius varies in his line 140 a line (401) from Aratus' didactic poem on astronomy, the *Phaenomena*. After all, Apollonius had likely learned in school that the Homeric shield of Achilles was an allegorical representation of the cosmos, and Eros' power over all gods and men had

12 Translation draws from two standard ones: Richard Hunter, trans., *Jason and the Golden Fleece (The Argonautica)* (Oxford: Clarendon Press, 1993), p. 69; and E. V. Rieu, trans., *The Voyage of the Argo (The Argonautica)* (New York: Penguin, 1971), pp. 112–13.

been a commonplace at least since Hesiod's *Theogony* (120–22) – indeed, part of the wit of this passage is that it is only because the same childish Eros also happens to be the uncontestable master of the universe that Aphrodite can be so sure that his intervention will be irresistible. Long before, Eros had played with a purple ball in Greek lyric poetry:[13] Apollonius' sublime yet witty transformation of that image into one of cosmic potency could not have been achieved without allegory.

The action of Virgil's *Aeneid* begins when Juno sees the Trojan fleet sailing away from Sicily and invokes Aeolus' help in creating a terrible storm to shipwreck them, at least delaying, if she cannot prevent it, their fated arrival in Italy. The parallels to the *Odyssey* are intentionally obvious, yet they are all slightly askew: Aeolus' residence comes from *Odyssey* 10.1–12, but the Homeric palace and city become an underground prison in Virgil; Aeneas' anguished outcry (*Aeneid* 1.94–101) recalls Odysseus' (*Odyssey* 5.306–12), but from a different storm; and above all Hera has nothing to do with the Homeric episode – in both epics the winds cause a storm and shipwreck, but in Homer they are released by human greed and stupidity, not by divine rancor. Indeed, what is Juno doing anyway stirring up a storm – something so little part of her own sphere of competence that she must devise a complicated stratagem in order to inveigle Aeolus into doing it for her? We can easily imagine reasons why, within the terms of the surface narrative, Virgil should have wished to introduce his human hero in conflict with his divine antagonist at the very beginning, and the storm and shipwreck do lead directly into Aeneas' meeting with Dido, an essential element of Virgil's immediate plot and larger historical design; and in terms of divine and human psychology, Juno's frantic passion is impressively externalized in this tumultuous meteorological tempest which leads even Aeneas, briefly, to abandon his typical self-control and composure. But Servius' commentary to the *Aeneid* demonstrates that at least some ancient readers of the epic explained Juno's role here differently, in terms of the Stoic physical allegory that saw her as the turbulent lower air in contrast to the serene aether of Jupiter (Servius on *Aeneid* 1.42, 47, 58, 78) – for example, it is said to be not without reason that Juno offers Aeolus a nymph as bride, since Juno is air, clouds are made of air, waters come from the clouds, and the nymphs are evidently waters (71); though when the storm makes even the aether gleam with frequent flashes (90) the commentator does not remark upon Virgil's sublime hyperbole but apologizes for the poet's frequently confusing aether and air (90). It is no doubt tempting to dismiss such an allegorical

13 Anacreon, Fragment 358, in Page, ed., *Poetae melici Graeci*.

interpretation as a late and irrelevant fancy. And yet the Stoic allegory of Hera as air (bolstered by the etymology of her name, *Hêra* < *aêr*) was well established long before Virgil's time and is well attested in our Homer commentaries (which, in some form, he had certainly studied). To suggest that Virgil himself may have meant something along these lines (though perhaps not in the particularly ham-fisted version Servius provides) allows us to link his intention more closely with the reception of Roman readers; and it both provides a physical correlate to Virgil's (pseudo-)scientific explanation of the winds as arising from subterranean caverns, and deepens the significance of the goddess' futile resistance to the fates, which Virgil emphasizes at the very beginning (*Aeneid* 1.16–31: according to Stoic dogma, fate guides the wise and drags the foolish). Put into these terms, Juno's storm symbolizes a force for disorder which cannot prevent the ultimate fulfillment of the design of universal *logos* but can make things difficult along the way, and thus coheres perfectly with the large-scale cosmological plan of the epic. All the wittier, then, and sadder, that Juno's rage for disorder should be exacerbated by an exquisitely feminine pique at Paris' snub during the judgment of the goddesses and Zeus's passion for the Trojan Ganymede (25–28).

Once the poets had adapted allegorical interpretation to their own compositional needs, the path lay open for the instructors of rhetoric to teach ambitious young pupils how to produce allegorical texts of their own or to introduce allegorical sections into larger contexts. Allegory, which had begun in philosophy and moved into poetry, could now establish itself as a rhetorical device. Writing sometime around 100 CE, Plutarch remarks that what used to be called *hyponoiai* (the term Plato had used at *Republic* 2.378D) had in his own time come to be named *allêgoriai* (*Moralia* 19E–F) – a terminological nicety denoting an epochal conceptual shift (attested as early as *c.* 100 BCE, in Demetrius' *On Style*): for if a *hypo-noia*, an "under-thought," is a kind of concept and hence belongs to philosophy, an *all-êgoria*, an "otherwise-speaking," is a kind of speech and belongs to rhetoric. Henceforth allegory pertained to the rhetoricians, and as a trope it appears in ancient and modern handbooks[14] and in numerous treatises, e.g. Heraclitus' *Homeric Allegories*. Yet its invariably unstable position within rhetorical systems – its definition is parasitic upon that of metaphor,[15] while its fuzzy characterization as saying one thing but meaning another

---

14 E.g., Cicero, *De oratore* 3.166; Quintilian, *Institutio oratoria*, 8.6.44, 9.2.46; Tryphon, *De tropis*, in Leonardus Spengel, ed., *Rhetores Graeci* 3 (Leipzig: Teubner, 1856): 193.9.
15 E.g., Quintilian, *Institutio oratoria*, 9.2.46.

makes it indistinguishable from irony[16] – suggests that it has arrived late at rhetoric, after all the best places have already been taken. Modern students usually come to allegory from rhetoric: but, in the ancient world at least, rhetoric is not the beginning of allegory's story, but the end.

16 E.g., Quintilian, *Institutio oratoria*, 8.6.44.

3

DANIEL BOYARIN

Origen as theorist of allegory: Alexandrian contexts

Within an early Christian context, one finds allegory judged by at least two quite different measures. It is, on the one hand, the powerful engine of Pauline reinterpretation that makes the Hebrew Bible into an "old" testament. On the other, it is a non-literal way of reading that raises a certain anxiety within a set of traditions that at regular intervals insist on different forms of literalism. Both kinds of measures are regularly applied to the vast corpus of Origen (185–c. 254), the formative thinker of early Christian allegorical exegesis. Among the anxieties that his non-literal interpretations have raised is that he too quickly abandons the literal sense of a text and is more informed by the spirit of Platonism than by the Scriptural letter. Frequently we even find him described as if a prior commitment to Platonic philosophy drove his theological enterprise and thus "distorted" his Christian theology, as well as his interpretative practice. This aspect of Origen's work highlights the transition of allegory from a pagan practice of interpreting difficult passages in Homer and Hesiod to a foundational piece of an emerging Christian biblical hermeneutics.

I would now propose that we think of this consequential relationship between Plato and Origen differently, in nearly opposite fashion: Platonism provided a framework within which Origen could think about the question of how we interpret; and Christian Logos theology, the notion of Christ as the incarnation of the Word, provided a solution to problems left unsolved by Platonism, precisely in that crucial area of epistemological theory, as well. Revised understandings of Christian Logos theology itself, as not even primarily a product of Platonism, fuel this re-vision. A crucial point that I will make early and often is that rather than seeing allegory as some bastard love-child or step-brother of interpretation, something marginal and bizarre, in my view allegory is in fact the very archetype, the purest form of interpretation. Another way of saying this is that all interpretation is allegorical in the sense that it says implicitly: This is the text and this is its meaning, but only the interpretation that people call allegorical does so frankly and openly, laying bare, as it were, the device. Let's get into a text here, and a gorgeous one at that. In a passage of Origen's commentary on Canticles, he writes:

> So, as we said at the beginning, all the things in the visible category can be related to the invisible, the corporeal to the incorporeal, and the manifest to those that are hidden; so that the creation of the world itself, fashioned in this wise as it is, can be understood through the divine wisdom, which from actual things and copies teaches us things unseen by means of those that are seen, and carries us over from earthly things to heavenly.
>
> But this relationship does not obtain only with creatures; the Divine Scripture itself is written with wisdom of a rather similar sort. Because of certain mystical and hidden things the people is visibly led forth from the terrestrial Egypt and journeys through the desert, where there was a biting serpent, and a scorpion, and thirst, and where all the other happenings took place that are recorded. All these events, as we have said, have the aspects and likenesses of certain hidden things. And you will find this correspondence not only in the Old Testament Scriptures, but also in the actions of Our Lord and Saviour that are related in the Gospels. If, therefore, in accordance with the principles that we have now established all things that are in the open stand in some sort of relation to others that are hidden, it undoubtedly follows that the visible hart and roe mentioned in the Song of Songs are related to some patterns of incorporeal realities, in accordance with the character borne by their bodily nature. And this must be in such wise that we ought to be able to furnish a fitting interpretation of what is said about the Lord perfecting the harts, by reference to those harts that are unseen and hidden.[1]

In this passage, Origen lays out with perfect clarity and concision both his interpretative theory and its practice. Invoking an analogy that would later become commonplace, Origen remarks that the ontological structure of Scripture is analogous (homologous) to that of the universe. Just as the latter is of a dualist structure with corporeal/visible related by analogy to incorporeal/invisible, so is Scripture too. The visible events narrated (the literal truth of which Origen does not deny) in both the Old Testament and the Gospels find their true meanings in correspondence to "hidden things." Moreover, just as in the case of the world, the hidden things are superior to the visible, "carry[ing] us over from earthly things to heavenly," so too the apprehension of the unseen meanings of Scripture.

David Dawson comments quite rightly that "Origen undermines any suggestion of radical separation of inner from outer by emphasizing the relation of a visible roe to 'the patterns of incorporeal realities' to which it is

---

1 Origen, *The Song of Songs: Commentary and Homilies*, trans. R. P. Lawson, Ancient Christian Writers 26 (Westminster, MD: Newman Press, 1957), p. 223.

related."[2] Dawson details the analogous relation and the fact that it has to do with a visceral fluid present in the hart that improves eyesight and "the vision that Christ both has and affords." Now, the crux:

> Although a Platonic worldview is a congenial context for such an analogy, there is nothing specifically Platonic about its details. Indeed, at the root of the analogy is specifically Christian theological reflection on the Son's capacity to know the Father and afford knowledge of the Father to others.[3]

I would, however, argue for a deep connection between the actual content of Origen's comment and a "Platonic" problematic – reversing precisely, as I've already mentioned, the usual pejorative intent of such an imputed nexus and proposing it rather as a celebration of the profundity of Origen's thinking about the epistemology of interpretation itself. Indeed, that very knowing of the Father and affording knowledge of the Father to others are, at least on one reading, the very essence of a hermeneutical dilemma, perhaps *the* hermeneutical dilemma.

Rather than seeing a commitment to a Platonic universe driving Origen's allegorical practice, I propose instead a reading of this relation in which a much subtler, finer, and more interesting relationship inheres between the Christianity of one such as Origen, and Platonism. This is a reading that reverses the previously imagined relation and makes philosophy the beneficiary of Christianity and not its benefactor. Rather than Platonism controlling and distorting (or even aiding) Christian theologizing, I am suggesting that Christian theology provided significant answers to philosophical problems. Dawson argues beautifully that,

> Just as Platonic *erōs* can be understood as a striving of the world of particulars for the forms of the Good and the Beautiful that would complete them, so allegorical reading can be seen as the striving of a reader confronted with incomplete or "thin" literal readings for the fuller or deeper meanings that would extend and complete them. Origen argues that allegorical readers should look for the spiritual (which is to say the *real*) import *of* the letter, rather than a meaning *in place of* the letter.[4]

As Mark Edwards has written too, "allegory in the Christian use of scripture is therefore not an exotic plant but the corollary of faith."[5]

2 David Dawson, *Christian Figural Reading and the Fashioning of Identity* (Berkeley: University of California Press, 2001), p. 53.

3 Dawson, *Christian Figural Reading*, p. 53.   4 Dawson, *Christian Figural Reading*, p. 54.

5 Mark J. Edwards, *Origen Against Plato*, Ashgate Studies in Philosophy and Theology in Late Antiquity (Aldershot: Ashgate, 2002), p. 132.

In a very interesting passage, Origen connects the theoretical problem of "true" interpretation with the general problem of epistemology. He finds a hermeneutics ungrounded in the Logos to be the source of disagreement within "Judaism," precisely analogous to the problematic of philosophy itself:

> Any teaching which has had a serious origin, and is beneficial to life, has caused different sects. For since medicine is beneficial and essential to mankind, and there are many problems in it as to the method of curing bodies, on this account several sects in medicine are admittedly found among the Greeks, and, I believe, also among the barbarians such as profess to practice medicine. And again, since philosophy which professes to possess the truth and knowledge of realities instructs us how we ought to live and tries to teach what is beneficial to our race, and since the problems discussed allow of considerable diversity of opinion, on this account very many sects indeed have come into existence, some of which are well known, while others are not. Moreover, there was in Judaism a factor which caused sects to begin, which was the variety of the interpretations of the writings of Moses and the sayings of the prophets.[6]

For Origen, obviously the written word alone gives rise to multiple interpretations and thus to multiple religious opinions and even sects, all in good faith, similar to the good-faith disagreement and sectarianism of physicians and philosophers. What needs to be noted here is the non-polemical and non-pejorative cast of Origen's characterization of Jewish sectarianism. It is no more fraught – but no less too – than the sectarianism of philosophy itself. Because there is no criterion with which to determine truth in interpretation, sectarianism must needs arise in all good faith.

The problem of interpretation is, accordingly, an epistemological problem, and a very ancient one by the time of Origen, indeed. A remarkable fragment from just about the time of Plato may help us win some insight into a non-platonic or even antiplatonic mode of thinking about language. I refer to the extraordinary text by Gorgias of Leontini which has come down to us under the title, *On That Which is Not or, On Nature*. Here is Sextus Empiricus' summary:

> Gorgias of Leontini belonged to the same troop as those who did away with the criterion, but not by way of the same approach as Protagoras. For in the work entitled *On What Is Not or, On Nature* he sets up three main points one after the other: first, that there is nothing; second, that even if there is

6 Henry Chadwick, trans. and ed., *Origen: Contra Celsum* (Cambridge: Cambridge University Press, 1965), p. 135.

[something], it is not apprehensible by a human being; third, that even if it is apprehensible, it is still not expressible or explainable to the next person.[7]

(Sextus Empiricus, *Against the Logicians* I.65)

In an excellent discussion, historian of rhetoric Richard Enos has interpreted these seemingly nonsensical statements. It would seem, at first glance, that Gorgias is denying the existence of the empirical, physical world, but not only would this be an absurd position, it would contradict everything else we know about his thought. In fact, however, it seems that Gorgias is, through this statement, asserting that there is nothing but the physical world. According to Enos' account, what Gorgias is denying is precisely existents in the philosophical (that is Parmenidean, thus Platonic) sense, essences, ideas or forms, that enable speech of essences. Gorgias claims that no essences exist, but only the physical reality that we see and touch:

> Platonic notions of ontological "essences" . . . were absurdities to Gorgias. He viewed humans as functioning in an ever changing world and manufacturing ideas that lose their "existence" the instant they pass from the mind of the thinker. Accordingly, ideals attain existence only through the extrapolations of the mind and are dependent upon the referential perceptions of their creator. As such, they cannot exist without a manufactured antithesis or anti-model. By their very nature, they can form no ideal at all since each individual predicated ideals based on personal experiences.[8]

The latter two points are closely related to the first. Based on his fundamental sensibility or understanding that the only objects of human cognition are sense-perceptions, Gorgias simply argues that even if there were some essence or idealities, there is no way that humans could perceive and understand them. In other words, we have here a statement of the limitations of human knowing because of the "*human media* of understanding – sense perceptions."[9] Beyond the positive experience of humans lie only the extrapolations of the mind, once again a system of representation or signification in which nothing exists except by virtue of that which it is not. Gorgias' third tenet is, then, simply a further statement about the inability of human language to communicate even sense perceptions, let alone whatever truths about reality that it might have been able (again contrary to plausibility) to divine. As must be obvious, Gorgias' rhetorical, or Sophistic, thought leads us in very different directions from the thought of philosophy. Plato

7 Translation from Sextus Empiricus, *Against the Logicians*, ed. and trans. Richard Arnot Home Bett (Cambridge: Cambridge University Press, 2005), p. 15.
8 Richard Leo Enos, *Greek Rhetoric Before Aristotle* (Prospect Heights, IL: Waveland Press, 1993), pp. 81–82.
9 Enos, *Greek Rhetoric*, p. 82 (emphasis original).

desired to discover, and believed he could, truths that would be always true without reference to speakers, hearers, or situations. Gorgias' thought leads us to understand that we must allow "for the contingencies of interpretation and human nature that are inherent in any social circumstances, which inherently lack 'ideal' or universally affirmed premises."[10] Gorgias' views clearly reflect a strong theoretical opposition to philosophy. I wish to suggest that Gorgias' three challenges to Parmenides and thus to philosophy raise the fundamental problems that a Judaeo-Christian theory of hermeneutics sets out to solve. Whatever Platonic or nonplatonic particular philosophical tenets we wish to ascribe to Origen, it seems to me absolutely clear that his quest for certainty in interpretive as well as theological knowledge puts him into the epistemological camp of Parmenides and not Gorgias, of philosophy and not of rhetoric. But Gorgias' challenges had to be answered, implicitly or explicitly.

Origen's Jewish Alexandrian predecessor Philo had understood the theoretical problem, and also proposed a solution to it. For Philo, something, of course, exists for sure, namely God and his Logos. Philo explicitly expressed a theory of the "magic language" of the Logos and its possible recovery. The philosophy of the "magic language" is essentially Platonism. This Platonism, however, has to be understood as including Aristotle, as exemplified most fully in his *On Interpretation*. This notion of ideal language bears a complicated relationship to the Stoic-Platonic Logos on the one hand and to the Judeao-Christian Logos on the other. For Middle-Platonists, such as Philo, it is the Logos as the independently divine Word of God. For Philo, only prelapsarian Adam among men had had direct access to the Logos. He had been able to see the nature of each thing, and had, therefore, been able to name everything with its perfect name, the name that corresponds perfectly to the language of *nous* or Logos. For Philo, God's language is entirely different from the language of humans:

> For this reason, whereas the voice of mortals is judged by hearing, the sacred oracles intimate that the words of God are seen as light is seen, for we are told that *all of the people saw the Voice* (Ex. 20:18), not that they heard it; for what was happening was not an impact of air made by the organs of mouth and tongue, but the radiating splendor of virtue indistinguishable from a fountain of reason. . . . But the voice of God which is not that of verbs and names yet seen by the eye of the soul, he (Moses) rightly introduces as "visible."
>
> (Philo, *On the Migration of Abraham*, pp. 47–48)

10 Enos, *Greek Rhetoric*, p. 73.

In his book on allegorical readers in Alexandria, Dawson explains that for all that human language is, however, inadequate for describing reality, one human, Moses, had the capacity for accurate knowledge of what he wished to say:

> But Moses is not like "most men," because his perceptions are superior to the language at his disposal. His name-giving flows from an accurate "knowledge that has to do with things," consequently, he "is in the habit of using names that are perfectly apt and expressive" (*Agr.* 1–2). Even so, Moses is forced to use ordinary language to express his extraordinary insights. As a result, his message is always clear and determinate once it is perceived, but it lies hidden in the very indirect linguistic expressions marked by various forms of semantic indeterminacy.[11]

The role of the interpreter – necessarily, then, an allegorist – is to perceive and then describe this clear and determinate message, to somehow divine the invisible "magic language" that underlies or lies behind the visible language and then to translate it in the form of allegorical commentary. The allegorist reaches this level of interpretation through a process of contemplation, as described in Philo's *On the Contemplative Life*. Thus too for Origen: "Even while we remain on earth the Christian life is grounded in a faithful and assiduous perusal of the scriptures, the depths of which cannot be mined unless we make use of the spiritual as well as carnal senses."[12] Or as Dawson has, once again, well put it, "Origen's imagination [as well, I would add, as his theoretical passion] is captured by Moses' ability to see God without a veil and by Moses' transformation in body no less than in spirit by virtue of his direct knowledge of the divine."[13] For Origen, as well, the biblical author(s) see God by "understanding him with the vision of the heart and the perception of the mind."[14] Philo was an important model for Origen, but a problematic one. As Mark Edwards has written, "From Paul to Clement allegory had been an indispensable tool for Christian expositors, all of whom, including Origen, were bound to hold that Philo's canon was incomplete and that no interpretation of the Prophets could be authoritative unless it yielded testimony to Christ."[15] Philo, of course, was also an allegorist, so where precisely can the incompletion be (unless we simply say that what was incomplete in Philo was simply that he was not a Christian – a

11 David Dawson, *Allegorical Readers and Cultural Revision in Ancient Alexandria* (Berkeley: University of California Press, 1992), p. 92.

12 Edwards, *Origen*, p. 111.   13 Dawson, *Christian Figural Reading*, p. 13.

14 Origen, *On First Principles*, trans. G. W. Butterworth (Gloucester, MA: Peter Smith, 1973), p. 99 (II.4.3); and see Dawson, *Christian Figural Reading*, p. 57.

15 Edwards, *Origen*, pp. 36–37.

weak answer in my opinion)? What seems to me lacking in Philo's thought, the "incompletion" – following out the implications of Dawson's account of Philo – is a way of accounting for the fact that he, via interpretation, claims to accomplish that which Moses himself could not. Christian theories of the Logos in flesh seem better equipped to address this issue. For Christians the divine language has appeared on Earth and spoken itself, thus answering to Philo's aporia. The prologue to the Gospel of John makes this point in its utterance that through the Torah it had proved impossible to communicate Logos to humans and that only through the Logos' actual taking on of human flesh was God made knowable to people.

Christian revisions of Philo's theory of the text and of interpretation thus had another answer than Philo's to the question of the source of knowledge of the allegorical meaning. If this reading has any cogency, then we can see that the "congenial context" that Platonism is for allegorical interpretation is actually much more than that: the problem of the Son's knowing of the Father and the question of how the Father can be made known to humans is a Christian formulation of a general fundamental problem in epistemology and language theory, and also a brilliant Christian solution to that problem. The Platonism and the Christianity of Origen's harts and roe-deers are actually tightly bound, and also more complexly integral to each other than earlier crude accounts of Origen's allegory would have had it. A coincidence, perhaps, of the elaboration of a Jewish theory of the Divine Word, the Logos as the given-to-know-and-be-known: Logos, when met with Greek thinking about language, provided very happy theoretical results in the imaginability of interpretation.

In my view, incarnational theology was crucial in the development of Origen's hermeneutical/allegorical theory and thus arguably for text interpretation in the West altogether. In Origen's hermeneutical theory, Logos theology functions in two ways. In his *First Principles*, Book IV, we can find one version of his three-fold theory of interpretation, whereby the "obvious interpretation" is called the flesh of the Scripture, but there are two more levels, the "soul" and the "spiritual law": "For just as man consists of body, soul and spirit, so in the same way does the scripture."[16] The very existence of allegory as a hermeneutical theory is made thus dependent on a Platonic universe of correspondences (not antagonisms) between things seen and things unseen, copies and originals, just as it had been in Philo's work as well. There is nothing new in *this* aspect of Origen's theory of interpretation other than the clarity of its articulation. For Origen, as for Philo, the external words of Scripture are "copies" of words and meanings

16 Origen, *On First Principles*, p. 276 (IV.2.4).

in the divine language. I would argue that some version of this ontology of language makes possible all thought of interpretation as translation and not only those methods that we would term allegory proper. Interpretation is always dependent on some articulated or post-articulated Logos. The ultimate figure for the ontotheological structure of Scripture is the Incarnation. In the words of R. P. Lawson: "If the Logos in His Incarnation is God-Man, so, too, in the mind of Origen the incarnation of the Pneuma in Holy Scripture is divine-human."[17] There is a virtual doubled Incarnation, then, in Origen's thinking. The Logos is incarnate in Jesus Christ and in Scripture as well.

However, Logos theology and in particular the notion of Christ as the Incarnation of the Word does more work for Origen. For one could imagine an ontological structure to both world and Word that would provide theoretically for the presence of a spiritual sense but not guarantee that anyone has access to that sense, as is virtually the case for Philo. However, as Karen Torjesen has written, for Origen,

> it is the power of the words of the Logos that makes the progression possible. It is the effect of his teaching which causes progress in the soul. If the word of the Logos were not effective, or he were not present teaching, then the steps of the progression would be an empty scaffolding into which the soul could gaze, but not climb.[18]

Not only, therefore, does Origen's Logos provide a theological structure and hermeneutical horizon for understanding the nature of Scripture and its dual and triple levels of meaning, but the Logos Incarnate in the actual "person" of Jesus, born in the cradle and on the cross, also provides Origen with a theoretical answer to the question of the source of allegorical knowing.

It will take some further work, however, before this point can be made in full. The first step is to show that Origen was aware of the epistemological problem that I attribute to him:

> This being so, we must outline what seems to us to be the marks of a true understanding of the scriptures. And in the first place we must point out that the aim of the Spirit who, by the providence of God through the Word who was "in the beginning with God", enlightened the servants of the truth, that is, the prophets and apostles, was pre-eminently concerned with the unspeakable

---

17 R. P. Lawson, "Introduction," in Origen, *The Song of Songs: Commentary and Homilies*, trans. R. P. Lawson, Ancient Christian Writers 26 (Westminster, MD: Newman Press, 1957), p. 9.

18 Karen Jo Torjesen, *Hermeneutical Procedure and Theological Method in Origen's Exegesis*, Patristische Texte und Studien (Berlin: Walter de Gruyter, 1986), p. 137.

mysteries connected with the affairs of men – and by men I mean at the present moment souls that make use of bodies – his purpose being that the man who is capable of being taught might by "searching out" and devoting himself to the "deep things" revealed in the spiritual meaning of the words become partaker of all the doctrines of the Spirit's counsel.[19]

Origen explicitly addresses the implicit problematic of Philo's theory, namely how may it be possible for a human writer to write in such a way that spiritual truths are, indeed, communicated; how, we might put it, can Origen hope to do better than Moses? Origen exposes this issue in another place when he writes:

As to the secret meaning which these things contain, however, and the teaching that these strange words labor to express, let us pray the Father of the Almighty Word and Bridegroom, that He Himself will open to us the gates of this mystery, whereby we may be enlightened not only for the understanding of these things, but also for the propagation of them, and may receive also a portion of spiritual eloquence, according to the capacity of those who are to be our readers.[20]

I am taking this, of course, as more than just a pious wish for divine assistance such as any religious writer might invoke, but rather a specific plea for the Father through the Word to solve a theoretical problem in Origen's hermeneutical theology. In yet another work, Origen articulates this clearly: "May you help with your prayers, that the Logos of God may be present with us and deign himself to be the leader of our discourse."[21] Of course, I have not yet established any role for the Incarnation in this meditation – except, perhaps, in the wording "deign" –, but it is the Logos present with us as the leader of our discourse who would guarantee us truth and insight in our interpretations.

This is, I suggest, the way that we need to understand also Origen's talk of interpretation as being via possession of the "mind of Christ," referring, as we shall see, to Paul's own Wisdom Christology. The richest text of Origen's for my purpose is adduced by Ronald Heine:

In this way, we can understand the Law correctly, if Jesus reads it to us, so that, as he reads, we may receive his "mind" and understanding. Or is it not to be thought that he understood "mind" from this, who said, "But we have the mind of Christ, that we may know the things which have been given to us by God, which things also we speak"? And [did not] those [have the same understanding] who said, "Was not our heart burning within us when he

19 Origen, *On First Principles*, p. 282 (IV.2.7).   20 Origen, *Song*, p. 151.
21 Origen, *Homilies on Genesis and Exodus*, The Fathers of the Church: A New Translation (Washington, D.C.: The Catholic University of America Press, 1982), p. 228.

opened the Scriptures to us in this way?" when he read everything to them, beginning from the Law of Moses up to the prophets, and revealed the things which had been written about himself.[22]

This key passage for Origen's hermeneutical theory needs to be read in the context of its several citations. The first is from Paul's Letter to the Corinthians and the second from the Gospel of Luke. In the second chapter of 1 Corinthians, Paul explains the difference between Christian knowledge and that of Jews previous to him:

> 1 When I came to you, brethren, I did not come proclaiming to you the testimony of God in lofty words or wisdom. 2 For I decided to know nothing among you except Jesus Christ and him crucified, and I was with you in weakness and in much fear and trembling; and my speech and my message were not in plausible words of wisdom, but in demonstration of the Spirit and of power, that your faith might not rest in the wisdom of men but in the power of God.

Paul continues a bit further on in the chapter:

> 10 God has revealed to us through the Spirit. For the Spirit searches everything, even the depths of God. 11 For what person knows a man's thoughts except the spirit of the man which is in him? So also no one comprehends the thoughts of God except the Spirit of God. 12 Now we have received not the spirit of the world, but the Spirit which is from God, that we might understand the gifts bestowed on us by God. 13 And we impart this in words not taught by human wisdom but taught by the Spirit, interpreting spiritual truths to those who possess the Spirit.

And finally Paul completes the argument with the verse crucial for Origen's reading: "16 'For who has known the mind of the Lord so as to instruct him?' But we have the mind of Christ."

It seems to me entirely plausible to read Paul's reference to "gifts" here as an allusion to the Torah, and he is, therefore, producing the earliest version of a Christian hermeneutical theory of allegorical reading, one that insists that Scripture can only be interpreted with the direct aid of the Holy Spirit, identified with the mind of Christ who alone knows the mind of the Lord and can, therefore, interpret the Torah as "a secret and hidden wisdom of God, which God decreed before the ages for our glorification" (1 Corinthians 2:7).

22 *Homiliae in Jesu Nave* 9. 8., cited Robert Heine, "Reading the Bible with Origen," in Paul M. Blowers, ed., *The Bible in Greek Christian Antiquity* (Notre Dame, IN: University of Notre Dame Press, 1997), p. 142.

Even more crucial, however, is the amazing narrative in the last chapter (24) of Luke:

> 27 And beginning with Moses and all the prophets, he interpreted to them in all the scripture the things concerning himself. 32 They said to each other, "Did not our hearts burn within us while he talked to us on the road, while he opened to us the scriptures?" [. . .] 36 As they were saying this, Jesus himself stood among them. 37 But they were startled and frightened, and supposed that they saw a spirit. 38 And he said to them, "Why are you troubled, and why do questionings arise in your hearts? 39 See my hands and my feet, that it is I myself; handle me, and see; for a spirit has not flesh and bones as you see that I have." 40 [. . .] 41 And while they still disbelieved for joy, and wondered, he said to them, "Have you anything here to eat?" 42 They gave him a piece of broiled fish, 43 and he took it and ate before them. 44 Then he said to them, "These are my words which I spoke to you, while I was still with you, that everything written about me in the law of Moses and the prophets and the psalms must be fulfilled." 45 Then he opened their minds to understand the scriptures.

These two passages together, I suggest, gave Origen everything he needed to "solve" the hermeneutical/epistemological problem that interpretation presented. The Spirit of God, identified in Paul's testimony with the mind of Christ is, for any Christian Logos theologian, the Logos himself. The passage in Luke provides Origen with an actual correlative for Paul's claim; both the incarnate Logos before the crucifixion and the resurrected but embodied Logos afterwards provided the disciples with the only possible and true interpretation of Scripture. Torjesen argues for three forms of the mediating activity of the Logos in Origen: the pre-incarnate activity of revelation to the Old Testament saints and prophets, the Incarnation itself, and the "present activity of the Logos, which is the disclosure of himself to us through the spiritual sense of Scripture."[23] What I think she doesn't sufficiently emphasize is the privileged nature of the Incarnation insofar as that is the only moment when the living voice of the Logos is directly present on earth, thus providing through Jesus' pedagogy precisely the hermeneutical guide that enables the "present activity of the Logos." In other words, the Incarnation is not only the "paradigm for this pedagogy" as Torjesen would phrase it but that which makes it possible *because he taught how to read Scripture.* It is not only that "in the taking on of flesh the Logos makes himself comprehensible to all those who wear flesh," a formulation that sounds almost Athanasian, but that in taking on flesh he could speak the magic language directly to human flesh and thus make himself, for he is the magic language, comprehensible to all those who speak human language.[24]

23 Torjesen, *Origen's Exegesis*, p. 114.   24 Torjesen, *Origen's Exegesis*, p. 115.

In the Incarnation, the Logos "offered himself to be known,"[25] in a way, I would add, that nothing but a physical body and voice *can* be known.

I am not claiming, of course, to have uncovered a new interpretation of Origen different from or even supplemental to Torjesen but only to be high lighting a particular element in his hermeneutical thought that I find crucial for articulating the way that the particular form of incarnational Christology was to reveal itself as the ma(r)ker of difference between "Judaism" and "Christianity." As Torjesen herself has put it, "In the incarnation the Logos speaks with his own voice. In Scripture he speaks through the mouth of the prophets and saints."[26] Given the universal Platonic understanding that the living voice of the teacher is superior to any "inscription" of that voice, the Incarnation then provides for Origen the guarantee of Christian allegorical access to truth and the Incarnation is a hermeneutical moment of full presence of meaning. This is why, again in Torjesen's words, "In the Gospels the Logos is speaking directly to the hearer, not mediated through a history other than his own,"[27] but also equally not mediated through a text other than his own. It seems plausible, then, that for Christian writers, the Incarnation of the Word, or the Holy Spirit which provides direct access to the Logos as well, provides a solution to what must remain a problem for Philo the Jew's theory of allegorical interpretation. The presence on Earth of the Word incarnate (or resurrected) in Jesus the spiritual reader who read Scriptures to the Christians and revealed the true interpretation has made it possible for other Christians to reach the spiritual meaning themselves, thus answering the question that Philo's allegorical theory must needs leave unsolved: "In the incarnation he has created the human conditions of his own perfect intelligibility for all time."[28]

Origen, we see, well understood that given the conditions of human speech, however much Christian speech has been learned from the Logos, it will be imperfect and thus multiple. Martin Irvine has recently made this point well:

> The unity of the Logos is fragmented into a multiplicity of temporal discourses which simultaneously attempt and fail to return to its unity; no repetition or multiplication of *logoi* is Logos. The transcendental signified remains beyond the reach of all temporal sign relations yet is immanently manifest in all of them.[29]

25 Origen, *Song*, p. 153.   26 Torjesen, *Origen's Exegesis*, p. 111.

27 Torjesen, *Origen's Exegesis*, p. 133.   28 Torjesen, *Origen's Exegesis*, p. 115.

29 Martin Irvine, *The Making of Textual Culture: "Grammatica" and Literary Theory, 350–1100* (Cambridge: Cambridge University Press, 1994), p. 266.

And yet, on Dawson's own account, "[Origen] identifies the consuming of the lamb with the allegorical reading of Scripture, which is contrasted with various deficient modes of reading, all of which have their subjective, experiential aspects."[30] I suggest that it is in that very drive for certainty, that desire to escape the subjective and the experiential, that we find the Platonic moment in Origen, precisely there, and that such a moment can only be grounded in a two-tiered universe (which is not, I emphasize, necessarily a dualism of value). One finds a useful contrast in another rich body of interpretive writings, the early Rabbinical commentaries collected in midrash. In sharp distinction with Origen's solution to hermeneutic plurality, in midrash, in its final development, *there is no transcendental signified.* God himself can only participate, as it were, in the process of unlimited semiosis and thus of limitless interpretation. The result will be not simply a multiplicity of interpretations that we cannot decide between, nor even a plethora of interpretations that all stand in the fullness of divine meaning, but finally a rabbinic ascesis that virtually eliminates the practice of interpretation entirely. Midrash, in its culminating avatar, eschews not only allegory and a discourse of the true meaning but renounces "interpretation" altogether and eats its Paschal lamb, to once more adopt an Origenist figure, raw.

The verse of the Torah says of the Paschal lamb, "You shall not eat thereof anything raw or boiled in water, but only roasted with fire" (Exod. 12:9). "If the lamb is Christ and Christ is the Logos, what is the flesh of the divine words if not the divine Scriptures" (*Treatise on Passover* 26.5ff),[31] and what is eating them, if not studying the Torah? Origen understands by the three ways in which the Paschal lamb might be consumed three kinds of readers: the first, a literalist who, like unto an irrational animal, violates the law by eating the text raw; the second, a "flaccid, watery, limp" moralizing reader, who eats the law boiled, and a third, the one who eats the Paschal text as it ought to be eaten, cooked in fire. Dawson writes of such a reader: "The ancient Passover continues to be celebrated, then, in the allegorical reading of Scripture, which is not a disembodiment through interpretation but instead a consumption of a body through reading."[32] And as for the one who reads the Torah cooked in fire:

> Clearly, the best readers are those who "roast" the meat of the lamb (Exod. 12:9a), that is, read the Word in Scripture "with fire." To read with fire means that the Word, through the reading of the text, becomes a speaker in the reader,

30 Dawson, *Christian Figural Reading*, p. 72.
31 Origen, *Treatise on the Passover; and, Dialogue of Origen with Heraclides*, trans. Robert J. Daly, Ancient Christian Writers 54 (Mahwah, NJ: Paulist Press, 1992).
32 Dawson, *Christian Figural Reading*, p. 71.

and the reader receives the Word as the voice of God. For example, Jeremiah received the words of God, who says, "Behold I have placed my words in your mouth as fire," and those who receive the lamb through reading "say, as Christ speaks in them" (2 Corinthians 13:3), "Our heart was burning in the way as he opened the Scriptures to us."

The Rabbis imagined their study of Torah in almost identical terms, as we read in the following story from the midrash on the Song of Songs:

> Ben-Azzai was sitting and interpreting [making midrash], and fire was all around him. They went and told Rabbi Akiva, "Rabbi, Ben-Azzai is sitting and interpreting, and fire is burning all around him." He went to him and said to him, "I heard that you were interpreting, and the fire burning all around you." He said, "Indeed." He said, "Perhaps you were engaged in the inner-rooms of the Chariot [theosophical speculation]." He said, "No. *I was sitting and stringing the words of Torah [to each other], and the Torah to the Prophets and the Prophets to the Writings, and the words were as radiant/joyful as when they were given from Sinai, and they were as sweet as at their original giving.* Were they not originally given in fire, as it is written, 'And the mountain was burning with fire'(Deut. 4:11)?"

In this text, allusions to the Song of Songs are deployed very skillfully in order to describe the experience of midrashic reading. The essential moment of midrash is the stringing together of parts of the language of the Torah, the Prophets, and the Holy Writings, forming new linguistic strings out of the old, and thereby recovering the originary moment of Revelation itself. The Rabbi was interpreting the Torah in accordance with the methods of midrash, stringing text to text and building new text as he strung. While doing this, he and the listeners had a visual experience indicating communion with God. Rabbi Akiva becomes suspicious that perhaps his colleague was engaging in forbidden or dangerous theosophical speculation and comes to investigate. He phrases his investigative question in the language of Song of Songs 1:4, "The King brought me into His chambers," the verse that gave rise to the mystical practice known as "being engaged in the inner-rooms of the Chariot." But Ben-Azzai answers that it was not that verse, that is, not a verse and practice that relate to mystical speculation, that brought him into communion with God but rather the application of another verse of the same Song, "Your cheeks are lovely with jewels, your neck with beads" (Song 1:10). The word for beads means that which is strung together into chains. Ben-Azzai's "defense" accordingly is that he was engaged in precisely the same activity as that exemplified by Rabbi Akiva's midrash above – linking "words of the Torah to words of the Holy Writings," as Rabbi Akiva linked the words of Exodus to the words of the Song of Songs. In order to recover the erotic visual communion that obtained between God and Israel at Mount Sinai, Ben-Azzai engages not in a mystical practice but in a hermeneutic one, the practice of midrash. This practice is accompanied by the visual experience also beheld at the giving of the Torah and particularly by the appearance of fire. This will be then a hermeneutics of recollected experience and visual perception.

In a striking – and perhaps not coincidental – convergence, both the Rabbi and the Father imagine the practice of holy reading as a moment of fiery encounter with God. Both imagine that through the properly intended study of the holy writ, direct contact with God the Father can be achieved; but the differences are interesting, as well. For the Rabbis, what is found are the words themselves, as radiant, joyful, and sweet – no interpretations and no knowledge of truth – as when given on Mount Sinai; for Origen, it is not finally the words but the Word and with it the Truth that is to be located in the otherwise so kindred a spiritual practice of reading. For Origen, those who find only the words and enjoy the words remain irrational beasts and only those who strip the meanings of flesh off the bones of word and read the text in allegorical fashion, which means in Christ, could ever even have hope for the experience of hot love that both he and his rabbinic interlocutor seek.

PART II

Philosophy, theology, and poetry
200 to 1200

4

PETER T. STRUCK

Allegory and ascent in Neoplatonism

In Late Antiquity a series of ideas emerges that adds a kind of buoyancy to allegorism. Readers' impulses toward other regions of knowledge begin to flow more consistently upward, drawn by various metaphysical currents that guide and support them. A whole manner of Platonist-inspired architectures structure the cosmos in the early centuries of the Common Era, among thinkers as diverse as the well-known Origen and the mysterious Numenius. Plato's understanding of appearances had always insisted on some higher, unfallen level of reality, in which the forms dwell, and to which we have no access through our senses. This other level seems to invite allegorical aspirations. Of course, Plato himself prominently declined the invitation, and it is no small irony that his work should have become the font of such heady visions. He consistently disparages poetry's claims to any kind of truth, let alone the grandiose varieties that allegorical readers tend to ascribe to it. The distance between the sensible world and the real source of truth operates for him as a chastening agent, a message of epistemological caution echoing over a chasm. (Plato typically leaves the task of mediating it to the colorless verb *metechô* "participate.") But his later followers do not feel such stringent compunctions. They will embrace Plato's metaphysics of fallenness, but then shift their emphasis from the distance that separates us and the highest truths to the notion that the world here and now is (somehow) connected to a higher order – a position inarguably Platonic but rarely more than implicit in the master's work. To greater or lesser degrees this group of readers will transform Plato's world of mere images, always and everywhere pale imitations of the real truth, into a world of manifestations, always potentially carrying palpable traces of that higher world.

This period represents something of a departure from the earlier ages, but it is worth noting also the important continuities with earlier allegorical readers. The Neoplatonists of late antiquity carry forward the Stoic ideas that myth might be a repository of profound truth, and that the dense language of poetry has the capacity to convey truths that exceed the grasp of plain speech. They carry forward an idea that we see in the Derveni commentator and in Stoic etymology: that language is naturally linked to its meanings and that single words might serve as discrete sites of interpretation and yield sometimes profound insights. Further, they continue and deepen a sense that allegorical ways of conveying meaning are not only capable of but particularly appropriate to discussing the divine.

Plotinus

Plotinus' (205–69/70 CE) interests in literature are not central in his corpus, but he leaves behind fascinating readings of traditional texts (especially Homer's) in articulating his philosophical system. The contemporary scholar Luc Brisson rightly points out the ease with which Plotinus engages in allegorical interpretation of myth as a mode of exposition of even his core philosophical ideas.[1] Myth gives Plotinus a means by which he can express synchronic realities in a diachronic narrative form. In the context of Plotinus' work, this is not the simple idea that a story might capture an abstract idea – since at the heart of his corpus Plotinus struggles with the idea of translating the utter transcendence on which his world centers into the discursive, sequential logic of language.[2]

Despite this attention to poetry in explicating his philosophy, Plotinus produces no discrete theorizing or criticism of poetry. He produces statements on aesthetics, in *On Beauty* and *On Intelligible Beauty*, which are notable especially for displacing proportion, which had been the centerpiece of classical aesthetics, in favor of the idea that beauty emerges from the radiance of the divine in a single point.[3] More important for the history of allegory, and in fact of central importance, are the positions he develops in metaphysics. While it may be too strong to say that Plotinus is responsible for the shape of the world in late antiquity, it is only a little too strong. He inherited from the Middle Platonic ferment that preceded him a few critical notions upon which he put a distinctive stamp, one that bore authority as a touchstone for centuries to come. In so doing he set out a universe that gave

1 Luc Brisson, *How Philosophers Saved Myths: Allegorical Interpretation and Classical Mythology*, Catherine Tihanyi, trans. (Chicago: University of Chicago Press, 2003).
2 The best summary treatment of Plotinian metaphysics remains A. H. Armstrong, "Plotinus," in the *Cambridge History of Later Greek and Early Medieval Philosophy* (Cambridge: Cambridge University Press, 1967), pp. 195–270.
3 The most serviceable translations are A. H. Armstrong, trans., *Plotinus*, Loeb Classical Library Series (Cambridge, MA: Harvard University Press; London: W. Heinemann, 1966–88).

allegorical strategies of reading a distinct resonance. I will give the whole picture first, then point out the elements of it that are most significant for allegorical interpreters.

According to Plotinus, the universe is constituted and sustained by a single, immaterial, and utterly transcendent entity, beyond even being itself, that eternally emanates pure being out from itself and so produces the entire cosmos in all its dimensions. This font of being, the One, radiates out a reality that precipitates a series of layers below itself: the tier closest to it is the realm of Mind (*nous*) in which all intellectual reality dwells, including Plato's forms; the region of the Soul (*psychê*) constitutes the third tier, and is where life emerges; last in this chain of being comes the material realm (*hulê*), a shadow world, as close to evil and pure non-being as any product of the One might become. The significance of this basic understanding for allegorical interpretation is hard to overstate. First, the tiered ontology means that any given entity here in the physical world always also has other, hidden aspects to it. Visible manifestations of objects increasingly take on the character of the tips of so many ontological icebergs. Second, the idea of emanation, claiming that the universe unfolds through an ontological flow, carries the corollary that invisible connections exist in the very being of things. Such ontological connections offer later thinkers a basis for semantic links. Such connections, which since Aristotle's time had had to settle for the thin beer of resemblance, could now rest on real ties in their very being. They constitute a new register to which those claiming hermeneutic connections will have appeal. Third, his view of the One as an entirely transcendent entity that also still (somehow) manifests itself in visible, tangible, concrete reality, sets out a paradox that is a natural incubator of allegorical thinking. It will give impetus and provide an authoritative parallel to an allegorical habit of claiming that allegorical literary constructions render the transcendent in the concrete, and use language to express what is beyond language. Finally, he produced lyrical meditations of unmatched power laying out the proper practice and purpose of human life as the pursuit of perfect union with the divine via mystical ascent. Philosophy has a mission of saving the soul, and reading and interpretation play a part in such a soteriological drama. This aspect of his thinking introduces an extraordinary development, nurturing the view in later figures that allegorical reading itself might offer a kind of pathway for this ascent, and that hermeneutic activity might lift one up through ontological layers, anagogically, toward the One. Plotinus produces a new and powerful possibility for understanding figuration according to a logic of synecdoche, as opposed to imitation. Such a possibility is not fully exploited in a literary context until two centuries later, in the work of Proclus.

Porphyry

Plotinus' literary executor leaves behind the most extended surviving allegorical commentary on a single passage from the whole of antiquity. Porphyry's (234–c. 305 CE) essay on Homer's Cave of the Nymphs in *Odyssey* 13 is a virtuoso performance, betraying a highly sophisticated literary mind, attuned to subtleties of language and sense.[4] He writes a densely argued interpretation of Homer's sparsely articulated image, that sees it as a meditation on the births of human souls into their bodily lives. In Porphyry's case, the influence of the new metaphysical developments of Neoplatonism is most keenly felt not so much in the methods he develops and puts to use as in the contents of those interpretations. Indeed, his practice of taking a word, image, or group of images from Homer and then making a set of associations from many registers of cultural experience past and present, does not separate him much from a figure like the Stoic Cornutus. Of course, the revolutionary possibilities for re-understanding representation that Plotinus' metaphysics offers were surely not lost on him and likely influenced his views on how expansively one might interpret a particular literary image, and expansive he surely was, but we find only in later figures explicit theoretical statements in this direction.

Porphyry's commentary runs for some twenty pages of detailed exposition on a proof text eleven lines long. He mentions a debt to the earlier thinkers Numenius and Cronius, but his version of this commentary remains authoritative for the rest of antiquity and beyond. Homer uses a few lines to depict a cave into which the Phaeacians deposit Odysseus and his loot when they return him to Ithaca. The description is both bare and peppered with extraordinary features: it is sacred to naiad nymphs, contains stone mixing bowls, stone jars used by bees to store honey, stone looms where the nymphs weave purple cloth, an eternal spring, and two entrances, one for mortals and one for immortals, and an olive tree sits adjacent to it. Beginning from a premise allegorical commentators hold in common, Porphyry takes the obscurity of the passage as a signal that the scene conveys some hidden message. This position stands in rich contrast to literary criticism in the ancient rhetorical tradition, in which something unclear is thought to be a flaw of style. He signals a defensive position, offering a justification of allegorical explanation, where some critics, he worries, will see only forced reading. He dismisses the idea that Homer's cave is a simple flight of poetic fancy, and

---

4 The most useful translation is Porphyry, *On the Cave of the Nymphs*, Robert Lamberton, trans. (Barrytown, NY: Station Hill Press, 1983). For the best text and commentary, see *The Cave of the Nymphs in the* Odyssey, Arethusa Monographs 1, L. G. Westerink and Seminar 609, eds., (Buffalo, NY: State University of New York Press, 1969).

therefore not to be seriously interpreted, on the grounds that Homer after all allowed his fancy to fly in a particular direction. These oddities compel the interpreter's attention.

Porphyry's goal is to reconstruct the senses which "the ancients" (*hoi palaioi*) might have attached to the cave and the elements inside it. This indicates a historical sense on his part. To understand the meaning of Homer's poem one needs to reconstruct what it may have meant during Homer's time. In method, Porphyry has a catholic approach to evidence. He is ready to argue from parallels within Homer's text (25–27) and from etymology (28–29), but his method is especially characterized by a broad exploration of whatever he is able to collect about caves from their many ancient cultural associations (Greek and non-Greek). He will then typically endorse the cultural associations he sees as most relevant with his own phenomenological arguments. He especially surveys religious and philosophical traditions surrounding caves. There are many examples. He enlists common treatments of the cave as a microcosm of the sensible cosmos (Mithraism, Plato, Empedocles) with its mutability and inscrutability, and then endorses this association by claiming that caves, as phenomena of nature, are indeed made of earthly matter and surrounded by a single mass whose outside border is functionally limitless, and whose dark interiors render them difficult to understand. Water, he says, is especially associated with the birth of souls and so this cave is populated by naiad nymphs. He adduces the opening of the Book of Genesis here, as well as Egyptian associations of gods with water, and Heraclitus' views, which he then endorses by pointing out the critical importance of fluids like water, blood, and sperm to living things. This double mode of argumentation – appeal to cultural associations and then approval of those senses with his own natural observations – produces a powerful ground of linkage, which marries the authority of the ancient ways of doing things and the evidentiary appeal of the natural sciences. Each of the components within the cave – honey, stone bowls and jars, stone looms and purple cloth, the ways for mortals and immortals – is then read in similar tandem fashion, with each piece adding to an overall picture that the cave represents a kind of birthing station where souls assume bodies and enter the material world.

As has been shown by Glenn Most above, among some Stoic readers, this wisdom conveyed by the poet may be due to his or her own intention or it may not. Porphyry shows some nuances on this question also. An urge to recover the author's intention (*boulêsis*) animates his hermeneutics, to be sure, but at one point he is willing to leave open just whose intention he is recovering. He is both curious about and willing to remain entirely agnostic on the question of the facticity of the cave (4, 21). Either Homer created a fictive cave with a hidden message, or some unknown ancient cave-makers produced a real cave with these strange characteristics, and Homer described it. Either way we have a readable cave, and either way the greatness of Homer's poetry is enhanced by it. This indifference illustrates a common allegorical sense that tends not to exclusively venerate the *technê* of poetic language or construction, but instead values the conveying of profound wisdom, through placement of potent symbols, coiled nodes of uncanny insight, waiting for an attentive reader to release the catch. At the close of the commentary he makes clear that, whoever made the cave, Homer should receive the credit for having placed it in the poem. Praising Homer's intelligence and excellence, he shows how precisely the cave fits into the poem's overall message. Having been stripped of all material possessions at this point in the story, his material self withered, Odysseus will now take Athena's counsel and turn to wisdom, in order to eliminate the soul's treacherous appetites (the suitors). This is a turn away from the material world and toward the intellectual world. His final task, to plant an oar for Poseidon so far inland that it could be mistaken for a winnowing fan, is read as an effort to move as far as possible from the world of corrupting material and change, for which the sea is said to stand. Finally, the cave lies in a harbor named after Phorcys, the cyclops Polyphemus' grandfather, as Homer tells us. It positions his turn to Athena after landing in the cave as a second try at escaping the material world, with his attempt to blind the concupiscent monster as a first, unsuccessful one. It is unsuccessful because it is a violent attempt to escape from matter – which only leaves one still enmeshed in the material world. Only a long and hard discipline, where one resists and beguiles the pleasures of the flesh one at a time (Odysseus' labors), will lead away from the body and to wisdom, which will allow for true and lasting liberation from the corporeal world. Porphyry sees Odysseus' story as a tale of a man passing through the stages of genesis, descending to the material body, and then returning to wisdom.

Interlude

Certain currents of pre-Plotinian Platonism, in which neither Plotinus nor Porphyry showed determinative interest, become central again for later figures, and so deserve some special mention before we move on. Before the third century CE a group of texts emerges, including the Hermetic corpus, Gnostic texts, and the works of Numenius, which draws from the same pool of Middle Platonic sensibilities. These writers set about elaborating medial layers of reality and installing within them choirs of exotic divine and quasi-divine figures like the demiurge, Hecate, the *junges*, Sophia, and the noetic father, ontological genealogies that succeeding generations of philosophers became more and more confident describing in proliferating detail. They rushed in where the more circumspect Plotinus and Porphyry feared to tread. Succeeding generations of Neoplatonists could eventually trace individual chains of being down through the heavens to their endpoints at particular points of the material realm. In this group, a text particularly important for the present purposes, known as the *Chaldean Oracles*, emerges in the second century. The later Neoplatonists make this collection of enigmatic sayings, which survives only in fragments, into a kind of wisdom text, rivaling the authority of Plato and Homer. A man named Julian claimed to have extracted the oracles via his son, also named Julian, after the son fell into a mediumistic trance. The father carried the fuller designation "the Chaldean." It is possible that the elder Julian could have actually been from Chaldea, a name the Greeks used for the region around ancient Babylonia, since Trajan's expeditions facilitated contact with the area. But because the text carries little that is verifiably Chaldean, and quite a bit that is identifiably Platonist, more likely the lineage emerges from the legendary aura of that region, which, since late classical times, the Greeks had associated with mystical insight. This lineage is of a piece with certain Egyptomaniacal currents that also ebb and flow through Greek philosophy during this period. These later figures looked to these exotic cultures, of which their knowledge was limited, as repositories of an ancient wisdom extractable via allegorical reading.

The *Chaldean Oracles* are elliptical statements on cosmogony (the origins of the cosmos), cosmology (its arrangement), anthropology, and theology.[5] Similar collections of dubious lineage had circulated since the earliest days of known writing in Greek, prominently including the *Sibylline Oracles*, and collections handed down under such names as Bacis and Orpheus – a phenomenon discussed by Dirk Obbink above. The prominence of these collections is proportional to their capacity to provoke allegorical interpretation. Iamblichus, Proclus, and many others produce allegorical commentaries on the work of the Chaldeans. These texts' status as oracles is often insufficiently emphasized. It reminds us of the connection between allegorical reading and divinatory interpretation, which is attested since at least the time of the Derveni Papyrus. In both practices, one finds dense and opaque texts and exuberant interpretive practices in a mutually reinforcing relationship.

Such a connection between divination and allegorism is also apparent in the extant Greco-Roman dream books. Artemidorus finds two kinds of

---

5 See Hans Lewy, *The Chaldean Oracles and Theurgy: Mysticism, Magic, and Platonism in the Later Roman Empire*, 2nd edn., ed. Michele Tardieu (Paris: Études augustiniennes, 1978).

dreams.[6] There are the straightforward ones, which require no interpretation, and the interpretable ones, which are the focus of his work, and are named, precisely, "allegorical" (*allêgorikoi*). The statements of method he makes for interpreting them are all but indistinguishable from statements of allegorical hermeneutics in a literary dimension. Macrobius' *Commentary on the Dream of Scipio* shows this elision even more starkly, since his introduction lays out, entirely paratactically, a statement of allegorical literary theory next to a theory of allegorical dreams (heavily indebted to Artemidorus).[7] Macrobius proceeds with his commentary without ever feeling the need to clarify whether he considers himself doing literary allegory or divinatory dream interpretation, an omission which could only be made in a case where the traditions were very close indeed. This elision in Macrobius will prove tremendously influential in the Middle Ages, where dream narrative is the field *par excellence* of allegorical poetics and interpretation. Macrobius is the key Latin figure in transmitting a distillation of the Greek traditions of allegorical reading and divination to the Western Middle Ages. Macrobius' effacing of difference between literary allegory and divination was precisely what authorized the medieval idea that poetic myth (*fabula*) contains a philosophical truth waiting to be divined by the attentive and wise reader (for more on this, see Whitman's essay below).

Iamblichus

An intense family squabble among Plotinus' heirs comes to light after the great man's death. The second of his two most prominent followers, Iamblichus (*c.* 245–*c.* 325 CE), disagreed seriously with Porphyry over a practice that Porphyry called magic (*goêteia*) and Iamblichus himself called "theurgy," coining a term from *theos* + *ergos* (meaning divine action) on analogy to "*theologia*" (meaning divine discourse). Iamblichus uses the new term to advance his advocacy of a set of ritual activities meant to aid in contemplation and bring devotees closer to Plotinus' goal of union with the divine. Porphyry strongly objects, opting for a pure contemplationist position, and produces a broadside attack. He writes with an expansive, scathing criticism, ridiculing in detail not only exotic practices – including standing on secret divine signs and calling down divinities – but also highly traditional religious acts, like sacrifice, set at the core of ancient religion. In short, he objects that *any* action we might perform in the physical world

6 Artemidorus, *The Interpretation of Dreams*, Robert J. White, trans. (Park Ridge, NJ: Noyes Press, 1975).
7 Macrobius, *Commentary on the Dream of Scipio*, William Harris Stahl, trans. (New York: Columbia University Press, 1990).

could affect the divine in any way. This position might be seen to maintain the Platonic penchant to see the phenomenal world as utterly separate from the source of real truth.

Porphyry's attack, preserved as the *Letter to Anebo*, provokes Iamblichus to his lengthy answer, the most important surviving philosophical treatment of ritual from antiquity, a tract known since Ficino's day by the title *De mysteriis*.[8] Interestingly, in a mystery which no scholar has conclusively unraveled, their entire debate is an act of ventriloquism. Porphyry writes his attack in the form of a letter to an Egyptian priest, and Iamblichus writes his defense of rituals in the voice of Anebo's supposed master, Abamon. While not focused on allegorical reading, their debate, which Iamblichus decisively wins according to their followers, has profound consequences for it. Taking the opposite side from Porphyry, Iamblichus' defense of rituals might be seen as a defense of the relevance of the physical world to the higher orders and the source of real truth. He advocates the rituals as a supplement to contemplation, and as an aid to upward-leading, anagogic ascent toward the One. He predicates their efficacy on the notion that the material world is connected to the divine, at least for those who know the secrets. He articulates his most important general principle concisely in book 5:

> The primary beings illuminate even the lowest levels, and the immaterial ones are present immaterially to the material. And let there be no astonishment if in this connection we speak of a pure and divine form of matter; for matter also issues from the father and creator of all, and thus gains its perfection, which is suitable to the reception of gods.... Observing this the theurgic art in exactly this way discovers receptacles fitted to the properties of each of the gods, and in many cases links together stones, plants, animals, aromatic substances, and other such things that are sacred, perfect and godlike, and then from all these composes an integrated and pure receptacle.　　　　(V.23)

This defense of cult objects in rituals, by far the most fully articulated in antiquity, will come to the aid of later interpreters of poetry trying to explain how material poetic images might be linked to transcendent truths.

Two final components of Iamblichus' work deserve special mention. First, he carries forward an idea he finds in the *Chaldean Oracles*, that the divine sprinkles seeds of itself throughout the cosmos in the form of "symbols" (*symbola*). These scintillas of the divine are thought to be hiding in plain sight among us. They are precisely the pieces of stone, herbs, etc., that

---

8 The first scholarly English translation of this pivotal text only recently became available. Iamblichus, *On the Mysteries*, Emma C. Clarke, John M. Dillon, and Jackson P. Hershbell, trans., Writings from the Greco-Roman World, 4 (Atlanta: Society of Biblical Literature, 2003). The translators include an improved text, and very helpful introductions and notes.

he mentions above, and are special intersections at which the divine tends to manifest itself more vibrantly than in the rest of the material world. Collectively they constitute an esoteric code, a metaphysical topography by which various rays of the divine are rendered materially. The theurgic art harnesses these points of radiance in ritual implements, and uses them to open up avenues of communication between this world and that one. Iamblichus' use of the term symbol, to mean a representational device that exceeds simple imitation and operates instead by synecdoche, borrows from two ancient contexts: the symbol as a magic talisman (such as is widely attested in the surviving magical papyryi), and as a passport to higher states of being in the mystery religions and Pythagorean cult, a use which dates back to the classical period. As we will see, this provides a gateway to a crucial allegorical path, though it will not be until the work of Proclus, who is the first to import this idea into literary theory, that the path is actually taken. In conjunction and finally, Iamblichus forwards a theory of language that builds on this use of the idea of the symbol. He justifies the use of special divine names for the gods, to which Porphyry objects on the grounds that if language is a human creation gods would not care what they are called. Iamblichus replies that certain language is *not* in fact a human creation, but is itself of the character of his material symbols. This symbolic language is not a mere *representation* of the gods, as a human-invented name would be, but is a shard from the higher orders sewn into our world, and carries an actual ontological trace of the divine in its material sounds and the letters that represent them.

Proclus

In the work of Proclus (410 or 412–85 CE), Neoplatonic allegorism comes into full flower. He brings synecdochic signification, made possible in Plotinus' metaphysics and elaborated by Iamblichus to justify theurgy, directly to bear on the power of allegorical literary constructions. He was extraordinarily prolific, and fortunately his works survive in abundance. As is typical of the time, he concentrates on commentary on the Platonic corpus, writing thousands of pages of interpretation covering even the most minute details, showing no less interest in Plato's dramatic staging and his use of story and myth than in his more straightforward moments of argumentation. In so doing, allegorical reading is his most powerful critical tool. Proclus also turns his attention to the poets, making extended readings of Homer and Hesiod. But unlike any of his predecessors and of most consequence, he produces detailed statements of theory, which stand out as the most fully elaborated theory of allegory to survive from antiquity.

Any serious student of Plato (as Proclus surely is) faces difficulty in producing a poetics. In the *Republic*, Plato is unsparing in his criticism of poetry's claims to truth. In a famous move, he maps it onto his ontological scheme, and states that just as the material world is a pale imitation of the real truth, poetry is a further imitation of the imitation, and so stands at a third remove from the real reality. It is through engagement with this problematic of imitation (*mimêsis*) that Proclus makes his most profound contribution. In a long excursus in the *Republic* commentary, he lays out a multi-layered analysis of poetry, claiming that only the lowest layer of it is mimetic.[9] Mimetic poetry attempts to produce images of the world around us and is what Plato was talking about (Proclus says) in his critique in the *Republic*. But there are other forms of poetry too. Above the mimetic is didactic poetry, which teaches the audience of intellectual and moral excellences through correct opinion. The very highest form of poetry is an inspired kind that indicates truths about the divine. It makes use of material representations but in this mode material things are not imitations of what they represent, but symbols of it. Such literary symbols signify their meanings not according to any economy of imitation (*mimêsis*), for how could any merely human representation resemble the divine and transcendent truth? Another, symbolic language is necessary.

When explaining how this language works, Proclus makes explicit reference to theories Iamblichus uses to justify the theurgic rites. Proclus, like all important Neoplatonists after Iamblichus, had been convinced by his arguments against Porphyry in the *De Mysteriis*, and vigorously deepened and extended his justifications of theurgy. Particularly interesting here, Proclus leaves behind more testimony than Iamblichus did on one theurgic practice, the animation of statues, that has a particular relevance to his literary theory. In it the theurgist constructs a material representation of a divinity, and then invokes the real presence of the god into it via a material token, a stone, plant, bone, or herb, called the *symbolon*, which like Iamblichus' symbol is the material node on which the real presence of the divine manifests itself. Just as they were for Iamblichus, these symbols are of a different ontological order from the rest of the material world. They are shards of the divine presence among us. When the theurgist inserts the symbolic token into the imitative statue, the statue no longer merely *resembles* the god, but actually *becomes* the god. Proclus claims that symbolic literary language works

---

9 The most succinct discussion comes at Proclus, *Commentary on the Republic*, I 192–93 (Standard pagination for this text refers to the edition by Wilhelm Kroll, ed., *Procli Diadochi in Platonis Rem Publicam commentarii* (Leipzig: Teubner, 1899–1901)). The best modern translation and notes are in French, *Commentaire sur la République*, A. J. Festugière, ed. and trans. (Paris: Vrin, 1970).

precisely the same way. When the inspired poet situates symbols in the material constructions of his language, he invokes the divinity's true presence via the pathways of being that descend from the heavens. Since these symbols carry a connection in their very being to the divinities they invoke, they escape the difficulties Plato had with mimesis. Just as the theurgist uses symbols to animate his representations of the divine, so also,

> the fathers of these myths . . . wanting to relate the myths to the entire chain [of being] issuing from each god, conceived the surface which the myths project, with its images, by analogy to the lowest classes that preside over the lowest level of experience, rooted in the material world, but the secret of the inaccessible transcendent essence of the gods, which is hidden from the masses of men and beyond their comprehension, they translated into perceptible form for those who aspire to such visions.
>
> (*Commentary on the Republic*, I 78.25–79.2)

Both the theurgist and poet reverse the process of emanation, and open up an avenue by which we might retrace the ontological movement that produced the universe back up from material to divine. An anagogical reading is now emphatically possible, and interpretation itself takes on a role in the soteriological aspirations of souls. Proclus has his answer to Plato, but of perhaps more consequence to the history of allegorism, allegory now has a theory of ontological connection between symbols and their meanings that claims for poets the power to not just represent, but to actually invoke the real presence of their subjects.

Symbol and allegory in the Neoplatonists

In closing it is important to note that this theory of the symbol is the only strictly *literary* theory attached to the term that survives from antiquity. Unlike metaphor (Greek *metaphora*), which since Aristotle was regularly theorized and argued over, ancient literary critics had little to say about "symbols" (*symbola*). In fact the term almost never appears in the work of the mainstream ancient rhetorical literary critics. When these writers discuss figuration, they do so under the heading of metaphor. By contrast "symbol" was an important part of the conceptual apparatus of allegorism from the third century BCE forward. The Stoics use it as a synonym for enigma (*aenigma*), the most powerful conceptual engine of ancient allegoresis, and Porphyry, as was also mentioned, used the symbol as his central concept of figuration in his treatise. But no literary thinkers before Proclus document their theories of it. I have emphasized the Iamblichean background, but Proclus also refers directly to the Pythagoreans, magicians, and mystery religions that lie behind Iamblichus. In later periods, allegorical readers will begin to make rich and productive distinctions between allegory on the one hand and symbol on the other. The ancient allegorists made no such distinction, but used the terms as synonyms.

Legacies

Given its extravagance, perhaps the most striking aspect of Proclus' theory of the symbolic is its afterlife. I will outline only the most important cases here. Some time in the century after Proclus' death a corpus emerges falsely claiming to be authored by Dionysius the Areopagite, a Greek character in the book of Acts who is provoked by Paul's caution against idolatry to convert on the spot. The deep indebtedness of this author (known to modern scholars as Pseudo-Dionysius) to the work of Proclus has been well documented for over a century. Prominent among his borrowings is the literary theory of the "symbol." In works on biblical hermeneutics, the author cautions against any objections to Scripture's portraying God in corporeal forms. Those who know how to read properly will recognize such images not as imitations of the divinity, but as symbols of it, and symbols indicate the truths they do, not through resemblance, but through direct ontological connection. Pseudo-Dionysius recapitulates the particularities of Neoplatonic metaphysics, especially Proclus' variety of it, that renders this notion of the symbolic comprehensible. Despite periodic objections from Christian thinkers who were dubious of the compatibility of his doctrines with Church teachings, Pseudo-Dionysius' reputation survives and thrives. As it happens, he becomes among the most authoritative figures in medieval Christendom. He is a wellspring of various Christian mysticisms, including those of Eckhart and John Scotus Eriugena, second only to Augustine in his importance in that tradition.[10] His interest in base material imagery sets him out as the authority on the Negative Way, and sets him apart from the other central ancient sources of apophatic theology. The Cappadocians had claimed that God is best described by negated terms – a rather different approach from Dionysius' Proclean claim to represent the divine in lowly matter. Thomas Aquinas cites Dionysius some 1700 times in the *Summa*, a frequency second only to Augustine, and finds him a particularly helpful guide in reading passages in the Bible where the divine is figured in the concrete.

10 See "The Dionysian Imagination," in A. J. Minnis and A. B. Scott, eds., *Medieval Literary Theory and Criticism c. 1100–c. 1375: The Commentary Tradition* (Oxford: Clarendon Press, 1988), pp. 165–96.

Invocationist theories of poetry percolate through many later thinkers, some of whom have familiarity with the Neoplatonists' work directly and some of whom know it through intermediaries. As Plato is periodically rediscovered in Europe, the Neoplatonists achieve the status of key interpreters to unlocking his often difficult and contradictory positions (a status against which modern philologists reacted strongly). They play this role for Ficino, and so the Florentine Renaissance knows them well. Schelling and other important Romantic figures like Coleridge find their own form of inspiration in Neoplatonic writings. Each of these cases is worthy of serious study, and filled with nuances, but in each one we find some form of an aspiration for a literary expression that transcends mere imitation and captures transcendent truths in corporeal form. Those that lay claim to ontological linkage between figurative devices and the realities to which they point, and do so via transcendental symbols, will owe some debt to the curious, but nonetheless powerful developments of Greek late antiquity.

5

DENYS TURNER

Allegory in Christian late antiquity

Writing sometime around 1330 in the general prologue to his first literal commentary on the Bible, the Franciscan biblical scholar, Nicholas of Lyra, summarizes what he understands to be the patristic and medieval consensus concerning the interpretation of Scripture. Any scriptural text may, he says, contain four senses, the "literal" (also "historical" or "narrative"), the "moral" (sometimes called "tropological"), the allegorical and the "anagogical" (aka "mystical"). "And these four senses," he adds,

> may be explained by way of illustration by the word "Jerusalem". In its literal sense it refers to a certain city which was once the capital of the kingdom of Judea, founded in the first instance by Melchisedech and later expanded and fortified by Solomon. But in its moral sense it refers to the faithful soul; it is in this sense that Isaiah says: *Rise up, Jerusalem, take your seat* (52:2). But in its allegorical sense it refers to the Church militant, as when it says in Revelation 21:2: *I saw the holy city, the new Jerusalem, coming down from heaven, like a bride dressed for her husband*. In its anagogical sense it refers to the Church triumphant, as Galatians 4:26 says: *She who is above is Jerusalem the freed-woman and she is our mother*. We have given as an example a single word; in the same way a single passage could be given, and as in the one case so in others.[1]

At least verbally, Nicholas is right: his account of the "four senses of Scripture" thus schematically set out would have been acceptable at any point in the western Christian tradition in the period from late antiquity to his own day in the fourteenth century. The broad distinction between "literal" and "spiritual" senses is there in general terms in Origen's *On First Principles* in the early fourth century, in Augustine's *De doctrina christiana* in the early fifth, and the distinction of the four senses in almost the exact

---

1 First Prologue to the *Postillae litterales*. I have translated from the printed text published in Rome, 1471. See my *Eros and Allegory, Medieval Exegesis of the Song of Songs* (Kalamazoo: Cistercian Publications, 1995), pp. 383–84.

terms in which Nicholas reports them is found in Gregory the Great in the late sixth century – which is not surprising, since in this connection Gregory is dependent on a famous text in Cassian's *Conferences*, foundational for the theory and practice of scriptural interpretation throughout the one thousand years of the Middle Ages. In fact, Nicholas' account is more or less a direct citation of Cassian. Thus Cassian:

> ...contemplative knowledge (of Scripture) is divided into two parts, namely, the historical and the spiritual. But there are three kinds of spiritual knowledge, the tropological, the allegorical and the anagogical... history embraces the knowledge of things past and visible... but the allegorical contains what follows thereafter, for the events of history are said to have prefigured the form of a mystery... the anagogical sense ascends from [those] spiritual mysteries to even more sublime and hidden secrets of heaven... [while] the tropological sense is the moral teaching which has to do with the emendation of life... And so these four figures interpenetrate... in one subject, so that one and the same Jerusalem may be understood in four ways: historically, it is the city of the Jews; allegorically, it the Church of Christ, anagogically, it is the city of God which is heaven... tropologically, it is the human soul...[2]

That obvious verbal continuity conceded, and granted that Nicholas' formulae are intentionally traditional and thus far uncontroversial, nothing else is simple in the history of the allegorical interpretation of Scripture in the medieval period of the Christian West. Of all biblical scholars in the late Middle Ages Nicholas is the least unaware that bare agreement on the terminology of Cassian's standardized schema of the "four senses" disguises vast differences concerning how the distinctions between those senses are to be understood, how they are related, and more particularly concerning how the other three senses are related to the first, the literal sense.

In fact Nicholas himself had an axe to grind, if not with the terminology itself, then with what he understood to be the prevailing employment of the hermeneutic of the "four senses" in the practice of biblical interpretation. On the score of priorities, Nicholas himself is firm, the literal sense comes first: "all of [the other three senses] presuppose the literal sense as their foundation; and as a building which tilts on its foundations is destined for collapse, so a mystical explanation out of true with the literal sense should be judged inappropriate and useless...."[3] But therein lies the point. For Nicholas believes that far too much of the practice of scriptural interpretation of his own times and earlier has suffered from a neglect of

2 Cassian, *Conferences*, 14.8, *Of Spiritual Knowledge*, Latin text in J.-P. Migne, ed., Patrologia latina (Paris, 1844–65) 49: 962C–64A (my translation).
3 Second Prologue to the *Postillae litterales*, see *Eros and Allegory*, p. 385.

the literal sense in its enthusiasm to exploit the other three, non-literal, or "mystical" senses, especially the allegorical.[4] " . . . [I]t is as well to know," he says,

> that the literal sense is much disguised [multum obumbratus] by the method of expounding generally handed down in the tradition by those who, though they have a good many things to say, to some degree have hidden the literal sense by virtue of the multiplication of mystical senses, the result being that the literal sense is almost suffocated, being entangled in so many mystical senses.

Therefore, he proposes in his own commentary on the whole of the Bible "to rest my case on the literal sense" and only "infrequently, to include the occasional, brief, mystical interpretation."[5]

It is not difficult to illustrate the sort of excessively allegorical-mystical reading of Scripture to which Nicholas takes exception, even if the following example comes from an author writing a century after Nicholas. Commenting on the second verse of the Old Testament Song of Songs (as construed by the Vulgate translation) "for your breasts are better than wine," Denys the Carthusian elaborates:

> According to Origen, the breasts of the Bridegroom are to be read as the secrets hidden in the heart or bowels of Christ, that is, they are the treasures of wisdom and knowledge which are hidden within him, by which he nourishes the hearts of the faithful. But it is also possible to interpret [them] as the two commandments of charity, or again, as the Old Testament interpreted in its spiritual [i.e., non-literal] sense, and the New; or again as the Saviour's commandments and the evangelical counsels, likewise as his mercy and truth; or, in yet another way, as prevenient and subsequent grace.[6]

Or, as Nicholas might well have put it, on *that* sort of account, anything at all in the Christian dispensation of which there are just two could every bit as well serve as the allegorical meaning of the Bridegroom's "two breasts." But Nicholas' problems are not over when once he has planted the flag of his exegetical practice firmly in the foundation of the Bible's literal sense. He has a further, prior, and much trickier problem of theoretical hermeneutics to deal with: how are we to identify the "literal sense" of Scripture in any particular case? Moreover, he is aware that

---

4 There is some slippage of terminology here. Nicholas is not alone among late antique and medieval authors in using the word "mystical" in two meanings. Sometimes the word is a synonym for the fourth sense, the so-called "anagogical," sometimes, as in the passage just quoted, as a generic term for all three non-literal senses.

5 *Eros and Allegory*, pp. 385–86.   6 *Eros and Allegory*, p. 426.

this is a question which can be answered only if we can say what in general counts as *literalness*. For Nicholas believes that it is confusion within the traditions of biblical interpretation concerning this last question that lies at the root of its excesses of free-range allegorizings in practice. It is, he says, for want of an adequate understanding of *how* the literal contrasts with the allegorical that an uncontrolled indulgence in allegory is motivated.

The reason, then, why the issue of literalness matters in the context of an essay on the hermeneutics of late antique and early medieval biblical allegory, is that it is impossible to understand what is meant within that tradition by allegory until one grasps in what way the allegorical is said to be distinguished from the literal. And the reason why it is relevant to the late antique conception of biblical allegory how that question is raised in so late a medieval scholar as Nicholas of Lyra, is that the chickens which come home to roost in Nicholas are all born of late antique eggs laid by Origen, Augustine, Cassian and Gregory the Great. What Nicholas identifies as confusion about the relation between the allegorical and the literal senses of Scripture in late medieval exegetical practice, is no less disguised by the assumption of continuity between that late medieval practice and that of those late antique authorities than it is by the apparent unanimity on the terminology of that distinction in his own times. The illusions whether of clarity or of continuity – and usually both – under which a thousand years of biblical exegesis laboured are exposed by Nicholas as being just that: illusions. And they are illusions which arise from unresolved ambiguities in the account of those key terms of the literal and the allegorical in the earliest Christian sources, in short, in Origen, Augustine, Gregory and, indeed, even in Cassian himself.

The multiplicity of senses in Origen, Augustine and Gregory

But why did theologians of late antiquity feel the need to distinguish "senses" of Scripture in the first place? One answer which is common ground to all four is that Scripture itself distinguishes its own literal and allegorical senses and thus provides at least the general principle of its own interpretation. Cassian had appealed in those general terms to Proverbs (22:20) as a basis for distinguishing the three spiritual senses from the literal, a text which instructs the reader to "describe these things in three ways according to the largeness of your heart." But less tenuously, and more specifically as construing the literal narratives of the Old Testament as allegories for the revelation of the New, his appeal, as later in Nicholas, is to Paul [Galatians 4:26]. Genesis, Paul tells us, recounts how Abraham had two sons, one born of a bondswoman, the other of a free woman, one born in the ordinary way, the other as the result of a promise. This, Paul adds, "can be regarded as an allegory: the women stand for the two covenants," Hagar the bondswoman for the Jerusalem which remains unconverted to Christ, Sarah the free woman, for the "Jerusalem above . . . [who] is free and is our mother," that is, the Christian Church. At any rate, so far as concerns the relationship between the Old Testament and the New, Cassian's appeal is to the New Testament not only as a fulfilment of the "promise" of the Old, but also, and by virtue of that relationship between promise and fulfillment, fixing the terminology for the later Middle Ages of what was already a fundamental principle of patristic and medieval biblical hermeneutics. In general the literal sense stands to the allegorical as promise stands to fulfillment. History, as literally narrated in the Old Testament, *means* more, because it *intends* more, than the events it literally records. What the Old Testament literally records is allegory for the New.

Cassian, of course, is no innovator in this connection. Behind him stands Origen, who goes even further than Cassian, in effect denying that the events of the Old Testament have any significance, at any rate in their own right, for understood in its spiritual sense – that is, in the light of its fulfillment in the New Testament – the Old Testament *is* the New Testament in disguised form:

> I do not call the law the Old Testament if I understand it spiritually. The law is only made the Old Testament to those who understand it carnally . . . But to us who understand it and expound it spiritually and with its gospel meaning it is always new; both are New Testament to us, not in terms of temporal sequence but of newness of understanding.[7]

In short, the Old Testament is, in terms of its true meaning, "other" than itself, it is allegory for other "mysteries" than its own.

But if thus in general terms the Bible, specifically in the relation between the two testaments, becomes the principle of its own interpretation, Origen has another, more directly exegetical, reason for distinguishing between its literal and its spiritual/allegorical sense: its literally anomalous character. Noting how much of the biblical narrative is at face value obscure, some of it plainly erroneous in matters of fact, some of it openly self-contradictory, Origen believes that respect for its veracity – that, after all, is guaranteed by its author, the Holy Spirit – demands that its true meaning be sought otherwise than in its literal meaning. Besides, common sense requires this. "[W]ho" after all, he asks,

7 *Homily 19 on Numbers*, quoted in *Cambridge History of the Bible* I (Cambridge: Cambridge University Press, 1970), p. 483.

will be simple enough to believe that like some farmer "God planted trees in the garden of Eden in the east" and that He planted "the tree of life" in it, that is a visible tree that could be touched, so that someone could eat of this tree with corporeal teeth and gain life, and further could eat of another tree and receive "knowledge of good and evil" [Genesis 3:8]? . . . Surely I think no one doubts that these statements are made by Scripture in the form of a type by which they point toward certain mysteries. Also Cain's "going away from the face of God" [Genesis 4:16] obviously stirs the wise reader to ask what "the face of God is" and how anyone could "go away" from it . . .[8]

Nor, for Origen, are the incongruities and anomalies of Scripture illustrative merely of the ignorance or literary failures of its human authors, thereby requiring of its human readers an emergency operation of allegorical retrieval with a view to rescuing its truth. Scripture is *strategically* designed by its principal author, the Holy Spirit, with an imperfect, fissured, literal surface so as to entice the reader's mind to enter through the cracks of anomaly into its deeper, spiritual, meaning: ". . . the divine wisdom," he says,

> has arranged for there to be certain stumbling blocks or interruptions of the narrative meaning, by inserting in its midst certain impossibilities and contradictions, so that the very interruption of the narrative might oppose the reader, as it were, with certain obstacles thrown in the way. By them wisdom denies a way and an access to the common understanding; and when we are shut out and hurled back, it calls us back to the beginning of another way, so that by gaining a higher and loftier road through entering a narrow footpath it may open for us the immense breadth of divine knowledge.[9]

Augustine is of much the same opinion: he tells us that one of the obstacles to his conversion had been his distaste for the stylistic and rhetorical crudities of the Old Latin version of the Bible, and that it was Ambrose who taught him to look past that vulgar surface of the literal text to its allegorical beauties, both disguised and at the same time revealed by that literal surface.[10] And in *De doctrina christiana*, observing the sheer difficulty of making out any coherent meaning from the more obscure passages of the Bible, he says he is in "no doubt that this situation [of scriptural obscurity] was provided by God to conquer pride by work and to combat disdain in our minds, to which those things that are easily discovered seem frequently to become worthless."[11] Gregory the Great, probably following

---

8 *Origen: An Exhortation to Martyrdom, Prayer and Selected Works*, trans. Rowan A. Greer (New York: Paulist Press, 1979), p. 189.

9 *On First Principles* IV.2.9, in Greer, pp. 187–88.   10 *Confessions* 6.3.

11 *On Christian Doctrine* II.vi.7, trans. D. W. Robertson (New York: Macmillan, 1958), p. 37.

Origen here in Rufinus' Latin translation rather than Augustine, has an even more particular and urgent reason in his commentary on the Song of Songs for adopting the same hermeneutic. For the Song of Songs is on the one hand a biblical text, hence inspired by the Holy Spirit; and on the other it is in *prima facie* an intensely erotic, not to say bawdy, collection of secular poems containing no reference to God, or Israel, nor does it offer any other clue as to its divine source or meaning. Consequently, Gregory says, in reading this book as Scripture, allegory is necessary, for

> allegory supplies the soul separated far from God with a kind of mechanism by which it is raised to God ... By that which we do know – out of such are allegories made – divine meanings are clothed and through our understanding of external speech we are brought to an inner understanding ... Thus it is that in this book, called the Song of Songs, we find the words of bodily love: so that the soul, its numbness caressed into warmth by familiar words, through the words of a lower love is excited to a higher. For in this book are described kisses, breasts, cheeks, limbs; and this holy language is not to be held in ridicule because of these words. Rather we are provoked to reflect on the mercy of God ... [12]

It would be easy to derive from such statements, especially those of Origen, the conclusion that all three regard allegory as a device of Christian tendentiousness, permitting, if not demanding, the evacuation of all literal meaning from the biblical text, especially the evacuation of the literal "Jewishness" of the Old Testament, the shell being thus emptied of literalness so as to be filled with its allegorical "otherness," its significance in terms of Christ. But this would be unfair at least to Origen and to Augustine. After all, one of Origen's principal legacies to the Christian tradition is his concern to establish a sound text, whether in the Bible's original languages or in its translations, on the grounds that what the Bible actually says and actually means in its own terms, must be the principal determinant of any allegorical significance it may thereafter be shown to contain. Augustine likewise, in a spirit close to that of the later Nicholas of Lyra, warns against too ready an appeal to "spiritual" and allegorical meanings just because we encounter difficulty with Scripture's less familiar metaphors. And in a distinction which becomes, as we will see, decisive for later medieval understandings of allegory, he insists that the presence in Scripture of what is nothing more than literary trope, especially metaphor, is neither the same thing as, nor in itself an occasion for indulging in, allegorical interpretations:

12 *Eros and Allegory*, pp. 217 –18.

... an awareness [of tropes] is necessary to a solution of the ambiguities of the Scriptures, for when the sense is absurd when it is taken verbally, it is to be inquired whether or not what is expressed is this or that trope which we do not know; and in this way many hidden things are discovered.[13]

It is as if to say that a license to allegory too easily granted is but the resort of the lazy, who find therein an excuse to neglect the demands of scholarship and research into text and context, into cultures of writing, rhetorical and literary, different from the reader's own by way of solution of literal anomalies: only when all such means have been exhausted may the "anomalies" remaining be allowed to provoke appeal to allegorical meaning. Thus, at any rate in principle, the Augustine of *De doctrina Christiana*. And it is no doubt this Augustine to whom Nicholas of Lyra is indebted when he complains of the uncontrolled allegorizing of too many of his theological contemporaries. They neglect their homework on the literal meaning of Scripture.

Theological allegory versus literary trope

It is just here, then, that we can see just why a late medieval scriptural interpreter such as Nicholas of Lyra, consciously drawing on late antique Latin Christian sources, should begin to see in them a significant ambiguity. Formulated in those later medieval terms, the question of the nature of theological allegory turns on the answer to another: "what constitutes the literal sense of Scripture?" For what counts as Scripture's allegorical sense will be very largely determined by the terms of contrast in which it stands to the literal sense, and without a clear account of the literal those terms of contrast will be indeterminable. But the question of what counted as the literal sense took a very particular form in the high Middle Ages – and Hugh of St. Victor in the twelfth century together with Thomas Aquinas in the thirteenth joined forces with Nicholas of Lyra in the fourteenth in asking it. It was a question the answer to which could not be found in the late antique sources on which all three claim to rely, for those sources are ambiguous. And that question was "in what relations of contrast does the literal stand with the metaphorical on the one hand, and with the allegorical on the other?" For Hugh, Thomas and Nicholas, the answer is clear: there are *two quite distinct* terms of contrast in which the literal can stand, and therefore two senses of the word "literal," one as getting its meaning by force of its contrast with metaphor, the other through its contrast with allegory. Moreover, if the literal and the metaphorical contrast in one way, and the literal and the allegorical in another it follows at least that the

13 *On Christian Doctrine*, III.xxix.41, p. 104.

allegorical and the metaphorical cannot be identified with one another, as Augustine had said. Now the significance of this is that in Hugh, Thomas and Nicholas there is at least the beginning of an awareness of the need for a more general distinction which cannot be found in the late antique sources on which they claim to rely, namely that between theological and literary forms of allegory. The two cannot be the same and the presence of the one in a text cannot claim justification for seeing the other's presence in it. Here it is important to remember that the word *allegoria*, transferred from Greek into Latin, carried two rather different meanings. When used in late antique Greek sources, it bore a theurgic value, relating to the concealment of divine or cosmic meanings, close in its value to "symbol." But in Latin, it had acquired a restricted literary or rhetorical sense of inferring another meaning than what is said. The word in Christian theological contexts carried the force of the Greek theurgic meaning, but was still susceptible to interference from its Latin rhetorical meaning [see in this volume Most, "Hellenistic Allegory" and Struck, "Allegory and Ascent in Neoplatonism"].

At any rate, Hugh, Thomas, and Nicholas are clear that allegory in the theological sense in which Scripture can sometimes demand to be interpreted is not a form of literary trope, a "figure of speech." Hugh of St. Victor, insisting with a vigor that matches Nicholas' that neglect of the literal sense of Scripture is both all too common and hermeneutically perverse, puts the widespread tendency to allegorize arbitrarily and without constraint down to the collapsing of the merely figurative into the allegorical: every time you spot a scriptural metaphor you have got an allegory; that seems to be the practice of too many. On the contrary, he says,

> ... even in the case where an utterance is accepted figuratively, it cannot be denied that the letter has its own signification; for when we claim that what is said is not to be understood at face value, nonetheless we still insist that it has some kind of *prima facie* [i.e., literal] meaning. Thus, something is said and signified literally, and this is so *even when the words uttered are not to be understood at their face values, but signify something else through what they say.*[14]

In short, for Hugh, figurative speech, metaphor, is part of the *literal* sense of scripture, allegory something which may or may not be legitimately constructed on the basis of that literal sense.

Just so for Thomas. Arguing against the view that it is not in Scripture alone that the four senses of Cassian can be found, but also in any form of secular poetry – after all, there too images which at one level signify one thing can at another level signify something else[15] – Thomas replies:

14 *Eros and Allegory*, p. 270 (emphasis added).   15 *Eros and Allegory*, p. 351.

... in no form of knowledge which is the product of human powers is any but the literal sense to be found, but only in those Scriptures of which the Holy Spirit is the author, man but the instrument. [Hence] ... poetic images refer to something else only so as to signify them; and so a signification of that sort goes no way beyond the manner in which the literal sense signifies.[16]

Implicit here is the distinction needed between theological allegory and literary trope, that is, between a theological hermeneutic and a literary theory, a distinction which he goes on to make explicit through an attempt at a clear definition of the literal sense. Anything at all that can be said to be contained in the meaning of the words of a text is part of its literal sense. This holds equally of the texts of Scripture or of secular poems: it therefore holds of scriptural poetry too, because scriptural poetry – such as the Psalms, or the Song of Songs – is just one of the means Scripture deploys of saying something about the world, whether this takes the form of historical narrative, moral instruction, or illuminating teaching about the nature of love, death, or whatever. Such deployment of the vernacular power of figurative speech, then, is one of the devices of the *literal* for Thomas, whether in Scripture or other writing. In *this* sense of "literal," then, the literal does not contrast with the metaphorical at all: rather it includes it. It follows that you cannot get to Thomas' contrast between the literal and the allegorical through any contrast, late antique, medieval, or modern, in which the literal stands to the metaphorical. In Scripture alone is allegory proper to be found.

Thomas explains why. Allegory, he says, is not strictly speaking, as metaphor strictly speaking is, a layer of textual meaning at all. It is not a semantic property of the *words* of Scripture, but is the meaning of the actual *events*, more generally the *res*, that Scripture literally narrates through those words, whether poetically or prosaically. And giving the allegorical meaning of the *res* of the Old Testament, recounted literally as the history of the people of Israel, in the proleptic terms of Christ, or the anagogical meaning of Christian history in the proleptic terms of the Kingdom of Heaven which it anticipates, these are not achievements of meaning which *any* human words could pull off, but only the Holy Spirit, working the providential designs of the Father through those events of human history. And so Thomas says:

The author of [all] things can not only make use of words to signify something, but also can arrange for things to be figures of other things. Because of this the truth is made plain in sacred Scripture in two ways. In one way insofar as things are signified by the words: and this is the literal sense. In another way

16 *Eros and Allegory*, p. 352.

by virtue of the fact that things and events [*res*] are figures of other things: and this is what the spiritual sense consists in.[17]

And so it seems to follow from this that, for Thomas, the spiritual senses of Scripture are not senses of the text itself – for only the literal sense is that. Anything at all which belongs to the text of the Scripture as part of its meaning is literal, metaphorical or otherwise: whereas allegory, tropology and anagogy are senses authored by the Holy Spirit alone in the text of providential history. And it is from the confusion of theological allegory with literary trope that follows the mistake we saw Nicholas of Lyra to have identified, of those who derive opportunity for freelance and arbitrary allegorizing from the mere presence of metaphor in the language of Scripture, who find in every utterance of scriptural poetry an alibi for generating a plurality of meanings which threatens theological discourse with equivocity. In short, for Thomas, poetry, even scriptural poetry, as such has no exegetical or spiritual significance.

Conclusion: the literary afterlife of patristic scriptural allegory

If even up to the end of the Middle Ages it is still felt to be incumbent upon all scriptural scholars of whatever hue to claim continuity with the foundational formulae of the late antique authorities – theologians as opposed to one another as Nicholas of Lyra and Denys the Carthusian both claim the legacy of Cassian – it is clear that in fact the consensus has broken down by the fourteenth century, if not two centuries earlier. And it is clear too that the seeds of later medieval differences on the score of the nature of allegory are sown in that same late antique, Latin patristic, soil to which all and sundry lay claim. Augustine himself may be clear in principle that theological allegory and literary trope are distinct, the one deriving alone from the divine power to shape the meaning of historical events to purposes and meanings beyond the capacity of human agents to shape, the other being simply a human device of the literary form in which those events are recorded. But Augustine in practice all too frequently fails to obey his own prescriptions, as one can see within a paragraph or two of the passage in *De doctrina Christiana*, quoted above, in which he is theoretically so precise: Augustine's exploitation of the riotous metaphoricity of the Song of Songs as allegory is no more sensitive of the text's own literary qualities than is the wooden and po-faced commentary of Denys the Carthusian.

Origen, too, is far less than clear about the distinction to which Hugh, Thomas and Nicholas of Lyra attach so much importance. Talk in Genesis,

17 *Eros and Allegory*, p. 344.

he says, about Cain "turning away from the face of God" is so obviously *literally* false, God having no face you could "turn away from," it follows that the meaning of the text must be "spiritual," allegorical. But that "literal falseness" is in fact nothing but the failure of literalness which is anyway *definitive* of metaphor, and gets its meaning of literalness from *that* contrast, not from any with allegory in its properly theological sense. In short, if there is ambiguity about the meaning of allegory to be resolved in later medieval theologies, it is in the sources in late antiquity to which all in common appeal that those ambiguities are already to be found.

A final comment. If what begins to clarify those earlier ambiguities is the late medieval distinction between the theological allegory of scriptural hermeneutics and the literary tropes of the poets, then the case of Dante must be of the utmost significance for the development of post-medieval forms of literary allegory. For in at least apparent defiance of Thomas' refusal to admit the poets into the company of the allegorists in the properly theological sense, Dante tells us that Cassian's four senses have application directly to his own *Comedy*. Now assuming that the *Letter to Cangrande* is indeed an authentically Dantean text [see, in this volume, Ascoli, "Dante and Allegory"], it is possible to read it in one or other of two ways. Either, as at face value it would seem, as an explicit rejection of Thomas' distinction – for it is certain that Dante had read Thomas on the subject – or else as a more or less explicit claim for his own poetry as having a quasi-scriptural standing. The latter reading is not beyond the bounds of credibility: Dante did not exactly suffer either a lack of self-esteem as a poet, or a low opinion of the poetic vocation itself. But whichever of these two ways of taking Dante's claim is correct, it can be seen from the hindsight of post-medieval literary development as a retrograde step. For though the intentions of Hugh, Thomas and Nicholas were to liberate theological allegory from its confusions with the literary, an unintended consequence was in turn to liberate the literary possibilities of allegory from their confusion with the theological: and Dante would seem to have intended the opposite. The post-medieval fortunes of allegory are, of course, another story. But it is one that needs to be told from the beginning, and that means at least from its sources in western Christian late antiquity. For it is there that the very ambiguities of Origen, Cassian, Gregory, and even of Augustine, open the way for a very different outcome than they for themselves had in mind.

6

PETER HEATH

Allegory in Islamic literatures

Allegory flourished in premodern Islamic literatures. Remarkably, however, neither premodern nor modern literary historians devote independent discussions to the genre per se, or even include the term in their indices. Allegorical praxis is simply treated under other generic categories, such as the mystical tale, the philosophical visionary recital, the poetic romance, or scriptural and textual commentary. Discussion here therefore requires drawing together variegated strands of literary practice to portray the history and development of allegory in Arabic, Persian, and Ottoman Turkish literatures, which are the major literary traditions of Islamic culture.[1] Other Islamic literatures exist, in Urdu, Malay, and Swahili, for example, yet neither space nor scope of personal expertise allows their treatment here.

Allegory in Islamic literatures as a developed literary practice begins at the turn of the eleventh century, four centuries after the death of the Prophet Muhammad. Yet allegory draws on earlier periods for crucial constituent narrative forms, topics, themes, source materials, and interpretational frameworks. An initial overview of relevant influences will clarify later developments.

---

1 My appreciation to F. Kesahvarz, V. R. Holbrook, and Marianne Heath for reading and commenting on this chapter. For general surveys and literary history, see for Arabic literature: A. F. L. Beeston, et al., *The Cambridge History of Arabic Literature*, 6 vols. (Cambridge: Cambridge University Press, 1983–2006; different editors for each volume; hereafter *CHAL*); and R. Allen, *The Arabic Literary Heritage: The Development of its Genres and Criticism* (Cambridge: Cambridge University Press, 1998; hereafter *ALH*). For Persian literature, see J. Rypka, *History of Iranian Literature* (Dordrecht, Holland: D. Reidel, 1956; hereafter *HIL*); E. G. Browne, *A Literary History of Persia*, 4 vols. (London, Cambridge, 1902–25); and J.T. P. de Bruijn, *Persian Sufi Poetry: an Introduction to the Mystical Use of Classical Poems* (Richmond, Surrey: Curzon Press, 1997). For Ottoman literature, see E. J. W. Gibb, *A History of Ottoman Poetry*, 6 vols., Gibb Memorial Series (London: Luzac, 1958); and A. Bombaci, *La litteratura turca* (Milan, 1969). Articles on individual writers are in the *Encyclopedia of Islam*, 11 vols., 2nd edn. (Leiden: E. J. Brill, 1960–2002; hereafter *EI²*).

Foundations and constituent elements

The Qur'an[2]

The Qur'an influences allegorical practice in Islamic literatures in three significant ways. First, it dramatically emphasizes the existential and experiential duality that informs all allegorical writing. The Qur'an finds humans immersed in the immediate pleasures of corporeal sensation and worldly ambition. It calls on them to transcend these alluring earthly attachments and return to the "rightly guided path." Humans, it states, must reorder their lives. Through divine mercy, God sends both prophets and revelation to guide this change in human orientation, with Muhammad being the last of such prophets and the Qur'an the final revelation.

This form of presentation enforces in readers habits of analogical and figurative thinking and offers potential emplotments.[3] The Qur'an uses varied rhetorical modes to achieve this reorientation. It exhorts and adopts the evocative, oracular, and forcefully hortatory styles of invocation and homily. It reminds by offering examples of past events, focusing especially on incidents in the lives of previous prophets and their own troubled relationships with their communities. It employs a legalistic style to reform deleterious practices in such areas as marriage, inheritance, or the treatment of orphans. Finally, it creates a symbolic language of striking power and stirring metaphor. Linguistically a forcefully emotive text, reading the Qur'an in the original is a unique experience. Yet understanding its format also requires training in and due appreciation of how the text interweaves its styles, symbols, and themes.

Such training in the art of reading is the Qur'an's second point of influence on allegory. The Qur'an demands from its audiences that they transcend literal approaches to reading. It assumes knowledge of narrative context and background. Its recitations of incidents in the lives of prophets such as Abraham, Moses, or Joseph, for example, assumes from its audience an already existing general acquaintance with the outlines of the stories.

2 The Qur'an has many translations. For background, see W. M. Watt and R. Bell, *Introduction to the Qur'an*, Islamic Surveys (Edinburgh: Edinburgh University Press, 1970); F. Rahman, *Major Themes of the Qur'an*, 2nd edn. (Minneapolis: Bibliotheca Islamica, 1989); and H. Gätje, *The Qur'ān and its Exegesis* (Oxford: Oneworld, 1996). Also valuable is J. D. McAuliffe, ed., *Encyclopedia of the Qur'ān*, 5 vols. (Leiden: E. J. Brill, 2001–06) and *EI*[2].

3 On simultaneity of historical perception and figuration, see E. Auerbach, *Mimesis: The Representation of Reality in Western Literature*, trans. W. Trask (Princeton: Princeton University Press, 1953), pp. 16–18, and the chapter "Figura" in his *Scenes from the Drama of European Literature* (New York: Meridian Books, 1959); "emplotment" is a central concept in P. Ricoeur, *Time and Narrative*, 3 vols., trans. K. McLaughlin and D. Pellauer (Chicago: Chicago University Press, 1990).

Hence, understanding the Qur'an accurately requires both an awareness of gaps in contextual knowledge and a willingness to fill in these gaps. Later commentary did so by introducing a fund of secondary narrative detail, supplementary information, and alternative interpretation.

This wealth of exegetical contextual detail highlights the third Qur'anic influence on allegory. The Qur'an and its commentaries provide an immense stock of culturally shared metaphors, symbols, textual references, narrative details, and stylistic modes. Qur'anic commentary supplemented this shared cultural reservoir and became a significant narrative resource for later writers of allegory.[4]

The anecdote

Long narratives exist in Islamic literatures; yet compilations of anecdotes (*khabar*, pl. *akhbār*) are also a significant narrative form (*adab*). In contrast to the deepening display of character that longer integrated narratives offer, the aesthetic aim of the allegorical anecdote is to provide glancing insights into moral character and practice. It achieves this by providing positive or negative examples of specific actions in the face of unexpected situations or ethical dilemmas. In Islamic literatures anecdotal composition remains crucial until the arrival of the modern novel and short story in the twentieth century.[5]

Interpretational contexts

Allegories in Islamic literatures create their polysemous structures by contrasting everyday experiences against several major cultural codes. Allegories seek to instill insight into the realms of practical morality, philosophical speculation, or mystical experience.

An early example of allegories of pragmatic morality are the writings of Ibn al-Muqaffa' (d. 750), especially his translation into Arabic (from Pahlavi or Middle Persian) of the *Book of Kalīla wa-Dimna*.[6] This work

---

4 On Qur'anic commentary, see A. Rippen, "Tafsīr," in *EI²* 10:83–88, and on interpretation, I. Poonawala, "ta'wīl," in *EI²* 10:390–92; also C. Giliot, "Exegesis of the Qur'ān: Classical and Medieval," in *Encyclopedia of the Qur'ān*, 2:99–124; and P. Heath, "Creative Hermeneutics: An Analysis of Three Islamic Approaches," *Arabica* 36 (1989), 173–210.
5 See R. Allen, *ALH*, pp. 222–47; and, on the genre *adab*, S. A. Bonebakker, "Adab," *CHAL* 2:16–30.
6 Often reprinted in Arabic, an English translation is: *The Fables of Kalilah and Dimnah*, trans. Saleh S. Jallad (London: Melisende, 2002); see also J. D. Latham's article in *CHAL* 2:48–77; for later Persian versions, see Rypka, *HIL*, pp. 660–61.

is essentially a collection of beast fables, yet it is also an early example of the genre of Mirrors for Princes that flourished in Muslim culture for centuries. In his introduction, Ibn al-Muqaffaʿ states that his fables serve two purposes: entertainment for the foolish and instruction for the wise (trans. p. 29). These stories, he says, should entertain children, amuse kings, and instruct all – whether royalty, gentry or the common people – but also train philosophers in wisdom (trans. p. 36).

Later examples of the Mirror for Princes genre, such as the Persian vizier Niẓām al-Mulk's *Book of Politics (Siyāsāt-Nāma)* or the *Qābūs-Nāma* of the prince Qābūs ibn Vushmgīr, rely on historical example or fictional anecdote to convey their messages, but the duality between the embedded narratives and overall moralistic theme implies an allegorical structure.[7]

A second intellectual framework for allegorical narrative consists of Greek traditions of ancient philosophy as integrated and developed in Islamic culture. A central analogy in this corpus is the Platonic correspondence among the different parts of the human soul, the social classes that constitute a city or state, and the multilayered cosmological structure of the universe. Key in this tradition is the conviction that the syllogistic demonstrations of philosophy mirror the truths of religion.[8]

Islamic mysticism (*taṣawwuf* or Sufism) is the third and historically the most influential frame of reference for allegory. At heart, the movement was (and is) experiential. Pietistic exercises resulted in spiritual insight and numinous inspiration, and over time mystics developed specific mental, emotional, and physical exercises to foster such experiences. Those who mastered mystical practices became guides for and teachers of aspirants; eventually

---

7 "Mirrors for Princes" is a rich but little studied genre in Islamic literatures, possibly because it is too literary for historians and too political for literary specialists. See Rypka, *HIL*, pp. 661–62 for brief comments. Ironically, although understudied, a fair number of English translations exist: see Kai-Kaʾūs ibn Iskandar, *A Mirror for Princes: the Qābūs-nāma*, trans. Reuben Levy (London: Cresset Press, 1951); Niẓām al-Mulk, *The Book of Government, or, Rules for Kings: the Siyāsat-nāma or Siyar al-mulūk*, trans. Hubert Darke (London: Routledge, 1960); Muḥammad ibn Ẓafar al-Siqillī, *The Just Prince: a Manual of Leadership, a Translation of the Sulwān al-Muṭāʾ fī ʿudwān al-atbāʾ (Consolation for the Ruler during the Hostility of Subjects)*, trans. Joseph A. and R. Hrair Kechichian (London: Saqi Books, 2003), and in Turkish, Yūsuf Khāṣṣ Ḥājib, *Wisdom of Royal Glory (Kutadgu Bilig): A Turko-Islamic Mirror for Princes*, trans. R. Dankoff (Chicago: University of Chicago Press, 1983); Dankoff's introduction above provides a useful overview and analysis.
8 A recent survey of Arabic/Islamic philosophy is P. Adamson and R. C. Taylor, *The Cambridge Companion to Arabic Philosophy* (Cambridge: Cambridge University Press, 2005). For translations, see R. Lerner and M. Mahdi, eds., *Medieval Political Philosophy* (Ithaca, NY: Cornell University Press, 1963); and M. A. Khalidi, ed., *Medieval Islamic Philosophical Writings*, Cambridge Texts in the History of Philosophy (Cambridge: Cambridge University Press, 2005).

this process formalized into training in the Sufi path (*ṭarīqa*). The goal of this path was to plumb the realities and truths (*ḥaqīqa*) of spiritual union with the divine, a process whose aim was mystical insight and ecstasy, within the boundaries of Islamic legal orthodoxy (*sharīʿa*). Ideally, the Sufi disciple would progress from an exoteric knowledge of *sharīʿa*, follow a prescribed path (*ṭarīqa*) under guidance from an experienced Sufi master, and finally attain pinnacles of esoteric ecstasy resulting from direct encounters with divine Reality (*ḥaqīqa*).

One challenge that mystics faced was how to express insights regarding their inner states and spiritual apperceptions. Mystical experience found articulation in spontaneous utterances produced in heights of ecstasy; in poetry, especially, love poems where the mystic expressed his or her passion for and devotion to the Beloved (God); and finally in allegory, which provided ways of depicting travel along the mystical path and methods for portraying various degrees of spiritual experience. One way that progress along the mystical path was expressed was through the development of technical terms for each "station" (*maqām*) along the way and for the various "states" (*ḥāl*) that the disciple progressively experienced at each station. As with the image of the heavenly ascent, that of the mystic's progress along stations and descriptions of its joys and travails provided an apposite structuring device for allegorical narrative.[9]

All three of the broad frames of reference briefly described above, and interlacements among them, underlie Islamic allegorical literatures. Dominant were philosophical and mystical allegory, so these will be the focus of the discussion that follows.

Philosophical allegory

Philosophical allegory emerges in the tenth century in an initial form in the lengthy *Epistles of the Brethren of Purity* (*Ikhwān al-Ṣafāʾ*).[10] Composed

---

9 Useful surveys of Islamic mysticism include A. Schimmel, *Mystical Dimensions of Islam* (Chapel Hill: University of North Carolina Press, 1975); A. T. Karamustafa, *Sufism: The Formative Period* (Edinburgh: Edinburgh University Press, 2007); and L. Massignon, B. Radtke, et al., "Taṣawwuf," in *EI*[2] 10:313–40. For translations, see M. A. Sells, *Early Islamic Mysticism: Sufi, Qurʾan, Miʿraj, Poetic and Theological Writings*, Classics of Western Spirituality (New York: Paulist Press, 1996). Several major early Sufi handbooks from the tenth and eleventh centuries, by al-Kalābādhī, al-Hujwīrī, and al-Qushairī, also exist in English translation.

10 *Ikhwān al-Ṣafāʾ*, *Rasāʾil*, 4 vols. (Beirut: Dār Ṣādir, n.d.). See also Y. Marquet, "*Ikhwān al-Ṣafāʾ*," in *EI*[2] 3:1071–76; and I. R. Netton, *Muslim Neoplatonists: an Introduction to the Thought of the Brethren of Purity*, Islamic Surveys (Edinburgh: Edinburgh University Press, 1991).

in tenth-century Baghdad by a group of intellectuals whose exact identity is still contested, the *Epistles*' overall theme is the universal unity and validity of rational knowledge across all religious divides. Despite this enlightened stance, the *Epistles* also exhibit a shallow hermeticism that invokes proto-allegorical symbolic correspondence indulged in for its own sake. References to the homology between the macrocosm (universe) and microcosm (human constitution) are constant. And analogies proliferate. At one point, for example, the human body is compared to a city, then to a house whose resident is the soul. This analogy proceeds for a page, enumerating how each feature of the body is comparable to a different part of a house. Thereafter follows another analogy comparing the body to a craftsman's shop, and then yet another comparing it to a city (2:380–85). Aiming for philosophical sublimity, the Treatises instead achieve superficial esotericism.

Embedded in the *Epistles* is the "Complaint of the Animals against Man" (2:203–377). The animals convene before a King of the Jinn to argue that Man enslaves them rather than treat them as interdependent fellow inhabitants of the world. Humans in turn contend that animals exist only to serve their needs. The two groups dispute their case using both religious and rationalistic arguments. Although the animals counter every assertion made by humans, the latter emerge victorious by reverting to religion: pointing out that only humans receive prophecy and divine revelation and that only they qualify for the afterlife. Man's victory is undercut by the final injunction of the treatise's author(s) that readers should understand its symbols and discern its true intent, thus intimating that the author may not truly believe in his own conclusion. Debates between classes of entities (sword versus pen, summer versus winter) form a separate genre in Islamic literatures, with semi-allegorical personification being common in them. In like fashion, in the "Complaint," each animal and human contender in the treatise represents a specific human trait (the lion kingship, the philosopher rational argument, etc.).[11]

If the Brethren of Purity were popular philosophers infused with analogical thinking, philosophical allegory appears in full force in the works of such thinkers as Ibn Sīna (Avicenna, d. 1037), Ibn Ṭufail (d. 1185), and

---

11 For a translation, see *Ikhwān al-Ṣafā', The Case of the Animals versus Man before the King of the Jinn*, trans. L. E. Goodman (Boston: Twayne Publishers, 1978). Debates (*munāẓarāt*) between contending personified entities – bow versus lance, night versus day – or human types – black versus white, slave girl versus slave boy – form a genre in premodern Islamic literatures that overlaps with allegory in many respects; see E. Wagner, "*munāẓara*," *EI*² 7:565–68.

Suhrawardī (d. 1191).[12] Ibn Sīna was a master of the rationalist philosophical traditions of his time and exerted a profound influence on later Islamic thought. Ibn Sīna composed several brief but brilliant and highly influential allegories in Arabic: the *Epistle of the Bird*, *Ḥayy ibn Yaqẓān*, and *Salāmān and Absāl*. He also offered interpretations of several verses of the Qur'an, most notably the Light Verse. Attributed to him as well are other commentaries, such as the Persian *Mi'rāj-nāma*.[13]

Underlying these allegories is the premodern philosophical theory of the human composite soul in which higher rational faculties contend with the temptations of the senses and lower passions. The protagonist of Ibn Sīna's allegories is the rational soul. Composed of the practical intellect, which deals with the affairs of pragmatic discursive reasoning, and the theoretical intellect, whose focus is attaining abstract knowledge, the rational soul is immortal and ineffable. Despite this, it finds itself immersed in corporeal form and harassed continually by the demands of bodily appetites, the attractions of emotional passion, and the vain illusions of the imagination. Its task is to extricate itself from these physical attachments and to turn its attention to its rightful orientation, the intellectual contemplation of divine causes and teleology, as represented by knowledge of the structure of the cosmos and a true understanding of the correct place for rational beings in it. A heavenly entity fallen into a terrestrial morass, the rational soul must return to its divine origins and in doing so find spiritual fulfillment in this world and eternal release in the afterlife.

Ibn Sīna's three epistles portray this trajectory from different perspectives. The *Epistle of the Bird* describes how its narrator, a bird, escapes from the snares of hunters to ascend with its flock through the heavenly spheres until it arrives above the highest sphere to encounter the Great King (God). In another work, the narrator meets Ḥayy ibn Yaqẓān (Alive, Son of Awake, i.e., the Active Intellect), a spiritual emissary and visionary guide who reveals with evocative imagery the structure and nature of the cosmos. Salāmān and Absāl in the third allegory are brothers representing, respectively, the practical and theoretical intellects. Salāmān's wife (the animal soul) first falls in love with Absāl and then when scorned arranges the latter's death. At this

---

12 For discussions of these thinkers, see Adamson and Taylor, *Cambridge Companion to Arabic Philosophy*. Historians of Arabic/Islamic philosophy tend to ignore allegory.
13 See P. Heath, *Allegory and Philosophy in Avicenna (Ibn Sīna), with a Translation of the Book of the Prophet Muḥammad's Ascent to Heaven* (Philadelphia: University of Pennsylvania Press, 1992). See also Henry Corbin, *Avicenna and the Visionary Recital*, trans. W. R. Trask (New York: Pantheon Books, 1960). For the "Bird," see S. Taghi, *The Two Wings of Wisdom: Mysticism and Philosophy in the Risālat uṭ-ṭair of Ibn Sīna*, Studia Iranican Upsaliensis 4 (Uppsala: Acta Universitatis Upsaliensis, 2000).

point, Salāmān "awakes" from his spiritual slumber, disposes of his wife, and retires to devote himself to study and contemplation.

Ibn Sīna's allegories are brief and allusive, but also compelling and numinous. They portray ideas already expounded in his philosophical works, yet their oracular style and their deep passion create powerfully emotive narratives. The philosopher's influence on subsequent writers of philosophical allegory was profound, but it appears in different forms. The Andalusian philosopher, Ibn Ṭufail, author of *The Treatise of Ḥayy ibn Yaqẓān*, retains the names of Ḥayy ibn Yaqẓān, Absāl, and Salāmān for different characters, and like Ibn Sīna he offers an account of the unfolding structure of the cosmos. Yet his focus differs. Clear and deliberate in style rather than allusive and evocative, the issues that Ibn Ṭufail pursues are philosophically straightforward but socially complex. His narrative first describes how the orphan Ḥayy ibn Yaqẓān, raised alone on an island but naturally endowed with perfect rationality, uses naturally endowed reason, empirical observation, and logical deduction to attain complete knowledge of the structure of the universe. He then exercises spiritual purification to achieve noetic unity with the divine. Thereafter, he delves into the relationship of those able to achieve such perfection with humans who constitutionally cannot. Ibn Ṭufail's conclusion may be viewed as either pessimistic or realistic. He advises perfected souls to retreat into quiet contemplation and instruct only a like-minded few while abandoning the multitudes possessing limited rationality to the normative, if spiritually limited, exoteric practices of revealed religion. This was a stance that echoed that of both predecessors such as Al-Fārābī and Ibn Bājja (Avempace, d. 1139) and Ibn Ṭufail's younger contemporaries, Ibn Rushd (Averroes, d. 1198) and the Jewish philosopher Mūsā ibn Maimūn, also known as Maimonides (d. 1204).[14]

Ibn Sīna's allegories also influenced the writing of the Jewish Andalusian philosopher, Abraham ben Ezra (d. 1164), who composed a poetic allegory entitled *Ḥay ben Meqitz*.[15] Ibn Ṭufail's allegory exerted its own influence on the thirteenth-century Syrian scholar and physician Ibn al-Nafīs (d. 1288), who composed a short analogous treatise, *The Perfect Treatise on the Prophet's Life (al-Risāla al-kāmaliyya fi al-sīra al-nabawiyya)*, titled by its

---

14 A partial translation is in Lerner and Mahdi, *Medieval Political Philosophy*, which also contains partial translations of relevant works by al-Fārābī, Ibn Bājja, al-Ibn Rushd, and Maimonides. See also Khalidi, *Medieval Islamic Philosophical Writings*. A full translation is *Ibn Tufayl's Hayy Ibn Yaqzān: a Philosophical Tale*, trans. L. E. Goodman (Los Angeles: Gee Tee Bee Books, 1991).

15 A. W. Hughes, *The Texture of the Divine: Imagination in Medieval Islamic and Jewish Thought* (Bloomington and Indianapolis: Indiana University Press, 2004).

editors and translators *The Theologus Auto-Didactus*.[16] Just as Ibn Ṭufail's protagonist, Ḥayy ibn Yaqẓān, grows up alone on a deserted island but is able to intuit philosophical truths through the use of natural reason, so Ibn al-Nafīs's hero, al-Kāmil (the Perfect), also alone on an island, comes to discern the theological verities of Islam. A final point of intertextual influence is that exerted by the seventeenth-century English translation of Ibn Ṭufail's treatise on Daniel Defoe in his creation of the story of Robinson Crusoe.

The last major examples of Islamic philosophical allegory are ten short allegories written in Persian by Shihāb al-Dīn Yaḥyā Suhrawardī, a charismatic and highly original philosopher who, as can happen with such individuals, was put to death at an early age.[17] Ibn Sīna's influence on Suhrawardī is demonstrated by his Persian translation of Ibn Sīna's *Epistle of the Bird*, as well as by direct references to Ibn Sīna's allegories in "A Tale of the Occidental Exile." Yet by Suhrawardī's time, Islamic mysticism had fully established its influence institutionally, culturally and intellectually. Therefore in his allegories, Suhrawardī uses both philosophical and Sufi frames of reference. He intertwines, for example, the sage–initiate relationship of Ibn Sīna's *Ḥayy ibn Yaqẓān* with the master–disciple teaching relationship prominent in Sufi training as a framing device in several allegories; typically, the narrator encounters one or more sages who instruct him on the mysteries of cosmological emanation. He is also fascinated by the duality of divine transcendence and manifestation. He uses as a symbol of this the image of Gabriel's wings, one of which is pure light while the other exhibits traces of darkness, indicating the intermixture of the divine ineffability with the realm of matter. Another symbol he employs is the "Red Intellect," the Active Intellect of Neoplatonic cosmology whose color stems from the mixture of divine light and material darkness.

Suhrawardī's allegories reflect the general absorption of philosophical concepts into mystical terminology that occurred during the twelfth

---

16 Ibn al-Nafīs, *The Theologus Auto-Didactus of Ibn al-Nafīs*, ed. and trans. M. Meyerhoff and J. Schacht (Oxford: Clarendon Press, 1968).

17 The allegories are edited in Sh. Suhrawardī', *Œuvres philosophiques et mystiques*, 2 vols. vol. 1, ed. H. Corbin (Tehran: Institut Franco-Iranien; Paris: Adrien-Maisonneuve, 1952) (one allegory); vol. 2, ed. S. H. Nasr (Tehran: L'Institut Français de Recherche; Paris: Adrien-Maisonneuve, 1970) (nine allegories). Corbin translations are in *L'Archange empourpré* (Paris: Fayard, 1976), with discussion in vol. 2 of his *En Islam iranien: aspects spirituels et philosophiques*, 4 vols. (Paris: Gallimard, 1971–72). An English translation is *The Mystical & Visionary Treatises of Suhrawardi*, trans. W. M. Thackston, Jr. (London: Octagon Press, 1982); some of its interpretations have been disputed, see H. Landolt, "Suhrawardī's 'Tales of Initiation'," *Journal of the American Oriental Society* 107 (1987), 475–86.

century.[18] Sufi allegory incorporated many of philosophical allegory's key concepts, such as the cosmological mixture of Neoplatonic hierarchical emanations with Ptolemaic astronomy, i.e., the system of heavenly spheres and intellects familiar to readers of Dante's *Divine Comedy*; and the structure of philosophical psychology, the Aristotelian divisions of the soul's faculties with its accompanying epistemological hierarchy of external and internal senses and the ascending levels of intellection. Certain narrative structuring devices also remain, such as the ascent through the cosmos or the encounter of sage and initiate. But in mystical works trust in spiritual intuition, insight, inspiration, and love replaces an anagogy that ascertains truth only through rational demonstration.

One other aspect of allegory during this period deserves mention. This is allegoresis, the allegorical interpretation of other texts, especially parts of the Qur'an. One example (of many) is the philosophical interpretation of the account of Muhammad's *mi'rāj*, or heavenly ascent attributed to Ibn Sīna. Another influential example is Al-Ghazālī's mystical commentary on the Qur'anic "Light Verse" in his *Niche of Lights (Miskāt al-anwār)*.[19]

Mystical allegory

The twelfth and thirteenth centuries witnessed a flowering of mystical poetry in Arabic and especially Persian literature, which replaced Arabic as the main literary language in Muslim lands east of Mesopotamia. For the study of allegory, four writers from these centuries are of especial importance: Ḥakīm Sanā'ī (d. 1131), Farīd al-Dīn 'Aṭṭār (d. *circa* 1220), Jalāl al-Dīn

18 For one example, see P. Heath, "Reading al-Ghazālī: The Case of Psychology," in T. Lawson, ed., *Reason and Inspiration in Islam: Essays in Honor of Hermann Landolt* (London and New York: I. T. Tauris, 2005), pp. 185–99.

19 On the *mi'rāj*, see B. Schreike, J. Horowitz, et al., "Mi'rādj," in *EI²* 7:97–105; for translations, see Sells, *Early Islamic Mysticism*, pp. 47–56 and 242–50. See also B. O. Vuckovic, *Heavenly Journeys, Earthly Concerns: The Legacy of the Mi'raj in the Formation of Islam*, Religion in History, Society, and Culture (New York and London: Routledge, 2005), and M. A. Amir-Moessi, ed., *Le voyage initiatique en terre d'Islam: Ascensions célestes et itinéraires spirituels*, Bibliothèque de l'École des Hautes Études, Sciences Religieuses 103 (Louvain-Paris: Peeters, 1996). On the "Light Verse," see S. M. Hajjaji-Jarrah, "*Āyat al-Nūr*: A Metaphor for Where We Come From, What We Are, and Where We Are Going," in Lawson, *Reason and Inspiration in Islam*, pp. 169–81. Al-Ghazālī's influential interpretation of the "Light Verse" has been translated into English by W. H. T Gairdner, *Al-Ghazzālī's Miskāt al-Anwār (The Niche of Lights)*, Royal Asiatic Society Monographs, 19 (London: Royal Asiatic Society, 1924; Lahore, 1952). For other translated examples of mystical Qur'anic interpretation, see Sells, *Early Islamic Mysticism*, pp. 75–96; for examples of non-mystical interpretation, see Gätje, *The Qur'ān and its Exegesis*.

Rūmī (d. 1273) – all writing in Persian – and Muḥyī al-Din Ibn Arabi (d. 1240), who wrote in Arabic.

Ḥakīm Sanā'ī is best known for his long didactic narrative poem (*mathnavī*) *Ḥadīqat al-ḥaqīqa va-sharī'at al-ṭariq* (*The Garden of Reality and the Law of the Path*), a combination of pious sermon and homily to anecdote. His contribution to allegory is the shorter *Sair al-'ibād ilā al-ma'ād* (*The Journey of the Servants to the Place of Return*).[20] The poem adopts for its narrative structure the model of mystical ascent already observed in the epistles of Ibn Sīna and Suhrawardī. Cast out of heaven, the protagonist (the rational soul) encounters first a nurse (the vegetable soul), and then a tyrant (the animal soul), until he encounters an aged sage (the Active Intellect) who guides him on a journey through the cosmos. At each stage, the protagonist encounters representatives, whether of one of the four elements or of the supernal spheres, each of whom correlates with one or more aspects of human nature. By journey's end, he both has learned how to cleanse himself of fault and has attained a clear vision of the purpose of human existence. Sanā'ī completes the poem with a long panegyric to his patron, who of course represents a state of human perfection.

Many mystical *mathnavī*s are attributed to Farīd al-Dīn 'Aṭṭār, although only four can be said with certainty to be his.[21] Three of these works employ allegorical frame stories to provide a measure of narrative cohesiveness for the many didactic anecdotes that fill the works. In terms of poetic aesthetics, these anecdotes rival the importance of the frame narratives, a point which modern readers accustomed to the dominance of strong overarching narrative lines should keep in mind. As mentioned, Muslim mystical theorists organized the path toward God into "stations" that indicate major spiritual stages (repentance, renunciation, trust in God, gnosis, love, mystical union, etc.) along the way. Within each station, however, the mystic experiences many "states," psychological moods or moments (doubt, fear, false optimism, joy, etc.). Using this framework, a poet such as 'Aṭṭār shapes major

20 The *mathnavī* is a narrative poetic form that consists of series of rhyming couplets that usually eschew enjambment so that each couplet must form a complete thought, a stricture that encourages a disciplined use of compressed imagery. Sanā'ī's *Sair al-'ubbād ilā al-ma'ād* is in *Mathnavīhā-i Ḥakīm Sanā'ī*, ed. Mudarris-i Raḍavī (Tehran, 1969), pp. 181–233. On Sanā'ī's corpus, career, and thought, see J. P. T de Bruijn, *Of Piety and Poetry: The Interaction of Religion and Literature and Thought in the Life and Works of Ḥakīm Sanā'ī* (Leiden: E. J. Brill, 1983); on *Sair al-'ubbād*, see especially pp. 200–18.

21 On 'Aṭṭār, see H. Ritter, *The Ocean of the Soul: Men, the World and God in the Stories of Farīd al-Dīn 'Aṭṭār*, trans. J. O-Kane, *Handbook of Oriental Studies* (Leiden and Boston: Brill, 2003). See also L. Lewisohn and C. Shackle, eds., *'Attar and the Persian Sufi Tradition: The Art of Spiritual Flight* (London: Institute for Ismaili Studies, 2007). 'Aṭṭār is frequently reprinted; see Rypka, *HIL*, pp. 775–76.

narrative events to symbolize attainment of a new station while using individual anecdotes (often stories from the lives of previous mystics or fables turned to mystical intent) to represent progress of psychological states. Narrative "stages" may appear initially more important than transient "states," but one must remember that although one may retrospectively divide mystic development into conceptual phases, moment by moment humans tend to be dominated by their immediate emotional moods. For most premodern Muslim mystic poets, using anecdotes to portray "states" is an essential artistic tool, since they represent deeply felt emotional junctures that the reader must understand correctly in order to apprehend the nature of spiritual progress.

`Aṭṭār's *Ilāhī-nāma* (*Book of God*) uses the frame story of a king counseling his sons with tales of instruction. His *Muṣībat-nāma* (*The Book of Affliction*) uses that of a spiritual guide advising a spiritual seeker along a path of cosmic travel. The most famous of `Aṭṭār's poems, *Manṭiq al-ṭair* (the *Speech of the Birds*), relates the decision of a flock of birds to seek the court of their king, the mythical Sīmurgh. After initial enthusiasm, each bird (representing a specific human trait or character type) argues for delay in beginning the journey. Their leader, the hoopoe, responds to each excuse with anecdotes that demonstrate the weakness of their arguments. Finally the birds set out and suffer a long and difficult journey through the seven valleys of the Way (Quest, Love, Insight into Mystery, Detachment and Serenity, Unity, Awe and Bewilderment, and Poverty and Nothingness). Each valley has its accompanying illustrative anecdotes. At journey's end only thirty birds survive. These thirty birds (in Persian *sī murgh*) finally encounter the Sīmurgh, who in fact constitutes a unified reflection of their purified selves.[22]

The greatest mystical poem in Persian, and one of the outstanding works of world literature, is the *Mathnavī-yi maʿnavī* (*The Narrative Poem of Spiritual Portent*) by Jalāl al-Dīn Rūmī.[23] Composed over a decade and consisting of some 27,000 lines, this poem is a virtual universe of mystical insight and allegorical thinking. Rūmī eschews the device of a frame story and as a result the work consists of series of tales and anecdotes. Instead

---

22 For a partial translation, see Farīd ud-Dīn ʿAṭṭār, *The Conference of the Birds*, trans. A. Darbandi and D. Davies (London: Penguin Books, 1984). See also *The Ilāhī-nāma or Book of God*, trans. J. A. Boyle (Manchester: University of Manchester Press, 1976). Also F. Keshavarz, "Flight of the Birds: The Poetic Animating the Spiritual in ʿAṭṭār's *Manṭiq al-ṭayr*," in Lewisohn and Shackle, eds., *Attar and the Persian Sufi Tradition*, pp. 112–34.
23 Jalāl al-Dīn Rūmī, *The Mathnavī of Jalālu'ddin Rūmī*, ed. and trans. R. A. Nicholson, 8 vols. (London: Gibb Memorial Series, 1925–40). On Rūmī's poetics, see F. Keshavarz, *Reading Mystical Lyric: The Case of Jalal al-Din Rumi* (Columbia, SC: University of South Carolina Press, 1998); also F. D. Lewis, *Rumi, Past and Present, East and West* (Oxford: Oneworld, 2000).

of one allegory he offers hundreds, each seeking to overturn the reader's superficial assumptions of reality and replace them with insights into the truths of the life of the soul. The first story, for instance, relates the tale of a king who falls in love with a slave girl (pp. 5–17, trans. 6–17). Despite loyal attention, the girl falls ill and no court physician is able to heal her. In despair the king prays to God and is told that a stranger will appear who can heal the girl. The new physician learns that the cause of the sickness is the girl's love for a goldsmith from Samarqand. This man is sent for and the physician gives him a potion that causes him to sicken and turn ugly, whereupon the girl is freed from her infatuation and falls in love with the king. Rūmī's allegories are often complex and purposely polysemous, open to multiple interpretations. One interpretation of this story is that the mystic aspirant (the girl) mistakenly becomes infatuated with the world (the gold-smith), but that through the guidance of religion (the physician) she finally turns to the love God (the king). Another interpretation is that the king rep-resents the rational soul whose lower side is in love with the lowly passions of the animal and vegetable souls and who needs the inspiration of the Active Intellect (the physician) to redirect love in the right direction. It is impos-sible to encapsulate in a few words the brilliance of Rūmī's masterpiece. One can only attest that it is an amazing achievement of spiritual insight, poetic imagination, and artistic genius. At heart, the poem is a multifaceted and highly sophisticated meditation on divine love and love for the Divine, before which other considerations pale.[24] Love had always been central to Islamic mystical practice and anecdote; after Rūmī it assumes prominence in allegory.

Ibn ʿArabī is less a poet than a mystic theorist and visionary. His allegories, however, are worthy of mention, in part for their didactic effect and in part for their periodic imaginative intensity. Didactic intent dominates his *Kitāb al-anwār* (*Book of Lights*), which employs the structure of spiritual ascent to instruct the reader about the stages of mystical development. More interesting is Chapter 367 of *al-Futūḥāt al-Makkiyya* (*Mekkan Revelations*), which again portrays the mystic's ascent, this time following more closely the narrative lines of the traditional story of Muhammad's ascent to heaven. Both philosopher and mystic traverse the heavens, but the philosopher stops at heaven's gates while the mystic, endowed with spiritual rather than purely rational insight, continues his ascent to attain proximity to God. Visionary and of greater complexity is *Kitāb al-isrā ilā maqām al-asrā* (*The Book*

---

24 Rūmī's concept of love is complex, cf. *Masnavī*, Book 1, line 111: "Whether love be from this (earthly) side or that (heavenly) side, in the end it leads us yonder." (trans. Nicholson, I:15; my thanks to F. Keshavarz for this reference).

of the Ascent to the Highest Station), which is composed in a mixture of rhymed prose and poetry. The protagonist is on his way to Jerusalem when he meets a youth who guides him first through spiritual states and then on to encounters with previous prophets until the traveler attains the highest stages of spiritual attainment.[25]

Ibn 'Arabī's mystical theology is intricate, and his writings at times difficult to understand; yet part of his complexity is that he is the rare mythopoetic thinker who effortlessly interweaves discursive and symbolic thought in rich and fascinating ways. Core to his thinking is an embrace of the divine and human creative imaginations. Rather than awarding priority to rationalist transcendence, as do the philosophers, he (and the mystics in general) give equal weight to transcendence and immanence. The world, therefore, is not something from which to escape in order to return to a primordial rationalist purity; rather it is a reflection of the omnipotent creative powers of God. "For wherever you turn is the face of God." (Qur'an 2:109). What humans must learn is how to recognize correctly the true nature of creation and their rightful place in it, rather than be restricted to apprehending it from either purely physical or purely rationalist perspectives. In this regard, Ibn 'Arabī and Rūmī share a similar stance, although the former uses mainly prose discussion to drive home his point while the latter relies more on poetry and imaginative illustrative anecdote.

Ibn 'Arabī has received much attention recently from scholars of religion, but his style and modes of expression would richly reward study by specialists in literature as well. One final work of note is his collection of love poems titled *Turjumān al-ashwāq* (*Interpreter of Desires*), for which the author wrote his own allegorical commentary to demonstrate that his poetry's intent was spiritual rather than profane.[26]

---

25 Both *Kitāb al-anwār* and *Kitāb al-isrā ilā maqām al-asrā* are in *Rasā'il Ibn al-'Arabī*, 2 parts in one vol. (Hyderabad-Deccan: Dā'iratu'l ma'ārif'l-osmania, 1948); a translation of *Kitāb al-anwār* is *Journey to the Lord of Power: A Sufi Manual on Retreat*, trans. R. T. Harris (Rochester, Vermont: Inner Traditions International, 1981). *Al-Futūḥāt al-Makkiyya*, 4 vols. (Cairo: Bulāq, n.d.); its ascent narrative is translated in J. W. Morris, "The Spiritual Ascension: Ibn 'Arabī and the Mi'rāj," *Journal of the American Oriental Society*, Part 1 107.4 (1987), 629–52; Part 2, 108.1 (1988), 63–77.

26 Ibn 'Arabī, *The Turjumān al-ashwāq*, ed. and trans. R. A. Nicholson, Oriental Translation Fund 20 (London: Oriental Translation Fund, 1911; repr., London: The Theosophical Publishing House, 1978); also translated in M. A. Sells, *Stations of Desire: Love Elegies from Ibn 'Arabi and New Poems* (Jerusalem: Ibis Editions, 2000). An excellent spiritual biography is C. Addas, *Quest for the Red Sulpher: The Life of Ibn 'Arabī*, trans. P. Kingsley (Cambridge: The Islamic Texts Society, 1993); also important is W. C. Chittick, *The Sufi Path of Knowledge: Ibn al-'Arabī's Metaphysics of Imagination* (Albany, NY: State University of New York Press, 1989).

One final poem from this period, in Persian, and based on the two themes of mystical guidance and ascent, is the *Miṣbāḥ al-arwāḥ* (*Lantern of Spirits*) attributed to Auḥad al-Dīn Kirmānī (d. 1238), but perhaps written by one Shams al-Dīn Muḥammad Īl-Ṭughān Bardasīrī. Again, the aspirant meets a spiritual guide who leads him on a journey of mystical progress.[27]

It is clear that many writers of allegories during this period favored narrative frames portraying encounters with sages and depicting ascents through the cosmos. In later centuries, however, the dominant allegorical frame became instead tales of desire, passion and love. The Persian poet Niẓāmī Ganjavī (d. 1209) created the template for such narratives with his renderings of the love story of the early Arab lovers, Lailā and Majnūn, and that of the Persian Shah Khusrau's passion for the Byzantine Princess Shīrīn, a love he shared with the noble Farhad (similar to the love triangle of King Arthur, Guinevere, and Lancelot). Niẓāmī's love stories, as well as those of his emulator Amīr Khusrau (d. 1325), focused on portraying how love leads to their protagonists' moral development and maturation. Although they could be read allegorically as representing not profane but mystical love, it is unlikely that this was their authors' intent. However, they did provide models for poets whose aims were explicitly mystical allegory.[28]

Some of these stories (all composed in Persian) use abstract allegorical characters. The poet Fattāḥī (d. *circa* 1448) composed the *Dastūr al-`ushshāq* (*The Counselor of Lovers*), a summary of which became known as *Ḥusn va-dil* (*Beauty and Heart*), which portrays the love of Prince Heart, son of King Reason, for Princess Beauty, daughter of King Love. Kātibī (d. 1434–35) tells the tale of the lovers Regarder and Regarded in his poem *Majma `al-baḥain* (*The Convergence of the Two Seas*). `Ārifī (d. *circa* 1449) relates of the passion of a dervish for a prince, using as symbols the ball and the polo stick, in *Gūy va-chaugān* (also known as the *Ḥāl-nāma*); Ahlī (d. 1535) the love of the moth for the candle in *Sham` va-parvān*; and Hilālī (d. 1529), following the model of `Ārifī, that of the beggar for the king in *Shāh va-gadā*. Each of these stories depicts a version of idealized romantic love, in which the lover is so consumed with passion that it burns away his personality to leave only utter devotion for the beautiful Beloved (God).[29]

---

27 See de Bruijn, *Persian Sufi Poetry*, pp. 95–96; and Rypka, *HIL*, p. 254.

28 On Niẓāmī' and Persian romance, see J. S. Meisami, *Medieval Persian Court Poetry* (Princeton: Princeton University Press, 1987), esp. pp. 77–236. For Amīr Khusrau, see S. Sharma, *Amir Khusraw: The Poet of Sultans and Sufis* (Oxford: Oneworld, 2005), esp. pp. 52–59.

29 These works have received little critical study; see Rypka, *HIL*, pp. 284–86; and de Bruijn, *Persian Sufi Poetry*, pp. 121–22.

Allegories that integrated portrayal of profane and mystical love were composed by the greatest narrative poet of this period, `Abd al-Raḥmān Jāmī (d. 1492). An expert in philosophy, mysticism, theology, and all branches of poetry, Jāmī was one of the many who attempted to equal Niẓāmī's feat of composing five high-quality *mathnavī*s. In his case, Jāmī outdid his predecessor – at least in terms of quantity – by completing seven poems rather than Niẓāmī's five. Collected under the title of *Haft Aurang* (*The Seven Thrones*, or *Ursus Major*), three of the narratives are allegories dealing with love. One is the story of Majnūn and Lailā, which recounts how the early Arab poet, Qais, goes mad as a result of his love for his cousin Lailā.[30] The second is the story of Joseph and Zulaikhā, based on the Joseph story as found in the Qur'an, which relates how Potipher's wife falls in love with the young Hebrew prophet Joseph. Both of these *mathnavī*s focus on the theme of how love for human beauty transcends itself to become love for the divine. Jāmī's third *mathnavī* relates the story of Salāmān and Absāl, but according to a version originally translated into Arabic from a hermetic Greek text rather than that composed by Ibn Sīna. In this version, Salāmān is a prince who falls in love with his nurse Absāl (once again the rational soul being infatuated by the lower animal and vegetable souls) whose father the king cures through an ordeal of fire in which Absāl perishes but Salāmān survives.[31]

Ottoman Turkish literature shared in many of the literary forms and styles of Persian literature. Hence it is little surprise that some of its poets tried their hand at allegory, often relying on models first written in Persian. The poet Ḥamdī (d. 1509), a contemporary of Jāmī, composed his version of Joseph and Zulaikhā as well as a version of Niẓāmī's Lailā and Majnūn, combining again in them themes of profane and mystical love. Āhī (d. 1517–18) reworked Fattāḥī's *Beauty and Love*. Lami`ī (d. 1531–32), in the next generation, did the same, as well as producing versions of the Candle and the Moth, the Ball and the Polo Stick, and Salāmān and Absāl. The poet Fazlī (d. 1563–64) took as his lovers the Rose and the Nightingale, while Yeḥyā Bey (d. 1575–76) composed an original version of the King and the Beggar. The great Fuzūlī (d. 1556) created a very highly regarded adaptation of Leilā and Mejnūn, basing it on the versions of Niẓāmī and of Hātifī

---

30 On Jāmī, see Rypka, *HIL*, pp. 286–87; his *Haft Aurang* is repeatedly published. For the history of the *Majnūn and Laila'* story, see A. E. Khairallah, *Love, Madness, and Poetry: An Interpretation of the Maǧūn Legend*, Beiruter Texte und Studien 25 (Beirut-Wiesbaden: Franz Steiner Verlag, 1980).

31 For translations, see Jami, *Yusuf and Zulaikha: An Allegorical Romance*, trans. D. Pendlebury (London: Octagon Press, 1980); and A. J. Arberry, *Fitzgerald's Salaman and Absal* (Cambridge: Cambridge University Press, 1956).

(d. 1520), Jāmī's nephew. Fuzūlī renders his characters' love as fully allegorical; profane love has now been completely displaced by Divine love.[32]

The literature of this late premodern period, whether Arabic, Persian or
Ottoman, has unfortunately received little study, either in the Middle East
or in the West. At its heart, the tradition embraces an increasingly intricate,
refined, and little-studied poetics that involves a high degree of intertextual
awareness and interplay, rhetorical sophistication, and stylistic nuance, with
each new poet being highly aware of the influence of predecessors as he
aspires to outdo their achievements. At issue for this poetics is less originality
of narrative plot (although there are certainly brilliant instances of this), than
the ability to create fresh images and improved formulations of language,
character, and event. Hence, although it is difficult to offer testimony as to
the comparative literary quality of the aforementioned allegories, it is clear
that further investigation would reward the effort.

Critics concur that the final major Ottoman allegory of the premodern
tradition is a masterpiece. This is the *Story of Beauty and Love* (*Hüsn ü
Aşk*) by the poet Şeyh Galip (d. 1799). Once again the elements of the
composite soul are personified and presented in the form of a quest. Here
the protagonist is not the rational soul but the youth, Love, who must find
his way through the temptations offered by the vegetable soul, the animal
soul, and most dangerous, the form-creating imagination, so as to attain the
hand of his beloved, divine Beauty, who all the while has been awaiting his
completion of his quest. Şeyh Galip had at hand mastery of an eight-century
poetic and spiritual tradition of assiduous and sophisticated exploration into
the meanings of mystical love. The poem is best read with an awareness of
the nuances and complexities of this tradition and represents a tour de force
that combines simplicity of plot with highly refined and creative intertextual
allusion.[33]

The last two centuries have been a period of intense change and experimentation in Middle Eastern literatures during which issues of political
reform, or the lack of such, have been central to literary expression. Hence
the allegories of the last century have tended to be political rather than philosophical or spiritual. Modern Arabic and Iranian writers and filmmakers,

32 For discussions and excerpted translations, see Gibb, *History of Ottoman Poetry*: Ḥamdī,
2:140–217; Āhī, 2:286–316; Lamiʿī 3:21–34; Fazlī, 3:108–16; Yeḥyā Bey, 3:116–32; Fuzūlī,
3:70–107. Gibb also summarizes eight Ottoman romances/allegories, 3:354–74. See also
Fuzūlī, *Leylā and Mejnūn*, trans. S. Huri (London: George Allen & Unwin, 1970), with an
excellent introduction by Alessio Bombaci.
33 Şeyh Galip, *Beauty and Love*, trans. V. R. Holbrook, MLA Texts & Translations (New
York: Modern Language Association, 2005). See also V. R. Holbrook, *The Unreadable Shores
of Love: Turkish Modernity and Mystic Romance* (Austin: University of Texas Press, 1994).

striving for the democratization of their respective societies, have composed allegories where the characters represent examples of political classes or competing ideologies. Whether in the fields of poetry, the novel, the theatre, or in film, authors rely on allegory to comment safely on the political and social issues of the day in the face of the political censorship that often reigns in modern Middle Eastern security states. Audiences are acutely aware of the true nature of these artistic messages; but their coded format generally allows them to survive the scrutiny of state censors who often view these messages as safety valves that do not directly challenge state security. Investigation into the details of the varied forms of modern political allegory, however, would require an essay unto itself.[34]

34 See Allen, *ALH*, 306–14 (on the novel) and 340–57 (on drama). For Persian, see in E. Yarshater, ed., *Persian Literature*, Columbia Lectures on Iranian Studies 3 (New York: Bibliotheca Persica, 1987), M. Hillman, "Persian Prose Fiction (1921–77): An Iranian Mirror and Conscience," pp. 292–317, and G. Kapuscinski, "Modern Persian Drama," pp. 381–402; for poetry, see F. Keshavarz, *Recite in the Name of the Red Rose: Poetic Sacred Making in Twentieth Century Iran*, Studies in Comparative Religion (Columbia, SC: University of South Carolina Press, 2006).

7

JON WHITMAN

Twelfth-century allegory: philosophy and imagination

Plato as a gentile counterpart to a Hebrew prophet, speaking a figural language . . . A rudimentary plea by a disorderly Prime Matter, providentially answered by the divine Mind . . . The divine words of Scripture not to be treated literally regarding the origin of Eve, who was created not from Adam but through the operation of nature . . . The figure of Nature herself circuitously complaining about the deviant grammar of fallen human nature . . . The whole *Metamorphoses* as an extended metaphor for the transformation of the soul . . .[1]

The transfiguration of allegory in twelfth-century Europe is so breathtaking that it can scarcely be framed in the conventional categories of an overview. It might be well to begin even a selective outline with an "inner view," a self-conscious account of the language of allegory from a commentary written in the twelfth century. However partial and schematic, the passage displays a revealing moment at which an allegorical commentary turns into a metacommentary on allegory itself.

Names and natures

The general context of the passage – a fragmentary but extensive interpretation of the *Aeneid* – may well originate early in the century, although its exact date and the name of its author are not known.[2] It is sometimes thought

---

1 For the texts and contexts of these developments, see my discussion below.
2 For the text, see *The Commentary on the First Six Books of the Aeneid of Vergil Commonly Attributed to Bernardus Silvestris*, ed. J. W. Jones and E. F. Jones (Lincoln, NB: University of Nebraska Press, 1977). For a translation, see E. G. Schreiber and T. E. Maresca, trans., *Commentary on The First Six Books of Virgil's Aeneid by Bernardus Silvestris* (Lincoln, NB: University of Nebraska Press, 1979). For a speculative dating of "*ca.* 1125–30,*" see Peter Dronke, "Bio-bibliographies," in Peter Dronke, ed., *A History of Twelfth-Century Western Philosophy* (1988; rpt. Cambridge: Cambridge University Press, 1992), p. 446; compare the complications discussed by Christopher Baswell, *Virgil in*

that the interpreter is Bernard Silvestris, the composer of the mid-twelfth-century *Cosmographia*, one of the most spectacular cosmic narratives before the *Mutabilitie Cantos* of the English Renaissance. Whatever its provenance, the commentary is one of the most elaborate allegorical interpretations of an ancient poem (outside the poetry of Scripture) that survives from any time until the twelfth century itself.

It should be noted (*Notandum est*), indicates the commentator as he pauses in his reading of Virgil's text,[3] that in this and other works with occult meanings (*aliis misticis voluminibus*) there are two kinds of complications in the relationship between words and things. One complication is the converse of the other.

On the one hand, the same name (*nomen*) can designate different natures (*naturas*). "Jupiter," for example, sometimes designates fire, and sometimes the supreme God. On the other hand, the same nature can be designated by different names. For example, the Creator is designated by both "Jupiter" and "Anchises" (the father of Aeneas). As the commentator observes at the opening of his account, the figurations of language are diverse in their reference points (*integumenta ad diversa respicere*).

At first glance, such reflections about the respective divisions of words and things may seem only one more expression of that familiar ambiguity which would lead Thomas Sprat of the Royal Society half a millennium later to wish for a return to that primal state "when men deliver'd so many *things*, almost in an equal number of *words*."[4] And it is true that the general notion of diverse yet converse relations between signs and subjects had been codified in allegorical writing long before the twelfth-century commentary. Already in a late antique interpretation of Scripture, Augustine had memorably formulated the view that there can be several ways of expressing one thing and, conversely, several ways of understanding one expression.[5]

But the twelfth-century commentator gives the general view a specific orientation different from that of Augustine. Though a Christian, the commentator applies the argument not to a scriptural text but to a pagan one,

Medieval England: Figuring the Aeneid from the Twelfth Century to Chaucer (Cambridge: Cambridge University Press, 1995), pp. 101–10.

3 See *Commentary*, ed. Jones and Jones, pp. 9–10; *Commentary*, trans. Schreiber and Maresca, pp. 11–12. Compare the related passage in *The Commentary on Martianus Capella's De Nuptiis Philologiae et Mercurii Attributed to Bernardus Silvestris*, ed. H. J. Westra (Toronto: Pontifical Institute of Mediaeval Studies, 1986), pp. 46–47, translated by Westra in his introduction, p. 25.

4 See the quotation from Sprat's *History of the Royal Society* (1667), in A. C. Howell, "*Res et Verba*: Words and Things," *English Literary History* 13 (1946), 140.

5 See *Confessions* 13.24.37, in Augustine, *Confessions*, ed. J. J. O'Donnell, 3 vols. (Oxford: Clarendon-Oxford University Press, 1992), 1: 199.

riddled with gods and goddesses. Though his reference here to natures (*naturas*) is broad, over the course of his work (as suggested in his association between Jupiter and "fire") he stresses far more than Augustine how diverse ways of "understanding" involve the objects of natural philosophy. And he frames his reflections (*Notandum est*) as an incipient act of critical theory, an assessment designed to clarify the operation of mythological discourse at large.

His argument concerns far more than the treatment of individual names. It informs the explication of the Virgilian narrative as a whole. "Venus" (designating different natures) and God (designated by different names) are two cases in point. When Venus is presented as the wife of Vulcan, continues the commentator in his excursus, she is to be understood as the pleasure of the flesh (*carnis voluptatem*), joined with natural heat (Vulcan). But when the text indicates that Venus and Anchises have a son, Aeneas, Venus is to be understood as the harmony of the world, that concord (*concordiam*) through which God (Anchises) enables the human spirit (Aeneas) to live in a body. Yet as the commentator later suggests in his account of the erotic affair between Aeneas and Dido, that embodied spirit eventually has its own steamy encounter with the pleasure of the flesh.[6]

Given a human figure divided between the demands of flesh and spirit, the divided identity of "Venus" is no mere convention; for Aeneas, such a mother is, so to speak, an invention of necessity. The dual reference of allegorical language is the very expression of the dual affiliation of a human soul.

If allegory of this kind were to be diagrammed, the diagram would not consist simply of a set of parallel lines connecting an array of individual "names" and "natures" in one-to-one correspondences. From a particular name there might be lines diverging toward multiple natures, while toward a particular nature there might be lines converging from multiple names. In such a diagram various lines of significance would potentially intersect with each other in a network of expanding and contracting relationships. The significance of the whole work would lie in the composite design of the intricate network as a whole.

Dimensions of language and dimensions of being

What kinds of worlds might be evoked by works conceived in such terms? It should be stressed that no single "metaphysic" underlies the aesthetic of

6 See *Commentary*, ed. Jones and Jones, pp. 23–25; *Commentary*, trans. Schreiber and Maresca, pp. 25–27.

this medieval commentary on an ancient poem, and the commentary itself only begins to suggest some of the radical ways in which names and natures come to be diversified in the twelfth century as a whole.

In more strictly philosophic forms of twelfth-century Christian writing, for example, the sense of a divided yet coordinated universe broadly draws upon certain Neoplatonic attitudes that develop already in late antiquity. From such Neoplatonic perspectives, "levels" of meaning in language are implicated with "levels" of being in the cosmos, and a carefully articulated discourse about the world displays by its own compositional design the complex differentiation of the cosmos itself. Variously adapted and transformed in Christian Neoplatonic thought of the early Middle Ages,[7] this sense of cosmic and compositional symmetry acquires one of its most striking formulations with the work of the twelfth-century philosopher Thierry of Chartres and his circle. In this view the universe is conceived as a vast system of divine enfolding (*conplicatio*) and unfolding (*explicatio*), in which different modes (*modi*) of the divine order correspond to different aspects of human comprehension. From such a perspective, the *explicatio* of an enigmatic work may be more than the explication of a text. It may be an act of mind disclosing the expansive features of a densely composed world.[8]

Yet while such philosophic views provide an important general context for allegory in this period, twelfth-century commentaries like those on the *Aeneid* and other ancient works imply more flexible negotiations with the nuances of literary language itself. In late antique Neoplatonic writing the single most influential expression of such concerns is a celebrated passage (indebted to a long history of prior interpretive theory) in the *Commentary on the Dream of Scipio* by Macrobius. There Macrobius seeks to clarify the conditions under which fabulous narrative (*narratio fabulosa*) may be suitable for explorations into the nature of things – explorations that he invests with the allure of a mystery rite. To Nature (*naturae*), he indicates, a frank, open exposition of herself (*apertam nudamque expositionem sui*) is distasteful. Just as Nature has "withheld an understanding of herself from the uncouth senses of men by enveloping herself in variegated garments (*vario... tegmine*)," so has she "desired to have her

---

7 On such ancient and early medieval developments (including the ninth-century work of John the Scot Eriugena) with particular reference to the movement of allegory, see the discussion and bibliography in Jon Whitman, *Allegory: The Dynamics of an Ancient and Medieval Technique* (Oxford: Clarendon-Oxford University Press, and Cambridge, MA: Harvard University Press, 1987), pp. 63–65, 95–104, 144–60.

8 For overviews see Whitman, *Allegory*, pp. 187–91, and Peter Dronke, "Thierry of Chartres," in Dronke, ed., *History*, pp. 368–74.

secrets handled by more prudent individuals through fabulous narratives (*fabulosa*)."[9] The erotics of such a conception acquire a flamboyant form in the late-twelfth-century *Complaint of Nature*, and later I plan to turn to that development. For the moment I wish only to stress the semiotics of this suggestive passage about enwrapping and exploring. By correlating the trappings of literary works with the trappings of the natural world, Macrobius provocatively associates the nature of textuality with the texture of nature itself.

Covering and discovering the cosmos

Over the course of the Middle Ages this semiotic turn[10] eventually helps to promote a distinctive approach to conventional notions of the "grammar" of nature. In twelfth-century natural philosophy that approach becomes systematic in detailed glosses on what are termed the *integumenta* (coverings) and *involucra* (wrappings)[11] of Plato's own account of the formation of the world, the *Timaeus* (partially available in a fragmentary Latin version by the late antique writer Calcidius). By the mid-twelfth century the "integumental" interpretation of the *Timaeus* acquires its most elaborate form with the "glosses on Plato" (*Glosae super Platonem*) of the avant-garde natural philosopher William of Conches.[12] For William the text of the *Timaeus* at large is virtually a fabric of *integumenta*, in which even apparent fabrications – from Plato's brief instances of conventional mythology to his exotic account of individual souls set upon stars (an *integumentum* for astral influence, argues William) – figure forth the interior workings of a tightly

9 See *Commentary* I.ii.6–18, in Ambrosius Theodosius Macrobius, *Commentarii in Somnium Scipionis*, ed. James Willis, 2nd edn. (Leipzig: Teubner, 1970); *Commentary on the Dream of Scipio / Macrobius*, trans. William Harris Stahl (New York: Columbia University Press, 1952), pp. 84–87.

10 On this and related aspects of early "philology," see, e.g., Winthrop Wetherbee, "From Late Antiquity to the Twelfth Century," in Alastair Minnis and Ian Johnson, eds., *The Cambridge History of Literary Criticism*, vol. 2, *The Middle Ages* (Cambridge: Cambridge University Press, 2005), pp. 99–144.

11 See especially Edouard Jeauneau, "L'usage de la notion d'*integumentum* à travers les gloses de Guillaume de Conches," orig. pub. 1957, rpt. in Edouard Jeauneau, "*Lectio philosophorum*": *Recherches sur l'Ecole de Chartres* (Amsterdam: Adolf M. Hakkert, 1973), pp. 127–92; Brian Stock, *Myth and Science in the Twelfth Century: A Study of Bernard Silvester* (Princeton: Princeton University Press, 1972), pp. 38–62; and Peter Dronke, *Fabula: Explorations into the Uses of Myth in Medieval Platonism* (Leiden: Brill, 1974), pp. 4–5, 23–28, 48–52, 56–57, 61–64, 119–22.

12 See *Guillelmi de Conchis: Glosae super Platonem*, ed. Edouard Jeauneau (Turnhout: Brepols, 2006), hereafter cited as *Glosae*.

coordinated universe.[13] In the case of William it sometimes seems (to adapt the later lines of Alexander Pope) that "when t'examine ev'ry part he came, / Nature and Plato were, he found, the same."[14]

Or rather, almost the same. For William and other philosophers of the early and middle years of the twelfth century, even integumentally inflected attempts to give the natural world depicted by Plato and other ancient authors a "deep structure" congruent with the tenets of Christian belief produce persistent tensions.

One of the primary focal points of such tensions is the concept of the World Soul (*Timaeus* 34B–37C), the vital spirit that animates and informs the body of the Platonic cosmos. The long-controversial question of whether this immanent *anima mundi* could be accommodated to a transcendent Christian God receives a particularly provocative response in the early twelfth century with the theological writing of Peter Abelard. Abelard treats Plato as a kind of philosophic counterpart to a Hebrew prophet, and he finds the words of such gentile philosophers about the *anima mundi* to apply to nothing more fittingly than the Holy Spirit, "by a most beautiful figural wrapping" (*per pulcherrimam involucri figuram*).[15] William of Conches, who seeks more than Abelard to probe the cosmological factors and authorial aims underlying the conception of the World Soul, struggles with that conception over the course of his career. Even within his *Glosae super Platonem* he turns strategically in different directions – in one comment seeming to associate it with the third person of the Trinity, in another, aligning it with the threefold powers of reason, sensation, and growth in this world.[16] Such a Soul is a mediating figure in more senses than one; with its divided natures, it is both divine and worldly in its very disposition. An *integumentum* of this kind is not to be simply uncovered; the discovery lies in the folds of the "covering" itself.

---

13 See, e.g., *Timaeus* 40E–41A, with *Glosae*, pp. 203–4, and *Timaeus* 41D–41E, with *Glosae*, pp. 213–17. Compare Jeauneau, "L'usage," 150–56, and Winthrop Wetherbee, *Platonism and Poetry in the Twelfth Century: The Literary Influence of the School of Chartres* (Princeton: Princeton University Press, 1972), pp. 43–48.

14 For Pope's original version, see *The Poems of Alexander Pope*, ed. John Butt (1963; rpt. New Haven: Yale University Press, 1974), *An Essay on Criticism*, ll. 133–34, where the ancient author, of course, is not Plato, and the meaning of "Nature" is conspicuously different.

15 See Tullio Gregory, *Anima mundi: la filosofia di Guglielmo di Conches e la scuola di Chartres* (Florence: Sansoni, [1955]), pp. 145–48; Wetherbee, *Platonism*, pp. 38–43; Dronke, *Fabula*, pp. 55–67.

16 See *Glosae*, pp. 124, 129–30; Jeauneau, "L'usage," pp. 159–61, 171–72; Wetherbee, *Platonism*, pp. 30–34, 40–47.

Not everyone liked the outfit. In 1140 the Council of Sens condemned the proposition that the World Soul is the Holy Spirit. Yet the very displacement of the World Soul from the divine sphere intensified its association with the natural sphere, where it was replaced in turn by a figure still more provocative in character: the figure of Nature itself. With twelfth-century commentators such as William of Conches, Hermann of Carinthia, and John of Salisbury, the kind of life-giving force once attributed to the *anima mundi* increasingly comes to be associated with the invigorating power of an animating *natura*. Even before the philosopher-poets Bernard Silvestris and Alan of Lille turn *Natura* herself into a full-fledged imaginative character, the conditions of her emergence are already developing in subtle but far-reaching shifts of language and thought. Eve herself, argues William of Conches early in his career, was not created from Adam's side, despite the scriptural account; that text is not to be taken literally (*Non enim ad litteram credendus est*). All men and women, then as now, are born through *natura*. For his attitudes toward nature William is censured by a contemporary theologian as a misguided "man of physics" (*homo physicus*), and later William himself repudiates this way of treating the text "metaphorically" (*translative*). But such censures are rapidly overtaken by events. About the middle of the century, when a treatise *On the Works of the Six Days* attributed to Thierry of Chartres aims to explicate the beginning of Genesis "according to physics and the literal sense," it boldly transfigures a range of direct injunctions of God into a sequence of interlocking natural processes that operate in their own right after the initial act of divine creation.[17]

At the same time, it should be stressed that for the philosophers of this period, to examine nature is finally to explore human nature – a nature itself divided between earthly attachments and heavenly aspirations – and the non-scriptural source texts for that open-ended exploration extend far beyond the *Timaeus*. The diverse imaginative reference points of such twelfth-century interpretation are not only individual figures like Orpheus or Castor and Pollux, shifting between lower and higher worlds.[18] They are also large-scale narrative structures. Whatever the generic diversity of those structures, from the perspective of twelfth-century intertextuality there is a shared vision of human spiritual ascent in works ranging from Virgil's *Aeneid* (with its agonized protagonist descending to the underworld to envision the future), to Martianus Capella's late antique *Marriage of Mercury and Philology* (with its multivalent deities passing up and down the cosmos to coordinate

---

17 For the points in this paragraph, see Gregory, *Anima*, pp. 123–246; Tullio Gregory, *Platonismo medievale: studi e ricerche* (Rome: Istituto storico italiano per il Medio Evo, 1958), pp. 122–50; and Whitman, *Allegory*, pp. 192–217.
18 See Wetherbee, *Platonism*, pp. 96–98, 114–15.

human life with the life of the gods), to Boethius' sixth-century *Consolation of Philosophy* (with its self-divided narrator needing to turn from destabilizing Fortune to uplifting Philosophy). In the words of a twelfth-century commentary on Martianus' work, "Martianus, then, imitates Virgil, and Boethius, Martianus."[19]

The writer of that commentary may be the same as the writer of the *Aeneid* commentary, for whom the descent of Aeneas suggests how a discerning individual can probe the creatural world in order to turn conversely toward the Creator.[20] Dante might have found such a text a useful subtext for his own version of how to transform a descent into an ascent. But whether or not his later poem looks back to the twelfth-century *Aeneid* commentary, it seems as if the allegorical commentary is already looking forward to the *Cosmographia*.

The texture of creation: the *Cosmographia*

With the mid-century *Cosmographia* of Bernard Silvestris, a philosophic commentary turns into a striking figurative composition in its own right.[21] The subject of the work, written in alternating poetry and prose (the *prosimetrum* format used by Martianus and Boethius), is the primordial composition of the cosmos itself, coordinated by a set of *dramatis personae* operating in their own sphere. In Book I, *Megacosmos*, "the greater universe," Nature expresses to Noys (*nous*; the divine Mind)[22] the appeal of Silva or Hyle (prime matter) for refinement. Noys organizes the amorphous state of matter into the elements; from Noys issues forth the animating presence of Endelichia (the World Soul); and the universe at large unfolds in panoramic detail. In Book II, *Microcosmos*, "the smaller universe," Noys promises to create man as the culmination of her work. Nature ascends to the highest level of the firmament to find Urania, the principle of celestial knowledge; together the two figures in turn descend earthward to locate Physis, the principle of earthly understanding. Suddenly Noys appears, directing

19 See *Commentary on Martianus*, ed. Westra, p. 47; translation drawn from Wetherbee, *Platonism*, p. 124.

20 See *Commentary*, ed. Jones and Jones, p. 30; *Commentary*, trans. Schreiber and Maresca, pp. 32–33.

21 For the text (completed perhaps in the late 1140s), see *Cosmographia / Bernardus Silvestris*, ed. Peter Dronke (Leiden: Brill, 1978); for a translation, see Winthrop Wetherbee, trans., *The Cosmographia of Bernardus Silvestris* (New York: Columbia University Press, 1973). My account draws upon the detailed discussion and bibliography in Whitman, *Allegory*, pp. 218–60.

22 In this and other cases my "glosses" are only broad ways of referring to multifaceted characters.

Urania to provide a soul, Physis to fashion a body, and Nature to unite the two. Though the making of this disparate, composite creature involves some strain, with the formation of man the universe is complete.

In the *Cosmographia* the interplay of diverse yet converse principles distinguishes not only the broad outlines of the plot, but also the inner conditions of the major characters. A striking case in point is the character of prime matter (Silva or Hyle), described in Nature's opening speech as "a mass discordant with itself" (*sibi dissona massa*), a figure who in her very formlessness (*informe chaos*) and turbulence (*Turbida*) "longs" for form and "yearns" for cultivation (*Optat . . . cupiens*).[23] While philosophically Prime Matter requires refinement, imaginatively she requests it; her "want" is not only her deficiency, but also her desire. The divided "personality" of matter – in tension between liability and longing – evokes the dynamics of its potentiality.[24]

The request of Prime Matter is complemented by the receptiveness of the divine Mind. Though theologically the Providence of God is transcendent, allegorically Noys is "troubled" (*Pertesum michi*) by the deprivation in the universe,[25] as if material disarray had its counterpart in empyreal dismay. Characters displaying this kind of self-qualifying flexibility are more subtly nuanced than the antithetical principles of Prudentius' late antique *Psychomachia*, yet more conceptually disciplined than the exotic gods of Martianus' *Marriage of Mercury and Philology*. Already at the opening of the *Cosmographia*, the other side of a Matter that appeals is a Mind that attends.

The interpenetration of figures in Bernard's story, which pervades the plot as a whole, is a radical expression of both a cosmic order and a compositional one. For all the sometimes unsettling divisions of his universe, the diverse "names" and "natures" that he recalls near the close of *Megacosmos* – Mind, Silva, the World Soul – finally develop a *continuum*, a realm of roundness (*rotunditas*)[26] in which there is ultimately no exclusive up or down. And this pervasive sense of a coalescent whole, indebted not only to Neoplatonic but also to Stoic and Hermetic versions[27] of a radically cohesive cosmos, suggests the expansive / contractive operation of the allegory itself. In this regard, the perpetual "weaving and unweaving" (*texit et retexit*) that Bernard associates with the cosmic process in the closing lines of *Megacosmos* seems almost a

---

23 See *Megacosmos* I.18–22 (trans., p. 67).
24 On some of the sources of this treatment of matter, see Whitman, *Allegory*, pp. 154–61, 169–92.
25 See *Megacosmos* II.ii (trans., p. 70). 26 See *Megacosmos* IV.viii–ix (trans., pp. 88–89).
27 See Stock, *Myth*, pp. 97–105, 137–62, 231–33, and Whitman, *Allegory*, pp. 32–38, 144–45, 177–78, 251–52.

self-conscious comment on the texture of his interwoven work at large.[28] Unfolding the work of creation, the author turns an act of exegesis into his own act of genesis.

Yet the constant transfiguration presented in the text has its darker implications. In the perpetual flux of the whole, all composite things – including man, with his signal but problematic twofold nature (*Naturis... duabus*) – must dissolve.[29] It is a measure of the complexity – the *conplicatio* – of Bernard's persistent sense of human disparities that his allegory nonetheless stresses not the impulse to escape the world but the effort to "explicate" it, to seek to "figure it out," like the figure of Nature in *Microcosmos*, learning to make her way about the universe. Passing up and down the realm of nature as she aims to compose human nature, Nature is in a sense both inside and outside her own world, developing a kind of dynamic standpoint from which to assess the very nature that she embodies.

With the figure of *Natura*, the *Cosmographia* promotes in large-scale allegorical narrative the development of a central character evocative of human *consciousness*. The groping spirit of *Natura* is the ancestress of the "I" that wanders through late medieval allegory and related narrative forms, from the lover of the *Romance of the Rose* to the dreamer of the *Parliament of Fowls*, who had intriguingly been reading about the cosmic ascent in Macrobius' *Commentary on the Dream of Scipio* before comically slipping into his own more mundane dream about the variegated realm of Nature. But long before that Chaucerian commentary on a commentary, a twelfth-century sequel to the *Cosmographia* is already exposing some of the acute liabilities of even an aspiring consciousness.

Fashioning nature and human nature: the *Complaint of Nature* and the *Anticlaudianus*

With the *Complaint of Nature*, written by Alan of Lille about 1160–1170, *Natura* appears as an expansive character conducting an extended dialogue with a figure of *humana natura* itself.[30] As if cut from more than Macrobian

---

28 On this translation of *texit et retexit*, see *Cosmographia*, ed. Dronke, p. 167, note to iv 14, 6–8. On the application of "weaving" (long applied to texts) to the texture of the cosmos, see Michael Lapidge, "The Stoic Inheritance," in Dronke, ed., *History*, pp. 101, 111–12, and Jon Whitman, "Present Perspectives: Antiquity to the Late Middle Ages," in Jon Whitman, ed., *Interpretation and Allegory: Antiquity to the Modern Period* (Leiden: Brill, 2000), pp. 53–54, nn. 70–73.

29 See *Microcosmos* X.21, with Wetherbee, *Platonism*, pp. 158–86.

30 For the text, see "Alan of Lille, 'De Planctu naturae,'" ed. Nikolaus M. Häring, *Studi medievali*, 3a ser., 19 (1978), 797–879, hereafter cited as *DPN*. My translations are based in

cloth, the *Natura* who descends to the narrator near the opening of Alan's *prosimetrum* text not only wears layers of intricate clothing depicting diverse creatures of the natural world. She herself aspires to "weave" the line of her own narrative (*seriem narrationis contexere*) as she elaborately describes how the divine artisan desired things to be "woven together" (*jingitur texeretur*) in a continuous sequence of cosmic generation. But the very "integument" (*integumentum*) of Nature's tunic – just at the place where it images man – has been violently torn; the natural sequence of generation has been broken by a wayward mankind; and her narrative line is interrupted by the human narrator's perplexity about the *involucrum* of the god of love.[31] After fashioning her own ingenious involutions about the "grammar" of erotic love and the conduct of gods (including her sexually insubordinate "subvicar" Venus), Nature finally summons Genius (the principle of generation) to excommunicate those who violate her generative principles and other norms.

The distinction of the *Natura* of the *Complaint* lies in her dramatization as both a full-fledged character and a full-fledged speaker. In the formative sense of the deployment of a character (*persona*) with speech, she is perhaps the most complex literary "personification" from antiquity to the twelfth century itself.[32]

As a character, she has important cosmic and moral functions, yet she repeatedly seems compromised by her own activity. Already when she descends (*delapsa*) to the hapless narrator, for example, she is so deeply implicated with a lapsed *humana natura*[33] that she almost seems to reenact the very fall that she wishes to remedy. That fall itself originates with the default of a constituent force of her own, her subvicar, Venus (who perversely double-crosses her by straying with a figure named Antigenius). The problematic operation of Nature suggests the dark possibility that in the world of the *Complaint* any divided "nature" that seeks to act within its own sphere is liable to turn in a circle.

part on Douglas M. Moffat, trans., *The Complaint of Nature by Alain de Lille* (New York: Holt, 1908), and James J. Sheridan, *The Plaint of Nature / Alan of Lille* (Toronto: Pontifical Institute of Mediaeval Studies, 1980); page numbers with "trans." refer to the Moffat translation.

31 For these passages, see *DPN* II.138–292; VIII.183, 221–22, 161–72, 247–54 (trans., pp. 11–17, 42, 44, 41, 45).

32 My account of the *Complaint* draws upon the detailed discussion and bibliography in Jon Whitman, "The Problem of Assertion and the *Complaint of Nature*," *Hebrew University Studies in Literature and the Arts* 15 (1987), 5–26. On "personification," see Whitman, *Allegory*, pp. 269–72, and the references s.v. in the index.

33 See, e.g., *DPN* II.2; VIII.4–5 (trans., pp. 5, 34).

This sense of circularity is intensified by her insistent turns of speech. In one sense, of course, the highly wrought discourse of Nature is a verbal counterpart to the cosmic articulation, the *ornatus mundi*, that informs the natural world itself. But the more Nature talks, the more she betrays the limits of her language and her world. Her circuitousness has a parodic element, of course; she anticipates the loquacious Nature of the *Romance of the Rose*, who in the course of a speech over 2500 lines long confides that it is good to "flee prolixity."[34] More deeply, however, Nature never formulates systematically the rationale of her own rhetoric. She had banned "metonymy" from the arts of Venus, for example, lest by "the pursuit of too harsh a metaphor," "excessive color" might be converted into "discoloration."[35] Yet the question of what makes a metaphor "too" harsh, what makes a rhetorical color "excessive," recurrently shadows her own speech – not only in her own explicit endorsement of "metonymy" in the arts of language, or in her luxuriant "grammar" of "transitive," "active," and "passive" sexuality, but also in her extravagant interior fable about a misbehaving goddess.[36] In language as in life, she keeps producing issues she cannot control. The ways of Nature, in effect, are corrupt "by nature."

It seems to me that Alan's interest lies in part in his intriguing effort to salvage the very nature he so artfully exposes. If the Nature who confesses that "I, Nature, am ignorant of the nature" of man's rebirth admits a fundamental disparity between physical and spiritual "nature," her very consciousness of that disparity seems to imply a receptivity to grace. If the internal divisions of her world and her words frequently undermine her, her dialogue with a figure of *humana natura*, and her closing appeal to Genius, her "other self" (*sibi alteri*), eventually suggest how the opening of an interior distance within the self can provide a context for introspection and self-assessment.[37] By the end of the *Complaint of Nature*, the remarkable dramatization of her character and speech – with all the divided "natures" and "names" in her world – provocatively suggests not only a way to make a personification out of Nature, but also a way to explore the nature of a person.

The daring effort to transform the divided nature of a person informs the *Anticlaudianus*, a widely influential work completed by Alan in the early

34 See *Le Roman de la Rose / Guillaume de Lorris et Jean de Meun*, ed. Félix Lecoy, 3 vols. (Paris: Champion, 1965–70), l. 18268.

35 See *DPN* X.112–14: *ne si nimis dure translationis excursu . . . in decolorationem color nimius conuertatur* (trans., p. 54).

36 On that fable, see Wetherbee, *Platonism*, pp. 193–97.

37 For the quotations, see *DPN* VI.146–47: *ego Natura huius natiuitatis naturam ignoro* (trans., p. 30); XVI.188 (trans., p. 85).

1180s.[38] In this intricate poem of epic hexameters, Nature urges the formation of a "divine man" (*diuinus homo*; I.236); Prudence, initially assisted by the Liberal Arts and Reason, eventually ascends beyond their realm to the wondrous citadel of God to seek a soul for this man; Concord joins that soul to a body ordered by Nature, and the "new man" (*nouus... homo*; VII.74) – after a battle of Vices and Virtues at the end of the poem – initiates a golden age.

Seeking to reverse the reversals of the *Complaint of Nature*, the author provocatively inserts an act of self-*explicatio* at the center of the central book of his work (V.265–78). As Prudence passes into the supernal realm, Alan declares that he is abandoning the role of "poet" and appropriating to himself "the new speaking part of the prophet," operating as the writing instrument of the divine artisan himself (V.268–69, 273). As his plot pivots between two worlds, his status as author turns inside-out; in his conception, a divinity speaks through his humanity. The "new man" toward whom the story is advancing seems increasingly designed to include the human writer himself, re-created by the transporting story he relates, and finally to encompass the readers of the story, insofar as an ethereal world "purer than pure" (V.395–96) informs their own vision.[39]

It has often been felt that after the intellectual ascent in the middle of Alan's poem, the descent to the earthly realm in the final books is philosophically and structurally a letdown. It should be stressed that the tension between an "ascent" to personal enlightenment and a "descent" to social engagement marks treatments of the philosopher-king since Plato's *Republic*; it is understandable that even the millennial earth/heaven of Alan's "new man" registers the strain. In the end, the imaginative difficulty of constructing the "new man" in the *Anticlaudianus* appears to involve persisting questions in twelfth-century thought about relations between diverse dimensions of the "individual" – cosmic and psychic, spiritual and social.[40] The "new man" himself has a somewhat shadowy existence, at times emerging into the foreground of the closing battle, at times receding into the background while one

---

38 For the text, see *Anticlaudianus / Alain de Lille*, ed. R. Bossuat (Paris: Vrin, 1955). For a translation, see James J. Sheridan, trans., *Anticlaudianus or The Good and Perfect Man / Alan of Lille* (Toronto: Pontifical Institute of Mediaeval Studies, 1973).

39 On such approaches to the "new man," see James Simpson, *Sciences and the Self in Medieval Poetry: Alan of Lille's Anticlaudianus and John Gower's Confessio amantis* (Cambridge: Cambridge University Press, 1995), although his argument that an informed reading of the poem involves reordering its narrative sequence seems to me to need revision.

40 On some of the implications of such questions for figures in the work, see, e.g., M. L. Fuehrer, "The Cosmological Implications of the Psychomachia in Alan of Lille's *Anticlaudianus*," *Studies in Philology* 27 (1980), 344–53, and Simpson, *Sciences*, pp. 48, 52–53, 62–63, 98–102.

of his constituent Virtues fights a corresponding Vice. If Alan of Lille finds it difficult to "put together" a divided "individual," his work nonetheless puts that pressing problem at the center of allegorical attention.

Worlds and works in flux

Even before the extended treatment of that problem in vernacular allegory of the thirteenth century, it is possible to sense some of its implications in a Latin work composed apparently almost immediately after the *Anticlaudianus*, the *Architrenius* of Jean de Hanville.[41] In Jean's poem of hexameters the main actor is not a cosmic or psychic principle but an inchoate person, the "Arch-Weeper" (Architrenius), whose search for *Natura* leads him satirically through a wide range of courtly, commercial, and clerical settings that mark the wayward world. Whereas the axis of narrative action in the universe of Bernard Silvestris or Alan of Lille tends to be vertical in orientation, in the landscape of Jean it tends to be horizontal. Even when the Arch-Weeper sees at the top of a lofty mountain a vision of cosmic order, in which "all the workings of fate are woven" (*fati exitus omnis / Texitur*), what Bernard and Alan conceive as the metaphysical weave of the world is for Jean the trompe l'oeil effect of an "actual" tapestry showily displayed in the Palace of Ambition.[42] The story of the poem, which ends when *Natura* arranges for Architrenius to marry Moderation, tends to exhibit less a metaphysical emphasis than an ethical one.

Such ethical concerns increasingly inform twelfth-century approaches to other complex forms of "nature" – the changing natures of gods and humans in ancient mythology. It is telling that the first detailed effort to allegorize the *Metamorphoses* of Ovid appears in a commentary of the latter twelfth century, a work composed by Arnulf of Orléans about the 1170s.[43] Unlike the sometimes more cosmologically oriented account of various gods in a twelfth-century compilation composed by the "Third Vatican Mythographer," Arnulf programmatically argues in his introduction that Ovid intends *mutatio* to refer not only to external (*extrinsecus*) change in bodies but also to internal (*intrinsecus*) change in the soul. Ovid might have been surprised to learn that Jove's love of Io indicates God's love of virgins and that Io's transformation into a cow and later into a goddess signifies her behavioral

---

41 See Johannes de Hauvilla, *Architrenius*, trans. and ed. Winthrop Wetherbee (Cambridge: Cambridge University Press, 1994); the poem was completed by 1184–85.

42 See *Architrenius* IV.214–83 (pp. 100–3).

43 See *Allegoriae super Ovidii Metamorphosin*, ed. Fausto Ghisalberti, "Arnolfo d'Orléans, un cultore di Ovidio nel secolo XII," *Memorie del Reale Istituto Lombardo di Scienze e Lettere, Classe di lettere, scienze morali e storiche* 24.4 (1932), 157–234.

turns toward bestiality and piety. But perhaps he would have appreciated the craft by which Arnulf maneuvers from physical to moral allegory in associating the intervening figure of Juno (who possesses the bestial Io) with "the lower air, that is, the baser and graver vices."[44] It should be stressed that Arnulf's interpretations in general (which include, for example, a large number of Euhemerist expositions, tracing stories of gods to histories of humans) are far more diverse and eclectic than this exercise. But his composite work helps to facilitate the "moralized Ovids" of the late Middle Ages, in which changes in nature are repeatedly divided into categories of good and evil (*in bono / in malo*) and in which the supreme model of metamorphosis is the loving Incarnation of the Christian God.[45]

The psychological and social turns to which Arnulf of Orléans and Jean de Hanville give expression suggest broader movements in the late twelfth century. Such movements can be traced, for example, in the contemporaneous emergence of courtly romance, with its interior dialogues between personified figures of reason and passion, its formative transactions between the established court and the tangled wood (*silva*) of individual adventure, and its increasingly intricate plots, which by the early thirteenth century involve forms of interlaced narrative (*entrelacement*) that use "weaving and unweaving" to display not cosmological but social and semiological complexities.[46] In large-scale allegorical narrative in its own right, it may seem that with the allegory of love of the early thirteenth-century *Romance of the Rose* the shift from *natura* to *humana natura*, from cosmic to courtly contexts, from the World Soul to individual souls, is complete. But hardly does the allegorical universe contract before it expands again – with the world-traversing narratives of Jean de Meun, Dante, Spenser, and others. Given the diverse yet converse relations between divided "names" and "natures" in allegorical writing, perhaps such complicating and explicating acts are to be expected. Yet twelfth-century allegory remains an imposing phenomenon. It does not just develop its own remarkable figurations; it finally promotes far-reaching transformations in later imaginative design.

---

44 For these passages, see Ghisalberti, "Arnolfo," pp. 181, 203 (*a Iunone id est inferiori aere id est viciis inferioribus et gravioribus*).
45 See, e.g., Paule Demats, *Fabula: Trois études de mythographie antique et médiévale* (Geneva: Droz, 1973), pp. 140–51, and Robert Levine, "Exploiting Ovid: Medieval Allegorizations of the *Metamorphoses*," *Medioevo Romanzo* 14 (1989), 197–213.
46 Compare, e.g., Wetherbee, *Platonism*, pp. 220–41, and Eugène Vinaver, *The Rise of Romance* (New York: Oxford University Press, 1971), pp. 68–98.

PART III

Literary allegory: philosophy and figuration

8

KEVIN BROWNLEE

Allegory in the *Roman de la Rose*

The thirteenth-century French verse *Roman de la Rose* involves striking new developments in the deployment of various allegorical constructs and procedures, within the context of a self-conscious and innovative expansion of dominant vernacular literary discourses, both lyric and narrative.[1] It is necessary to stress at the outset the *Rose*'s unique status in the medieval French literary corpus – in terms of authority, of prestige, and of influence. Not only does it exist in a greater number of manuscripts (nearly three hundred) than any other single work from this corpus, but it generated a remarkable number of poetic, philosophical, theological and political responses in a variety of key European cultural contexts: Italian, English, and Dutch, as well as French.[2] In all of these contexts, it is particularly significant that the Rose is a work by two authors: the "courtly" Guillaume de Lorris, whose romance (of about 4,000 lines, apparently incomplete) dates from *c.* 1225–30; and the "clerkly" Jean de Meun, who self-consciously continued and completed his predecessor's kernel text between *c.* 1270 and 1280 with an additional 18,000 lines. It was only the conjoined *Rose* text of which Jean was the architect that succeeded so spectacularly (and so quickly) in dominating the French vernacular literary scene.

Guillaume's extraordinarily innovative Prologue (vv. 1–44) deploys the language, structure, and truth claims of Macrobian dream discourse (in

---

1 Among many studies of allegory and rhetoric in the *Rose*, see Daniel Poirion, *Le Roman de la Rose* (Paris: Hatier, 1973), pp. 8–39, 98–144; Michel Zink, *La Subjectivité littéraire. Autour du siècle de Saint Louis* (Paris: PUF, 1985), pp. 127–47; Armand Strubel, *La Rose, Renart et le Graal. La littérature allégorique en France au XIIIe siècle* (Paris: Champion, 1989), pp.199–224; Douglas Kelly, *Internal Difference and the Meanings of the Roman de la Rose* (Madison: University of Wisconsin Press, 1995).
2 For the *Rose*'s reception, see Pierre-Yves Badel, *Le "Roman de la Rose" au XIVe siècle* (Paris: Champion, 1980); and Sylvia Huot, *The "Romance of the Rose" and Its Medieval Readers: Interpretations, Reception, Manuscript Transmission* (Cambridge: Cambridge University Press, 1993).

which dreams can be interpreted as having oracular or prophetic value) to authorize a new combination of courtly erotic lyric subject matter with the narrative procedures of courtly romance narrative. The authorial voice – in a standard romance opening gambit – first evokes his named Latin *auctor* (v. 7), to "guarantee" (v. 6) the power of dreams to "signify" (*senefiance*, v. 16) future truth in waking life, to figure *covertement* things that later reveal themselves *apertement*.[3] The vocabulary of allegorical hermeneutics in a Macrobian context is thus introduced at the very outset of the *Rose* text.[4] Then, in a striking discursive shift (vv. 21–27), the *je*-narrator presents the subject matter of his romance as the dream of initiation into love that he himself had dreamed when he was five years younger: the romance's narrative line will be the dreamed initiatory love experience of this *je*-protagonist. With the explicit affirmation that everything in the dream later came true (vv. 28–30), a basically lyric *matière* is established. The Prologue's final section (vv. 31–44) focuses on the present of the time of writing, and on the *je*-narrator both as poet and as lover. Following the commandments of Love (*Amors*, v. 33), he will compose a verse romance, "rhyme the dream" (v. 31). The overall result will be simultaneously didactic, directed at a general audience (a new Ovidian, vernacular *Ars amatoria* ("le *Romanz de la Rose* / ou l'art d'Amors est tote enclose," vv. 37–38)), and lyric, aimed at a single, privileged female addressee (an extended love request intended to move an extra-textual Lady, herself so worthy of love that she should be called "Rose" (v. 44)).

Guillaume's Prologue conflates into a new, unified (but visibly hybrid) speaking authorial subject: 1) the learnèd narrator figure of courtly romance and 2) the first-person lover/poet of the twelfth- and thirteenth-century courtly lyric poetry. In the *Rose* Prologue, the vernacular lyric first-person subject matter (Love) is articulated through vernacular romance narrative procedures and constructs, but in a Macrobian prophetic dream that allows (even "requires") both the hermeneutic claims and the technical terminology of allegoresis.

But if Guillaume uses the language of allegorical exegesis in an erotic lyrico-narrative context, the *Rose* is not a Neoplatonic work employing literary techniques to articulate philosophical truth. Rather, Guillaume de Lorris' text is a first-person courtly romance (addressed to a Lady outside the frame of the story) that utilizes claims to allegorical truth in the service

---

3 All citations are from Félix Lecoy, ed., *Le Roman de la Rose*, 3 vols. (Paris: Champion, 1965–70). All translations are mine.

4 See J. Willis, ed., *Commentarii in Somnium Scipionis* (Leipzig: Teubner, 1963), 1.2.7–21, 1.3.1–20. Cf. John V. Fleming, *Reason and the Lover* (Princeton: Princeton University Press, 1984), pp. 160–65.

of courtly values, claims which cannot ultimately be sustained – and whose very inadequacy functions ultimately to produce meaning for the text as a whole.

Before moving to a direct consideration of the ways in which different (and varied) programs of allegorical discourse function semantically in Guillaume's *Rose*, a brief treatment of the poem's unfolding narrative is, I think, required in the interests of clarity.

The text (that is, the dream) falls into two major episodes (each with its own mimetic strategy). First, we have the representation of what can be termed "Love as Initiation" (vv. 45–2008). The first-person protagonist dreams that he awakens one morning in May – emphatically characterized as the canonical literary season of love – and walks through a beautiful landscape (the *locus amoenus* ("beautiful place"), the conventional setting of love poetry) until he reaches a garden enclosed by four walls decorated with portraits of ten allegorical figures representing the anti-courtly attributes excluded from the garden. Upon being admitted into the garden (vv. 629ff.) by the poem's first fully anthropomorphized personification character, Leisure/Idleness (*Oiseuse*), the Dreamer meets the other courtly personifications who inhabit the garden, finally joining them in a celebratory dance (*querole*). Among them is their "Lord," the God of Love (v. 864), who is a distinctive figure in this poem: he is the mythographic, Ovidian winged archer, the son of Venus, not a personification allegory of "Love."

The Dreamer's final initiation (his actual transformation into the Lover) ensues, depicted in three complementary – but different – mimetic modes, three different sign systems – each tied to a distinguishable, traditional literary discourse. First, within the economy of desire based on seeing the beloved, the gaze of the desiring male subject encounters the image of the "female" object of desire, which instantly (and conventionally) results in his *innamoramento*. In a complex transformation of Ovid's story of Narcissus in *Metamorphoses* 3, the *Rose*'s desiring male subject looks down into what is presented as Narcissus' original fountain and ultimately sees not his own reflection, but rather a figuration of the female Other as the object of his desire: a specific, individual rosebud. If calling the beloved a "rose" is a metaphor, that metaphor has here been realized in concrete terms.[5] Outside the frame of the narrative, the *je*-narrator's Lady is "like a rose"; inside the narrative frame, at the level of plot in the mimetic economy of the poem itself, that Lady is figured for the *je*-protagonist as the flower itself. Second,

---

5 For Narcissus' Fountain see David Hult, *Self-Fulfilling Prophecies: Readership and Authority in the First Roman de la Rose* (Cambridge: Cambridge University Press, 1986), pp. 263–300.

the God of Love shoots the new Lover with five allegorical arrows that go through his eye and into his heart: Beauty, Simplicity, Courtesy, Company, and Fair Seeming. The mimetic conventions of Ovid's *Amores* are thus rewritten in yet another of the *Rose*'s (increasingly diverse) allegorical registers. Third and finally, the God of Love requires the Lover to perform an amatory version of the feudal ceremony of homage, as he solemnly enters into the god's "service" – becomes the "man" of this "lord" – thus representing the experience of falling in love through the transformative rewriting of yet another mimetic register authorized by literary tradition.

The second and final major episode of Guillaume's *Rose* (vv. 2754–4028) can be placed under the rubric of "Love as *Récit*." The first-person protagonist, having been initiated into his new identity of Lover, and having been instructed by the God of Love, the Ovidian *magister amoris* on the love experience, now proceeds to narrativize, to "illustrate," to act out (the entire sequence is highly theatrical) "his" love experience in terms of the hybrid mimesis that is part of Guillaume's literary innovation. Having then, at the level of plot, become coterminous with his new identity as (evolving) Lover, the *je*-protagonist now sets out to possess the object of his desire, failing repeatedly. The same basic sequence of narrative events is enacted twice (the second time with considerable elaboration): a cyclical structure is established. The action is initiated (indeed, made possible) by the sudden appearance of a new character, Fair Welcome ("Bel Acueil"), son of Courtliness, and a personification of the positive aspect of the Lady's reaction to her suitor.[6] The majority of the new "characters" encountered in this episode each figure ("allegorize") different (and often conflicting – hence the drama) features of the complex psychological response of the beloved object of desire to the advances of the desiring subject.

Guillaume de Lorris' *Rose* develops multiple programs of allegory, which function in different ways to produce different (and different kinds of) meanings. First, the prophetic dream discourse derived from Macrobius results not in "truth," but in a Macrobian *narratio fabulosa* (fabulous narrative),[7] which, in one important sense, employs the powerful rhetoric of structural irony both for erotic and for literary purposes. The triple temporality set up in the Prologue (past dream time of the *je*-protagonist; present writing time of the *je*-narrator; an intermediate time between this past and this present, in which all the events narrated "proleptically" in the dream "came true" in the non-dream world, but before the narrator began his composition of the

---

6 See Simon Gaunt, "Bel Acueil and the Improper Allegory of the *Roman de la Rose*," *New Medieval Literatures* 2 (1998): 65–93.

7 See *Commentarii in Somnium Scipionis*, ed. Willis, I.2.7–11, shortly before Macrobius' descriptive taxonomy of dreams in I.3.1–11.

text) ultimately collapses under the pressure of the narrator's courtly love request, beyond the narrative frame, to his Lady, Rose.[8] Any representation of the Lady yielding to her aspiring Lover at the level of plot within the narrative (i.e., the capture of Jealousy's castle by the God of Love) would violate (and undermine) the system of courtly discourse, and thus render the entire poem dysfunctional in courtly erotic terms. Instead we have two opposite endings, which, as it were, exist simultaneously. As narrative, the poem must be incomplete. The "authorial intention" to continue the story until it ends with the castle falling to the troops of Amors works, finally, as the sign of a persuasive courtly discretion that requires the absence of narrative closure.[9] As lyric, on the other hand, the poem functions quite effectively – and in this sense may be regarded as "finished." The concluding plea for mercy conflates the *je*-protagonist's voice in the past (explicitly addressing Bel Acueil at the level of plot) with that of the *je*-narrator in the present (implicitly addressing his Lady, Rose).[10] At the same time – and throughout Guillaume's poem – the use of the technical vocabulary of Macrobian allegoresis (especially from *Somnium Scipionis* 2.7–11,17) reinforces the status of the dream as containing deeper, hidden meanings, as inviting (as well as being about) allegorical hermeneutics.[11]

Second, Guillaume's *Rose* also involves a program in which the author/narrator also functions as textual interpreter. In a series of key passages, the authorial voice intervenes to present plot events as requiring interpretive glosses, which are always deferred (see 975–81, 1596–99, 2071–76). In the final passage of this program, the ten commandments of the God of Love are introduced by the authorial voice, speaking initially to his reading public in a general didactic register that presents the entire "dream" as a text (even, a *fabula*, i.e., a fable or fiction) that will require a gloss. The narrative *récit* will be followed by an interpretive exposition. Thus the full revelation of the meaning of the dream will only occur after the narrative concludes: when

---

8 For Guillaume's triple temporality, see Emmanuèle Baumgartner, "The Play of Temporalities; or, The reported Dream of Guillaume de Lorris", in Kevin Brownlee and Sylvia Huot, eds., *Rethinking the "Romance of the Rose": Text, Image, Reception* (Philadelphia: University of Pennsylvania Press, 1992), pp. 22–38.

9 This proleptic "end point" is explicitly articulated in the narrator's voice in vv. 3500–02. See Douglas Kelly, " 'Li chaistieus... Qu'Amors prist puis par ses esforz': The Conclusion of Guillaume de Lorris's *Rose*", in Norris J. Lacy, ed., *A Medieval French Miscellany* (Lawrence: University of Kansas Press, 1972), pp. 61–78.

10 See Hult, *Self-Fulfilling Prophecies*, pp. 186–250.

11 Namely, "lies" vs. "truth," "fable" vs. "senefiance," "covered (or veiled)" vs. "revealed," the "beautiful ornaments of clothing, jewelry, etc." vs. the "naked body of Nature or Truth," etc.

the narrator becomes an interpreter.[12] The repeated articulation of the text–gloss opposition (which derives from hermeneutical traditions) marks the dream narrative as allegorical, that is, having a deep meaning below the surface. This strategy works, even though it is problematized in Guillaume's *Rose* by the "incompleteness" of the narrative.

The third, and most spectacular, allegorical program involves the consistent deployment of personification characters at the level of plot. For this reason (among others) it has long been a critical commonplace that the first-person lover-protagonist is the only true subjectivity in the "allegorical" dream narrative. It must be stressed, however, that the dramatic figures in Guillaume's story collectively involve a hybrid, rather than a single, coherent, mimetic economy. Personifications of courtly characteristics and values co-exist with personifications of the stylized psychological components of the Lady as "reactive" object of desire, both courtly and anti-courtly. Male Bouche, the personification of a whole category of slanderers (*Lozengiers*), a constitutive component of courtly lyric as well as courtly romance, co-exists with Chastity, a religious (even a Christian) value personified. Reason and, especially, Friend are both differentiated mimetically from the more standard personifications with allegorical dimensions. And finally, interacting with all of the personifications are the two key mythographical figures of Cupid and Venus, who carry with them (modified) Ovidian genealogies, literary and other. Coherent or monumental allegorical interpretations of Guillaume's *Rose* thus tend to be elusive. Rather, the author appears to deploy various allegorical discourses in order to bestow greater significance on his vernacular poetic enterprise as such. At the same time, he highlights the poem's innovative character as a courtly and erotic production that places lyric and narrative modes in continuous tension with each other.

Jean de Meun "continues" Guillaume's text by expanding and transforming its discursive and ideological ground rules, using it as a point of departure for a new vernacular poetics of (often playful) philosophical and theological inquiry into the nature of desire, knowledge, language and the production of meaning as such. In relation to his model text (Guillaume's poem), Jean deploys the rhetorical devices of amplification and digression as structural principles. Jean creates a vast, new vernacular encyclopedia, organized (ultimately) around the forms of scholastic exercises such as the

---

12 That is, when "j'espoinge . . . dou *songe* la *senefiance*: / la *verité* qui est *coverte* / vos sera lores toute *aperte* / quand *espondre* m'orroiz le *songe* / car il n'i a mot de *mençonge*" (vv. 2071–76; emphasis mine). It is worth noting the two rhyme word pairs which recall and "correct" the Prologue, by making fully explicit the author figure's claims to interpretive authority.

disputatio – an extravagantly prolonged university-style debate in vernacular verse involving a plethora of opposing positions. These positions (in principle, all dealing with the nature of love) are articulated by a series of "speech characters" who dominate Jean's poem.

The first two are transformed and expanded versions of the Reason and Friend introduced in Guillaume's poem, who speak directly to Amant, the first-person protagonist. Jean's Reason is represented as a combination of the Boethian Lady Philosophy with the Thomistic logical practice of the mid-thirteenth-century University of Paris. She argues that Amant's love of the rose should be rejected as inherently illogical, then proposes herself to him as a "substitute" *dame*, a superior object of desire. This proposition involves self-representation through the discourses of courtly poetry and the bawdy *fabliau* genre, to place Reason as a desiring subject within the economy of sexual desire. Jean's character Friend incarnates the Ovidian strategy of deception as a technique for seduction. Both courtly discourse and mythographic fables of history are thus implicated as rhetorically powerful, but referentially unreliable.

The Ovidian mythographic God of Love reenters the narrative in a key scene that visibly redefines Guillaume's first-person protagonist in a number of interrelated ways. The God of Love's reappearance fundamentally alters the mimetic status, semantic content, and inner hermeneutical workings of the conjoined *Rose* text as conceived by Jean. In the speech (vv. 10465–648) of the God of Love to his assembled troops (requesting that they help the first-person author/protagonist), the entire ontological self-presentation of Jean's text is transformed: the two authors are named for the only time in the poem, and differentiated from each other in a visibly artificial temporal construct that foregrounds the fictionality of Guillaume's first-person love experience, while stressing the primacy of Jean's identity as a writer to the production of the text we are in the process of reading. Equally emphasized, however, is the constructedness of Jean as author figure who, within the explicit temporality of the narrative frame, will not be born for forty years. [13]

The next speech character, False Seeming, engages in a dialogue not with Amant but with the God of Love, a passage implicitly addressed to Jean de Meun's contemporary reader: urban, Parisian, University-oriented. As a character, False Seeming figures deceptive linguistic practice within religious, or theological, discourse: the limits of linguistic referentiality as such are

---

13 Kevin Brownlee, "Jean de Meun and the Limits of Romance: Genius as Rewriter of Guillaume de Lorris", in K. Brownlee and M. S. Brownlee, eds., *Romance: Generic Transformation from Chrétien de Troyes to Cervantes* (Hanover, NH: University Press of New England, 1985), pp. 114–134.

paradoxically (and dangerously) represented in the parody of both confession and scholastic debate that constitutes False Seeming's dialogic encounter with Love.

The introduction of the speech characters Nature and Genius constitutes a radical departure for Jean de Meun as author figure, with Alan of Lille's *De planctu Naturae* (*c.* 1160–65) displacing Guillaume de Lorris' *Rose* as model text. The allegorical poetics and Neoplatonic myth-making of the twelfth century are thus brought into the mimetic and discursive compass of Jean's poetic *summa*. In terms of narrative framework, Nature is situated outside of, indeed, with no reference to, Guillaume's allegorical garden, and the first-person protagonist has completely disappeared. Rather, we have a first-person authorial voice meditating on the mimetic art that enables him (within its inherent limitations) to figure – in French vernacular verse – his transformed version of Alan's mid-twelfth-century Latin *Natura* in terms of mid-thirteenth-century Parisian scientific cosmology.

Genius, Jean's final speech character, is a vastly expanded version of Alan's mythic personification of the process of giving birth, of giving individual form to every new life, presented as Nature's necessary collaborator. In Jean's *Rose*, Genius preaches a "gospel" of procreative sexual activity leading to "human redemption" in a Christological and Trinitarian paradise figured as a "beautiful park," which explicitly displaces Guillaume's courtly garden. Jean's character Genius treats Guillaume's part of the conjoined *Rose* exclusively as a written text that he is correctively rewriting. Guillaume de Lorris, author of the first *Rose* text, thus becomes himself a courtly "speech character" in the global context of Jean's new poetic *summa*, moving towards closure.

When considered collectively, as configured by Jean de Meun's master text, each of his speech characters, I would argue, embodies a seemingly coherent discourse, ideology, or moral philosophy which, in the final analysis, undermines itself. No single inscribed "argument" is presented by the text, globally speaking, as authoritative in absolute terms. Jean's *Rose*, which contains them all, does not privilege one "speech character" by associating it with an "authorial" perspective. Indeed, the poem's careful and complex structure makes it impossible to locate such a perspective in global interpretive terms. Rather, we confront (among the speech characters) a multiple set of *disputationes*, with no final intervention by the *magister* to effect a single, definitive resolution with his *respondeo* ("I respond").

At the same time, Jean's *Rose* also makes use of a second (and complementary) hermeneutic strategy, in fruitful contrast with the poem's dominant dialectic structure: a programmatic foregrounding of an "integumental" poetics of allegoresis, which posits a beautiful but fictional *fabula* at the literal level of the poem that both conceals and reveals the truth at the allegorical level. This kind of "rhetorical" hermeneutics is – paradoxically, or ironically, associated with Guillaume's courtly poetics – introduced in Jean's text by Reason at the end of her debate with Amant on language, semiotics, and referentiality (vv. 6898–7174), when she advises him against a mere "literal" interpretation (*a la letre*, v. 7127) of her words. In this context, she contrasts the surface "fables" with the deep-structure "*verité*" that they contain: the "fables" "clothe" (*vestirent*) the "truth" (*le voir*) (v. 7148), which thus needs to be "interpreted" (*esposte*, v. 7136; from *espondre*). The poets' "integumanz" contain the philosophers' "secrez" (vv. 7138, 7140). The articulation of this theory of two-fold allegorical signification is continued by a series of three inscribed promises (emanating from Jean's first-person author figure) that the dream will be glossed, its significance revealed, only after its full narrative exposition (*récit*: see vv. 10573–74, 15143–53, 20787–21180).

The fact that Jean's *Rose* (in dramatic contradistinction to Guillaume's) imposes narrative closure in explicit and emphatic fashion (vv. 20755–21750) means that the failure to deliver the oft-promised gloss undermines any fixity for the allegorical hermeneutics of integument-text vs. truth-gloss. At the same time, however, the process of continual reading and rereading is valorized as constituting the (open-ended) work of interpretation of Jean's text.[14]

14 Kevin Brownlee, "Pygmalion, Mimesis, and the Multiple Endings of the *Roman de la Rose*," *Yale French Studies* 95 (1999), 193–211, and Daniel Heller-Roazen, *Fortune's Faces: The Roman de la Rose and the Poetics of Contingency* (Baltimore: Johns Hopkins University Press, 2003), pp. 100–31.

9

ALBERT R. ASCOLI

Dante and allegory

Since the seminal work of Charles Singleton in the 1950s, the subject of allegory has been at the controversial heart of Dante scholarship.[1] The debate focuses on the *Commedia* and in particular on the question of whether Dante is there writing an allegory "of theologians," that is, an imitation of the fourfold model of Scriptural signification, or not. Around this central question several others are arrayed. Is the "letter" of the "holy poem" to be taken as "true" like that of the Bible or as a "beautiful lie"? If the *Commedia* is modeled on the Bible, does it include all or some of the three allegorical senses (allegorical or Christological; moral or tropological; anagogical or eschatological) attributed to Scripture in the exegetical tradition? Is it more appropriate to talk about the *Commedia* in terms of allegory per se or rather in those of the typological ordering of God's two books – the Bible and creation as a whole – *sub specie aeternitatis*,[2] which provides the ontological and epistemological basis out of which the fourfold scheme is developed?

Most of what has been written – far more than can be summarized here – has been aimed at determining the *Commedia*'s intrinsic mode of signification and has consistently begged the question of how Dante might have come to displace into the domain of lay vernacular poetry an exegetical practice designed for exclusive application to Holy Scripture, and what might the wider significance of such an extraordinary displacement have been. In examining these latter issues, this essay will not consider the *Commedia* itself – in which the word *allegoria* does not appear – but rather the two theoretical statements, in which Dante explicitly defines his own allegorical

1 Charles S. Singleton, *Dante Studies 1: Elements of Structure* (Cambridge, MA: Harvard University Press, 1954).
2 A. C. Charity, *Events and their Afterlife: The Dialectics of Christian Typology in the Bible and in Dante* (Cambridge: Cambridge University Press, 1966); John Freccero, "Allegory and Autobiography," in Rachel Jacoff, ed., *The Cambridge Companion to Dante*, 2nd edn. (Cambridge: Cambridge University Press, 2007), pp. 161–80.

practice, situating it in relation to two different types of allegory and/or allegoresis: the first chapter of the second book of the unfinished treatise, *Convivio* (written *c.* 1303–06, in the period just preceding the *Commedia*) and the *Epistle to Cangrande* (*c.* 1316–18; attribution contested),[3] which presents itself as accompanying, introducing, and beginning to comment upon a gift of the early cantos of *Paradiso* to Cangrande della Scala, Lord of Verona.

These texts, which have been invoked time and again in scholarly battles over the *Commedia*, have not usually been considered on their own terms and/or in wider historical perspective, which, though understandable, is nonetheless regrettable. Just to begin with, before Dante no practicing medieval poet, and, *a fortiori*, no poet writing in a vernacular, ever undertook systematic interpretations of his own works (in *Convivio*, of three philosophical *canzoni*; in the *Epistle*, of the *Commedia* itself), much less offered a theory of allegorical writing and/or reading to underpin it. I will not attempt here to describe how this came to be, although it falls under the general rubric of transformative appropriation of high Latin cultural authority for a medieval vernacular author, and is addressed amply elsewhere in this volume [see within essays by Brownlee, Kamath and Copeland, and Zeeman].[4] My focus, instead, is Dante's manipulations – at once brilliant, innovative, and deeply confused – of received models of poetic and biblical signification and exegesis.

My argument is twofold: first, that, in an apparent paradox, Dante's invocation of biblical allegory has as much to do with affirming the importance of the literal sense, true or false as may be, as with discovering hidden meanings beneath the textual surface; second, that what is usually called Dante's allegory, meaning his mode of signification, is better understood as an attempt to conflate allegoresis, a practice of reading, with allegory, a practice of writing,[5] so as to suggest that the text's author is also its best

3 Albert Russell Ascoli, "Access to Authority: Dante in the *Epistle to Cangrande*," in Zygmunt Barański, ed., *Seminario Dantesco Internazionale/International Dante Seminar I* (Florence: Le Lettere, 1997), pp. 309–52; Luca Azzetta, "Le chiose alla *Commedia* di Andrea Lancia, L'*Epistola a Cangrande* e altre questioni dantesche," *L'Alighieri* 44 (n.s. 21) (2003), 5–73; Zygmunt Barański, "Dante Alighieri: Experimentation and (Self) Exegesis," in A. J. Minnis and Ian Johnson, eds., *The Cambridge History of Literary Criticism*, vol. 2: *The Middle Ages* (Cambridge: Cambridge University Press, 2005), pp. 561–82.

4 Alastair J. Minnis, *Medieval Theory of Authorship*, 2nd edn. (Philadelphia: University of Pennsylvania Press, 1988); Rita Copeland, *Rhetoric, Hermeneutics and Translation in the Middle Ages* (Cambridge: Cambridge University Press, 1991).

5 Rita Copeland and Stephen Melville, "Allegory and Allegoresis, Rhetoric and Hermeneutics," *Exemplaria* 3.1 (1991), 157–87.

reader.[6] Put another way, Dante's career-long obsession with defining how his texts signify and how they should be interpreted points to a relatively novel investment, historically speaking, in the power of the author to realize his intentions in writing and to control the reception of that writing by readers.

The *Convivio*, projected to be fifteen books in length, and to comment upon fourteen of Dante's *canzoni*, actually consists of an introductory, justificatory book, plus commentaries on three *canzoni*. In its commitment to turning vernacular poetry into an instrument for the communication of philosophical knowledge, the *Banquet* resembles Jean de Meun's *Rose*, but in its poem-commentary form it is more closely aligned with a Scholastic tradition which provided elucidating commentaries on classical literary and philosophical authors (Ovid, Virgil, Aristotle, et al.), as well as on the Bible. As Dante begins the first book of commentary proper (book 2, commenting upon "You who by understanding move the third heaven"), he stops to explain the exegetical method which he will use. I reproduce a large portion of the explanation in order to convey its density, complexity and, perhaps most importantly, its daring innovations:

> I say . . . that this exposition ought to be literal and allegorical. And so that this may be understood, it is necessary to know that writings may be understood and must be expounded primarily according to four senses. The first is called the literal [and this is that sense which does not go beyond the letter of the fictitious words, as in the fables of the poets. The next is called allegorical][7] and this that which is hidden beneath the mantle of such fables and is a truth hidden beneath a beautiful falsehood: such as when Ovid says that Orpheus tamed the beasts with his lyre and made trees and stones move towards him, which means that the wise man makes cruel hearts grow tame and humble with the instrument of his voice, and how he makes those that have no life in science or in art move according to his will: and they who have no rational life are little better than stones . . . Truly speaking, the theologians take this sense otherwise than the poets, but because it is my intention here to follow the manner of the poets, I take the allegorical sense in the way that it is used by those poets. The third sense is called moral; and readers must watch out for this most carefully as they go through writings, both for their own benefit and for that of their pupils. So, for example, one may note in the Gospel that when Christ

6 Alastair J. Minnis and A. B. Scott, with David Wallace, eds., *Medieval Literary Theory and Criticism, c. 1100–c. 1375: The Commentary Tradition* (Oxford: Clarendon Press, 1983), especially ch. 10 (written by David Wallace); Barański, "Dante"; Ascoli, *Dante and the Making of a Modern Author* (Cambridge: Cambridge University Press, 2008), ch. 4.

7 Brackets indicate editorial interpolations in the notoriously corrupt manuscript tradition. My arguments do not rely on the interpolations. Translations of *Convivio* and *The Epistle to Cangrande* are adapted from Minnis, et al., *Medieval Literary Theory*, chs. 9–10.

ascended the mountain to transfigure himself he took three of the twelve apostles with him. The moral sense of this is that we should have few companions
in our most secret undertakings. The fourth sense is called anagogical, that
is, above the senses, and this sense appears when one expounds the spiritual
meaning of a text which, even though [it may also be true] in the literal sense,
nevertheless points through the things signified to the supernal things of eternal
glory. This may be seen in that song of the prophet which says that Judea was
made holy and free in the exodus of the people of Israel from Egypt (Psalm
113:1–2). And although it is manifestly clear that this is true according to the
letter, that which is understood spiritually is no less true: that the soul in her
exodus from sin is made holy and free . . . And in demonstrating this, the literal
sense must always come first as that which contains in its meaning all other
meanings, and without this literal sense it would be impossible and irrational
to attend to the others, especially the allegorical,[8] without first coming to the
literal.

Most criticism of this passage focuses on two obvious features: on the one
hand, the use of a fourfold model of exegesis which derives from biblical
commentary; on the other, a distinction between how poets and how "theologians" take allegory, with Dante claiming to follow the poets. However,
in the rush to establish what Dante "means" here, the peculiarities, the ambiguities, the confusions of the passage – which are its most telling features
from both the historical and the conceptual point of view – are frequently
glossed over – and in particular the importance of the examples given is not
well understood.

The first point to establish is that, while the most common references
to this passage suggest that it can tell us how Dante's poetry signifies, or
how Dante wishes us to believe his poetry signifies, it is in fact concerned
with explaining how Dante as prose commentator intends to explicate his
canzoni: in other words, it begins as a discussion not of "allegory" but of
"allegoresis." This confusion, however, is generated by the text itself. When
Dante says he does not take the allegorical sense(s) as the "theologians" do,
he seems to be referring to biblical exegetes, although "theologus" is also
sometimes used to refer to the human authors of the Bible. But when he says
he *does* take that sense as the "poets" do, he is clearly referring to writers
of poetry, not to its interpreters. In other words, he presents the distinction
between allegory and allegoresis, only to elide it. What allows this? The
fact that in *Convivio*, as against typical medieval examples of allegorical
commentary, Dante is both the glosser of poetry and its author. In other
words, the "confusion" is underpinned by an assumption that in glossing
the text he is simply making known his own intentions.

8 I.e., the first of the three allegorical senses.

A second point is that while the critical tradition would suggest that the passage is largely concerned with the allegorical sense(s), whether poetic or biblical, Dante in fact says that exposition must be *both* literal and allegorical, and spends a full half of the chapter explaining why it is that all understanding of the hidden senses depends directly upon first coming to grips with the letter. This emphasis is borne out in his subsequent practice. In books 2 and 3, both fifteen chapters long, ten chapters each are dedicated to expounding the letter, with only four and five respectively given over to allegorical exegesis, while book 4, which is as long as the other two put together (thirty chapters), is entirely taken up with literal interpretation. In other words, whether or not the textual surface may be considered a "beautiful lie," it is nonetheless the engine which generates all meanings. This second point, of course, is closely intertwined with the first: if the poet's intended allegory and the exegete's allegoresis are to coincide anywhere but in Dante's mind, the letter must serve as the mediator between them – indeed, the letter must, in some sense, already reveal what is by definition hidden.

Finally, but not briefly, we should consider the status of the illustrations that Dante offers of the "four senses." These are, again, typically taken to illustrate the difference between the allegories traditionally attributed to poetic texts (such as the moral and/or spiritual readings of Ovid and Virgil) and those produced in biblical exegesis. However, *both* the poetic and the biblical examples, and the collection of the three examples (illustrating the allegorical, the moral-tropological, and the anagogical senses respectively), are idiosyncratic and deeply problematic, and suggest that in bringing together these two traditions Dante ends up deforming and transforming both.

The most extraordinary, and least appreciated, of these examples is the first: that of the Ovidian Orpheus moving rocks and stones with his music, allegorized as the wise man who tames the ignorant with his voice. In the fourfold biblical scheme, this would be the Christological and/or ecclesiological sense (*quod credas*: "what you should believe"), on which the tropological (*quid agas*) and anagogical (*quo tendas*) senses are based – but though the text points to a difference of the Orphic example from theological intentions/interpretations, it does not specify in what that difference consists. At first glance, Dante's example seems to be a perfect illustration of the typical allegorization of poetic texts, which largely confines itself to uncovering a single hidden sense, usually "moral" in its applicability to the behavior of the reader.[9] This sense, logically speaking, should correspond to the second

9 Judson Allen, *The Ethical Poetics of the Later Middle Ages* (Toronto: University of Toronto Press, 1982).

of the three senses of biblical exegesis – the moral-tropological (what *you*, the Christian everyperson, should do) – rather than the first.

Further consideration, however, suggests that this is not so much an example as a "meta-example" of poetic allegory, a characteristically Dantean "allegory of allegory" in Martinez's felicitous phrase:[10] what we are presented with is *not* a lesson for the reader, but rather an illustration of how the poet-philosopher or poet-theologian goes about instilling such lessons through the power of his language. In other words, Orpheus allegorizes Dante as the poet whose beautiful verses will "delight, instruct, and move," in the Ciceronian formulation. Moreover, once we have recognized this departure from the standard "allegory of poets," we can also recognize an implicit assimilation to the Christological sense of biblical exegesis. In fact, Orpheus, because of his descent into and return from Hell, was often treated as a *figura Christi* in medieval allegorizations.[11] In the present context this means that the poet himself, in this case Dante, is the allegorical referent, where in the usual fourfold scheme it would be Christ. This does not mean, of course, that Dante is equating himself with God made flesh; it does mean that the separation between "allegory of poets" and "allegory of theologians" is breached in the very moment it is supposedly illustrated – and that this happens in the name of justifying Dante's ambitions for himself and his writings.

In exemplifying the first of the three allegorical senses, Dante uses a poetic text not a biblical one, and no *explicit* reference is made to how a "theologian" would treat this sense differently. In exemplifying the next two senses, exactly the reverse occurs: both are illustrated with reference to biblical texts (the Transfiguration; the Exodus) and the relationship to Dante's exegesis of his poems is not evident. Even so, this is by no means a straightforward use of the biblical model. Usually, illustrations of the biblical exegetical model begin with a single literal passage of the Bible and then show how all three allegorical senses proceed from it, as does the *Epistle to Cangrande* in illustrating the polysemous character of the *Commedia*:

[T]he first meaning is that which is conveyed by the letter, and the next is that which is conveyed by what the letter signifies; the former is called the literal, while the latter is called the allegorical or mystical. And for the better illustration of this method of exposition we may apply it to the following verses: "When Israel went out of Egypt, the house of Jacob from a people of

10 Ronald L. Martinez, "Allegory," in *The Dante Encyclopedia*, ed. Richard Lansing (New York: Garland, 2000), pp. 24–34.
11 John Block Friedman, *Orpheus in the Middle Ages* (Cambridge, MA: Harvard University Press, 1970).

strange language, Judah was his sanctuary, and Israel his dominion" (Psalm 113:1–2). For if we consider the letter alone, the thing signified to us is the going out of the children of Israel from Egypt in the time of Moses; if the allegory, our redemption through Christ is signified, if in the moral sense, the conversion of the soul from the sorrow and misery of sin to a state of grace is signified; if anagogical, the passage of the sanctified soul from the bondage of the corruption of this world is signified.   (Par. 7)

Dante, on the other hand, illustrates each sense with a different literal text: first, Orpheus; then, for the moral-tropological sense, the Transfiguration of Christ; finally, for the anagogical sense, the same passage from Psalms which is then used for all four senses in the *Epistle*.

From this peculiar configuration, one might infer that Dante did not (yet) understand the logic of the three allegorical senses in biblical exegesis, where the first entails the second, which entails the third: the example of Christ in the first allegorical sense gives rise to an *imitatio Christi* in the life of the individual which in turn, if successful, gives rise to the salvation of "the sanctified soul." Another way of construing it, however, would be that Dante is deliberately blurring the conceptual boundaries between the two modes of allegory and/or attempting to compensate in some way for his initial substitution of a classical text and a "moral" sense for the usual Christological gloss. This would help to account for the oddity of the second example, where a literally Christological text (Christ unveiling himself as the Messiah in the company of the Old Testament prophets and the three most favored Apostles – Peter, James, and John) is made to yield up an allegorical meaning that seems more Machiavellian than biblical, signifying "that we should have few companions in our most secret undertakings." Indeed, this example could also be read meta-poetically, since it provides an implicit justification for the obscurity of allegorical discourse. Only the final, anagogical, example represents an unproblematic reproduction of the biblical model.

Having examined each of Dante's illustrations of the three allegorical *sensus*, it is tempting to posit an ascending "typology" (in the modern classificatory meaning) of examples: one strictly "according to the poets"; one that mingles elements of poetic and biblical exegesis; and one that keeps strictly to the paradigm of "i teologi," even apparently referring to the signifying structure of an *allegoria in factis* (allegory of facts), which is characteristic of God's writing alone ("by the [literally] signified things, signifying the supernal things").[12] Even here, however, the "allegory of theologians" is

---

12 Jean Pépin, "La Théorie dantesque de l'allégorie, entre le *Convivio* et la *Lettera a Cangrande*," in Michelangelo Picone and Tatiana Crivelli, eds., *Dante, mito e poesia: atti del*

immediately deflected back toward Dante's allegory and allegoresis, because it becomes the occasion for the insistence, noted earlier, that allegorical interpretation, of whatever kind, must begin from the letter.

One way of understanding what I have described here is as a confused "hybrid" of two types of allegory,[13] a transitional moment in Dante's movement from standard poetic allegory toward the theological allegory implemented in the *Commedia* and described in the *Epistle to Cangrande*. My emphasis, however, is different. Wherever Dante's engagement with the allegorical tradition would ultimately take him, and it is not so easy to say exactly where that is, *Convivio* 2.1 serves purposes that point more or less directly toward modern notions of authorial self-reflexivity and intentionality and of the textual letter as the basis for all interpretation.

There is no doubt that both the *Commedia* and the *Epistle* go further down the road to imposing the categories of biblical typology and Christian exegesis on the vernacular poetry of a secular writer. Even then, however, it is the exceptional and idiosyncratic elements that stand out, and beg to be understood in historical perspective (as against the endless wrangling over whether the "holy poem" claims biblical status and literal truthfulness, or not). On the one hand, it is surely significant that the *Commedia* can be said to express both the moral-tropological and anagogical senses not allegorically at all, but *literally*: in Dante-pilgrim's *imitatio Christi* (descending into Hell on Good Friday, emerging to the light on Easter morning); in Dante-poet's representation of "the state of the souls after death."[14] On the other, in the midst of that "literal" journey Dante presents us with his representation of Geryon which is not only an allegory of the sin of fraud, but also the embodiment of poetic allegory: "truth hidden beneath a beautiful lie" only barely displaced into "that truth with a lying face" (*Inferno* 16.124). Similarly, the famous paragraph 7 of the *Epistle to Cangrande* claims not, as is usually argued, to describe the "mode of signifying" of the *Commedia*, but rather to exemplify the meaning of the word "polysemous." The *Epistle*'s gloss on *Paradiso* then makes no attempt at all to apply the model of biblical exegesis: rather, it is resolutely, explicitly, *literal*.

secondo Seminario dantesco internazionale, Monte Verità, Ascona, 23–27 giugno 1997 (Florence: Cesati, 1999), pp. 51–68.

13 Joseph Mazzeo, *Medieval Cultural Tradition in Dante's "Comedy"* (Ithaca: Cornell University Press, 1958); Robert Hollander, *Allegory in Dante's "Commedia"* (Princeton: Princeton University Press, 1969).

14 Ascoli, "Access."

10

STEPHANIE GIBBS KAMATH AND RITA COPELAND

Medieval secular allegory: French and English

Behind the *Roman de la Rose* lies a tradition of philosophical allegory. The *Rose* in turn inspired a tradition of secular allegory, in narrative and lyric forms, across Europe. This essay will focus on French poetry of the fourteenth and early fifteenth centuries, and the extension of these poetic conventions into England. Both Guillaume de Lorris and Jean de Meun, the authors of the two parts of the *Rose*, experiment with the claims of philosophical truth in poetry. In their hands, vernacular poetry rose to new heights of ambition: the *Rose* combines classical myth with philosophical reflection, dream vision with allegorical interpretation, and erotic story with cosmological themes.[1] Their experiments provoked innovative responses in the vernacular secular allegory produced for the aristocratic milieus of France and England. One key element that distinguishes this new vernacular tradition from earlier Latin allegory is the role of its singular first-person voice. In the *Roman de la Rose* and the allegories that followed it, this voice is identified with the historical writer, not only narrating as writer but acting as a character, participating in the drama that structures the narrative. While these writers are interested in the experience of love and desire, they increasingly focus on love for its relation to artistic production or as a pretext for evaluating other forms of worldly or spiritual wisdom, as an opening for ethical, philosophical, or political debate. Not only the beginning of love but its ending, through age or loss of the beloved, becomes a subject for figuration.

The shifting role of love in vernacular poetry is clearly visible in the works of Guillaume de Machaut (*c.* 1300–77), master poet and composer of the fourteenth century. Machaut never sought to recreate the encyclopedic span of the conjoined *Rose* in a single work. Instead he used allegory to dramatize the connections among the many works of his large corpus, which

---

1 On medieval philosophical allegory see the essay above by Jon Whitman; on the *Roman de la Rose*, see the essay above by Kevin Brownlee.

encompassed ten narrative poems and four more compact *dits*, an extensive collection of short lyrics, twenty motets, and a polyphonic setting of the Mass.[2] Machaut writes a prologue for his oeuvre in which he depicts his formation as a writer through a dialogue with the mythic god of Love and the personification of Nature. Nature replaces the role played by the human beloved in the *Rose* – she is the lady whom Machaut serves. Significantly, the first of the children/gifts Nature offers her servant is *Scens*, which can mean knowledge, sense, science, or craft. Machaut accepts *Scens*, together with rhetoric and music, by making a pledge to use these three to produce well-ordered *dits amoureus* (love poetry) (II.6).[3] Immediately following, he depicts the entrance, exhortation, and emotional gifts of Love. In the prologue, then, knowledge precedes feeling, and both Love and Nature ask for textual, rather than sexual, production. This focus on the poet's own artistic development goes beyond the terms of the erotic narrative in the *Rose*, as Machaut valorizes understanding and poetic skill over actual erotic engagement.

The prominent place of music, along with knowledge and rhetoric, in Machaut's vision of production represents another expansion beyond the erotic narrative model of Guillaume de Lorris and Jean de Meun. Machaut's lyric-infused allegories recall not only Boethius' *Consolation of Philosophy* (with its prose and lyric form), but also his *De institutione musica* (*Fundamentals of Music*). In this way Machaut's work displays an affinity with Jean Renart's thirteenth-century *Roman de la Rose*, an innovative combination of narrative allegory with inset songs that shares the earlier allegory's title.[4] In practice, Machaut's allegories maintain the interest in musical expression found in the earliest complete French translation of Ovid's *Ars amatoria*: this translation prominently included song refrains in its glossing commentary.

But even while Machaut's work absorbs other cultural influences, he still maintains some crucial thematic links with Jean de Meun's *Rose*. One of these is the image of Love as a patron for textual production, which the *Rose* itself had borrowed from Ovid's *Amores* 3.9. Machaut's use of this figure suggests how important Ovid was to writers wanting to announce their own poetic lineage as well as claim authority on love. Here, in imitation of Ovidian poetics, the mythic god takes the role of the writer's patron. Within

---

2 On the importance of the author-centered collection, see Ardis Butterfield, *Poetry and Music in Medieval France* (Cambridge: Cambridge University Press, 2002), and Kevin Brownlee, *Poetic Identity in Guillaume de Machaut* (Madison: University of Wisconsin Press, 1989).
3 Guillaume de Machaut, *Prologue*, in *Oeuvres*, ed. E. Hoepffner, 3 vols. (Paris: Firmin-Didot, 1908–21).
4 See Butterfield, *Poetry and Music*, and Sylvia Huot, "Guillaume de Machaut and the Consolation of Poetry," *Modern Philology*, 100 (2002), 169–195.

his allegorical poems, however, Machaut figures his patrons in the role his prologue attributes to the god of Love, exhorting and evaluating love lyrics with the aid of supporting personifications.

In his *Dit de la fonteine amoureuse* (*The Fountain of Love*) (c. 1360), Machaut deploys allegory to celebrate the literature of love, its production and patronage. In this allegory, Machaut returns to the *Rose*'s vision of the *locus amoenus* ("pleasant place," an idealized setting for love) surrounding the fountain of Narcissus. But Machaut's narrator enters the garden not guided by a personification within a dream but hand in hand with the noble lord to whom he has already pledged his service. Machaut identifies the pair as himself and his patron, the Duke of Berry, through a game of poetic anagrams at the opening. The joint artistic production of these two men, rather than erotic experience, is the primary significance of Machaut's fountain, which displays not only the lifelike ivory statue of Narcissus, but also the epic Trojan story in marble. Instead of either man drinking at the fountain, as happens in the *Rose*, the Duke explains that Pygmalion constructed the fountain with the help of Cupid to honor Venus.[5] In allegorizing the labor of these mythic creators, Machaut rewrites the individual desire for the female beloved as the joint service of poet and patron. Thus he frames love and royal lineage together. The patron replaces the god of Love as the lord of the allegorical garden, and the demand of the narrator's heart is replaced by a request for a textual creation to unburden the heart of his patron. The "grant merveille" (great marvel) (1542) in this allegory is not love, but rather the narrator's perfect and pre-produced record of the patron's love.[6] The narrator and patron also dream together, wrapped in each other's embrace, and the lady who appears in their dream combines their roles, as she composes lyrics and grants the duke her ring. Machaut's allegory thus recombines elements of the *Rose* – the garden, the retelling of myth, the dream – to envision a new *translatio* of love and chivalry in his fertile vision of the artistic relationship between himself and his patron. Machaut's last great work, the *Voir dit* (*True Story*) (c. 1362–65), features the narrator's most extended performance as the lover-protagonist, but even here the use of myth, personified figures, and narrative arc produce more reflection on the experience of writing than of love. The narrator's opening discomfort arises not from love but his lack of writing inspiration. The lady who re-inspires him loves him for his literary skill rather than for his person

5 For study of the fountain's significance and the mythic tradition, see Renate Blumenfeld-Kosinski, *Reading Myth: Classical Mythology and Its Interpretations in Medieval French Literature* (Stanford: Stanford University Press, 1997), p. 151.
6 Guillaume de Machaut, *Le livre de la fontaine amoureuse*, ed. Jacqueline Cerquiglini-Toulet (Paris: Stock, 1993).

(he is depicted as exactly the sort to be excluded from the *Rose*'s garden of Love).[7] The work finds its culmination in the consummation of their textual relation, the book's creation, rather than in a vision of sexual union.

Jean Froissart (*c.* 1337–1404), best known today for his prose chronicles, consciously imitates Machaut in several allegorical poems. Also influenced by the *Rose*, Froissart nonetheless expresses his longing for literary service far more memorably than his erotic desire. Froissart innovatively recombines *Rose* personifications, Ovidian mythology, and ethical/political discourse in *La Prison amoureuse* (*The Prison of Love*) (1372). This work echoes the title of Machaut's *Fonteine amoureuse* as well as its internal imagery. Froissart opens his allegory with his first-person narrator's meditation on two texts – a maxim on achieving worth through service he attributes to Aristotle and the scriptural command to Moses that he love the Lord with all his heart (11–12).[8] The narrator immediately glosses the command to love as a command to serve. With the aid of Aristotelian philosophy, he interprets the relation of Moses and God as the image of his service to the mythic god of Love; here he renders scriptural reference as mere marginal commentary on authoritative emotional experience. Froissart further inverts discourse relations as the narrator explains his devotion to Love's service by example of the loyal service that was given to two historical rulers, Alexander the Great and John of Bohemia. The persons of scriptural and political history thus become types fulfilled by the mythic god.

Ultimately, Froissart represents a relationship between two male lovers, the narrator-poet and his noble *ami*, that is far more developed than the relation of either to his respective female beloved. Early one morning, the narrator enters a garden where the image of a single rose captures his attention. The rose is actually the seal on a letter sent to the narrator by a man who has assumed the name of Rose and its image to represent his beloved. The narrator declares Rose more or less his equal in love even if Rose's concealed identity should turn out to be the Duke of Brabant (811), Froissart's patron. The Rose seen in the garden, but as a sign on a page, thus represents the patron and his beloved; but this is also an unmistakable allusion to the beloved and the text of the *Roman de la Rose*. Froissart's narrator underscores the complexity of signature: he adopts the name *Flos* (Latin for flower), but he defers explaining its significance and instead visually describes his own newly crafted seal ring which bears the image of a small *marguerite* flower (daisy). Like Machaut, Froissart also composes lyric poetry to ladies

---

7 Machaut depicts himself as an "elderly, weak, cowardly, unattractive, one-eyed, non-noble clerk," Blumenfeld-Kosinski, *Reading Myth*, p. 155.

8 Jean Froissart, *La Prison amoureuse*, ed. Laurence de Looze (New York: Garland, 1994).

represented as *marguerites*; this sign, like Froissart's Rose seal, refers not only to the beloved, but to a tradition of text. This self-conscious literary exchange of signatures between two poets of love is another way in which they can claim that their work is equal in status to the *Rose*. Froissart also rivals Ovid, composing at the Rose's request the pseudo-classical myth of Pynotheüs. Rose glosses the myth with an allegorical dream of battling personifications that reflects the experiences of the Duke of Brabant in the 1371 Battle of Baesweiler.[9] The allegory concludes with the narrator expanding on the intertwined meanings of both myth and dream in relentlessly figurative terms. Pynotheüs is Desire, for example, and the ornamented room of the dreamer represents the sweet thoughts furnishing his mind. Froissart's daring recombination of the modes of allegorical discourse to serve the vernacular composer and his aristocratic patron thus not only competes with Latin philosophical and erotic discourse but repeatedly inverts both commentary and narrative traditions.

Eustache Deschamps (*c.* 1346–1406), famed for his division of poetic and musical composition in *L'Art de dictier* (*The Art of Composing*) (*c.* 1392), never completed an extended allegorical narrative, but created an enormous collection of *ballades* and other lyrics, richly varied in subject and tone, which offer a kaleidoscopic view of court life, university experience, and aristocratic politics. Deschamps' lyrics draw constantly but not synthetically upon the personifications, myths, dream frames, and landscapes arising in the wake of the *Rose* tradition. His contemporaries praised him for his moralizing thought, and in his longest piece of narrative allegory, the unfinished late fourteenth-century *Miroer de mariage* (*Mirror of Marriage*), Deschamps envisions personified counselors debating the conjugal rather than erotic quest. Deschamps borrows rather more from Scriptures and patristic, even mystic thought than his predecessors, but the moments when he engages the comedy of the obscene or delves into mundane detail are equally extreme in comparison.

It is common to use the term "allegory" to talk about practice and outlook in the poetry of Geoffrey Chaucer (*c.* 1340–1400). Sometimes this is intended in a fairly strict technical sense, as in the encoding of contemporary political events, or to consider localized personifications (as in some of the short poems, notably "Complaint unto Pity," "Complaint to his Lady," and the Boethian lyric "Fortune"), or to designate clear references in Chaucer's texts to allegorical interpretation (e.g., the end of the *Nun's Priest's Tale*: "Taketh the fruyt, and lat the chaf be stille," Fragment VII,

---

9 See Claude Thiry, "Allégorie et histoire dans la *Prison amoureuse* de Froissart," *Studi Francesi*, 61–62 (1977), 15–29.

3443) or, conversely, to the literal sense (*Prologue* to the *Legend of Good Women*: "For myn entent is, or I fro yow fare, / The naked text in English to declare / of many a story," G 85–87).[10] Perhaps the most radical and long-influential reading of Chaucer's works in terms of sustained allegory was D. W. Robertson's *Preface to Chaucer*, which argued for a universal medieval Christian aesthetic of writing (and reading) for doctrine, for inner or deeper spiritual truth. The ultimate effect of such reading is to place Chaucer (along with the *Rose* tradition) in a direct line reaching back to Augustine and to even earlier esoteric traditions.[11] Chaucer is also often linked more generally with philosophical allegory, stressing the intellectual sources of his writing and his continuous conversation with several traditions: not only the *Rose* (especially as a resource for natural philosophy) and Dante's *Commedia*, but also Neoplatonist mythography and the tradition of Boethius' *Consolation of Philosophy*.[12] In a different vein, the notion of Chaucer as "allegorist" has been used to point forward to modern conceptions of allegory (derived, e.g., from Walter Benjamin or Paul de Man) as the condition of textual and hermeneutical opacity, and the sign of linguistic fragmentation or partiality.[13]

But apart from such a multiplicity of theoretical models for allegory in Chaucer, there are basic and important questions that still persist about Chaucer's literary response to his immediate inheritance from the French tradition. On the one hand, Chaucer looks back to the French poets in his use of the traditional elements of allegorical narrative: the dream frame, the allegorical landscape, mythographical narrative, and even the incorporation of the patron (or patron figure) into the fictional frame, as in *Book of the Duchess* and *Legend of Good Women*. But on the other hand, to what extent can we call Chaucer an allegorist in the strict sense of those French predecessors to whom he was so deeply indebted in many ways?

10 Chaucer quotations are from *The Riverside Chaucer*, 3rd edn., ed. Larry D. Benson (Boston: Houghton Mifflin, 1987). On political allegory in Chaucer, see Ann W. Astell, *Political Allegory in Late Medieval England* (Ithaca, NY: Cornell University Press, 1999), pp. 94–116.

11 D. W. Robertson, *A Preface to Chaucer: Studies in Medieval Perspectives* (Princeton: Princeton University Press, 1962); John V. Fleming, *The Roman de la Rose: A Study in Allegory and Iconography* (Princeton: Princeton University Press, 1969).

12 For example, Sheila Delany, *Chaucer's House of Fame: The Poetics of Skeptical Fideism* (Chicago: University of Chicago Press, 1972); Kathryn L. Lynch, *The High Medieval Dream Vision: Poetry, Philosophy, and Literary Form* (Stanford: Stanford University Press, 1988).

13 For example, James Paxson, *Poetics of Personification* (Cambridge: Cambridge University Press, 1994); Joel Fineman, "The Structure of Allegorical Desire," in Stephen J. Greenblatt, ed., *Allegory and Representation* (Baltimore: Johns Hopkins University Press, 1981), pp. 26–60.

While critical interpretation of Chaucer's dream poems has never remained stable, the facts of his sources are clear. The *Book of the Duchess*, the earliest of his dream poems, derives much of its setting and circumstances from Froissart's *Paradys d'amours* (*Paradise of Love*); the Ceyx and Alcyone episode from Machaut's rewriting of Ovid in the *Dit de la fonteine amoureuse*; the dreamer-narrator's overhearing of the Black Knight's complaint from Machaut's *Jugement dou Roy de Behaingne* (*Judgment of the King of Bohemia*); and the themes of the complaint from Machaut's *Remede de fortune* (*Remedy against Fortune*). The *House of Fame*, in its grandest ambitions, is a meditation on Dante (and Dante's mediation of Virgilian epic), and on the formal allegory of Petrarch's *Trionfi* (*Triumphs*) and Boccaccio's *Amorosa visione* (*Amorous Vision*). But its opening is also a response to the *Rose* and Guillaume de Lorris' mediation of the Macrobian analysis of dreams, their truthfulness, and their interpretability. The *Parliament of Fowls* takes its start from Macrobius (again) and the matter of Cicero's *Dream of Scipio* (which had survived with Macrobius' commentary), and then proceeds to the next dimension of that legacy, the cosmographical allegory of Alan of Lille's *Plaint of Nature*. The *Prologue* to the *Legend of Good Women* returns to the earliest fields of Chaucer's literary inheritance, the French courtly poetry of the fourteenth century: the *marguerite* themes of Machaut, Deschamps, and Froissart in which the beloved is represented as a daisy (see p. 139 above), as well as Machaut's "court of love" in the *Jugement*.

As clear as the sources are, the question remains how we are to read Chaucer's works against the foregoing allegorical traditions. Chaucer's ambiguity about the interpretability or even meaningfulness of dreams in the *Book of the Duchess* (270–90) might suggest a resistance to the terms of allegorical narrative; does the dream fiction (integument) necessarily answer to a higher philosophical or spiritual reality, or is it simply generated by the narrator's Ovidian reading?[14] Yet the *Book of the Duchess* certainly harks back to the rich context of French patronage allegory. Like Froissart's *Prison*, the narrative of the *Book of the Duchess* glosses the reading of a myth with a dream that suggests the patron's historical experience and opens with the dream's narrator in another richly decorated room. But this room visualizes the mind of the narrator, not the patron, and the decorations reveal thoughts more explicitly textual than emotional (e.g., walls depicting scenes from the *Rose* and windows depicting scenes from the story of Troy).

14 Suzanne Conklin Akbari, *Seeing Through the Veil: Optical Theory and Medieval Allegory* (Toronto: University of Toronto Press, 2004), pp. 187–88; see also J. Stephen Russell, *The English Dream Vision: Anatomy of a Form* (Columbus: Ohio State University Press, 1988), pp. 74–81.

The *House of Fame* might be seen to take such ambiguity even further, to meditate on the impossibility of giving figurative expression to the multivalent truths of a transcendent philosophy and of cosmic and epic history.[15] But nevertheless this meditation on the impossible takes the classic form of a visionary journey that holds out – even if only parodically – the promise of a fullness of meaning – if only about the incompleteness of historical and textual record – to be revealed beneath the shifting figurative surface. The *Parliament of Fowls* clearly acknowledges its debt to the apotheosis of *Natura* in twelfth-century Neoplatonic poetry and philosophy, but it also enfolds that debt in a broader response to the *Roman de la Rose* and Jean de Meun's "natural" critique of the brittle erotic allegory of Guillaume de Lorris. The finale takes this further, substituting the ekphrastic representation of the birds in Alan of Lille's *Plaint of Nature* with vocal debate infused with class humor.[16] Here Chaucer combines two of his sources, Alan's *Plaint* and Jean de Meun's *Rose*: he foists Nature's lamentation about social division, from Jean's *Rose*, upon the birds who, in Alan's poem, emblematize Nature. Thus he uses one allegorical source to gloss – open the meaning of – the other.

In the *Prologue* to the *Legend of Good Women*, the mythographical narrative is focused inward, to illuminate the shape of Chaucer's own poetic career. Even figurative and interpretive categories are blurred: Alceste is the *marguerite* inclining towards the sun; she is a mythographic type of Love but also of sacred sacrifice; and even as daisy she blurs the rhetorical boundaries between the trope "allegory" (otherness) and metaphor (similitude).[17] Chaucer's Alceste, interceding on the narrator's behalf with a god of Love who is harshly critical of Chaucer's own forays into love poetry (his translation of the *Rose*, his story of Criseyde), is a hybrid figure who represents Chaucer's skill in remastering classical myth as well as the "daisy" worship of French contemporaries like Froissart and Machaut. Chaucer, like the writers of the *Rose* and their successors, uses the intersection of myth and dream allegory to direct attention to the value and authority of his poetry in relation to his predecessors. Yet he conspicuously conscripts the

---

15 Akbari, *Seeing Through the Veil*, pp. 205–10; see also Christopher Baswell, *Virgil in Medieval England: Figuring the Aeneid from the Twelfth Century to Chaucer* (Cambridge: Cambridge University Press, 1995), chapter 6.

16 Cf. Maureen Quilligan, "Allegory, Allegoresis, and the Deallegorization of Language: The *Roman de la Rose*, the *De planctu Naturae*, and the *Parliament of Foules*," in Morton W. Bloomfield, ed., *Allegory, Myth, and Symbol* (Cambridge, MA: Harvard University Press, 1981), pp. 163–86.

17 Akbari, *Seeing Through the Veil*, pp. 178–84; see also Peter W. Travis, "Chaucer's Heliotropes and the Poetics of Metaphor," *Speculum* 72 (1997), 399–427.

tradition of allegory to his own purposes, embedding within his responses new and always productive ambiguities about the capacities and limitations of allegory as literary form.

John Gower's *Confessio amantis* (*Confession of a Lover*) (1386–90) also takes its force from the philosophical and erotic traditions of earlier centuries. It carries over distinctive traces of Latin and French narrative allegories. It features the figures of Venus and especially Genius, both composites from Alan of Lille and Jean de Meun. As in the *Rose*, the Lover (Amans) is the first-person narrator of his own amorous quest. Indeed, the most frequent colophon to the *Confessio* draws special attention to its focus on love, distinguishing this poem from Gower's other major figurative works, the Latin *Vox clamantis* (*Voice of One Crying*) and the French *Speculum hominis* (or *Mirour de l'omme*) (*Mirror of Humankind*). But the Lover of *Confessio amantis* is revealed, at the end, to be John Gower himself (8:2321, 2908), and someone too old for love. Unlike the lover of Guillaume's *Rose*, Gower as Amans ultimately stands outside his amorous subject matter: not only is he too old, but he has seen too much political disruption, and he positions himself at the vestigial end of a literary tradition rather than at its origin. He has to abandon that tradition in favor of the more pressing ethical matter of saving his soul through penance, praying for the peace, and recovering his cultural memory through books where "vertu moral duelleth" (8:2925).[18]

If Gower's work refuses the erotic invitation of the *Roman de la Rose*, it also circumvents the structural mechanics of narrative allegory in a way that tells us a great deal about how that tradition could be received and processed. Gower's *Confessio amantis* works the pre-conditions and the effects of allegorizing without investing very much in the actual dynamics of narrative allegory. It uses key elements associated with the traditions of philosophical and erotic allegory, but it seems to forgo allegorizing itself in favor of the end product of late medieval integumental reading: the moral truth that is understood to lie beneath the fictive surface.

While the *Confessio amantis* has much in common with contemporary vernacular frame narratives (*Decameron, Canterbury Tales*), it also has very strong generic affinities with Ovidian anthologies: the *Metamorphoses* and the *Heroides*. And here lies a key to the allegorical underpinnings of Gower's work. By the late Middle Ages, readers would be likely to encounter Ovid or other anthologies of classical myth through allegorized commentaries and glosses. Such collections present a "moralized" Ovid or (more generally) classical fable, the product of reading the fiction integumentally,

---

18 *The Complete Works of John Gower*, ed. G. C. Macauley, vols. 2–3 (Oxford: Clarendon Press, 1901).

that is, "translating" plots and characters into the moral or philosophical equivalents for which they supposedly stand. In addition to late antique and medieval allegorizing mythography such as Fulgentius' *Mythologies* and the Vatican Mythographers, a learned reader of the fourteenth century would have available an array of recent and contemporary sources: Arnulf of Orléans' allegorizing commentaries on Ovid and Lucan (twelfth century); John of Garland's *Integumenta Ovidii* (early thirteenth century); and from the first half of the fourteenth century, Ovidian commentaries by Giovanni del Virgilio, John Ridewall, Pierre Bersuire, and others.

Like the mythographers, Gower combines narration of the story and moralizing commentary. But unlike his mythographic models, Gower does not directly or explicitly engage in the mechanics of allegorical exegesis, that is, of stating "this signifies that." The procedure that produces significative equivalence has been absorbed, assimilated, one might say sublimated, and what remains is the moralized application. Thus (among countless examples) the story of Deianira and Nessus is taken as an illustration of one aspect of the sin of envy, deceit or "Falsesemblant": "It oghte yive a gret conceipte / To warne alle other of such deceipte" (2:2311–12); and the story of Pygmalion is treated as a counter-example of the vice of sloth, because Pygmalion was so persistent in his pleas that he prompted Venus to bring the statue to life (4:437–41). Thus we might think of the *Confessio amantis* as a "post-allegorical" anthology, a work structured not as continuous allegorical narrative (like the *Rose*), but as a compilation of moralized myths and fables that emphasizes the conceptual relations that link the narratives together. Such conceptual understandings and moral truths are the effect or end product of a dynamic exegetical process that Gower's mythographic sources would have featured, but which Gower's own text does not perform for us.

Christine de Pizan (*c.* 1364–1430), the first professional woman writer in French, produced her own collection of one hundred retold myths, the *Epistre Othea* (*Epistle of Othea*) (*c.* 1399), united as the epistle of her invented goddess Othea rather than through an amorous framework. By contrast, her major narrative allegories use myth to craft a landscape and setting for a first-person voice identified with the name of the writer. These narratives claim a new literary lineage for the vernacular writer of allegory, rivaling the influence of the *Rose*, a poem fiercely debated in the letters she wrote and collected as the *Querelle de la Rose* (*Quarrel of the* Rose) (*c.* 1402). The concern with female identity is one motivation for this new lineage, most visible in her *Cité des dames* (*City of Ladies*) (*c.* 1404–5), which depicts its narrator, advised by personified virtues, triumphantly constructing a utopian city of women, combining mythology and hagiography in founding narratives. But Christine's interests in personal gender and philosophical thought also mingle productively in the *Mutacioun de fortune* (*Mutation of Fortune*) (1400–3), recounting the narrator's service in the court of Fortune, including her Teiresian transformation into a male writer. The connection is more explicit in the *Avision Christine* (*Christine's Vision*) (1405), which contains both the largest amount of biographical detail and Christine's most extensive rewriting of Boethian philosophy, as its preface explains, its significance operates on three levels, relevant to the individual, to the kingdom of France, and to the cosmic order. The *Chemin de long estude* (*Path of Long Study*) (*c.* 1402–3) deserves particular attention for its displacement of the *Rose*'s allegorical influence, being the first sustained French response to Dante's *Commedia*. Christine's narrator establishes overtly that her guide is not Ovid's Pallas but Virgil's Sibyl after a moment of visual confusion; the narrator is a lover, but she loves not the rose but *long estude* (long study), a translation from Dante's opening greeting to Virgil in the *Inferno*. The fountain the narrator beholds in her dream as the font of poetic inspiration is not the *Rose* fountain of Narcissus but the Helicon – Christine's muses, so to speak, are not drowning but waving. The Sibyl, Italian like Christine in both her ancient birthplace and literary antecedents, is not only Christine's guide to the inspiring fountain (and a cosmic tour) but also her patron figure, handing her precious jewels and entrusting her with a message for the French court. Like Machaut's *Fontaine* narrator, Christine's writings produce what her patrons require before the request is even voiced: she has perfectly recorded the debate between Riches, Nobility, Chivalry, and Wisdom, ready to refer it to the judgment of Charles V. The creation of the allegory is thus again located in the person of the poet's dedicatee, although its substance is transformed from the personal grief of love to the concern for public welfare. The transformation is also mirrored in Christine's narrator. She is the lady who has lost the perfect love in the death of her husband, like the ultimately triumphant lover imagined in Machaut's *Jugement* allegories or the mythic Alcyone. But Christine's allegory alleges not her personal sorrow but public misfortune as the distress that sends her beyond her late-night reading of Boethius' *Consolation of Philosophy* into the dream of the mythic fountain, the debate of the court of personifications, and, ultimately, the king's literary service.[19]

Thomas Hoccleve (*c.* 1366–1426), by contrast, gives far greater place to his personal misfortune in figuration and is aptly famed as the "first

---

19 Much of Christine de Pizan's corpus is represented in *The Selected Writings of Christine de Pizan*, ed. and trans. Renate Blumenfeld-Kosinski with Kevin Brownlee, trans. (New York: Norton, 1997); see further references there.

autobiographical poet" of the English language.[20] His three major works, *La Male regle (The Unruly Regimen)* (*c.* 1406), the *Regiment of Princes* (*c.* 1411), and the compilation of texts known as the *Series* (*c.* 1419), employ a first-person voice that assumes the name of the poet and offers an unparalleled wealth of self referential detail, expressing personal and topical concerns through a language of "small-scale personification," invoking abstract or imagined figures as characters, although their interaction never develops into an extended, continuous narrative.[21] The *Series* includes a translation of a short allegory by Christine de Pizan but sets the entire tradition of first-person allegorical narratives involving myth and personifications in opposition to universalizing spiritual allegoresis through a dialogue between the narrator and a friend, who proposes general moralizing interpretations for the additional tales the narrator translates. Hoccleve's prolific contemporary, John Lydgate (*c.* 1371–1449), more closely imitates the structure and images of dream allegories from the Chaucerian canon in his "The Complaint of the Black Knight" and "The Temple of Glass," short visionary narratives at times included in early prints of Chaucer's works.[22] Yet Lydgate's lengthy adaptations of historical chronicles and topical drama, often compared to the humanist and classicizing impulses of England's sixteenth-century Reformation, are also interfused with the medieval tradition of philosophical allegory mediated by the *Rose*: Lydgate's London mumming, for example, presents Fortune "lyche as þe Romans of þe Roose / Descyveþe hir, with-outen glose" being conquered by the English king Henry V, in the company of personified virtues.[23] The late medieval tradition of secular allegory in the vernacular played a highly visible role in defining both writer and patron in the courts of France and England, lingering long in aristocratic audiences' expectations.

20 Jennifer E. Bryan, "Hoccleve, the Virgin, and the Politics of Complaint," *PMLA*, 117 (2002), 1172–87 (1185).

21 A. C. Spearing's phrase in his *Medieval to Renaissance in English Poetry* (Cambridge: Cambridge University Press, 1985), p. 119.

22 On Lydgate's use of the tradition, see Susan Bianco, "A Black Monk in the Rose Garden," *Chaucer Review*, 34 (1999) 60–68, and Larry Scanlon, "Lydgate's Poetics: Laureation and Domesticity in the *Temple of Glass*," in Larry Scanlon and James Simpson, eds., *John Lydgate: Poetry, Culture, and Lancastrian England* (Notre Dame: University of Notre Dame Press, 2006), pp. 61–97.

23 John Lydgate, "A Mumming at London," *The Minor Poems of John Lydgate, Part II: Secular Poems*, ed. H. N. MacCracken (Oxford: Oxford University Press, 1934), pp. 682–91, line 167.

11

NICOLETTE ZEEMAN

Medieval religious allegory: French and English

In the second recension of Guillaume de Deguileville's *Pelerinage de la vie humaine* (translated by John Lydgate) the narrator cannot understand his allegorical pilgrim's bag of faith and staff of good hope until Grace Dieu tells him that she will "Bothe thyn Eyen take awey . . . And in thyn Erys I shal hem sette." This surprising course of action is an allusion to St. Paul's statement that "faith comes by hearing": the physical senses may be unreliable, but for Paul and Deguileville hearing connotes both a literal and a figural "hearing" of the "word" of God – and the imaginative, internal "seeing" this brings. After an extended explanation by Grace Dieu, the narrator tells us, "Myn eyen two she gan translate / Into myn Eryn, ther they stood."[1]

This bizarre sequence involves several mutually commenting discourses; its narrative is "glossed" by the doctrinal proposition that "faith comes from hearing," but the doctrinal proposition is also "glossed" by the strange and unnatural images and narrative – faith is counter-intuitive and contrary to the order of nature. Further allegorical commentary is provided by the informed words of Grace Dieu and the uninformed words of the narrator, while the rest of the narrative tells us about the position from which they speak: such allegorical speakers represent and reify within the narrative the very business of interpretation. This passage is also a direct riposte to, and commentary upon, the secular love allegory on which the whole of the *Pelerinage* is modelled, the *Roman de la Rose*: in the *Roman*, eyes are the dominant sense and the narrator finds love by looking in the optically enhancing crystal(s) of the pool of Narcissus; in Deguileville "seeing" has to occur in the ears, the symbolic organ of revelation. Just as Grace Dieu

1 *The Pilgrimage of the Life of Man*, trans. John Lydgate, ed. F. J. Furnivall, 3 vols., EETS ES 77, 83, 92 (London, 1899, 1901, 1904), lines 6254–56, 6578–79; Romans 10:17; Susan K. Hagen, *Allegorical Remembrance: A Study Of The Pilgrimage Of The Life Of Man As A Medieval Treatise On Seeing And Remembering* (Athens: University of Georgia Press, 1990), pp. 1, 67–68, 118. Thanks to Jane Gilbert and Stephanie Kamath for their help and advice in the preparation of this piece.

"translates" eyes into ears, Deguileville "translates" secular, vernacular textuality to religious ends (on *translatio*, see below, p. 153). There is also an ironic or iconoclastic dimension to the Deguileville passage, with its implicit repudiation of natural seeing in favor of spiritual, "heard seeing": if allegory always works by juxtaposing unlike terms, religious allegory seems especially often to foreground the unlikeness and the possible discrepancies between the terms it brings together. This passage exemplifies several features found in later medieval vernacular religious allegory.

The discursive multiplicity we see here is underpinned by later medieval exegetical practice. Patristic scriptural commentary, still circulating independently and in compendia, models a variety of techniques for multiple reading, and these techniques develop and proliferate in the later Middle Ages.[2] The Bible is read literally/historically, morally/tropologically (for ethical exempla) and allegorically (as an extended metaphorical narration of events in the life of the soul, Christ or the Church, including final things); the distinctively Christian form of allegory, according to which both signified and allegorical signifier have a historical existence, is often called figural or typological.[3] If much later scriptural interpretation draws on a highly affective, mystical hermeneutic that goes back to Augustine and Gregory the Great, there is also from the thirteenth century onwards a burgeoning interest in literal and historical reading of the Bible. Commentary on Classical Latin poetry also reveals a concern, not just with "science" and philosophy, but also with history, ethics and psychology.[4] While such commentary practices involve analytical and preceptive forms of expression, therefore, they also include discourses that are ekphrastic and narratival – descriptions of inner mental life, "experience," image and action that in many respects replicate the ekphrastic and narratival forms of the texts under commentary.

Medieval "glossatory" modes of composition[5] mean that the impact of these commentary practices can be seen in many places, not least in vernacular religious allegorical narratives. Indeed, the formal multiplicity of scriptural and poetic commentary means that its influence is manifest not just in the internal glosses of these allegories, but also in their action, imagery

---

2 A. J. Minnis and A. B. Scott, eds., *Medieval Literary Theory and Criticism c.1100–c.1375. The Commentary-Tradition* (Oxford: Clarendon Press, 1988), chapters 3 and 6; Gilbert Dahan, *L'Exégèse chrétienne de la Bible en Occident médiéval. XIIe–XIVe siècle* (Paris: du Cerf, 1999).
3 Erich Auerbach, "Figura," in his *Scenes from the Drama of European Literature* (Manchester: Manchester University Press, 1984), pp. 11–76.
4 Minnis and Scott, eds., *Medieval Literary Theory*, pp. 200–7; chapters 1, 2, 4, 7 and 8.
5 Rita Copeland, *Rhetoric, Hermeneutics and Translation in the Middle Ages: Academic Traditions and Vernacular Texts* (Cambridge: Cambridge University Press, 1991).

and psychology. These allegories' discursive multiplicity is further enhanced by the fact that they draw on secular literature, both classical and vernacular; they are part of a general devotional and pastoral tendency to appropriate the inventive richness of non-religious literature. Like the use of the vernacular, this is typical of the laicizing, disseminatory intent of later medieval spirituality.

"Allegory" – whether allegoresis on another, separable text, or an allegorical narrative in which several mutually commenting discourses are embedded – is the site of intersection for two or more distinct discourses. As in the Deguileville, each discourse refigures, but also unpacks, the others involved. The allegorical text has been characterized as both concealing and revealing, a combination of myth and elucidation that plays "compositional and interpretative strains off each other."[6] However, such a description conforms to a long tradition according to which allegory is read through its explicatory discourses: these discourses, with their bias towards the analytical, abstractive or instructional, tend to lay claim to interpretative primacy, masking their partialities and discursive coloring by appearing to be "literal" or "direct," deflecting attention from their own rhetorical productivity by seeming merely to explicate other, anterior languages. As a result of this, allegory is often thought to be strongly intellectualist or didactic. But this is not necessarily the case. While the allegories that I discuss here do use an interpretative language to comment on their figures and narratives, they also use figures and narrative to comment on the language of interpretation.[7]

Although later medieval vernacular religious allegory does work towards some central synthetic meanings, it also often exploits discrepancies within its components. Not infrequently, it has a critical, ironic or iconoclastic dimension. Allegory has been described in terms of polysemy and the pun, which foregrounds its potential fragmentariness, its interest in thought-provoking conjunctions of things unlike. "Ironic" allegory also links dissimilar phenomena, and here the "absurd possibility of similarity" undermines complacent formulations, but also produces some of "the richest allegorical paradoxes . . . the transfiguration by Dante of the courtly ideal of love, Arthurian symbolism interlaid with Revelation symbolism . . . " The effects can be simultaneously "exhortatory" and "satirical."[8] There are

6 Jon Whitman, *Allegory: The Dynamics of an Ancient and Medieval Technique* (Cambridge, MA: Harvard University Press, 1987), p. 9.

7 Maureen Quilligan, *The Language of Allegory: Defining the Genre* (Ithaca: Cornell University Press, 1979), p. 53; Jill Mann, "Langland and Allegory," Morton W. Bloomfield Lectures on Medieval Literature 2 (Kalamazoo, MI: Medieval Institute Publications, 1992).

8 James Simpson, "Spirituality and Economics in Passus 1–7 of the B Text," *Yearbook of Langland Studies* 1 (1987), 83–103 (p. 93); also Quilligan, *Language of Allegory*, chapter 1;

many maneuvers by which such an internal split may be opened up: texts may resist interpretation, terms may prove equivocal or inadequate to the task at hand, protagonists may refuse to "hear," allegorical narratives may simply disintegrate. Such moments are often both distinctively challenging and revelatory.

An allegory dominated by the mode of allegoresis is the *Ovide moralise*, a 65,000-line, early fourteenth-century French re-narration and commentary on Ovid's *Metamorphoses*, whose anonymous author describes himself as "le maindre des menours," (?) "the least of the Franciscans."[9] Its narrative style and even content owe much to earlier French romance and go far beyond its interpolations (such as the *Philomela* attributed to Chrétien de Troyes); it has been claimed that even its ethical commentaries owe much to romance psychology, which means that both its retelling of classical stories and its commentary vividly engage with the secular.[10] Its exegesis is enormously varied. Some of it draws on traditions of historical and euhemeristic glossing for classical literature that stretch back to antiquity itself, and some of it draws on later ethical and philosophical medieval commentary on the classics. More unusually, some of it is overtly Christian, pastoral and preacherly. Although this is in itself not entirely new (Christian reading of Ovid begins with the twelfth-century commentary of Arnulf of Orléans), earlier commentaries tend to be sporadically Christian rather than systematically so, as the *Ovide moralisé* is.[11] Inserting elements of commentary into the narrative, the fourteenth-century text moves confidently from Ovidian myth to euhemeristic reading, to moral commentary, to Bible story and gloss; it makes no structural distinction between story and gloss, repeatedly using narrative to gloss narrative: "The fable and the holy scriptures . . . agree." (I, 1462–63). However, none of this prepares us for the famous incongruity of the text's Christian interpretations – the incestuous Myrrha or Venus, the pagan goddess of love, interpreted as the Virgin Mary, and Oedipus or the Emperor Augustus interpreted as Christ (X, 3748–809; XV, 7254–65; IX, 1932–47; XV, 7177–253). Nevertheless, although the text has long been

Edwin Honig, *Dark Conceit: The Making of Allegory* (London: Faber and Faber, 1959), pp. 129–30, 107.

9 *Ovide moralisé. Poème du commencement du quatorzième siècle*, ed. C. de Boer, 5 vols., Verhandelingen der Koninklijke Nederlandse Akademie van Wetenschappen, Afdeeling Letterkunde, Nieuwe Reeks, 15 (1), 21, 30 (3), 37 and 43 (Amsterdam: Johannes Müller, 1915–38), XV, 7432.

10 Marylène Possamaï-Pérez, *L'Ovide moralisé. Essai d'interprétation* (Paris: Champion, 2006), p. 404.

11 Paule Demats, *Fabula. Trois études de mythographie antique et médiévale* (Geneva: Droz, 1973).

criticized for its supposedly crude allegorical "impositions," recent scholarship suggests that such critiques will not hold up. The *Ovide moralisé* "romance" retellings of Ovid are subtle and in many cases elaborated, sometimes so as to enhance their aptitude for moralization, but often so as to enhance their "Ovidian" and "romance" effects:[12] instead of being deaf to the contrast between these materials and their moral and Christian readings, this author highlights them.

He elaborates Ovid's already extended description of Apollo's love for Daphne, daughter of the river Peneus. He reduces Ovid's epic similes, but develops the story's "romance" psychology, inspired by the *Roman de la Rose*;[13] Apollo is a typical Ovidian and French romance lover, denying Daphne's refusal and obsessively detailing her attributes; however, when she metamorphoses into a laurel, with "fueilles verdoians," he elaborates, "I want you in all seasons to have the verdure of evergreen leaves" (I, 3030; 3058–59). The text then offers four interpretations, which contrast not only with the story but also with each other: Peneus is a river surrounded with laurels; Daphne was a girl who died protecting her chastity and was buried under some laurels; Daphne is virginity, "born of coldness," and Apollo "is wisdom and charity, which should always be virginal" (I, 3116, 3131–32). Now it transpires that the amplification of Ovid's evergreen laurel was introduced to facilitate interpretation: "just as the laurel is green and never loses its greenery . . . verdant in all seasons, without producing fruit, so by reason, virginity should be green and live without producing fruit" (I, 3194–200). The one exception to the rule of virginity, of course, is the Virgin Mary – which brings the author to his fourth interpretation: Daphne is the Virgin Mary herself, and Jesus Christ is a lover, who loved human nature so much "that he wanted to join himself carnally to her, and let himself be wounded and pierced to the heart with the stab of love" (I, 3233–35). The Virgin in turn "is the laurel, full of greenery, with which the son of God crowned himself, for the Virgin contained him within her body . . . " (I, 3246–49). The *Ovide moralisé* glosses one narrative with another, flamboyantly embracing textual and conceptual difference, repeatedly finding startling points of connection.

This author treats the *Metamorphoses* as a compilation of metamorphic mythic *material*, a "natural" world of change ready for interpretation. He is not interested in Ovid's writerly intention or authority. Earlier glossators had sophisticated ideas about Ovid the "philosopher," his authorial

---

12 Possamaï-Pérez, *Essai d'interprétation*, pp. 46, 70; on the enhancing of romance effects, pp. 154–56, 263–77.
13 Compare Ovid, *Metamorphoses*, I, 452–567 and *Ovide moralisé*, I, 2737–3115.

intention and about the way the classical poets veiled their ethical, scientific or even historical teaching under poetical *integumenta*. But here, Ovid is sidelined and, in an act of vernacular self-assertiveness, the introduction now heralds, not, as is usual in commentaries, the author, Ovid, but the *Ovide moralisé* itself.[14] This is an expansive, pastorally oriented and preacherly enterprise. The *Ovide moralisé* enacts *translatio* in the medieval sense of a creative re-telling, refiguring or "carrying over" of text, not just from one language to another, but from one set of forms and meanings to another; Ovid's mutatory text is itself metamorphosed into a vehicle for moral, typological and Christian teaching, one that is organized round the ultimate metamorphic figure of the God-man, lover and son to his virgin mother, Christ.[15] This is a highly "rhetorical" textual hermeneutic.

The text is marked by a (Franciscan?) sense that all spiritual understanding should also be "sapiential" and desirous,[16] and many of its readings focus on the "frenzy" and "drunkenness" of divine love. Semele, burnt up because she asked Jupiter to appear to her in all his glory, can signify the dissolute body of the drinker and glutton, but also:

> a soul drunk and full of divine love, which is always afraid, fearful and anxious about losing the love to which her heart should fix itself, and whose mouth and heart never do anything except speak of her love and think of his commands . . .
>
> (III, 906–13)

This is a spiritual version of the psychology of obsessive desire to be found in the tales, whether in Ovid's Latin or in the French.[17] Biblis, who "loved her brother beyond measure" (IX, 2083) and wept herself into a fountain, is divine wisdom "sweet and desirable, more delicious [*savoureuse*] and drinkable than wine, milk or spiced wine" (IX, 2586–89). Biblis' incestuous love is the divine Wisdom that shaped the world and so loved humanity,

> that she held it her sovereign delight to join herself to the human race in siblinghood and marriage. She who was the creator and mother of all creatures made the human race her brother. Against nature she wanted to join herself carnally to man and resemble creatures. (IX, 2602–10)

---

14 Copeland, *Rhetoric, Hermeneutics*, pp. 107–26.

15 Possamaï-Pérez, *Essai d'interprétation*, pp. 587–619, 657–69; on the pastoral dimension, pp. 789–868; on *translatio*, Copeland, *Rhetoric, Hermeneutics*, pp. 88, 102–3, 235, n. 74.

16 On *sapientia* as a loving wisdom (and later the "sapiential" pun of the French term *savour*), see Nicolette Zeeman, *Piers Plowman and the Medieval Discourse of Desire* (Cambridge: Cambridge University Press, 2006), p. 2.

17 Compare the episodes of Bacchus (III, 1965–2914) or Myrrha (X, 1080–1959, 3678–953, especially 3748–810).

The Christological "banquet that was spread on the cross for our salvation, the very fountain out of which comes everlasting life and which gives life to those who drink from it," she is also a trinitarian source that recalls the life-giving well of Jean de Meun's sexual garden of nature in the *Roman de la Rose*: "all the water is clean and pure, of one taste [*savour*], of one nature; all three are one thing" (IX, 2662–66, 2689–91). Along with Gower's *Confessio amantis*, Jean de Meun's shocking conflation of *fin'amors*, natural philosophy and creation theology is perhaps the best parallel for the work of this poet, who seems not so much oblivious to the differences in his materials as exhilarated by the challenge of bringing them together.[18]

The dynamic pedagogy of Deguileville's enormous and widely disseminated fourteenth-century allegorical narrative, the *Pelerinage de la vie humaine*, juxtaposes bizarre, enigmatic, and often amusing, iconography with moral and Christian exegesis.[19] The first recension makes clear the poem's secular inspiration: "I hadde in wakinge rad [read] and considered and wel seyn the faire romaunce of the rose."[20] The narrator dreams that he journeys to "Jerusalem," in the course of which he meets a fabulous array of personifications, including Grace Dieu, Resoun, Nature, "Aristotyles," Penance, Rude Entendement, the vices (including an ugly old Venus riding on a pig and Avarice with her six hands) and Idolatrye; he finally arrives at the ship of Religion (monasticism), where Death swings his scythe, and the dreamer awakes. Deguileville's emblem-like iconography is purposely difficult to decipher, and functions as a visual tool for devotional imagining and remembering. Deguileville defers naming or explaining his images in such a way as to excite the dreamer and reader's curiosity.[21] Sometimes the strange imagery conveys the counter-intuitive nature of faith and its objects, as with Grace Dieu's 1,330-year-old house hanging in the air (second recension, translated by Lydgate, lines 849–76), but its effect is also to produce the desire for exegesis: Penance has a hammer and a besom broom in her mouth and Memory's eyes are at the back of her head; the Body is a monstrous adversary, but dead and blind without the soul, and Youth is a feathered girl who plays with a ball (lines 4006–573, 8713–816, 8989–10242, 11068–212). The action too involves moments of high

18 Other relevant devotional contexts are provided by Barbara Newman, *God and the Goddesses: Vision, Poetry, and Belief in the Middle Ages* (Philadelphia: University of Pennsylvania Press, 2003), chapters 5 and 6.
19 Deguileville became a Cistercian monk at the Abbey of Chaalis; he wrote the *Pelerinage* in 1331 and revised it in 1355.
20 Middle English translation in *The Pilgrimage of the Lyfe of the Manhode*, ed. Avril Henry, EETS OS 288, 292 (London: Oxford University Press, 1985, 1988), I, 1.
21 Hagen, *Allegorical Remembrance*, pp. 30–31, 38–41.

comedy – the dreamer struggling with the painful armour of the virtues or tied up and dragged along at the back of Venus' pig (lines 8194–367, 13512–44). Like the author of the *Ovide moralisé*, Deguileville exploits the disjuncture between fantastical imagery and explication: if the odd visuals bring their own pleasures, then they also demand in-house commentary:

> 'Reporte off me, and sey ryht thus,
> That I am callyd Dame venus...'[22]

In the French prose *Queste del Saint graal* and the English verse *Pearl*, imagery and narrative seem to be more integrated with exegesis, but also contribute to meaning very much on their own terms. Indeed, they often work against the synthesising claims of the exegesis, as these texts too exploit tensions within their materials.

Probably written between 1220 and 1230, possibly by someone with connections to the Cistercian order, the *Queste* was almost certainly conceived not as a separate religious appropriation of Arthurian materials but as part of the prose "Vulgate Cycle" of Arthurian romance; it is preceded by the *Estoire dou graal* (*The History of the Grail*), the *Merlin* (although these two are probably written later), and the *Lancelot*, and it is followed by *La mort le Roi Artu* (*The Death of King Arthur*).[23] A version appears in Malory's *Morte Darthur*. The *Queste* re-imagines the chivalric adventures of the Arthurian Round Table as a spiritual quest inspired by the "saint graal," the vessel in which Joseph of Arimathea caught Christ's blood at the crucifixion. In fact, the *Queste* draws on the latent Christian associations found in even secular Arthurian narrative, where the body and the shedding of blood often have semi-sacramental, Christological connotations.[24] However, these materials are also substantially reoriented. Inspired by a miraculous vision of the *graal* at Camelot, knights seek another sight of this legacy of the embodied Christ; the quest is really for Christ himself, and those who fully succeed, Percival and Galahad, do not return – they have died and been taken up to heaven. This new version of the Arthurian quest thus develops and stands in tension with secular Arthurian narrative. Secular chivalric *aventure*, for instance,

22 Trans. Lydgate, lines 13,117–18. On allegorical "geography" on the rhetoric of these two texts, see Sarah Kay, *The Place of Thought: The Complexity of One in Late Medieval French Didactic Poetry* (Philadelphia: University of Pennsylvania Press, 2007), chapters 2 and 3.

23 Edited as *La Quête du Saint graal. Roman en prose du XIIIe siècle*, ed. Fanni Bogdanow, trans. Anne Berrie, Lettres Gothiques (Paris: Librairie Générale Française, 2006); referred to as *Queste*; *The Quest of the Holy Grail*, trans. P. M. Matarasso (Harmondsworth: Penguin, 1969). For date and development, Carol Dover, ed., *A Companion To The Lancelot-Grail Cycle* (Cambridge: D. S. Brewer, 2003), chapters 2, 5–10.

24 Jill Mann, "Malory and the Grail Legend," in *A Companion to Malory*, ed. Elizabeth Archibald and A. S. G. Edwards (Cambridge: D. S. Brewer, 1996), pp. 203–20 (pp. 208–9).

acquires its meaning (its "gloss") only when knights return for acknowledgement to the restless, homosocial and transient world of the court. The *Queste* too is valorized by witnesses, but, unless they are deceivers, these are holy men from outside the court and their immutable authority derives from God. "Sir, you asked me just now the meaning of the mysterious task you fulfilled, and I will gladly inform you ... " (*Queste*, p. 156; translation, p. 63).

And yet these holy men with their schematic and (often literally) black-and-white glosses scarcely sum up the meaning and spiritual or affective impact of these narratives. The *Queste* knights who seek and suffer become part of a reiterative, typological narrative of sacramental wounding and sacrifice that stretches back to the crucifixion. The now overt Christological allusions are focused on the mysterious, eucharistic *graal*, which has – in a religious version of the romance *translatio imperii* ("transmission of power") by which the descendants of Troy arrive in Britain – acquired a back-narrative according to which it was personally brought to England by Joseph of Arimathea. The *Queste* narrates a series of pursuits of Christ across history, and the knights themselves – especially the most perfect knight, Galahad – become types of Christ. In an enhanced form of quest, according to which the quester, more advanced in pursuit, himself becomes an object of quest, the *graal* knights are often themselves pursued.[25] This reworks those passages of secular Arthurian romance where the court seeks out knights who have been long on adventure, sometimes traveling incognito. The name, identity and even paternity of Galahad, "le Chevalier desirré" (the Desired Knight) remain mysterious for quite a while; everyone knows and asks about him, but he is absent for most of the *Queste* (*Queste*, p. 96; translation, p. 37). In the near-contemporary *Perlesvaus*, the eponymous hero also circles endlessly round the margins of the narrative: "we are daily awaiting the arrival of the Good Knight... there is nothing in the world I desire to see more."[26] In both texts, the narrative nuances meaning in ways not summed up by the hermit commentators, describing adventure as an active submission to events beyond one's control, a singular pursuit of the unknown mostly satisfied only in brief visionary encounters.

What is more, the *Queste* continues to recognize the call of the secular. Even as his knights prepare to depart, King Arthur laments, "Ah,

---

25 Psychoanalytic analysis in Miranda Griffin, *The Object and Cause in the Vulgate Cycle* (London: Modern Humanities Research Centre, 2005), p. 54 (and chapter 2).

26 *Le Haut livre du graal. Perlesvaus*, ed. William A. Nitze and T. Atkinson Jenkins, 2 vols. (Chicago: University of Chicago Press, 1932–37), pp. 148–49; *The High Book of the Grail. A Translation of the Thirteenth-century Romance of* Perlesvaus, trans. Nigel Bryant (Cambridge: D. S. Brewer, 1978), p. 97.

Gawain...you have deprived me of the best and truest companions a man could find...I am well aware that of those who leave my court when the hour comes, all will not return" (*Queste*, p. 114; translation, p. 45). The *Queste* acknowledges the incomplete synthesis of its components – sometimes humorously, as when the imperfect knights who carry on in the old modes of adventuring encounter each other confusedly in the wilderness to ask why all the adventures have disappeared (*Queste*, pp. 380–82; translation, p. 162). The most important example of this ambivalence must be Lancelot, father to Galahad and superannuated "best knight in the world." Despite his desire to achieve the quest, he is repeatedly reminded that his love for Guenevere means that he will never succeed. However, the text cannot bring itself to dismiss him: "you have ever been the most wondrous of men, therefore it is no marvel if more wondrous things are said to you than to another" (*Queste*, p. 218; translation, pp. 90–91). Here too, the *Queste* draws on a feature of the secular Arthurian tradition, the fact that many of the difficulties experienced in the chivalric world derive from the complexity or contradictoriness of its chivalric requirements. So, when at Corbenic Lancelot is offered his last vision of the grail, but forbidden to pass through the door, he is seized with sympathy for the priest ("so weighed down...that he seemed about to fall beneath the burden") and crosses the threshold with a prayer: but "he felt a puff of wind which seemed to him shot through with flame, so hot it was...He stood rooted to the ground like a man paralysed..." Lancelot remains in a coma for twenty-four days (*Queste*, p. 606; translation, pp. 262–63). In comparison to such poignant scenes, even the glorious apotheosis of Galahad seems slightly one-dimensional. The emotional focus on Lancelot makes him not just an instance of failed questing, but the site of a division at the heart of the inspirational narrative of the *Queste*.

Something similar occurs in the anonymous fourteenth-century English alliterative verse *Pearl*, found in only one manuscript, British Library Cotton Nero A.x.[27] In a pastoral *erber* (herb garden), the narrator, a "joylez juelere," describes how he has lost a *perle*, "thurgh gresse to grounde hit fro me yot (fell)" (lines 38, 252, 10); he dreams that he is taken to a bejewelled landscape where a river separates him from an even more fabulous scene containing the lost *perle* maiden, now crowned and adorned with pearls. It becomes clear that the *perle* herself, usually assumed to be a daughter, died when she was two, but that she is now in the heavenly Jerusalem,

---

27 *The Poems of the Pearl Manuscript: Pearl, Cleanness, Patience, Sir Gawain and the Green Knight*, ed. Malcolm Andrew and Ronald Waldron (rev. edn., Exeter: University of Exeter Press, 1978), pp. 52–110.

"married" to Christ. The poem concludes with a luminous vision of the holy Jerusalem itself, drawn from the Apocalypse, along with the Lamb of God and his 144,000 saved "maidens." The poem is thus a study in numerology, a spiritual consolation and a theological treatise – not just on the salvation of those who die young, but also on the mystery of saving grace itself.[28]

However, it is also a poetic amalgam of secular modes – the complaint, the elegy, the lapidary and the courtly poetry of *fin'amors* – reworking, in alliterative form, elements from the *Roman de la Rose* and fourteenth-century French "marguerite" poetry.[29] It reworks these secular modes to create a vision of spiritual ascent with its own intensifying "typology" of pearls: the earthly *perle* is now discovered to be a spiritual, "*saved*" *perle*; she is adorned with *perles* and surrounded with other *perle* maidens; it turns out that heaven itself is a *perle*, "For hit is wemlez [flawless], clene, and clere, / And endelez rounde" (lines 737–38). The concentric circles of these various pearls are echoed in the circular structures of the poem, which is made up of twenty sections, each (except one) containing five twelve-line stanzas linked at beginning and end with a theme-word; the last line of the poem links back to the first in referring both to *perles* and to the *pay* ("pleasure") of the "Prince" of heaven. Although the dreamer constantly uses the language of possession to describe her ("Art thou my perle that I haf playned," line 242), and queries what the *perle* tells him, these final lines have often been read as a signal of his final acquiescence to the will of God.

And yet, this allegory too seems un-reconciled with itself. I am not only referring to its portrayal of the disjuncture between earthly and spiritual ways of "imagining," understanding and loving: the narrator cannot understand how a two-year-old could merit salvation or be a queen in heaven and married to Christ, and he cannot comprehend a love that includes 144,000 souls in all their individuality; what is more, her explanations do not really elucidate – they only demand submission. Nor am I only referring to the discursive gap between them, as he pleads with her to be his, and she roundly rebukes him. Surely most disturbing is that desperate moment near the end when, despite all her teachings – "Delyt me drof [drove]... My manez mynde to madding malte [melted]" (lines 1153–54) – he leaps into the stream to reach her and the dream ends. Although the poem attempts to use human imagination, reason and desire to lead the dreamer to some kind

28 For religious sources, see Ian Bishop, *Pearl in its Setting* (Oxford: Blackwell, 1968).
29 On the *Roman de la Rose*, the poet's use of "courtly" literature, even his "courtly theology," see Ad Putter, *An Introduction to the Gawain-Poet* (London: Longman, 1996), pp. 18–20, 153–56, 182; Nicholas Watson, "The *Gawain*-Poet as Vernacular Theologian," in *A Companion to the* Gawain-*Poet*, ed. Derek Brewer and Jonathan Gibson (Cambridge: D. S. Brewer, 1997), pp. 293–313.

of divine encounter, not even desire for the soul in heaven can be co-opted to make the leap. Human desire still needs to possess the things it loves, and is, if at all, only taught by its failures.

This may also be true of *Piers Plowman*, the obsessive life-work of the writer usually named Langland, assumed to originate in the West Midlands, but writing in English in London in the later fourteenth century.[30] Unusually structured in terms of a series of dreams and dreams-within-dreams, the poem is a political analysis of Christian history and later medieval society, but also a practical and spiritual journey to discover what humans must do to be saved. It begins with a series of only partially successful attempts to reform secular society, takes an inward turn to explore the question of "doing well" and climaxes dramatically in a simultaneously historical and devotional vision of God in man, Christ being crucified and harrowing hell; at no point, however, does it lose sight of the social dimension, and in the last two *passūs* ("steps," "sections") it returns to a dark vision of a corrupt and apocalyptic world.

Although the poem is punctuated with authority figures who offer a series of interpretative sermons or excursus, this is a dialogic text and each speaks from a particular perspective: none has the last word. Allegorically, the poem is far more eclectic and diverse than any of the texts described so far, mingling personifications with exemplary individuals,[31] allegorical narrative with mimetic scenes, "diagram" allegory with typological narrative, secular vision with biblical history.[32] Not only is its allegorical narrative the unpredictable product of many different layers of discourse, occurring simultaneously and in sequence, but Langland is uninterested in narrative continuity. Readers have stressed the grounding of *Piers Plowman*'s allegory in issues of epistemology and wordplay; as a result of the verbal equivocity of terms such as *mede* (reward, bribe), *pardon* or *dowel*, for instance, the narrative surface repeatedly breaks down.[33] Not only does Langland frequently use narrative to comment on narrative, but he is also disorientingly flexible in the way he allows one narrative to vanish and be replaced or continued by

---

30 William Langland, *The Vision of Piers Plowman. A Critical Edition of the B-Text based on Trinity College Cambridge MS B.15.17*, ed. A. V. C. Schmidt (2nd edn., London: Everyman, 1995).

31 Lavinia Griffiths, *Personification in Piers Plowman* (Cambridge: D. S. Brewer, 1985).

32 Elizabeth Salter, "*Piers Plowman*: An Introduction," in *English and International: Studies in the Literature, Art and Patronage of Medieval England* (Cambridge: Cambridge University Press, 1988), chapter 5.

33 Mary Carruthers, *The Search for St. Truth: A Study of Meaning in Piers Plowman* (Evanston: Northwestern University Press, 1973); Quilligan, *Language of Allegory*, chapter 1; James Simpson, *Piers Plowman: An Introduction to the B-text* (London: Longman, 1990).

another. In B, 6 the idea of pilgrimage is subverted to reveal that true "pilgrimage" is enacted not literally in concrete pilgrimages but metaphorically in the good life of the ploughman. In B, 16 even a pre-glossed image such as the spiritual "tree of charity" alters before the reader's eyes, as it turns into the tree of the Garden of Eden at the moment of the Fall.[34] Tropology and typology provide some of the main terms of analysis as words and protagonists engage, metamorphose and echo each other: Piers Plowman, for instance, is the vernacular Piers, a good working man, but also a spiritual "worker" engaged in the tending of the "fruit" of love, St. Peter – the guide for an inspired Church – and the form in which Christ comes to Earth.[35] But these are only types and echoes, and no meaning remains fixed for long.

Even at the climactic "joust" of the crucifixion, for instance, speakers offer conflicting readings of what is happening. The dreamer asks with whom Christ will joust, and Feith announces that it is "fals doom to deye" (false condemnation to death); according to Feith, Deeth says he will take all, but Lif claims that in three days he will fetch "Piers fruyt the Plowman," humanity, from the fiend (B, 18, 27–35). However, at this point, we can only have faith – we cannot know. The dead then rise out of the ground to tell of a "bitter battaille" occurring in the darkness: Langland's great originality is to present the outcome of the crucifixion as still uncertain, seen from the partial perspectives of those caught within time on Earth: "Shal no wight wite witterly who shal have the maistrie / Er Sonday aboute sonne-risyng" (B, 18, 66–67). The dreamer slips down into hell where, even as the light of Christ appears mysteriously at a distance across the landscape, the "Four Daughters of God" argue about what these events can mean, regarded in the light of divine justice and mercy; finally, all they can do is be silent, listen, watch and "suffer" events to occur (B, 18, 260–61).

This poem too is dominated by division and disjuncture. Even more than in *Pearl*, the dreamer of *Piers Plowman* is characterized in terms of unstable desire – his good intentions suddenly and unexpectedly turn out to be misdirected. Repeatedly his expressions of enthusiasm or even dissatisfaction are followed by a rebuke from an authority figure, an aggressive confrontation that results in narrative breakdown; and yet, "going wrong" is one of the mechanisms by which the poem creates the need, the sense of loss, to go on

---

34 J. A. Burrow, "The Action of Langland's Second Vision," in *Essays on Medieval Literature* (Oxford: Clarendon Press, 1984), pp. 79–101; David Aers, *Piers Plowman and Christian Allegory* (London: Edward Arnold, 1975), pp. 79–107.
35 Carruthers, *Search*, pp. 65–80, and chapters 5 and 6; Griffiths, *Personification*, chapters 4 and 5.

and start afresh.[36] However, in Langland's endemically satirical and critical allegory there are also narrative equivalents to these failures of desire; at crucial moments – usually in the presence of some failing or corrupt protagonist – terms, personifications and even narratives turn out to be less than they seemed. Such is the effect when the venal lady personification Mede suddenly reveals that the authoritative figure Conscience might in fact be "bad conscience." Similarly, when a literalistic priest looks at Piers's spiritual "pardon," obtained from divine Truth, the inspiring idea that "doing well" is itself a form of divine pardon turns flat and un-pardon like: " 'Do wel and have wel...' / And 'Do yvel, and have yvel...after thi deeth day the devel shal have thi sowle.' " At the conclusion of the feast with the gluttonous doctor of divinity, the personification Clergie (revealed teaching) momentarily reveals a myopic, fetishistic side, "ar ye coveitous nouthe / After yeresyeves [presents] or yiftes, or yernen to rede redels [riddles]?" (B, 3, 180–96; B, 7, 112–14; B, 13, 184–85). In the final apocalyptic meltdown, Pees lets a false friar into the "barn" of the church and, as a result of his too-gentle penitential "glossing," the personification Contricion forgets to be himself:

> Thus he gooth and gadereth [collects money], and gloseth there he shryveth
> [gives confession] –
> Til Contricion hadde clene foryeten to crye... (B, 20, 369–70)

Langland integrates multiple interpretative discourses into his allegorical narrative in a highly unsettling fashion. His disintegrative narratives purposely subvert expectation, illustrating the extremes to which he is prepared to go in order to probe understanding and interrogate desire.

What we see in the vernacular religious allegories discussed here is an intense religiosity coupled with a sense of how difficult it is to access the divine from a complexly material and embodied world. All of these texts draw in various ways on secular vernacular narrative models that are often already ironized or conflictual; nevertheless, they co-opt such models for a newly religious engagement with the world – one that is almost invariably critical, iconoclastic and painfully uncertain.

36 Anne Middleton, "Narration and the Invention of Experience: Episodic Form in *Piers Plowman*," in Larry Benson and Siegfried Wenzel, eds., *The Wisdom of Poetry: Essays in Honor of Morton Bloomfield* (Kalamazoo, MI: Western Michigan University Press, 1982), pp. 91–122; Zeeman, *Piers Plowman*, pp. 1–19, 27–28.

MICHAEL MURRIN

Renaissance allegory from Petrarch to Spenser

Introduction

In such a long stretch of time, over 250 years, from roughly the middle of the fourteenth to the end of the sixteenth century, so much happened in allegorical theory and practice that I will have to be very selective, working by example rather than offering a comprehensive picture. I will discuss only heroic poetry with occasional glances at pastoral, the two classical genres commonly associated with allegory. For allegorical interpretation, the objects of study are the *Aeneid* and the *Divina commedia*. For allegorical writing, the discussion here will cover Petrarch and Boccaccio, Boiardo, Camões, Tasso, and Spenser.

My approach will be topical. I will begin each topic with Petrarch and Boccaccio, who developed their position out of that created by Dante and his circle, and then proceed to show how later interpreters and poets made significant changes or explored special problems. Petrarch and Boccaccio set the parameters that involve two interlocking concepts and practices. First is the theory and practice of allegory itself and its varieties, the moral-psychological, the historical or euhemeristic, the physical and cosmological;[1] and the second, the consequences of that theory, the varied attempts to control audience response.

Part one: The theory and interpretation of allegory

Ethical and psychological allegory

I begin with some remarks on terminology. The tendency in the fourteenth century was to talk of a literal and an allegorical sense, but the situation was

---

[1] In his "Letter to Raleigh," Spenser indicates that his poem includes political allegory, which Petrarch had used in some of his pastorals but which had since virtually disappeared. Since most of the discussion concerns Spenser and since I am not the only one writing on him here, I will have to omit it from discussion.

still fluid enough so that other terms could be used as well. *Allegory* (Greek, *allêgoria*) (one thing in words, another in meaning) had become overshadowed for poetry in the late antique period by *symbol* (*symbolon*) among the Neoplatonists. In the twelfth century *integumentum* had been a common term, and Petrarch and Boccaccio will still use variants of the term on occasion. *Allegory*, however, had remained a standard term in biblical criticism, either as a general indicator of all levels beyond the literal or more specifically for a sense Protestant commentators later called *typological*. Dante in the *Convivio* drew on this usage, listing the four levels of interpretation but then distinguishing his own usage from that of Aquinas and the scholastics. In the exposition of a *canzone* he talks of two levels, the literal and what he calls the allegory of the poets, which he illustrates by the myth of Orpheus taming the animals (*Conv.* 2.1.2–4). Poets see in this story an allegory of the wise man who by voice softens cruel hearts and moves to his will those who do not have a life of science and art.

More important than the terms is the thinking behind the terms. At the end of Book One of his *Contra medicum* (1352–53) Petrarch argues that poets veil truth and in so doing fulfill their particular role.[2] The Bible has many allegorical fictions, but *all* poetry is allegory. Boccaccio agrees. In his definition poetry consists of both verbal ornament and the invention or fable, which is allegorical (*Genealogie deorum gentilium* 14.7, dated 1347?–1371). He ends his discussion distinguishing poetry from rhetoric. Both require inventions, but "tegumenta fictionum" belong only to poesis, and he concludes: "mera poesis est, quidquid sub velamine componimus et exquiritur exquisite." ("Whatever is composed as under a veil, and thus exquisitely wrought, is poetry and poetry alone.") All poetry is by definition allegorical. The Florentines, picking up from the late antique Neoplatonists, would later concur with this view. Poetry *essentially* requires obscurity.[3]

A logical inference follows: whole poems are allegorical, not just certain scenes within poems. The interpreter finds the hidden meaning in the plot or story, and this is exactly what Petrarch and Boccaccio do. In a letter to Federigo of Arezzo, Petrarch provided the young poet with a brief but comprehensive reading of the whole *Aeneid* (*Rerum senilium* 4.5, dated circa 1370). Boccaccio was doing the same in his public lectures on the *Commedia* just before he died.

One's approach to the hidden meaning, however, varied, depending on the lapse of time that separated the interpreter from the text. Boccaccio

2 Petrarch, *Contra medicum* in the *Opere latine*, ed. Antonietta Bufano (Turin: UTET, 1975), vol. 2, p. 844.
3 André Chastel, *Marsile Ficin et l'art* (Geneva: Droz, 1954), p. 141.

assumed he could recover Dante's intention in the *Commedia*,[4] but both writers agreed that an ancient poet's intention could not be recovered. In his letter to Federigo of Arezzo, Petrarch claims that none can affirm a particular interpretation after so many years and in a work where the truth is studiously concealed and where so many alternatives are possible.[5] The two differed, however, in the rules to follow in such a situation. Petrarch tells Federigo he will not give the opinions of other people. New readings are acceptable as long as the letter brings them and they are true. One must allow the possibility that the author had another reading in mind. Boccaccio takes the scholar's approach in the *Genealogie deorum gentilium*. He will give ancient opinion, and, where that fails, his own. He includes in his collection only those myths he could find in ancient sources.[6] Hence he adopts a learned approach to classical stories.

The kind of readings the two writers looked for likewise followed from their theory of poetry. In the *Genealogie deorum gentilium* Boccaccio classes poetry with the speculative sciences, with theology and philosophy (*GDG* 14.4). Philosophy here is the crucial comparison. Poetry shares with philosophy a common subject matter. This subject is physics and ethics, with all the emphasis given to the latter.[7] The practical example is Dante's *Commedia*, where the final end is moral, to remove its audience from misery to felicity, and of which Boccaccio normally does a single-level ethical reading, despite his preliminary discussion of the other levels. This ethical basis presupposes a reorientation of philosophy. Humanists stressed praxis as the end of education, not speculation, hence their interest in ethics and in Cicero, the orator immersed in the politics of his day but also the one who composed philosophical treatises. Petrarch does not include the scholastics in his list of those philosophers who favored poetry but does cite Cicero,[8] who appears again in his speech on the Crown (*Collatio laureationis* 2.4, 7, dated 1341). Boccaccio similarly cites Cicero's *Pro Archia*, in the chapter where he defines poetry. The two did make room, however, for Aristotle,

---

4 Boccaccio says so at the beginning of his discussion of allegory in *Inferno* 2 (*Comento*, p. 241), and on Acheron he remarks that the poet's *intention* was to show how one gets to hell proper (p. 282). I cite from *Il comento di Giovanni Boccaccio sopra la "Commedia,"* ed. Gaetano Milanesi (Florence: Le Monnier, 1863).

5 For Boccaccio there is the Proem to the *Genealogie deorum gentilium*.

6 *Genealogie*, Proem; 14. Proem; and 15.5; *Boccaccio on Poetry*, trans. Charles G. Osgood (Indianapolis: Bobbs-Merrill, 1956), 15.5, pp. 110–11.

7 For the list of topics there are Boccaccio's *Vita di Dante*, 1.37, in *Delle opere di M. Giovanni Boccaccio* (Florence, 1723) and Petrarch's *Contra medicum* 3 in the *Opere latine*, vol. 2, p. 908.

8 Petrarch also cites Seneca, who composed dramas, and Solon, who turned to poetry in his old age. See *Contra medicum* 3, in the *Opere latine*, vol. 2, p. 904.

probably for two reasons. First, they knew about Aristotle's *Poetics*. Their friend and correspondent, Benvenuto da Imola, would use the *Poetics* in his public lectures on Dante.[9] Second, if one's concern is ethics, Aristotle and Cicero reinforce each other, since the *De officiis* reworks Aristotle's *Ethics*. Dante had already used both treatises, when he worked out the ethical organization of the *Inferno*, and Boccaccio uses the *Ethics* in his *Comento sopra la "Commedia,"* that is, the rapprochement of poetry and philosophy presupposes the new humanist view of philosophy, Cicero rather than Thomas Aquinas. It is only philosophy thus redefined that fits the argument.[10]

Petrarch provides a good example. In his Letter to Federigo of Arezzo he reads the *Aeneid* as a psychomachia and, therefore, stresses the books of personality clashes and battles: *Aeneid* 1–2, 4, 7, 10–12.[11] In this respect he differs markedly from previous tradition. Earlier commentators had emphasized the books that allowed for symbolic readings: 1, 3, 6. Most shocking, Petrarch completely ignores *Aeneid* 6, which had absorbed 50 per cent of previous criticism and helped Dante compose his *Commedia*. Petrarch's *Aeneid* is dramatic and involves a set of oppositions rigorously worked out. Aeolus must control the winds, and Aeneas must leave his lover Dido. In Italy, King Latinus and Amata quarrel over whom she should marry. Latinus favors Aeneas and the Trojans, but his wife supports Turnus and the locals and goes mad in the process. Finally, the two competitors meet, and Aeneas kills his rival Turnus.

It is further a drama of Everyman. For the Iliadic *Aeneid* Petrarch drops all personal names. It is not Latinus, Amata, Turnus, and Aeneas but husband, wife, local, and stranger.

Petrarch reads these figures psychologically, as symbols of passions that Aeneas must strive to control. In his flight from Troy, Aeneas loses his wife Creusa, that is, he loses the habit of pleasures. At Carthage, Aeneas dozes on the poop of his ship, a situation which indicates that his mind sleeps till he makes a firmer choice and sails off. Dido then cremates herself, or shameful pleasure perishes by itself. Aeneas looks back and sees the fire, but reason drives him on to Italy. Petrarch's reading of these figures is traditional. Earlier commentators had read Dido's self-cremation in similar fashion. And like his predecessors Petrarch tends to systematize these figures. Both he and Boccaccio are close to a grammar of symbols. High places signifiy

9 See especially chapter 4 of Benvenuto's *Comentum super Dantis Aldigherij Comoediam*.
10 Boccaccio, for example, notes that the five poets in Limbo guide Dante to the castle of moral and natural philosophy (*Comento*, 427–28).
11 *Rerum senilium*, Book 4, Letter 5 to Federigo of Arezzo, in *Opera* vol. 2 (Basel, 1554).

reason: the citadel of Aeolus, Limbo in the *Commedia*,[12] Reason's tower in the *Roman de la Rose*. Darkness indicates mental and moral ignorance, and death signifies the extinction of a passion in the soul.

In the following century Cristoforo Landino developed interpretations of both Vergil and Dante, basing his moral exegeses on Platonic philosophy. His readings transformed the moral and psychological interpretations of Petrarch and Boccaccio and had a profound effect on writers in the sixteenth century. In his *Disputationes Camaldulenses* (1480) Landino found two senses in the *Aeneid*, the literal or political, which concerns the active life, and the allegorical or purgative, which concerns contemplation. Dante presented these two senses successively, the political in the *Inferno*, the purgative, of course, in the *Purgatorio*, and then added a third in the *Paradiso*: the virtues of the soul already purged.[13] The purgative sense is original and redefines the moral virtues in a Platonic fashion. Man is mind, but the body poisons the soul through its passions. Hell, therefore, is this world, which explains why the *Inferno* concerns political virtue, since a trip to hell is really a study of humankind here on Earth. In the *Aeneid* the political dimension is the literal level of the poem. This Platonic viewpoint changes the moral readings by then traditional for allegory and common to Vergilian commentators, who stressed the growth of the hero.[14] It automatically alters the very definition of the virtues because it changes the goal, which is now the mind's disengagement from this world. Aeneas wishes to find his true home (Latium), where he has never been, and in Dante "the hero's mind awakes and realizes it has lost the way, oppressed by ignorance and vices," well symbolized by the wood.[15] The goal then is not participation in the affairs of this world but escape.

Platonic purgation is both intellectual and moral. Aeneas is constantly at the crossroads, choosing between opposed alternatives, often deceptive. Renaissance heroes will do the same. Here the poets involved are Torquato Tasso (1544–95) and Edmund Spenser (*circa* 1552–99). Tancredi and Rinaldo in Tasso's *Gerusalemme liberata* (1580–81) and the Red Cross Knight in *The Faerie Queene* (1590 and 1596, 1609) must constantly decide between alternatives and often choose the wrong one. Landino considers these repeated and difficult situations as part of a massive negative dialectic.

---

12 Boccaccio reads Limbo as the human brain, the seat of reason (*Comento sopra la "Commedia,"* pp. 249–50).

13 He gives the grand schema in his "Praefatio in Vergilio" (1488) reprinted in *Scritti critici e teorici*, vol. 1 (Rome: Bulzoni, 1974): 17–28.

14 The older commentators and Dante in the *Convivio* all assume this reading.

15 Michael Murrin, *The Allegorical Epic: Essays in its Rise and Decline* (Chicago: University of Chicago Press, 1980), p. 44, n. 58.

Aeneas must reject all that humans love, all attachments, but he never sees his goal, a city and civilization to be realized in the remote future. For a Platonist the goal is actually not in this world. God or the One, the true goal, cannot accept predication and, therefore, must remain concealed. Hence, the story of Aeneas' search for his home must be allegorical.

This situation carries within itself a crucial inference. The *horizontal* journey of the hero Aeneas diagrams what a standard Platonist would call a *vertical* movement, that of the mind's journey out of matter and upward. In this sense Aeneas and Dante the Pilgrim follow the *same* path, a possible inference, since Dante based his *Commedia* on the *Aeneid* and made Vergil his interpreter for the first two *cantica*.

Tasso and Spenser continue this tradition, both the general moral and psychological line formulated by Petrarch and Boccaccio and the Platonism revived by the Florentines. For Tasso, his male characters represent different Platonic faculties of the soul, and the plot dramatizes their integration under reason.[16] In Spenser each book has its own hero, who represents a particular virtue imperfectly at the beginning and must develop a more mature version of it. Books One and Two, Five and Six are particularly clear manifestations of this pattern, since the Red Cross Knight, Guyon, Artegall, and Calidore must constantly make choices, not all of them correct, till they reach their goal.

Euhemerism and its problems

Petrarch and Boccaccio incorporated euhemerism into their notions of allegory. A historical event or series of events became one of the secrets hidden behind the veil of fiction. These secrets were either elusive and personal or historical and public. In the way he read some of Vergil's eclogues Servius provided the model for the first category, and Petrarch and Boccaccio would give similar explanations for their own Latin pastorals. So in Petrarch's *Bucolicum carmen* (1346–57) Silvius and Mincius in Eclogue One stand for Petrarch and his brother Gherardo,[17] but the method could be applied to heroic poetry as well. Boccaccio assures Fiammetta that she will see in one of the lovers of Emilia, the lady of his *Teseida* (btw. 1339 and 1341) what was said and done by Boccaccio to her and she to him.[18] The second

---

16 See the "Allegoria del poema" and the analysis in Murrin, *Allegorical Epic*, chapter 4, especially pp. 94–127.

17 Petrarch so explains this eclogue in a letter to Gherardo (*Familiares* 10.4, in *Le familiari*, ed. Vittorio Rossi (Florence: Sansoni, 1926)).

18 *Teseida*, ed. Alberto Limentani, letter to Fiammetta, pp. 246–47, in *Tutte le opere*, gen. ed. Vittore Branca, vol. 2 (Milan: Mondadori, 1964).

category is the one originally called euhemeristic, and it is the way Boccaccio reads the *Aeneid* in his *Genealogie deorum gentilium*. He argues, for example, that Aeneas did not escape Troy but that the Greeks allowed him to leave, either because he betrayed the city or because at the original embassy he spoke for the return of Helen and was kind to the Greek ambassadors.[19] Dido was a widow who committed suicide rather than break her vow and marry again.[20] In fact, Vergil's lovers were not contemporaries, since Aeneas lived in the twelfth and Dido in the eighth century BCE. Nor did Aeneas ever visit Carthage. Boccaccio supports his readings with a range of Latin authorities. This turn to history had a contemporary parallel in biblical exegesis. Nicholas of Lyra read the Apocalypse as a history of the Church.

Yet there were problems. Euhemerism had begun as a separate tradition, for ancient allegorists did not class historical events as one of the secrets hidden behind the veil of fiction. This is a development from within Christian exegesis. Later in the sixteenth century the poet Luís Vaz de Camões (1524 or 1525–80), who published *Os Lusíadas* (*The Lusiads*) in 1572, illustrates the imperfect union of these two critical approaches. He used the old gods as actors in his epic about the Portuguese discovery of the sea route to India, and two of them, Bacchus and Tethys, make the tension explicit.

The story of Bacchus would seem to fit easily into a euhemerist reading, needing very little interpretation. The son of a god and a mortal woman, he initially had to win recognition as a god from human beings. He did so by first conquering India and then returning in triumph to Greece, where most people then accepted him as divine. In the poem of Camões he now opposes the Portuguese, who are sailing around Africa to India, a much more difficult technical enterprise than the land expeditions led there by Bacchus and Alexander. As antagonist, Bacchus initiates all the counteractions in the *Lusíadas*, trying to stop or destroy the Portuguese. He makes his motives and thinking most explicit when he addresses the sea gods in Canto Six, trying to persuade them to release such a storm that it will sink all the Portuguese ships. Here is his argument:

> Vistes que, com grandíssima ousadia,
> Foram já cometer o Céu supremo;
> Vistes aquela insana fantasia
> De tentarem o mar com vela e remo;

---

19 *Genealogie* 6.53.
20 *Genealogie* 2.60–61, 14.13; Petrarch, *Rerum senilium*, 4.5 (the Letter to Federigo of Arezzo) in the *Opera*, vol. 2: 871–72.

> Vistes, e ainda vemos cada dia
> Soberbas e insolências tais, que temo
> Que do Mar e do Céu, em poucos anos,
> Venham Deuses a ser, e nós humanos.

You saw that with greatest audacity they have already attacked high heaven,
You saw that mad fantasy to attempt the sea with sail and oar; you saw, and
indeed we see every day such arrogance and insolence that I fear in a few years
they will become the gods of sea and sky, and we, human.

(*Os Lusíadas* 6. 29)

Bacchus refers to Daedalus, who made waxen wings and flew, and to the
Argonauts. Bacchus assumes he is a god only by *fame*, but now the Portuguese will surpass his exploits and through Camões' poem enjoy a greater
fame than the god. In effect, Camões' own plot requires a euhemerist
assumption to function at all.

Later in the poem, moreover, the poet himself expresses this view
(*L* 9. 89–92). Some human beings by their great deeds were later imagined to be gods living on starry Olympus. He then turns around and gives
the other side of this thinking to Tethys. She has been portraying the
cosmos to Vasco da Gama and has described the empyrean where pure
souls live and contemplate the God beyond the universe. She then says
that these are the only genuine gods, while she and the Olympians exist
only for poetry and are mere fables (*fabulosos*), feigned by blind error
(*engano*) (*L* 10. 82). The gods serve only to fashion delightful verses, like the
painter, who with biblical precedent, gives angels the names of the ancient
gods (*L* 10. 84).

All this fits quite awkwardly into the poem, since Tethys has just shared
a marriage bed with Gama and will soon go on to explicate a global vision
of Portuguese achievements much in the manner that Michael later explains
the future to Adam in *Paradise Lost*. It is one thing to look for a probable
historical event behind a myth, quite another to make one's characters within
the story themselves aware that they are only interpretive fictions.

The revival of physical allegory

In the *Collatio laureationis* Petrarch allows for physical allegory (9. 7),[21]
but in fact he ignores it in the *Bucolicum carmen* and in his interpretations.
The revival of this ancient mode had to wait for Boiardo in the following
century. The first part of his story about the nymphs of Riso provides a

---

21 "Poetas, sub velamine figmentorum, nunc physica, nunc moralia, nunc historias
comprehendisse," in the *Opere latine*, vol. 2, p. 1270.

good example (*Orlando innamorato* 2. 31. 44–48, dated 1483 and 1495).[22] Orlando, decoyed from a battlefield, finds a fountain of water, encircled by laurel trees that make a little grove. It is hot, and Orlando is thirsty. He enters the grove and bends down to drink. To his wonder he sees through the clear water a hall of crystal full of women, who play music and dance. The hall itself is sculpted with gold and precious gems. Wishing to explore this new marvel, Orlando jumps into the fountain, fully armed. He lands in a meadow with more flowers than any other place in the world. The Count is so happy he forgets why he had come there and where he came from. The door of the hall stands open before him, made of gold and sapphire. He enters, and women dance around him in a circle. Here Boiardo cuts off the story and ends Book Two.

Boiardo, of course, knew about fountain nymphs from Ovid and probably from Greek sources as well. The Italian poet, however, makes the fountain a door to another world, like the lake entrance he imagines for Morgana's underground kingdom or Alice's looking glass. Here the glass walls, the translucent blue stones, and the gold allegorize water seen under different atmospheric conditions: clear like glass, blue like the sky, or lit by solar rays. The dance and music of the nymphs represent flowing water, ever in motion with its own kind of sound. Orlando forgets his background, that is, he leaves the historical world of battles and Charlemagne and enters the natural cycle outside human time. Boiardo later says, in fact, that the nymphs are a natural power. They live in water like fish but lack men, hence their practice of waylaying heroes (*OI* 3. 7. 7). At the end of the story in Book Three the place does not vanish like Dragontina's and Falerina's magical gardens. This fountain and its nymphs are part of the natural order and therefore survive.

Camões specializes in physical allegory, and in one place he transforms Boiardo's presentation, turning a fairy tale into an epic sequence. Instead of a palace inside a fountain he has a city at the bottom of the ocean, where the marine deities live (*L* 6. 7–26).

As often, however, physical allegory was really cosmological, reflecting both Neoplatonic influence and medieval interests. Dante had associated the sun and planets in the *Paradiso* with the astrological dispositions associated with them, Mars with the warlike, Venus with lovers, and the like. Boccaccio in his *Teseida* thinks along the same lines, though normally he stresses human dispositions, the means of astrological influence in scholastic

---

22 It is also a complex moral and psychological allegory. See Murrin, *The Allegorical Epic*, pp. 118–19 and n. 68.

theory. Boccaccio explains that the poets feign Mars has his house in Thrace because the men of the north, who live under a cold sky, are full-blooded, wild, and eager for war.[23] In his presentation of the Temple of Mars, for example, where Arcite prays before the tournament, Boccaccio sticks to humoral theory (*Teseida* 7. 25 30). It is Chaucer who turns this sequence into astrology.[24]

The Florentine Platonists, while also avoiding astrology, nevertheless made cosmology central to their theory and with it the possibility of polysemeity. Ficino went back to the source of the scholastic theory used by Dante and Boccaccio, when he translated the *Phaedrus* and wrote a special commentary for it.[25] In its cosmological myth, souls, as they fall into genesis and human bodies, pick up their appropriate dispositions from the planets on the way. The cosmological determines the psychological and at the same time suggests that a single image, symbol, or story, may have more than one meaning. Pico della Mirandola worked out the theoretical implications of this view in the Second Proem to his *Heptaplus* or "The Sevenfold Narration of the Six Days of Genesis" (1489). Pico refers to the first chapter of Genesis and its description of the six days of creation. There he enunciates a general theory, not limited to the biblical criticism that it introduces. The three worlds – the supercelestial, celestial, and sublunary – are all parallel to each other, so names in one can be applied to another. Particulars on one level can have meanings on other levels, meanings which are *already* determined. Similarly, in the microcosm which is man the three levels exist and imply psychological and moral interpretations.

In numerous places Spenser illustrates how the psychological grows out of the cosmological. The episode of Colin Clout on Mt. Acidale provides a useful example. In it Spenser includes his wife, Elizabeth Boyle, who appears as Rosalind at the center of a round dance, performed by the Graces with the three named ones, Euphrosyne, Aglaia, and Thalia, singing as well as dancing within the circle and around Rosalind herself. In this scene Spenser does to

---

23 *Teseida* 1. 15 and n. and Jean Seznec, *Survival of the Pagan Gods*, trans. Barbara F. Sessions, 1953 (New York: Harper Torchbooks, 1961), chapter 2.

24 *Knight's Tale*, lines 2367–2437 and ns. to 2217 and 2367 in *The Riverside Chaucer*. The basic study remains that of Walter Clyde Curry, *Chaucer and the Medieval Sciences*, rev. edn. (New York: Barnes & Noble, 1960). For later discussions see the brief bibliography in *The Riverside Chaucer*, p. 775.

25 Michael J. B. Allen, ed. and trans., *Marsilio Ficino and the Phaedran Charioteer* (Berkeley: University of California Press, 1981) covers both the relevant part of the translation and all of Ficino's discussions of the myth elsewhere.

the Florentines what Chaucer had done to Boccaccio, giving cosmological allegory an astrological dimension.

Spenser shows us geometry in motion. The hundred Graces move in a circle around the inner three, who form a moving triangle about the woman at the center, who wears a rose crown. In a series of similes Spenser carefully works out the significance. The outer circle he compares to a garland (*TFQ* 6. 10. 12), then he switches perspective, looking down at the dancers and compares Rosalind, the one in the center, to a gem in a ring. In the third simile he compares the whole diagram to Ariadne's Crown, also called the Corona borealis or Northern Crown, one of the constellations in the Northern Hemisphere that never sets, so the poet can claim the other stars circle about it. Spenser meditates on the scene, transposing it from one image to another but always with an eye to geometry, a science Platonists favored, and one that here ends among the stars.

At this point the poet turns to the *Astronomica* of Manilius, a contemporary of Ovid, and develops nuances in his two passages which concern the Corona borealis. In the first, Manilius describes the bright star that with its red color outshines the white fires of the others,[26] as Rosalind does the Graces in the second simile, that of the ring:

> ... nam stella vincitur una
> circulus, in medio radiat quae maxima fronte
> candidaque ardenti distinguit lumina flamma.

For the circle is dominated by a single star, which with passing splendor sparkles in the mid forehead and enhances with its blazing flame the bright lights of the constellation. (*Astronomica* 1. 320–22)[27]

In the second passage Manilius himself works out the astrological meaning of the constellation (*Astronomica* 5.251–66). The Crown gives the following gifts to those born under its sign: the cultivation of flower gardens, the making of garlands, and the distillation of perfumes from flowers. The latter two fit Spenser's passage, especially the third:

> ... And ever, as the crew
> About her daunst, sweet flowres, that far did smell,
> And fragrant odours they upon her threw.
> (*The Faerie Queene* 6.10.14)

26 The star is Alphecca or aCrB.

27 At the same time Spenser creatively misreads the phrase "in media fronte / candidaque," in transposing the passage to the Crown itself and puts it on Ariadne's "yvory forehead" (*Faerie Queene* 6.10.13).

Rosalind has the disposition and interests of those born under the constellation Corona borealis, and the poet weaves into his poem another compliment to his wife, parallel to the astronomical razzle-dazzle of the *Epithalamion*.[28]

Part two: The problem of the audience

Most poets in this period tried to control audience response. Dark conceits can confuse a reader or lead to misinterpretations. Dante had set the pattern with his *Vita nuova*. He surrounded his lyrics with commentary and explication, partly to correct false readings of some lyrics which had previously circulated separately,[29] partly following the classical model, taking on the role both of Vergil and of Servius.

As we have seen, Petrarch and Boccaccio similarly provided their own interpretations for their Latin pastorals, and Boccaccio composed a commentary for his own *Teseida*, giving his heroic narrative the trappings of the medieval *Aeneid*. All three poets may have been reacting against Bonaventure's *Collationes in Hexaemeron*, his conception of an infinite text, itself based on a notion of inspiration, of God as the true author of the Bible, so an infinite source. Bonaventure had tried to convey this sense of boundlessness through his commentary, a dizzy cycle of interpretations controlled only by the index he had to his Bible. By the mid fourteenth century, however, Nicholas of Lyra had limited Apocalypse to a single hidden sense. One could argue that he too wished to control and restrict interpretation, just like his contemporaries, Petrarch and Boccaccio. The problem would reappear, however, once Ficino revived Platonic theory.

When Ficino composed his *Commentarium in Phedrum* (1493),[30] he outlined in Chapter Ten a very complicated mode of analysis based on late antique Neoplatonists and on Proclus in particular.[31] He gives there a brief explication of the twelve Olympians through a threefold set of categories: the first based on their distribution through various substances, the second through the ideas of species in the intelligible world, and the third through an ampler consideration of more general properties. Accordingly, the reader of Plato's myth of the charioteer could interpret a god like Saturn differently depending upon which grid he had in mind. Ficino complicates the possible

---

28 A. Kent Hieatt, *Short Time's Endless Monument* (New York: Columbia University Press, 1960) provides the discussion.

29 Justin Steinberg, *Accounting for Dante* (Indiana: University of Notre Dame Press, 2007), especially chapter 2, section 4.

30 Published in the *Opera* (1496); Allen, *Marsilio Ficino*, pp. 19–20 and n. 90.

31 Ibid., pp. 112–13 and n. 33. Proclus is behind Ficino's discussion of the supramundane gods (Ficino, *Commentarium* 10. iii).

analysis further by his observation that in the visible universe, where Saturn occupies the second celestial sphere, he is served by various *daemones*, who represent different functions of the god, and who all, therefore, bear his name. As a result the name *Saturn* could in a particular context refer not to the god but to one of his servants. Furthermore, Saturn could represent an aspect of any single god, that of looking selfwards. Ficino here cites "Orpheus," who claims that all the supernaturals are in any one god.[32] At this point the average reader might give up. Despite the logical presentation, the reader, dizzied by all these possibilities, might assume that only Platonic scholars could possibly explicate Plato's myth.

Ficino's friend, Giovanni Pico della Mirandola, was, if possible, even more daunting. He could talk like Ficino, as in one comment on the magical reading of the Orphic hymns,[33] but it was his biblical criticism that reopened the door to the infinite, albeit with the appearance of rigorous control in his sevenfold reading of the *Hexaemeron* (the six days of creation in Genesis). In his Second Proem to the *Heptaplus* he argued that the creation narrative used the *same* words in the *same* order to symbolize the secrets of all the worlds.[34] He closed his reading with a kabbalistic interpretation of the first word of Genesis, *beresith*, yet another road back to infinity.[35] It is not surprising that Protestants with their interest in a wide audience would soon insist on the plain sense of Scripture, and the great secular allegorists of the later sixteenth century got the point. Like their fourteenth-century predecessors, they did everything they could to control the interpretation of their works, and Tasso kept the Bible as much as possible out of *Gerusalemme liberata*.

Tasso and Spenser composed prose explications of their poems. Tasso's "Allegoria del poema" regularly appeared with the *Gerusalemme* and so did Spenser's "Letter to Raleigh" with *The Faerie Queene*. Tasso waited till he had completed his poem (1575) before he explained its allegory, and his guide provides a comprehensive sketch of its moral and psychological meanings for a reader. Spenser, however, composed his letter while he was still writing his poem, so, as scholars have long recognized, it is not an accurate guide for *The Faerie Queene*, not even for the first three books

---

32 Ibid., pp. 118–19 and n. 46 (*Commentarium* 10. xii). The reference is to the Orphic hymns that circulated in late antiquity.

33 Michael J. B. Allen, *Synoptic Art* (Florence: Leo S. Olschki, 1998), p. 123, n. 61.

34 *Heptaplus*, Proem to Book 2, in the *Opera omnia* (1557–73), vol. 1, reprint (Hildesheim: Georg Olms, 1969), p. 16. For an English translation see that of Douglas Carmichael in Pico della Mirandola, *On the Dignity of Man, On Being and the One, Heptaplus* (Indianapolis: Bobbs-Merrill, 1965), pp. 94–95.

35 The notion of an infinite text had already been a commonplace among kabbalists in the thirteenth century.

for which it was written.[36] The "Allegoria del poema" and the "Letter to Raleigh," nevertheless, both fall within the tradition set by Petrarch and Boccaccio. The poets kept their explications separate from their poems.

Spenser, however, went further. In the "Letter to Raleigh" he had already envisaged an allegory that could shift from the ethical-psychological to the political and personal, since he claimed that he shadowed Elizabeth as queen through Gloriana and as private person through Belphoebe. It is perhaps for this reason, because of the complicated and varied character of his allegory, that he inserted many personifications into *The Faerie Queene* to guide the readers of his "darke conceit,"[37] as in the paradigmatic presentation of Medina and her two sisters, Elissa and Perissa (*TFQ* 2. 2. 12–39), a set piece to illustrate the Aristotelian notion of the mean, which he then complicates in the narrative that follows. Sometimes he creates pageants like that of the Seven Deadly Sins (1. 4. 16–36) or the procession of the seasons, months, and days (7. 7. 28–46), sequences more or less modeled on the city pageants he would have remembered from his childhood in London.[38] Occasionally, the personifications tell a story, like that of the Masque of Cupid, part of the allegorical climax of Book Three (3. 12. 1–26).

This was a clear break with the tradition. Neither Dante, nor Petrarch, nor Boccaccio, nor Boiardo, nor Camões had ever used personifications systematically as a reader's guide to the story or allegory. In the whole *Divina commedia* there is really only the procession of personifications that greets Dante on his arrival in Paradise. Boccaccio might fill three stanzas with them, describing the Temple of Mars (*Teseida* 7. 33–35), but Camões and Tasso avoided them.

In all cases where they were used, such personifications functioned in a manner opposite to that of allegory. A figure like Excess, who sits at the inner gate or porch of Acrasia's garden, requires no interpretation:

> Clad in fayre weedes, but fowle disordered,
> And garments loose that seemd unmeet for womanhed.
> (*The Faerie Queene* 2. 12. 55)

Allegory, on the contrary, requires an interpretation, and all the other terms that have been used in its long tradition, terms like *aenigma, hyponoia* (undermeaning), *symbolon*, have the same implication. Spenser could use personifications because the authors of this period saw allegory in stories,

---

36 An example would be the diverse presentations of the initiation of Guyon's quest between the letter and the poem (*Faerie Queene* 2. 1. 39–2.11; 2. 42–45).

37 He uses this phrase in the "Letter to Raleigh."

38 C. S. Lewis, *Spenser's Images of Life*, ed. Alastair Fowler (Cambridge: Cambridge University Press, 1967), pp. 2–7.

whether episodes within a longer work like the *Orlando innamorato*, or an entire long poem like *The Faerie Queene*. With this view Spenser could include personifications, if he wished, but it was the story, not the personifications, that made the allegory.

Later in the long eighteenth century all this would be reversed. Nicolas Boileau-Despréaux (1636–1711), the defender of the ancients against the moderns, provides an early example in his *L'Art poétique* (1674). In a passage where he is defending the use of the old gods in heroic narrative, he presents them as if they were simple personifications:

> Chaque vertu devient une divinité:
> Minerve est la prudence, et Venus la beauté.
> (*L'Art poétique* 3. 165–66)

> Each virtue a divinity is seen:
> Prudence is Pallas, Beauty Paphos' queen.[39]

Now a major cult goddess like Minerva or Athena had *many* functions. She was a war goddess, a city goddess, and many other things besides *phronesis* or prudence. The poet could either limit her role or present her in all of them, as does "Homer" in the *Iliad* and the *Odyssey*.[40] She was not a personification. Eighteenth-century writers, however, following Boileau's line of thought, would stress clarity in allegory, as they did in everything else. They therefore favored personification fiction and, being neoclassicists, invented a genre for it which they called allegory,[41] again in sharp contrast to their predecessors, who, though they tended to associate allegory with pastoral and heroic narrative, made it part of their general definition of poetry. By such thinking the use of personifications proved that Spenser wrote allegory, and their absence in the *Gerusalemme liberata* indicated that Tasso did not, despite his "Allegoria di poema." And the world turned upside down.

---

39 The editors of *The Continental Model* (Ithaca: Cornell University Press, 1970), Scott Elledge and Donald Schier, include the English trans. by Sir William Soame and John Dryden (1683) along with the French text.
40 Michael Murrin, "Athena and Telemachus," *International Journal of the Classical Tradition* 13 (2007), 499–515.
41 Angus Fletcher, *Allegory* (Ithaca: Cornell University Press, 1964) throughout but, perhaps, especially chapter 4, pp. 181–219, and Gordon Teskey, *Allegory and Violence* (Ithaca: Cornell University Press, 1996), chapter 5, pp. 98–121 for extensive discussions of neoclassical allegory in theory and practice.

13

BRIAN CUMMINGS

Protestant allegory

Properly speaking, the definitive position on protestant allegory would seem to be that it is a contradiction in terms. Does not the theory of biblical interpretation developed in the early years of the Reformation begin by denying allegory's validity? Certainly, in the hermeneutic works of Martin Luther it is not difficult to find somewhat negative sentiments on allegory: "An interpreter must as much as possible avoid allegory, so that he may not wander in idle dreams."[1] Again, from a lecture on Genesis: "Allegory is a sort of beautiful harlot, who proves herself especially seductive to idle men" (WA 42.667; *LW*, 5, 347). Or, most succinctly: "Allegories are empty speculations, and as it were the scum of holy scripture" (WA 42.173.31).

The rejection of allegory by Luther appears at first sight to be motivated primarily on theological grounds: it wrests attention away from the words of God, which left to themselves will render forth truth complete and in its own terms. Luther's own mantra, repeated many times, is "The literal sense of scripture alone." Not only *sola scriptura*, then, but alongside it an equally significant principle, *solus sensus litteralis*. Luther does not stand alone in this respect, and the observation is found not only in theology but also in handbooks of rhetoric. Thus Philipp Melanchthon, Luther's junior associate in Wittenberg, wrote in *Elementa rhetorices* of 1531, what is virtually a manifesto for protestant hermeneutics: *Nam oratio quae non habet unam ac simplicem sententiam nihil certi docet* ("any discourse which does not have a single and simple meaning teaches nothing for certain").[2] Luther and Melanchthon were followed in this doctrine by all wings of Reformation theology: by Huldrych Zwingli, Joachim Camerarius, Andreas Osiander, Martin Chemnitz, Martin Bucer, John Calvin and Theodore Beza; and into

---

1 All citations from Luther's works are from *D. Martin Luthers Werke*, Weimarer Ausgabe, 80 vols. (Weimar: Heinrich Böhlau, 1880–2007), using the standard citation formula; here WA 42.174. English translations are from *Luther's Works*, ed. Jaroslav Pelikan, 56 vols. (St. Louis: Concordia Publishing House, 1955–86); [here I, 233, abbreviated as *LW*].
2 *Elementa rhetorices* (Lyon: Sebastian Gryphius, 1539), p. 76.

the later sixteenth- and seventeenth-century protestant confessions by Julius Caesar Scaliger, Jacobus Arminius, Hugo Grotius, Isaac Casaubon, Georg Calixt, Johannes Drusius, Simon Episcopius and John Lightfoot.

This, at least, is the way that Luther's commentators, past and present, have wished to see things. Indeed, there can be found lurking in this account a deeper wariness towards allegory in the protestant world, located perhaps in Thomas Hobbes or John Locke, which passes over in part into both English and German romanticism, and lingers into the "higher criticism" of the Bible in the late nineteenth century. All of the citations from Luther at the beginning of this chapter are in fact to be found in Frederic Farrar's *Bampton Lectures* of 1885 and published as the *History of Interpretation*.[3] The modern academic study of vernacular literature that emerged in the United Kingdom and in the USA in the twentieth century is not immune to this bias. It only disappears altogether in the English-speaking world with the advent of literary theory on campuses in the 1960s. In all of this, an anti-allegorical sentiment has relied on what might appear now (and especially in a book like this) a very narrow and reductive division between intellectual epochs, between medieval obscurantism and Renaissance clarity. Such a sentiment nonetheless influences many present-day accounts of the origins of protestant theology, however well submerged or endowed with scholarly or philosophical sophistication.

The first thing that might be said in reply to this is that the picture of allegory that Luther possesses is in fact much more complicated. For instance, Luther dismisses the use of allegory in the scriptural interpretations of the scholastic theologians not only because of theology, but also for much more humanist reasons. Luther's distaste is founded on common sense (allegory involves manifestly absurd distortions of meaning); good taste (it produces vulgar, fantastical readings); literary propriety (these readings are redundant and fabricated); and intellectual chic (allegories just sound so old-fashioned). His barbs aimed at his opponents also do not lack rhetorical energy. All of the citations at the beginning of this chapter are complexly figurative. Elsewhere he calls allegory *Affenspiel* – a monkey game.[4] If we use allegories, we must remember that they are *Schmuck und schöne Spangen* ("paste jewelry and pretty bangles").[5] If he rejects allegory, he does not appear to mind alliteration or metaphor. As ever, it is best to remember that Luther is a creature of the sixteenth century rather than a bolt from the pure blue sky of evangelical Christianity. To understand Luther's polemic here, then, we have

---

3 Frederic W. Farrar, *History of Interpretation*, Bampton Lectures (London: Macmillan, 1886), p. 327.
4 WA, Tischreden, 2.317. 5 Cited in Farrar, p. 327.

to understand something about the history of literary method and rhetorical analysis in the sixteenth century more widely, and not just about the history of protestant thought.

Secondly, the harsh sound bite of Luther's radical stance should not be allowed to shout down other more modulated views which he voices about methods of reading. Context is everything in his denunciation of allegory. Luther dismisses the allegorization of the Koran by Turkish commentators; he pours scorn on the books of the Brigittines (WA 43.669; *LW*, 5, 348); he rejects Rabbinic etymologies of the word "Gad" (WA 24.669; *LW*, 5, 349). Yet this does not mean that he never uses allegory in his own scriptural exegesis. To illustrate this, I will leave alone examples from his earliest lectures (when he might still be felt to have been operating within the scholastic system himself). I will refer instead to the lectures on the book of Genesis which he began in Wittenberg in June 1535.

In the very first lecture he takes an anti-allegorical stance, commenting on the number of the days of the creation, rejecting Hilary and Augustine on the simultaneity of creation, and insisting that Moses speaks literally. With a characteristic combination of plain-speaking and figurative complexity, employing a German-Latin pun, he says that Moses calls a spade a spade: *appellat Scapham scapham* (WA 42.4; *LW*, 1, 5). On the other hand, in Genesis 2:7, when God breathes into man and man becomes a living soul, Luther comments: "And here by a very beautiful allegory, or rather by an anagoge, Moses wanted to intimate dimly that God was to become incarnate" (WA 42.66; *LW*, 1, 87). Luther makes an important distinction in the meaning of allegory here, one which becomes a commonplace in later protestant usage. The scholastics, he says (later protestants would say "catholic method" here) apply allegory extrinsically. They change the meaning by means of allegory to suit the position they wish to uphold. Luther's interpretation (later protestants would generalize to call this "protestant method") accepts allegory only when it can be shown to work intrinsically: when Scripture itself intends the allegory. We could call this allegory as an extension of the literal sense: indeed, the literal meaning *is* an allegorical one. Yet is he really calling a spade a spade here? Only if you accept that Scripture has in some final sense only one author; so that Genesis proleptically understands a meaning which only embodies itself many centuries later in the incarnation. God's meaning, if you like, was always the same. Protestant writers, of course, usually took for granted that Scripture is all one writing (many still do). But in any historical and rhetorical sense (using the arguments of Erasmus never mind the higher critical school) this is nonsense: an Old Testament writer cannot be referring to the incarnation, even figuratively. So is this not a case of extrinsic allegory after all: Luther is allegorizing the Old

Testament to make sense of the New, in order to iron out any inconsistencies or contradictions in his theology. How can he maintain that this is still the literal sense? Yet in the very next verse (Genesis 2:8), he changes tack again. He cites Origen, in taking (allegorically) paradise to be heaven, the trees to be angels, and the rivers, wisdom: "such twaddle is unworthy of theologians" (WA 42.68; *LW*, 1, 90).

Luther nonetheless attempts to develop his assertions into a kind of theory, one that repays further study. Jerome and Origen justified their method by reference to the verse in Paul, "the letter kills"; but for Luther, the letter is a lifesaver. This is not because he does not understand allegory; in fact, he says, with donnish vanity, he used to be rather good at it. But now he prefers, he says, to use the "historical meaning, which is the real and true one" (WA 42.173; *LW*, 1, 231). Otherwise, there are "such a variety of interpretations" that the interpreter will easily get lost. In the face of the confusion of possibilities we need "sure and plain meanings." Intriguingly, he makes this distinction in the application of figures in rhetoric by means of a maneuver that excludes rhetoric from its own proper domain:

> The historical account is like logic in that it teaches what is certainly true; the allegory, on the other hand, is like rhetoric in that it ought to illustrate the historical account but has no value at all for giving proof.
>
> (WA 42.174; *LW*, 1, 233)

Like many other philosophies of language, this denies that rhetoric is part of language, correctly understood, at all. It is something extraneous to language, an adornment, or an accretion. Language, in its logical structure, is simple, unadorned, and non-figurative.

Luther in this ambiguous legacy follows Erasmus. For Erasmus, too, is in at least two minds about allegory. In *De copia rerum ac verborum commentarii duo* (1512), his most substantial and influential treatise on rhetoric, Erasmus at first treats *allegoria* as a simple rhetorical figure. He places it immediately after metaphor, and defines its effect as similar to metaphor. With a little more confidence than he perhaps feels, he declares that allegory "is nothing more than a metaphor carried beyond the bounds of a single word."[6] A little allegory is always a good thing, he says: for even when you are writing for the general reader, you do not want the reader to understand everything straightaway. In Book II of *De copia*, he expands at considerably greater length, emphasizing the classical lineage of allegory. He extracts well-known examples from the *Odyssey* and the *Metamorphoses*.

---

6 References to Erasmus from *Collected Works of Erasmus* (Toronto: University of Toronto Press, 1974–; hereafter *CWE*), 29, 336.

Such allegories are not always hard to discover or to unravel: no one is in any doubt, he says, that when Icarus falls into the sea, we take it that "no one should rise higher than his lot in life allows" (*CWE*, 29, 611).

In the sphere of Scripture, too, Erasmus in his early work approved the use of allegory to explain theological meanings. The *Enchiridion militis christiani* (first published in 1503) recommended a spiritual interpretation of Scripture well beyond the literal sense, citing Jesus, Paul, Origen, Jerome, Augustine, Ambrose and even Pseudo-Dionysius as examples of practice to follow. In the Bible, Erasmus declared, some things are simply absurd if understood superficially.[7] In the Preface to the 1508 edition of the *Adagia* printed by Aldus Manutius, Erasmus announced his intention to comb the sacred scriptures and ancient theologians for allegories.[8] He never completed the task. Instead, in the methodology of biblical exegesis that he expounded in relation to his famous edition of the New Testament (1516), he positioned allegory more ambiguously. The most developed form of this argument came in the *Ratio verae theologiae* (1518), an expanded form of the *Methodus* (one of the prefaces to the *Novum instrumentum*). All the old theologians, he says, were rhetoricians. His own principle of the literary interpretation of the Bible is resolutely rhetorical: he wants to find out by whom something is said, to whom it is said, in what words it is said. Erasmus makes the obvious if no less central point that Jesus himself uses *similitudines* and *parabolae*.[9] He lists a series of rhetorical tropes and figures which are commonplace in New Testament idiom (I6r). Among them are many allegories. In fact, Erasmus says, insisting on the *sensus simplex* will in many cases lead to manifest absurdity (K2v). Yet Erasmus also gives warnings the other way, against the excesses of scholastic interpretations – what he calls "Sorbonicisms" (K6r). The 1523 edition of the *Ratio* increased these warnings, adding some passages singling out problems in Origen, Ambrose and Hilary.[10] The *Ratio* went through many changes from edition to edition through the rest of Erasmus' life, and in the revisions and expansions we can see the etiolations in his account of allegory. This proves to be a premonition of the career of allegory in protestant thought and literature.

This contestation over the process of figuration in the Bible finally reached its head in the argument between Erasmus and Luther on free will, which

---

7 CWE, 66, 68–69. See J. H. Bentley, *Humanists and Holy Writ* (Princeton: Princeton University Press, 1983), p. 188.

8 André Godin, *Érasme lecteur d'Origène*, Travaux d'humanisme et renaissance, 190 (Geneva: Droz, 1982), p. 256.

9 *Ratio seu methodus compendio perveniendi ad veram Theologiam* (Basel: Johann Froben, 1522), H8v.

10 Bentley, *Humanists*, p. 188.

began in 1524. Erasmus tried to protect his interpretation of a passage in Exodus (which otherwise appeared to deny free will) by way of an allegorical explanation in Origen. When God hardens the heart of Pharaoh in Egypt, this cannot be meant literally, Erasmus asserted. It is absurd to think that a good and just God could make a man worse deliberately. Erasmus invoked a figure. Just as the coming of the rain brings forth good fruit in one place and thistles and weeds in another, and just as the action of the sun both melts wax and yet hardens mud, so God's action has one result in one man and another in another.[11] This, Erasmus says, is the classic application of a figure of speech, no less to be observed in Scripture than elsewhere. The hardening of the heart is a trope: God is said to be an agent of destruction when in reality he provides an opportunity, which Pharaoh may or may not take, according to his free will. It is no more to be meant literally than when we say that a father "spoils" his child by failing to apply the rod.

Luther's reply to this has often been misunderstood. He rejects Erasmus' interpretation scornfully: we would expect nothing less of him. But he does not reject a figurative reading of Scripture out of hand. He makes the now familiar move of asking whether a literal interpretation of the passage would include the figure of speech. He recognizes the presence of figures of speech in many parts of the Bible; the question is whether a figure is at work here. In other words, he sees a figurative explanation, when it occurs, as being part of the literal sense. But that is not the case in Exodus, he declares. There is no need for the figure, for we know what God is saying without it. Bringing the figure in is not a way of releasing the meaning, but of "twisting" it.[12] Here, of course, he makes use of a nicely literal reading of the Greek word *tropos*, that is, a "turn" or "twist." The figure is included within the literal. Whenever it is affixed instead *from outside*, as we might say extraneously, it is a deviation from the truth. Of course, we could rightfully notice here that this is a deeply figurative understanding of the workings of the literal.

Rhetoricians in England follow directly on Erasmus' model. They use a conservative and derivative definition, which continues to express allegory in its narrowest sense as a figure of speech. Richard Sherry in 1550 borrowed his phrasing, word for word, from Quintilian: allegory comes second in the order of tropes, "an inuersion of wordes, where it is one in wordes, and another in sentence or meanynge."[13] Allegory says one thing

---

11 Erasmus, *De libero arbitrio*, in *Luther and Erasmus: Free Will and Salvation*, ed. Gordon Rupp and Philip S. Watson (Philadelphia: Westminster Press, 1969), p. 65.

12 *Free Will*, pp. 223–24.

13 Richard Sherry, *A treatise of Schemes & Tropes very profytable for the better vnderstanding of good authors* (London: John Day, 1550), C7r.

and means another. Thomas Wilson in 1560 is even closer to Erasmus (the popular handbook by Johannes Susenbrotus is more likely to be his immediate source): "In allegory is none other thing but a metaphor used through a whole sentence or oration."[14]

Humanist rhetoric, with its rigid typology characterized by lists of schemes and figures, attempted two things: to ingratiate itself among schoolmasters and students as an indispensable teaching aid, and to re-imagine the universe of language as a world of discourse, in which the conventions of speech rather than the principles of logic dictate the limits of the sayable. In practice, however, whereas the first of these principles was reductive, the second principle, of staying true to actual usage, tended to complicate this idealized simplicity. In particular, the elucidation of rhetorical figures in practical demonstrations tended to obscure the clarity found in theoretical analysis. This tendency increased when rhetoricians of a Puritan bent began to cite scriptural examples of allegory alongside the classical paradigms borrowed from Virgil or Horace via Quintilian. Henry Peacham's *The Garden of Eloquence* of 1577 remarks on Christ's habit of using allegory when issuing a moral rebuke.[15] In the expanded and revised edition of 1593, which showed the influence of the Ramist rhetorics emanating from France, Peacham amplified this analysis of biblical examples of figurative language, for instance, Matthew 7: "Giue ye not that which is holy to dogs, neither cast ye your pearles before swine."[16]

Yet doubts soon preoccupied Puritan rhetoric. Dudley Fenner's *The artes of logike and rethorike*, which appeared in 1584, attempted to demonstrate the usefulness of Christian rhetoric through a detailed rhetorical analysis of some of Scripture's "hard places." Rhetoric was now delving deep into protestant theology. Among the explications is Fenner's extended interpretation of the Lord's Prayer. Here he defines "forgive us our trespasses" (for which he uses the translation, "Father remit us our debtes") as a form of allegory: Christ uses the analogy of paying back borrowed money to clarify the doctrine of justification.[17]

---

14 Thomas Wilson, *Arte of Rhetorique (1560)*, ed. Peter Medine (University Park: Pennsylvania State University Press, 1994), p. 201. This is the revised version of a work originally printed in 1553.

15 Henry Peacham, *The Garden of Eloquence: Conteyning the Figures of Grammer and Rhetorick* (London: H. Jackson, 1577), D2r.

16 *Henry Peachams "The Garden of Eloquence" (1593): Historisch-kritische Einleitung, Transkription und Kommentar*, ed. Beate-Maria Koll (Frankfurt-am-Main: Peter Lang, 1996), p. 33.

17 Dudley Fenner, *The artes of logike and rethorike plainelie set foorth in the English tounge* ((Middelburg: R. Schilders), 1584), D2r.

In what sense, then, is he taking Christ literally, here? The problem encountered in Luther's assertion of the literal sense is reaffirmed in English protestant thought with a vengeance. Even before the English Reformation, William Tyndale set the tone with a declaration of independence for the literal sense in *The Obedience of a Christian Man*. The climax of this view came in the work of William Perkins, who for a decade at the end of the sixteenth century was the best-known theologian in England and also a phenomenally successful preacher. He was therefore ideally placed to unite the arts of theology and rhetoric in a single analysis, a *summa* which he attempted in his treatise on preaching, *The arte of prophecying*, first published in Latin and then in an English translation. This included a full-scale theory of protestant allegory. Holding his nose, he rehearses the four-fold interpretation of Scripture, "the literall, allegoricall, tropological, & anagogical," in the exegesis of the Catholic Church. This methodology "must be exploded and reiected."[18] He continues with what is a manifesto of protestant hermeneutics: "*There is one onelie sense, and the same is the literall*" (C5r). An allegory, he explains, "is onely a certaine manner of vttering the same sense," in other words allegory is a specialized type of the literal. In the same way, anagogical and tropological meanings are simply "applied" forms of the same, single, literal sense.

Like Luther before him, Perkins does not find the literal sense so simple that he does not need about five qualifying adjectives (proper, germane, and so on) to identify it. Perkins, whatever his radical Calvinist commitment to the literal sense, is troubled by it. He made his fullest account in a work left unfinished at his death, a *Commentary on Galatians*, which was then published and completed by Ralph Cudworth, father of the future Cambridge Platonist. Perkins repeats his description of catholic procedure and its division of the four senses, and repeats his counter-assertion that there is in fact only one sense, and that always literal. But he does not thereby deny the figurative, or even the allegorical. The allegorical is a necessary function of the literal. In this way the literal sense broadens to take in other senses. The literal sense is "sometimes expressed in proper, and sometimes in borrowed or figuratiue speaches."[19] The so-called "spiritual senses" – the allegorical, anagogical and tropological – "are not senses, but applications or vses of scripture." Like so many before him, Perkins has no intention of reading the Song of Songs as it were *literally*. For him, too, this notorious book of the Bible is readily sanitized to figure the communion between Christ and

18 William Perkins, *The arte of prophecying, or, A treatise concerning the sacred and onely true manner and methode of preaching* (London: Felix Kyngston, 1607), C4v.
19 William Perkins, *A commentarie or exposition, vpon the fiue first chapters of the Epistle to the Galatians* (Cambridge: John Legate, 1604), XX1r.

his church. The books of Daniel and Revelation are also accommodated by Perkins as allegorical histories.

Much more radically, perhaps, Perkins acknowledges the power of metaphor in Christ's own words, of all the words of Scripture those that place most pressure on the reader to take them properly, truly, literally. Christ's words in John 15:1, "I am the true vine," if they are taken properly, Perkins says, "are absurd in common reason" (XXiv). They only make sense as a simile, a figurative comparison. Lurking in the next sentence is the fiercest quarrel over literal and figurative meanings of the age, perhaps of any age: what does Christ mean when he says *Take, eate, this is my body?* Perkins' response is unequivocal: if this is their proper sense, Christ's own words are against the articles of his own faith. Christ cannot mean his words in this way: for he cannot be in the bread (since he is sitting at the right hand of the Father); and we cannot "eat" him, for in that case we would be murderers. He concludes: they can therefore only be expounded by a figure, thus, *This bread is a signe of my bodie.*

It is only by the narrowest of finesses that Perkins can assert that this is still the literal sense. What is the difference between saying that the literal sense is here "expounded" by a figure, and saying that it is a figurative rather than a literal sense? Yet Perkins is adamant that the distinction is valid. Rather than scoffing at his dogged literal-mindedness, we might instead realize that his definition of the literal is much richer than at first sight seems to be the case. We can also recognize in this the reason why the proposition with which we began, namely that "protestant allegory" is a contradiction in terms, turns out to be anything but the case. The simplest proof of this is that the three most notable examples of protestant English literature up to the end of the seventeenth century, the *Faerie Queene*, *Paradise Lost*, and *Pilgrim's Progress*, are all at least partly allegories.

The brief history of Reformation hermeneutics offered here suggests, however, that far from this fact being a strange paradox about protestant literature, as is often claimed, it is a natural consequence. Protestant literalism is nowhere near so literal as it wants to appear. If simple-minded adherents then and now wished for plain and simple meaning, language itself always got in the way. Once a figurative reading was subsumed as part of the act of interpretation demanded by the literal, the literal sense was encountered as already rich and complex. In this sense literary writers were working in the same vein as rhetoricians and theologians. In working out a position on allegory, they were all participating actively in protestant culture rather than pursuing a diversion from it or a return to more classical and aesthetic concerns. All show themselves disturbed by allegory yet also drawn towards it. There is no clear division between these writers: the rhetorician Abraham

Fraunce quoted equally freely from Sidney and Spenser or from the Bible; Fenner mixed prosody with presbyterianism; Perkins was read by poets as well as parsons.

George Puttenham in *The Arte of English Poesie* called allegory "a duplicitie of meaning or dissimulation vnder couert and darke intendments."[20] Yet he also called it a "common figure," indeed one of the most common (p. 186). Allegory is a fact of life. It is so natural to the world of the court and its politics that it becomes a figure for the court itself and vice versa: allegory "not impertinently we call the Courtier or figure of faire semblant" (p. 299). Such a folding in of the figure on itself could not be more Spenserian, but it turns out that this went with the grain of Spenser's protestantism rather than against it. Protestant commentators were fond of saying that Scripture was its own commentary, but in this they were also admitting that commentary is a natural by-product of the reading process. Like many rhetoricians of the time, Puttenham distinguished "mixt allegory" (p. 188) – when the author glosses his own allegorizing and offers an interpretation of the meaning of the figure even in the act of making a figure of his meaning – and full allegory, when everything is left to the reader's imagination and conjecture. Yet allegory always seems to be tempting its readers into ad hoc acts of glossing, and then making that very gloss disappear in further conjurations of figuration.

Something of the same can be seen in Spenser's first exercise in this mode, *The Shepheardes Calender*. A scriptural frame of reference is already in evidence. When Piers addresses Pan in the fifth eclogue, "Maye," the prose gloss by E. K. explains: Great Pan "is Christ, the very God of all shepheards, which calleth himselfe the greate and good shepherd."[21] This is neither exactly simile, nor mere allusion. Pan and Christ are put in metaphoric conflation, in which one term may be substituted for another. Christ as Pan goes into free play: Pan in Greek equals "all"; and Christ is both "all" and "one"; ergo Pan and Christ are one and the same.

Commentators are tempted to see a conflict between classical Spenser and protestant Spenser. However simple the theological doctrine the poet wishes to project, his classical frame of reference cannot help reverberating in divergent directions. Spenser's allegory, critics helpfully suggest, is therefore never as simple as the act of translation required in protestant theory. By now we can see that the complexity of the translation process is thoroughly part of the protestant traditions Spenser was participating in. We

20 *The Arte of English Poesie*, ed. Gladys Doidge Willcock and Alice Walker (Cambridge: Cambridge University Press, 1936), p. 154. Further citations refer to this publication.
21 Spenser, *The Shorter Poems*, ed. Richard A. McCabe (London: Penguin, 1999), p. 82.

can see this in E. K.'s gloss to "Maye," which parodies yet also revels in theological and etymological pedantry, such as a gleefully obscure reference to Eusebius.

This provides the context for understanding the principles behind the allegory of *The Faerie Queene*. Spenser's notorious comments on his allegorical methods, which appear in the "Letter to Ralegh" in the 1590 (but not in the 1596) edition, have also been taken as unduly simplistic. Each of the twelve Aristotelian virtues is represented in a different knight; and each knight "stands for," in metaphorical equivalence, an idea or concept, a single word-for-word translation. Spenser offers here as it were the literal meaning of the poem. His first example is Redcrosse, the knight of the first book, "in whome I expresse Holynes."[22] Redcrosse is told that he can only succeed if he wears the armour his Lady brings. This armour is then glossed by Spenser as "the armour of a Christian man" specified by St. Paul in the letter to the Ephesians. The biblical reference appears to solve the problem; the literal level lying beneath the allegory must be identical with the meaning in Scripture.

Yet the case is hardly so straightforward when we refer to the biblical text in question. Paul's line in Ephesians, "Put on the whole armour of God, that ye may be able to stand against the wiles of the devil" is after all itself an allegory. There is no untranslated place we can go to, before the work of translation begins. We are in the midst of translation even as we encounter the letter of the text. The first physical description in the poem can therefore be seen as emblematic of the figurative technique of the whole:

> But on his brest a bloodie Crosse he bore,
> The deare remembrance of his dying Lord,
> For whose sweete sake that glorious badge he wore,
> And dead as liuing euer him ador'd:
> Vpon his shield the like was also scor'd,
> For soueraine hope, which in his helpe he had:
> Right faithfull true he was in deede and word,
> But of his cheere did seeme too solemne sad;
> Yet nothing did he dread, but euer was ydrad.
> *(Faerie Queene*, I.i.2)

It is not at all simple to say where the boundaries of the literal and the figurative are here. What is figured in the "bloodie Crosse"? Christ's blood shed on the cross, clearly; but then also, at a literal level, St. George always has a red cross emblazoned on his shield. The figure conceals another figure behind it. To add to the difficulty of finding a more literal meaning, the

22 *The Faerie Queene*, ed. A. C. Hamilton, 2nd edn. (Harlow: Pearson, 2001), p. 716.

verbal icon is itself represented physically in the printed book. A woodcut of St. George killing the dragon is included at the end of Book I – complete with red cross on his shield and on his horse's armor. This is the only woodcut illustration appearing in either the 1590 or the 1596 edition. The wearing of a badge, the taking on of the wounds of Christ, the bearing of the cross of suffering, all become semantically conflated. The knight signals his affiliation with Christ, but also suffers like Christ, but also imitates, that is, becomes one with Christ.

All of these are of course perfectly conventional ways of describing Christian identity. All are also in some degree figurative expressions. It is Spenser's gift to protestant theology not to shy away from this figurative language but to immerse the reader in it. This is where he leaps ahead of Perkins. For Perkins in his exposition of the Eucharist attempts to reduce it to the level of figurative signification, as the only way of making the literal acceptable. He renders the bread as sign alone. Spenser, while proclaiming in the "Letter to Ralegh" a sharp division of the literal level and the figurative levels in his description of the Redcrosse Knight, in the surface of the poem he redeems his own figurative language. The reader is fully aware that a symbolic transaction is taking place, and fully aware that there is no alternative.

Protestant theology was troubled by this, but after an initial effort at denial, gradually came to terms with its burden. Literary history has been too keen to take Calvinism at its word in this respect. Lip service to the letter is not the same as rigid conformity. Having decided that a literal interpretation necessarily involved close attention to figures of speech, all kinds of things brought themselves into the purview of protestant thought. What was left behind was a sense of anxiety about figuration. On one side there was a frequent invocation of the plain style as the proper garb of the Christian writer. This style has been much discussed and well described, especially by American literary and intellectual historians such as Yvor Winters or Perry Miller.[23] On the other hand, there is that less-acknowledged tendency in the seventeenth-century Puritan mind towards extremes of fancy. One feature of this is that while the first generation of protestants – Luther and Calvin among them – cast doubt on the canonicity of the last book of the Bible, Revelation, later protestants loved it, often above all other books. In the middle years of the century, when civil war opened up new avenues of publication and new modes of religious expression as well as new political possibilities, it is to this book that the latter-day prophets turned. One

23 Yvor Winters, "The Sixteenth-Century Lyric in England," first published in 1939, reprinted in *Forms of Discovery* (Chicago: Swallow Books, 1967); Perry Miller, *The New England Mind: From Colony to Province* (Cambridge, MA: Harvard University Press, 1953).

example is the Ranter writer, Abiezer Coppe and his *A Fiery Flying Roll*. The second of these two tracts especially, addressed in 1650 "to all the inhabitants of the earth; specially to the rich ones," comes close to breaking the ordinary bounds of language in its rejection of the commonplace religion of conformity and orthodoxy.[24] From its sub title on ("A sharp sickle, thrust in, to gather the clusters of the vines of the earth") it never leaves the allegorical mode to show the reader the plain path of its argument.

Yet it is not only the wilder non-conformists who strain for new worlds of the figurative. Milton's *Paradise Lost* famously includes full-scale personification allegory in its description of Sin and Death at the gates of Hell in Book X.[25] Joseph Addison was the first of many subsequent readers to feel allegory improper for epic.[26] The invocation of the word "improper," a mantra against the evils of prosopopoeia, is a characteristic marker of the purity of diction that followed Locke's attack on metaphor at the end of the seventeenth century. Yet it is only a shift in taste that finds the direct allegory of the ill-born progeny of Satan so different in kind from the epic similes and complex involuted metaphors that are the norms of Milton's high style. Milton's poem is constantly on the edge of allegory even when not indulging in personification: and what is the story of the forbidden fruit in the paradisal garden if not a powerful allegory?

In the assumption of the inimical attitude of Puritanism to the imagination, it is easy to forget that its most popular work, perhaps the most widely read book in English history outside the Bible, is John Bunyan's *The Pilgrim's Progress*. This declares itself outright as a "Dream" or "Similitude."[27] In the accustomed manner it justifies itself straightaway by means of scriptural precedent, quoting Hosea on the title-page, "I have used Similitudes." Bunyan appends an "Apology" for allegory in the form of a verse preface to the book. He never meant to write an allegory: it just came into his head. Once there, he could not get rid of it, indeed it multiplied into twenty more. He shows a characteristic protestant wariness of literature here. He assures his readers that he did not write it for their pleasure; still less for his own. He is in an author's quandary, and his friends were no help, he said,

---

24 *A Fiery Flying Roll* (London, 1649 (1650)); *A Second Fiery Flying Roule* (London, 1649 (1650)), title page.

25 *Paradise Lost*, ed. Alastair Fowler, rev. 2nd edn. (London: Longman, 2007), ll. 229–640.

26 Addison, *The Spectator*, Nos. 273 (12 January 1712) and 309 (23 February 1712), reprinted in *Milton: The Critical Heritage*, ed. John T. Shawcross (London: Routledge & Kegan Paul, 1970), pp. 152 and 177.

27 *The Pilgrim's Progress from this World to That which is to come: Delivered under the Similitude of a Dream* (London: Nathaniel Ponder, 1678), title page.

being divided themselves about whether his book would do any good. Their indecision made Bunyan's mind up: he will publish and see for himself.

This is a witty preface to a book, and a winningly self-mocking one. Yet it is also defiant of convention and respectability. He knows what his enemies are saying: "*Metaphors make us blind.*"[28] But is not Christ a fisher of men, and a shepherd of his flock? Holy writ once again certifies his method. The gospels themselves put themselves forward into the minds of men "*by Types, Shadows and Metaphors*" (p. 5). Bunyan finishes his "Apology" with an unapologetic invocation of the rule of the imagination and its power to move, and a splendid charge to his readers to try not enjoying his book if they can.

The ebullience of Bunyan's method is matched by his opening paragraph: "As I walk'd through the wilderness of this world, I lighted on a certain place, where was a Denn; And I laid me down in that place to sleep: And as I slept I dreamed a Dream" (p. 10). It is a literary opening as confident as any ever made. Yet at the same time it contains the same tension about where the figure stops and the meaning begins that we find in Spenser. This tension is not unconnected with its success. It is partly the resistance to the style that accompanies the stylistic affect that gives Bunyan his vigor and relish. Even so unregenerate a skeptic about allegory as Samuel Taylor Coleridge could not help to take some tincture of enjoyment from Bunyan's book. In his 1818 *Lectures on European Literature*, he condemns as "the dullest and most defective parts of Spenser" those places where we see his "agents as allegories."[29] He struggles to make an exception for Milton's Sin and Death but finds them, too, prone to censure. Yet toward Bunyan he is strangely sympathetic. It is a book which "delights every one" (not a view perhaps any longer in fashion). Coleridge concludes that Bunyan's "piety was baffled by his Genius" (1, 103).[30] It is still faint praise: Bunyan succeeds despite himself, and despite his principal literary method. Yet Coleridge perhaps himself mistakes the basis of this method. He allows Bunyan to be baffled only when he relinquishes allegory, and thus to be saved by genius from allegory. Yet the bafflement could be said to be part of the allegory in the first place, and part of the paradoxical legacy of protestant theology to the history of interpretation.

28 *The Pilgrim's Progress*, ed. W. R. Owens (Oxford: World's Classics, 2003), p. 5.
29 Coleridge, *Lectures 1808–1819 On Literature*, ed. R. A. Foakes, 2 vols. (London: Routledge & Kegan Paul, 1987), 1:103.
30 Seamus Perry, "Coleridge, Bunyan, and the Arts of Bafflement," *The Wordsworth Circle* 32 (2001): 89.

14

BLAIR HOXBY

Allegorical drama

Prudentius' *Psychomachia*, Guillaume de Lorris and Jean de Meun's *Roman de la Rose*, Dante's *Divina Commedia*, and Petrarch's *Trionfi* invest combats, triumphs, dances, and other festive and dramatic forms with allegorical significance. But the costumes they describe, the personifications they introduce, and the mystical visions in which they culminate appear only in the mind's eye. In allegorical dramas, on the other hand, actors change their costumes in order to make the states of their characters' souls visible; they perform stage business like hiding a board beneath the earth to discourage Mankind's labors; and they descend from the heavens in machines. The symbolic loci that so often stand out from narrative allegories and ask to be mapped in the imagination are actually arranged in the space of the playing area, which may oppose the mansion of the World to the Heavenly Paradise or may use platforms and scaffolds to create different planes of action proper to demons, mortals, and heavenly spirits. In some cases, allegorical plays turn the conditions of their own performance into an extended metaphor. In *El Gran Teatro del Mundo* (The Great Theatre of the World) (*c.* 1640–45), for example, Calderón de la Barca presents life as a play in which Men are the actors, the World is in charge of the properties and the stage, and the producer is God: the actors are assigned parts, but they must perform them without a script and without rehearsal.

Almost all the drama produced in the late Middle Ages and the Renaissance invites the audience to interpret particular moments allegorically. A revenger may employ allegory as a rhetorical figure, apostrophizing Vengeance as the quit-rent of Murder and the tenant of Tragedy; he may transform a skull into a *memento mori*; and he may be observed by Revenge himself. Villains may fall through trapdoors that resemble hell's mouth. And presenter-figures may direct audiences to see Old Testament figures like Adam, Eve, and the Tree of Knowledge as shadowy types of Christ, Mary, and the Cross on Calvary. Yet it is just as important to recognize that the converse is also true: even the most resolute and sustained allegories of the period inevitably contain a residual of dramatic action, ritual, or ceremony that resists allegorical interpretation. This plenitude and recalcitrance is one of their pleasures and one of the bases of their claim to lead us circuitously toward a truth that eludes direct approach.

In this chapter, we shall be concerned exclusively with dramas whose fiction appears to point toward a system of non-fictional ideas; the existence of such a system is suggested by the "rudiments" of an interpretation provided in the play itself. We shall not be concerned with dramas that contain an occasional action or stage picture that invites moralization.[1] We shall see that in some medieval morality plays, these "rudiments" are substantial and discursive, while in some Renaissance courtly allegories they are as iconic and mysterious as hieroglyphs, but the difference remains one of degree. The roots of such extended allegories extend back to the Hellenistic age, when encyclopedic commentators sought philosophical truths in the myths of Homer. Jewish and Christian exegetes in turn adopted these methods when they sought to discover an organized structure of meaning running through even the darkest passages of Scripture. This genealogy is important, for it helps to explain why many of the dramas we shall consider treat their own difficulty as a proof of sublimity, aspire to be encyclopedic in scope, and display a drive toward the *eschaton*, or last things of history.

Religious allegories

The sustained religious allegorical plays of the late Middle Ages typically center on a representative character who is tempted, falls, repents, and finds redemption. This story is told by dramatizing extended metaphors: that the soul and the body converse with each other; that the World, the Flesh, and the Devil tempt man to sin; that the struggle between the Vices and the Virtues is a chivalric combat waged in the soul; that life is a pilgrimage; that death dances with all the estates. The protagonist may be doubled in order to contrast the consequences of good and bad choices, as he is in *Bien-Avisé, Mal-Avisé* (Well-Advised, Badly-Advised) (1439) and *L'Homme Juste et l'Homme Mondain* (The Just Man and the Worldly Man) (1476). Or he may be played by a group of actors who give life to each of his faculties, as they do in *Wisdom* (1450–1500), a play that anatomizes its protagonist into the Soul, the Three Mights (Mind, Will, and Understanding), and the Five Wits.

1 Gordon Teskey, "Allegory," in *The Spenser Encylopedia*, gen. ed. A. C. Hamilton (Toronto: University of Toronto Press, 1990), p. 16.

The Castle of Perseverance (*c.* 1400–25), one of the earliest examples of the genre to survive, commences before the birth of Mankind and follows him after death. It was staged on a circular *platea* or playing area with a Castle at its center and the mansions of the World, the Flesh, Belial, and the Heavenly Paradise placed around the periphery at the four points of the compass. In the first half of the play, Bad Angel leads Mankind into the unholy company of the World, the Flesh, and the Devil, but fortunately Confession and Penance reintegrate Mankind into the body of the Church and take him to a castle where he is guarded by seven virtues. In the second half of the drama, the Seven Sins besiege the castle; Mankind dies in sin; and Bad Angel carries him off to hell. In heaven, Mercy and Peace prevail over Justice and Truth because they impute the identity of Christ to Mankind, thus reprieving him from hell.

We can draw a useful if misleadingly simple contrast between *Perseverance* and the last great morality play written before the Protestant Reformation, *Everyman* (*c.* 1495–1520). Whereas *Perseverance* is encyclopedic in ambition, *Everyman* achieves its dramatic power by limiting its scope to the last day of Everyman's life. Its message is simple: "Man, in the beginning / Look well, and take good heed to the ending, / Be you never so gay!" (ll. 10–12).

In the first half of the sixteenth century, northern humanists like John Rastell, John Redford, and John Skelton analyzed the trials of humanist study and the perils of secular rule in allegorical interludes that were the direct descendants of such moralities, and some Protestant reformers rewrote older plays like the Flemish *Elckerlijk*, the source of the English *Everyman*, so that Faith, not Good Deeds, was the only reliable companion of Everyman.[2] Others, like John Bale, ridiculed Catholics' allegorical interpretations of scripture without rejecting allegory outright as a mode of dramatic composition.

Protestant criticisms of the mystery cycles, the Council of Trent's determination to enforce the true doctrines of the Church, and the desire of secular authorities to avert civil discord led to the suppression of overtly religious drama in the mid sixteenth century not only in many Protestant lands but also in some Catholic regions that felt vulnerable to reform.[3] Many of the dramatic patterns of the morality play persisted, however, in

2 Thomas H. Best, "Everyman and Protestantism in the Netherlands and Germany," *Daphnis: Zeitschrift für Mittlere Deutsche Literatur* 16 (1987), 13–32; and John Watkins, "The Allegorical Theatre: Moralities, Interludes, and Protestant Drama," in David Wallace, ed., *The Cambridge History of Medieval English Literature* (Cambridge: Cambridge University Press, 1999), pp. 767–92.
3 Harold C. S. J. Gardiner, *Mysteries' End: An Investigation of the Last Days of the Medieval Religious Stage* (New Haven: Yale University Press, 1946).

the popular theater: plays like Marlowe's *Dr. Faustus* may be described as *psychomachia* (battle of the soul) dramas that have been transformed into homiletic tragedies by lopping off their redemptive close. Indeed, *Everyman* has been the most widely admired of moralities since its stage revival in 1901 not because it offers us consolation but because it displays what V. A. Kolve has described as "that movement-into-aloneness generic to tragedy" – and therefore bears witness to the structural debt of Elizabethan tragedy to the morality play.[4]

Despite the widespread suppression of overtly religious drama in Europe in the second half of the sixteenth century, allegorical drama continued to thrive in Rome, where a dialogue of the Soul and the Body provided the vehicle for one of the earliest experiments in the *stile rappresentativo* (the theatrical style of musical text setting employed by the first opera composers), Emilio de' Cavalieri's *La rappresentazione di Anima e di Corpo* (1600). It also received support in the hundreds of Jesuit colleges across Europe that staged Latin plays, operas, or ballets for prize day, Carnival, or Shrovetide. Some of these, like Jakob Bidermann's *Cenodoxus* (1602), were homiletic tragedies with a cast of personifications like Conscience and Death; others, like Jakob Masen's *Androphilus* (1664), represented all of history as a play; and still others, like *Le Tableau Allégorique des Moeurs* (The Allegorical Display of Manners) (1714), were pure ballets depicting different kinds of human character (for example, the rage of Achilles or the madness of Ajax).

The most important religious allegories of the period were the *autos sacramentales* (sacramental acts, that is, dramatic representations of the mystery of the Eucharist) sponsored by Spanish cities. Although the earliest surviving examples date from the first quarter of the sixteenth century, the most accomplished are those of Lope de Vega and Calderón de la Barca. *Autos* could dramatize biblical history, saints' lives, parables, or dogma like the Atonement. Because they were staged in honor of the Feast of Corpus Christi, however, they usually asked the audience to infer the connection between their subject and the Eucharist as a central mystery of the faith.

No single example can suggest the form's range, but because the allegorical interpretation of Scripture was so controversial after the Reformation and so central to Calderón's Catholic dramaturgy, I want to consider an *auto* that dramatizes two of the parables for which Jesus apparently provided his own allegorical interpretation, thus providing some authority for the claim

---

4 V. A. Kolve, "*Everyman* and the Parable of the Talents," in Jerome Taylor and Alan H. Nelson, eds., *Medieval English Drama: Essays Critical and Contextual* (Chicago: University of Chicago Press, 1972), p. 321.

that Scripture may have not only a literal sense but also allegorical ones referring to the deeds of Christ, the state of the soul, and the final events of Christian history.

In *La Semilla y la Cizaña*, which reworks the parable of the Sower and the Weeds (Matthew 13:19 23, 36–43), Calderón celebrates the polysemous quality of Scripture while insisting on the essential coherence of the Bible and the Catholic Faith. For if the seed is many things in the parable, all these things refer to and are made significant by the sole source of meaning in the universe: the Word, the Flesh, and the Eucharist. Calderón's Sower preaches the doctrine of the Eucharist to the Four Continents, where, for the most part, it falls on barren ground. Even in Europe, it is allowed to become mildewed. When the Sower (Jesus) is executed, Judaism, the leader of Asia, transforms the fruit of the seed into instruments of mockery and torture: she gives the Sower a straw stalk as a scepter, a crown of thorns as a diadem, and so forth. After the death of the Sower, God charges Gentiledom to sow the seed. Whereas the vessel that initially carried the seed was Mary, it is now the Church Militant. As the play unfolds, signs do not change their signifiers, they accumulate them, acquiring a fullness and unity of meaning through a dramatic time that compresses sacred history.[5]

Calderón's *autos* share the urge of most morality plays to illustrate matters of faith and morals in an accessible form; in this sense they resemble the pictures and sculptures that Church officials approved as the scriptures of the unlettered crowd. But they also create a sense of power through mystery – an effect they share in common with the drama of the court to which we now turn.

Courtly entertainments

Each form of courtly allegorical drama that the Renaissance inherited from the late Middle Ages had its own dramatic logic. The royal entry took the form of a processional drama in which the advent of the ruler at the city gates transformed everything: the terrestrial city became another Jerusalem and he became more and more like Christ as he penetrated the city. In the pageants that were inspired by allegorical poems like Petrarch's *Trionfi*, on the other hand, each pageant wagon superseded the previous one while remaining in a meaningful relationship to it. The final wagon often arrived with the force of a revelation. Thus, in the *Trionfo de' Sogni* (Triumph of

5 Donald Thaddeus Dietz, *The Auto Sacramental and the Parable in Spanish Golden Age Literature*, North Carolina Studies in the Romance Languages and Literatures (Chapel Hill: University of North Carolina Department of Romance Languages, 1973), pp. 98–107.

Dreams) which Georgio Vasari devised for the Medici in 1565, the pageants of Love, Beauty, Fame, Wealth, and Conquest were exposed as vain dreams when Madness and her band of fools appeared in their wake.

In tournaments, which began as schools of the martial arts but became increasingly theatrical after King Henri II of France died jousting in 1559, combats, assaults on castles, and forms of imprisonment all assumed allegorical significance. Knights might battle to win access to the Temple of Fame, or if the occasion were a wedding, they might style themselves the Knights of the Mount of Love, assault a castle held by fair ladies, and celebrate the erotic surrender of the ladies in a dance. In the hands of a Renaissance poet like Tasso, who was probably responsible for *Il Tempio d'Amore* (The Temple of Love), a *tournament à theme* (chivalric tournament on a theme) staged in Ferrara in 1565, this simple scenario could be transformed into a complex allegory by the introduction of sorceresses, a wood of error, a labyrinth, and false rivals to the Temple of Love, but Tasso still had to dramatize the problems of making a Platonic ascent in terms of the basic situations in which a knight could find himself in a tournament: fighting in the open field, assaulting a defended position, or resting captive.

The key elements of a masquerade, on the other hand, were disguise and dance. Typically, one or more members of the court would appear in disguise, present some fictional explanation of their visit, perform a choreographed dance, and then commence revels that transformed the court. During a feast that the Duke of Burgundy held in 1454, for example, God's Grace entered leading twelve knights and twelve veiled ladies impersonating the Virtues. When the masquers danced with the rest of the assembly, they taught the lessons in virtue that the court would need to achieve its objective: the recapture of Constantinople from the Turks.

The courtly ceremonies and aristocratic entertainments that the court of Burgundy sponsored in the fifteenth century were emulated by the Hapsburgs in Spain and the Netherlands, by the Tudors in England, and by the Este, Gonzaga, and Medici in Italy, but they were also transformed by the political and intellectual developments of the Renaissance.[6] The first of these took its roots from the desire of Florentine humanists like Leonardo Bruni to defend the building projects of Cosimo de Medici in the early fifteenth century against the censure of preaching friars who considered them contrary to the ethic of Christian poverty. Bruni defended such expenditures as expressions of what Aristotle called *megaloprepeia* (or magnificence), the spirit displayed when leading citizens financed dramatic productions and

6 See Roy Strong, *Art and Power: Renaissance Festivals, 1450–1650* (Woodbridge: Boydell Press, 1984).

similar public undertakings with fitting greatness. The full force of this intellectual development was only felt in the next century, however, when the Protestant Reformation divided the universal Church and monarchs became the arbiters of religion and the guarantors of civil peace. Secular rulers then attracted much of the artistic talent and ceremonial energy that had hitherto flowed to the Church, staging shows that exalted their own persons by inspiring awe of their magnificence.

While monarchs and princes naturally looked to Scripture to legitimize their own authority, they also embraced the burgeoning interest of humanists in the Hebrew wisdom and pagan theology that had descended from Moses and Zoroaster through Hermes Trismegistus to Orpheus, Pythagoras, Plato, and his followers. The attempts of Florentine Neoplatonists like Marsilio Ficino to synthesize these traditions, following in the footsteps of the late antique Neoplatonists, proved particularly consequential to the development of courtly entertainments. Ficino reconciled Plato's idea that thought consists of forms received by the mind as images with the philosopher's observation (developed by Boethius and Macrobius) that the audible harmony of voices or instruments (*musica instrumentalis*) captured something of the harmony of the cosmos (*musica mundana*) and could therefore regulate the motions of the soul (*musica humana*).[7] Ficino did this by assuming that all the arts, not just music, were grounded in Pythagorean consonances of number and proportion. That meant that verse, iconography, music, and dance could be coordinated to tell allegories of the cosmos that could harmonize both the soul and human society.

These allegories differed in kind from the *exempla* of medieval sermons. Through his familiarity with the texts of Proclus and Iamblichus, Ficino believed that names, barbarian words, and talismans were more than just signs, they were repositories of meaning and power linked through an occult network of sympathies to what they represented in the cosmos. By skillfully manipulating them, man the microcosmos could in turn attune himself to the spiritual influences targeted. One reason why dances based on the Druid alphabet were performed at the French court was that they did not have to be understood to be potent (see Figures 14.1 and 14.2). For an aristocratic art form that was constantly insisting on the distance between those near the seat of power and those excluded from the palace hall, between those privy to state secrets and those in the dark, mysterious signs had their own political force.

7 Plato, *Timaeus* 34b–37c, *Republic* 398b–412b, *Laws* 788–827; Boethius, *De Institutione musica*, sec. 2; Macrobius, *Commentary on the Dream of Scipio*, trans. William Harris Stahl (New York: Columbia University Press, 1952), pp. 73–74, 185–200.

tres pierres fines, que de diuers émaux, felon le naturel defdites penfées : Le troifiefme cercle, remply de petites rozes de diamans brillans, & de plufieurs perles rondes. Le fôd couuert de petites enfeignes de pierreries & d'or, & la cime de plumaches de toute façon, & de longues & petites aigrettes, au haut defquels il y en auoit vn d'exceffiue groffeur & haulteur. Les fraizes qu'ils portoient faites de fine dentelle fort grande, & les manches plifées femblablement: Ils tenoient chacun vn mouchoir de poind coupé d'or & d'argent dans la main: les mafques dorez & decouppez à piece emportée par compartiment, tous lefquels ainfi parez faifoiét vne entrée fuperbe, auec plufieurs entrelaffemens, tant qu'ils fe venoient ranger en haye, fix d'vn cofté & fix de l'autre. Alors les viollons fonnoient la premiere partie de leur Ballet: & lefdits Cheualliers changeant de pas & de mefure, alloient former leur premiere figure, laquelle fuiuant l'Alphabet des anciés Druides (trouué depuis quelques années dans vn vieil monument) reprefentoit vn caractere d'iceluy Alphabet poincté du nombre de douze, fignifiant

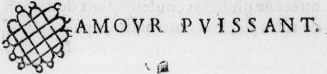 AMOVR PVISSANT.

Figure 14.1 One of several allegorical figures danced in the *Ballet de Monseigneur le Duc de Vendosme* (1610): Mighty Love, an allegorical figure danced in the Ballet.

38

plus parfaict caractere qui fuſt audit Alphabet, qui ſignifioit

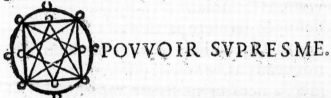

POVVOIR SVPRESME.

A la fin de laquelle ils ſe trouuoient au
plus proche du theatre, où ils ſe repoſoient
iuſques à ce que le Roy commandoit qu'õ
dançaſt des branles: & les violons commen-
çans à en ſonner, leſdits Cheualiers alloiẽt
chacun prendre pour dancer auec eux telle
Dame de la Cour qui leur plaiſoit : & ayant
cõmencé la dãce, pluſieurs autres ſeigneurs
& Gentils-hõmes qualifiez des plus diſpots,
prenoiẽt auſſi d'autres Dames à leur fantai-
zie, & ſe meſloiẽt auec leſdits Cheualiers &
ſeigneurs ſuſdits audit bal, où toute ſorte de
dance fuſt dancée en apres, tant en general
qu'en particulier, iuſques à tant qu'il pleuſt
à ſa Majeſté de ſe retirer.

F I N.

Figure 14.2 One of several allegorical figures danced in the *Ballet de Monseigneur le Duc de Vendosme* (1610): Supreme Power, another of the allegorical figures danced in the Ballet.

This ideological climate helps to explain Tasso's definition of allegory as an expressive mode that can only be understood by initiates, for it "reflects the passions, the beliefs, the manners, not only in their appearances, but chiefly in their intrinsic being, and signifies more obscurely through (so to speak) mysterious signs which can be fully comprehended only by those who know the nature of things."[8] This mode of courtly Neoplatonic allegory reached its height in the *ballet de cour* (court ballet) of the Valois, the masques of the Stuart court, and the *intermedi*, or spectacular intermissions, with which the Medici relieved their productions of learned comedies.

The French *ballet de cour* achieved its definitive form under Catherine de Medici. After the death of her husband Henri II at a tournament, Catherine made repeated attempts to reconcile the religious and political factions of the realm. When she temporarily succeeded, she mounted what she called *magnificences* that were intended to affirm the sacral power of the monarch, depict the bankrupt Crown as a source of plenty, and impute the serenity of the heavens to her troubled realm. The artists associated with Jean Antoine de Baïf's *Académie de Poésie et Musique* and the group of poets known as the *Pléiade* (whose most notable members were Pierre de Ronsard, Joachim du Bellay, and Baïf) used these occasions to try to marry verse, music, and dance as the Greeks had done. The *ballet de cour* began to emerge from these *magnificences* in a recognizable form with the *Paradis d'amour*, an allegorical combat and dance performed for the wedding of Henry of Navarre and Margarite de Valois in 1572, but it was Catherine's daughter-in-law Queen Louise of Lorraine who sponsored the best-documented of the period's ballets in 1581, the *Balet Comique de la Royne* (Queen).[9]

An engraving of the event shows that the royal family sat at one end of a hall opposite an artificial garden flanked by entrances for the personages of the ballet. Circé, who tempted men to live a life of the passions that transformed them into beasts according to Natale Conti's allegorical interpretation, sat enthroned like a rival to the king. The ballet opened when a gentleman who had escaped Circé's clutches appealed to the king to rescue him. This appeal initiated a series of *entrées* in which mythological figures asserted their own powers only to be subdued by Circé's ability to incite a desire for change. The see-saw struggle continued until an alliance of gods and personified virtues, strengthened by the king's justice, assaulted

---

8 Torquato Tasso, "Allegoria del poema," in *Opere*, ed. G. Rosini, 33 vols. (Pisa: Niccolò Capurro, 1830), 24:v–vi.

9 See Balthazar de Beaujoyeulx, *Le Balet Comique*, facs. with intro. by Margaret M. McGowen (Binghampton: Medieval and Renaissance Texts and Studies, 1982); and Thomas M. Greene, "The King's One Body in the *Balet Comique de la Royne*," *Yale French Studies* 86 (1994), 75–93; earlier studies are cited in the notes.

her bower. Circé was finally forced to hand over her wand to the king. The entertainment, which lasted more than five hours, culminated in a Grand Ballet that the ladies of the court addressed to the king as the single guarantor of meaning to which all the signs in the court pointed. They imitated the order and harmony of the cosmos by forming, breaking, and re-forming forty figures that were so "exact and well planned in their forms" that "the spectators thought that Archimedes could not have understood geometric proportions any better." As they did so, they invested the king's person with the eurhythmic energy of the cosmos itself.[10]

The similarities between the *ballet de cour* and the masque are apparent in the entertainment that Ben Jonson and Inigo Jones created for the marriage of the Earl of Essex to Frances Howard in 1606.[11] *Hymenaei* is a paean to a notion of Union that becomes increasingly expansive and exalted until it encompasses the wedding of these two aristocrats, the ideal marriage of James I and Queen Anne, the political union of England and Scotland, and the great Chain of Being that stretches from the hand of God to the lowest form of nature. The masque commenced with a Roman marriage rite that was disrupted by contentions in the human "Microcosme" that were only set to rights when the figure of Reason enjoined the warring factions of the human being and the body politic to recognize the power of Union, the force that makes souls and bodies mix, contracts the world in one, and is the spring and end of all things. The consummation of the marriage was then enacted when Order supervised figured dances that terminated in a circle that took Reason as its center: these dances represented the union of loving marriage, the harmonious ordering of man's nature and human society under the guidance of reason, the correspondence between the microcosm and the macrocosm, and the girdle of Venus – at once an erotic force of nature and the abstract power of the World Soul that animates and unites the order of creation.

We find a similar ambition to tie the microcosm to the macrocosm, the mythical to the natural, in the *intermedi* that were staged to celebrate the marriage of Grand Duke Ferdinand I to Christine of Lorraine, granddaughter of the French queen Catherine de Medici, in 1589.[12] But in this case, the unifying force was music. Count Giovanni Bardi, who devised the *intermedi*, was the patron of the Florentine Camerata, an informal academy that met

---

10 Beaujoyeulx, *Le Balet Comique*, p. 56.

11 See D. J. Gordon, "*Hymenaei*: Ben Jonson's Masque of Union," *Journal of the Warburg and Courtauld Institutes* 8 (1945), 107–45. All citations are from *Ben Jonson*, ed. C. H. Herford, Percy and Evelyn Simpson, 11 vols. (Oxford: Clarendon, 1925–52), vol. 7.

12 See James M. Salow, *Florentine Festival as Theatrum Mundi: The Medici Wedding of 1589* (New Haven: Yale University Press, 1996), with earlier studies listed in the bibliography.

Figure 14.3 The first *intermedio* of 1589, Florence.

to discuss ancient music, and these *intermedi* were, among other things, a forum in which he and others could attempt to recreate various aspects of the ancient theater – including its machines, choral songs, and mimetic dance. Like all *intermedi*, Bardi's were intercalated between the acts of a learned comedy. The first, fourth, and sixth were Neoplatonic allegories about the music of the cosmos (see Figure 14.3). The second, third, and fifth used legendary material to celebrate the music in nature and culture alike and to demonstrate its effects on the human soul. Bardi's *intermedi*, in other words, embraced both the Platonic view of music as a principle of the cosmos and Aristotle's rhetorical conception of music as a means for the singer to bring his listeners to feel the same passions of the soul. They thus represent the high-water mark of courtly Neoplatonic allegory and an intimation of its mortality.

While they remained independent genres, the *ballet de cour*, the masque, and the *intermedio* all borrowed from one another. They were courtly forms whose outward show was expected to be magnificent, whose "*voice*" had to be "taught to sound to present occasions," yet whose "*sense*," said Jonson, ought to "lay hold on more remov'd *mysteries*" (*Hymenaei*, ll. 17–19). With the search for these mysteries came an expansion of the court, which became the world, and an idealization and abstraction of the ruler, who, whether he was watching or dancing for all to see, became Heroic Virtue, Pan the universal god of Nature, Apollo the sun god, Jupiter the Thunderer – even the Prime Mover. These entertainments sought to bring the harmony of the cosmos down to earth, but they also longed for a return of the Golden Age: this desire for an idealized past that would return in the present reign was the structural equivalent of religious allegory's drive toward the *eschaton*, for it too betrayed an urge to escape the burden of time.

Spatial allegories

One of the things that distinguishes dramatic allegory from narrative allegory is that it makes its meaning in part by imputing allegorical significance to the performance space in which the actors will move and their audience will watch. Here are three examples of the way dramatic space matters.

The royal entry took the form of a processional drama in which the ruler was presented with the keys to the city and he affirmed the privileges of the citizens and clergy.[13] The crucial trope of the royal entry in its first centuries was that the advent of the king transformed the city into a New Jerusalem. So when Henry VI made his entry into London in 1432 after being crowned king of France, he was greeted as a Davidic king returning to Jerusalem after victory. On Tower Bridge, he received blessings from Nature, Grace, and Fortune, who were flanked by the Seven Gifts of the Holy Ghost and the Seven Gifts of Grace. As he approached subsequent pageants, his royal charisma animated the tableaux and turned water into wine at a fountain. The entry reached its climax when the king passed from the heavenly Jerusalem to a likeness of the Trinity enthroned and surrounded by a hierarchy of angels who assured the king of divine protection.

The rediscovery of ancient texts describing Roman triumphs led to a revision of the royal entry in sixteenth-century Italy so that the ruler was greeted as a *triumphator* entering Rome. In 1535, the Farnese Pope Paul II even ordered that houses and churches be demolished so that the Holy Roman Emperor Charles V might make his Roman entry along the ancient *via triumphalis*. It was not long before the antique style was emulated farther north. But classical trappings did not change the essence of the drama: excitement commenced when the royal body crossed the limen of the city and it mounted as he approached a spot of sacredness at its heart. As the ruler penetrated the city, he more nearly approached divinity and the city became more ideal.

13 Lawrence Manley, *Literature and Culture in Early Modern London* (Cambridge: Cambridge University Press, 1995), chapter 5; and Gordon Kipling, *Enter the King: Theatre, Liturgy, and Ritual in the Medieval Civic Triumph* (Oxford: Clarendon Press, 1998), with earlier studies listed in the bibliography.

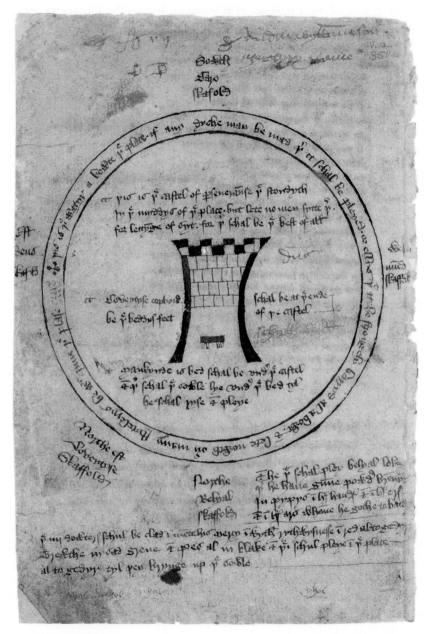

Figure 14.4 Diagram for a performance of *The Castle of Perseverance* (*c.* 1400–25).

The Castle of Perseverance makes an entirely different use of space. According to a diagram following the text (see Figure 14.4), the Castle stands at the center of a circular *platea* demarcated by a ditch filled with water.[14] At the foot of the Castle is a bed for the birth of the "human soul," and on the periphery of the circle are five mansions. To the east, the position of the altar in a church and of Jerusalem on a medieval map, stood Heavenly Paradise, which may have been represented by an elevated scaffold with an upper tier for a choir. To the west, and diametrically opposed to Heaven, lay the World (Mundus), flanked by the house of Flesh (Caro) to the south and that of Belial to the north. This arrangement pitted the World, the Flesh, and the Devil against Heaven in a struggle for control over the soul of Mankind. Between the World and the Devil stood the scaffold of Covetousness, the most puissant vice of the play. The setting of *Perseverance* asked its spectators to see the arena before them as both the world and a spiritual cosmos corresponding to the world. It suggested that the temporal struggle of Mankind was just a chapter in a great mystical combat between the forces of good and evil that would only be decided at Doomsday.

The audience of *Perseverance* would have been forced to move their eyes with the actors: no seat would have been ideal at all times. Such a theatrical space differs markedly from court theaters with perspective scenes like the Teatro Uffizi or the Banqueting Hall of Inigo Jones.[15] These had only one perfect line of sight which was reserved for the ruler, who sat in a raised platform, or even (a little later) in a royal box framed by a proscenium arch. This seating arrangement created a hierarchy of knowledge with the ruler seated at the head and those farthest away from him at the base. What the audience watched was not so much a performance on stage as two spectacles at either end of the hall that invested each other with meaning and enhanced each other's status. The machinery that was used for these court spectacles was essential to the action of the drama, for the ascents and descents, changes of scene, and metamorphoses in plain view that they permitted reinforced the metaphysical and ethical contentions of their courtly allegories: that kings transcend common men as far as men do beasts; that, thanks to their virtue and their charisma, they can impose a beneficent order on society and restrain the bestial and demonic forces that threaten it; that the ideal can transform the real. The steps that led down from the raised stage to the

---

14 See A. M. Nagler, *The Medieval and Religious Stage: Shapes and Phantoms* (New Haven: Yale University Press, 1976), pp. 49–52, which surveys earlier studies.
15 Stephen Orgel, *The Illusion of Power: Political Theater in the English Renaissance* (Berkeley: University of California Press, 1975), chapter 1.

level of the hall were just as significant, for they permitted the erasure of the distinction between the idealized fictions of the scene and the audience when the masquers joined in the revels of the court.

The shifting sands of allegory

The late Middle Ages and the Renaissance thought about allegorical signs in two basic ways. The first was grounded in Aristotelian logic. In the introduction to *Iconologia* (1593), Cesare Ripa says that if we wish to form the image of a concept we must analyze it logically as we would when trying to frame a verbal definition: the human figure stands for the essence of the concept and the items that she holds are its attributes. These attributes are to be found by rationally arriving at the qualities that abstract ideas and concrete objects have in common. As we watch an allegorical play, we decode it. Neoplatonists emphasized, on the other hand, that allegorical signs shared a genuine identity with the things they resembled. "Whatever exists in the inferior world will also be found in the superior world, but in a more elevated form," says Pico della Mirandola. "In our world we have fire as an element, in the celestial world the corresponding entity is the sun, in the supra-celestial world the seraphic fire of the Intellect. But consider their difference: The elemental fire burns, the celestial fire gives life, and supra-celestial loves."[16] Guided by ancient allegorical commentators, they ransacked the classics for myths, images, and the smallest details of costumes because they believed that these held the secrets of the super-sensible world. They were not embarrassed by the difficulty of their allegories because they took their mysterious quality as a sign of potency and wisdom.[17]

It would be misleading to suggest that authors in the late Middle Ages and the Renaissance felt a sharp distinction between the Aristotelian and Neoplatonic views of allegory. Even Christians who felt little interest in the occult wisdom of the pagans believed that God revealed himself in the book of Nature, and even Neoplatonists made use of Ripa's iconography. But it is still fair to say that the morality play and most of the other religious allegories produced after the Council of Trent thought of dramatic allegories not as representations but as symbols that changed and developed through time – pictures that could teach the illiterate what the letter of Scripture could likewise teach readers. When these allegories made use of the apparently inappropriate symbols and similes to be found in books like Revelation,

16 Giovanni Pico della Mirandola, *Heptaplus*, ed. Eugenio Garin (Florence: Vallecchi, 1942), p. 188.
17 E. H. Gombrich, "Icones Symbolicae: The Visual Image in Neo-Platonic Thought," *Journal of the Warburg and Courtauld Institutes* 11 (1948): 163–92.

it was, as Dionysius the Areopagite explained, so that the audience would refuse to accept these as actual representations and would search for a higher truth by following the *via negativa* or negative theology. The Neoplatonic authors of courtly allegories were also interested in erecting ladders, but their dramas were intended to create a two way traffic between the court and the heavens, and they believed that the geometric forms of their dances and the "fiue hundred severall hiewes" created by stage machines like the sphere of Fire in *Hymenaei* (ll. 674–75) were more than just stimuli to thought; they were acts and images of Intelligence that had "a wonderful power to calm, move, and influence our spirit, mind and body."[18] This faith in the reality and efficacy of perceptible manifestations of truth also distinguished the court masque from Jacobean tragedy and the contemporary *Trauerspiel*, or mourning play, which might stage allegories and transform the corpse into its ultimate "emblematic property" but displayed a melancholy disbelief that these spectacles of ruin could empower, liberate, or console.[19]

Belief in the Neoplatonic order of creation was not undermined in a day, but we can point to several developments that had eroded it by the beginning of the eighteenth century. The first was the growing authority of Aristotelian criticism after the publication of the first commentary on the *Poetics* in 1548. Although many of the masters of the masque and the *intermedio* had a thorough knowledge of the *Poetics*, Aristotelian criticism did slowly promote a shift from the intimation of mysteries to the representation of the actions, characters, and affections of men, and it set up the passions as the universal reference point of the arts in lieu of Pythagorean consonances of number and proportion. Descartes' philosophical method, Locke's theories of epistemology, and experimental science also undermined the assumptions that underwrote a masque like *Hymenaei*. Although courts continued to present allegorical dramas in the eighteenth century – the last great festival in the Teatro Farnese was held in 1732 – the movement away from Neoplatonic allegory toward the operatic expression of the passions was already under way when the Teatro Farnese was inaugurated in 1628. The Mars and Mercury of the *opéra-tournoi* that Claudio Achillini and Claudio Monteverdi created for the occasion represented war and learning, to be sure, but the vital energy of the work was devoted to testing the persuasive power of the arts – not to laying "hold on more remou'd *mysteries*," as Jonson said masques should.

---

18 Marsilio Ficino, *Three Books on Life*, ed. and trans. Carol V. Kaske and John R. Clarke (Tempe, Arizona: Arizona Center for Medieval and Renaissance Studies, 2002), p. 331.
19 Walter Benjamin, *The Origin of German Tragic Drama*, trans. John Osborne (London: Verso, 1998), pp. 217–18.

By the early eighteenth century, the abbé Dubos could see no point in allegories that did not have an instantly recognizable sense accepted by tradition; all other attempts to represent concepts with images were "a kind of ciphers, whereof nobody has the key, and very few are desirous of having it. It will suffice to observe... that their inventor generally makes a bad use of his abilities, in spending his time in the production of such beings."[20] Dubos enjoyed great prestige as a theorist of the arts in France, England, and Germany, and many of the allegorical dramas that were produced in subsequent decades answered his call for clarity. These allegorical dramas often warranted Coleridge's charge that "allegory is but a translation of abstract notions into a picture-language, which is itself nothing but an abstraction from objects of the senses; the principal being more worthless even than its phantom proxy, both alike unsubstantial, and the former shapeless to boot."[21] For the authors who created allegories in the eighteenth century no longer assumed with Jonson that "the conceits of the mind are Pictures of things, and the tongue is the Interpreter of those pictures."[22] They no longer believed in signs that, like the hieroglyphs that Plotinus described, were immediate unities, not aggregates of discursive reasoning and detailed willing (*Enneads* 5.8.6). The epiphanies that allegory had once delivered would henceforth have to be sought in the misty recesses of the romantic symbol.

20 Jean-Baptiste Dubos, *Critical Reflections on Poetry, Painting and Music*, trans. Thomas Nugent, 3 vols. (London, 1748), 1:153–54.
21 Samuel Taylor Coleridge, *The Complete Works*, ed. W. G. T. Shedd (New York: Harper, 1884), 1:437.
22 *"Discoveries"* in *Ben Jonson*, 8:628.

PART IV

The fall and rise of allegory

15

THERESA M. KELLEY

Romanticism's errant allegory

They look at [*The Faerie Queene*] as a child looks at a painted dragon, and think it will strangle them in its shining folds. This is very idle. If they do not meddle with the allegory, the allegory will not meddle with them.

William Hazlitt[1]

Introduction

Neoclassical writers took a dim and limited view of allegory, insisting that it was most decorous when strictly iconographic and immobile, like a pictorial representation of Justice holding scales. Allegorical "persons" that move and act troubled Neoclassical strictures about the need to separate abstract figures from realist narratives or, indeed, narrative of any kind. Both Spenser's *The Faerie Queene* and the allegorical episode Satan, Sin and Death in Milton's *Paradise Lost* were common targets. When the Romantic writer Leigh Hunt suggests that *The Faerie Queene* is "but one part allegory, and nine parts beauty and enjoyment; sometimes an excess of flesh and blood," he exposes a dimension of allegory that Neoclassicism rejected.[2] The unaccommodated remainder in this equation registers what his contemporary William Hazlitt wryly suggests readers might safely ignore – the specter of allegorical figures alive and on the move. This essay charts the Romantic understanding of allegory as a genre and narrative figure that tacks between realist narratives and details and the abstractions with which allegory has long been identified.

Romantic writers and artists devise allegorical figures whose unaccommodated remainder of "flesh and blood" is a striking index of their "otherness," an excess defiant of the law of abstraction and the law of genre. This figural practice bends toward a version of allegory whose differences from the Neoclassical model are emphatic. Like Proteus, Romantic allegory is bound to successive visible and material shapes that hover over the boundary between

---

1 William Hazlitt, "Chaucer and Spenser," in *The Complete Works of William Hazlitt*, ed. P. P. Howe, 21 vols. (London: J. M. Dent, 1933), 5:38.
2 Leigh Hunt, "Spenser," in *Imagination and Fancy*, 2nd edn. (London: Smith, Elder, 1845), p. 50.

abstract idea and material form. Temporizing and excessive, it eludes capture by changing shape. The imagined proximity of allegorical shapes to real people and events corrodes the barrier between the general and the particular which Neoclassical critics had hoped to secure. By way of allegory, Romantic writers investigate a problem that becomes more pressing with the rise of nineteenth-century realism, whose epistemological faith in real particulars William Carlos Williams echoes in a modernist key when he calls for "no ideas but in things."[3]

To the world of Spenser's faery romance, as mediated by eighteenth-century neo-Spenserian poets, Romantic allegory offers the flesh and blood that Hazlitt's formula for reading Spenser tries to minimize. To the decorum of Neoclassical allegory, it replies with phantasmagoric and monstrous figures. Working against or with the emergent demand for realism, it co-opts realistic details only to deform or transform them, in spite of themselves, into something "other" such that the role of abstraction in all acts of representation cannot be put aside. To the emptying of human traits and motion from later eighteenth-century poetic personification, it replies with figures animated as well as prompted by passion such that they cannot be excluded from the scene of Romantic figuration. To the presumption that allegorical meaning is elsewhere, visionary, or hidden, Romantic allegory offers in opposition its hunger for spectacular images and figures. This oppositionality is creative and double-jointed: it ratifies the prominence of visual images in allegory since the Renaissance, but uses those images to reorient (and disorient) that tradition. Even as Proteus adopts then sheds successive shapes to evade those who would capture him and force him to reveal the future, so does Romantic allegory evade the fixed, ahistorical and determinate meaning toward which allegory tends and toward which it was impelled by the Neoclassical insistence on simple allegorical ideas and images.

Allegoric shapes

From the obviousness of punning allegorical names like Urizen (Your Reason) to the more subtle and varied allegorical claims he makes for Enitharmon and Los in the prophetic poems, William Blake's characters inhabit shifting allegorical frames. As the fallen poet-artist, Los is a minute and vast "particular" instance of Blake's allegorical method. Unlike Urizen, whose rigid schematism brilliantly satirizes Enlightenment values and, not incidentally, Neoclassical allegory, Los tests critical preconceptions about

---

3 William Carlos Williams, *Paterson*, ed. Christopher MacGowan, rev. edn. (New York: New Directions, 1992), p. 9.

what allegory is or can be. Watching what Los does and doesn't accomplish from poem to poem exposes the fragile, if sustained allegorical enterprise at work in Blake's prophecies. Driven by the Romantic bias toward particularity, he works against Neoclassical abstraction by inventing words and images that grapple with the hermeneutic difficulty for which allegory is both a metafigure and a scapegoat in modern culture: how particular forms give shape to ideas beyond their boundaries. The labor required to produce illuminated poems may in this way assist Blake's sometime vision of a "Sublime Allegory." As he solicits "corporeal understanding" of his labor and forms, he imagines an optical relay between the small images presented in his books and the gigantic beings those images represent – Albion, the four fallen Zoas and the cast of larger-than-life characters who struggle to divide further or to reunite.[4]

Blake's frontispiece for *Visions of the Daughters of Albion* (1793), reproduced on the cover of this volume, invites just such a relay or, perhaps more accurately, difficult conversation. The trio of tormented figures huddled at the opening of a cave compresses the story of slavery, abolition and the British slave trade to North America into a sexual triangle between the unwilling slave Oothoon, her owner and rapist Bromion, and the isolated figure of Theotormon, Oothoon's beloved. Theotormon, recoiling prudishly from the rape of Oothoon, does not take in the argument that ensues between Bromion, who presents a confident view of the limits of knowledge, and Oothoon, who argues passionately for knowledge beyond the (literal and visible) chains that bind her. The poem also invites an allegorical reading and re-reading of its frontispiece, where breaking clouds and the sun may visually pre-figure the opening horizon of knowledge and possible futures that Oothoon imagines in the poem, but which none of the three physically embodied beings can see as the poem begins and only one of them still imagines as it ends. More defined in later copies, those bodies insist on the material and local conditions that bind all the poem's speakers, even as the poem develops competing allegorical visions of how beings (might) experience existence. Here allegorical tendency is bound to its stubborn material and historical ground. The skull-like shape of the cave that surrounds these figures in Blake's frontispiece implies too that these divergent allegorical narratives play out in mind and world.

Blake's late tempura painting, titled *Allegory of the Cave of the Nymphs, The Sea of Time and Space* (1821) or, more neutrally, the Arlington Court painting, presents a rather different tableau of figures beside sea and cave that

---

4 William Blake, *The Complete Poetry and Prose of William Blake*, ed. David V. Erdman, rev. edn. (Berkeley: University of California Press, 1982), p. 730.

may reflect the pictorial interest in allegorical subjects that emerges clearly in 1824, when he begins to illustrate Dante's *Commedia*. The allegorical claim of the Arlington Court painting's sometime title directs readers, or at least some readers, back to Porphyry's treatise on Homer, which Blake's friend or acquaintance Thomas Taylor translated and published in 1788. Kathleen Raine traces the spiraling composition of the figures in Blake's painting to Porphyry's Dantesque account of souls moving toward the sea and back up to an eternal realm.[5] For those readers who accept this lineage, Blake's allegorical method reaches back, via Taylor, to Neoplatonist exegeses of classical and biblical texts.

Blake's frontispiece for *Visions of the Daughters of Albion* and the Arlington Court painting occasion present, then, quite distinct allegorical trajectories. In the first, allegorical meaning remains tethered to its difficult realist substrate; in the second, an allegorical vision moves swiftly away from embodied, physical existence. Reading between them, as the shared iconography of cave, sea and figure also invites us to do, the Neoplatonic vision of the soul's rebirth and renewal in one speaks to Oothoon's visions in the other of a state of being and knowledge beyond the visible restraints on her present existence.

A newspaper headline in Mary Shelley's *The Last Man* suggests how such inversions advertise an allegorical frame of reference. In the novel, which chronicles the spread of plague across the globe, the newsprint itself becomes a compellingly unstable material sign of the plague itself: "diminutive letters grew gigantic to the bewildered eye of fear: they seemed graven with a pen of iron, impressed by fire, woven in the clouds, stamped on the very front of the universe."[6] What makes those letters expand to that "bewildered eye of fear" is their referent – news of the plague on the Continent and the likelihood that it will soon reach England. As Romantic allegorical figures often do, the ballooning size of these letters mimics the approach of the plague and points elsewhere, in this case just across the Channel to the plague itself.

This enlargement, which occurs in a fantastic, not verisimilar, register, also reduces the figure of the newspaper reader to an abstracted, condensed and disembodied synecdoche – the "eye of fear" – whose figural reduction mirrors in reverse the effect of the as-yet-absent plague made "present" by newspaper headlines. This strange semiotic cross between iconicity and

5 Martin Butlin, *The Paintings and Drawings of William Blake*, 2 vols. (New Haven and London: Yale University Press, 1981), 1:549 and 2: plate 969; Kathleen Raine, *Blake and Tradition*, 2 vols. (1969 rpt.; London: Routledge, 2002), 1:75–78.
6 Mary Shelley, *The Last Man*, ed. Hugh J. Luke, Jr. (Lincoln: University of Nebraska Press, 1965), p. 171.

indexicality – that is, between signs that represent something visually and signs that point elsewhere for their meaning – is as fundamental to allegory and emblem as it is to Blake's prophetic poems, where the iconic function of engraved images and texts defers to their indexical status as signs for future, imaginative restoration. Indeed, the imaginative sign of this restoration may be, David Clark has suggested, not universal harmony but minutely articulated differences that sheer off one from the next to manifest energies that lie buried or obscured after the Fall and even in *Jerusalem*.[7]

Romantic reservations about allegory often compete with the depiction of absent things or ideas as though they were present, the rhetorical strategy and figure called *phantasia*.[8] Mary Shelley invokes its English cognate and vividness and mental vision, its trademark effects on readers and viewers, to describe the image or dream that prompted her to write *Frankenstein*:

> My imagination, unbidden, possessed and guided me, gifting the successive images that arose in my mind with a vividness far beyond the usual bounds of reverie. I saw – with shut eyes, but acute mental vision – I saw the pale student of the unhallowed arts kneeling beside the thing he had put together. I saw the hideous phantasm of a man stretched out.[9]

Shelley's account aligns *phantasia* with monsters like "that hideous phantasm" that grotesquely exceed human norms. Although such exaggerations are not necessarily allegorical, distortions of human scale and proportions are one way that Romantic allegory occupies the border between what appears to be true to life or verisimilar and what is not.

Wordsworth's uneasiness about personification conveys a broader Romantic ambivalence about the rhetorical vividness of figures that seem animated, but are nonetheless unlike the human beings those figures are said to imitate or represent. In his 1800 *Preface* to *Lyrical Ballads*, he says that personifications of "abstract ideas" do not "make any regular or natural part of" ordinary conversation. Eighteenth-century poets who used a stock lexicon of "poetic" personifications with scant attention to situation and affect are the obvious target of this disclaimer. When Wordsworth revises this statement in later editions, he grants, with Longinus' treatise *On the*

---

7 David Clark, "The Innocence of Becoming Restored: Blake, Nietzsche, and the Disclosure of Difference," *Studies in Romanticism* 29 (1990), 91–114 (at 111).
8 Pseudo-Cicero, *Rhetorica ad Herennium*, trans. Harry Caplan (Cambridge, MA: Harvard University Press, 1954), p. 405 and *De Oratore*, trans. and ed. H. Rackham, 2 vols. (Cambridge, MA: Harvard University Press, 1954), 4.20–21; Quintilian, *Institutio oratoria*, trans. H. E. Butler, 4 vols. (Cambridge, MA: Harvard University Press, 1921), 8.3.61 and 9.2.40.
9 Mary Shelley, 1831 "Preface," *Frankenstein*, ed. James Rieger (Chicago: University of Chicago Press, 1974), pp. 227–28.

Sublime in mind, that powerful, even exaggerated figures are appropriate (albeit distinctly not "regular" in the sense of being ordinary or usual) when "prompted by passion." With this self-correction Wordsworth joins *pathos*, the classical rhetorical term for strong passion, to the most fully Romantic argument of the *Preface*: that good poems need strong figures to convey passion.[10]

Whether *pathos* or passion, this familiar Romantic category is linked on one side to human beings, and on the other to allegory. This second affiliation is clear in Joanna Baillie's "Introductory Discourse" for *Plays on the Passions*, published two years before Wordsworth's *Preface*. Baillie argues that assigning a master passion such as envy, love, or hatred to a single protagonist should be avoided because audiences find such displays unbelievable and therefore unaffecting. The reason is not hard to work out: a character who is dominated by a single passion like fear may well look like Fear and nothing else. Yet she presents the tragic passions that impel her protagonists in allegorical terms: they are "those great masters of the soul," even "tyrannical masters" whose "irresistible attacks . . . it is impossible to repel."[11]

The proximity between allegory's palpable shapes and real or material details is especially telling in French revolutionary propaganda. For a brief time Liberty was a woman; cheap pamphlets, broadsides, and almanacs extolled pro-revolutionary allegorical virtues; and one remarkable deck of playing cards replaced the traditional images of kings, queens, and jacks with allegorical virtues that inhabit a post-revolutionary view of culture and class. The jacks, now called "equalities," include the *égalité* of rank or power and color represented by Courage, a former African slave who has been, the advertisement and accompanying rule book explain, relieved of his chains and given arms. At the same time and for similar ends, allegorical figures also packaged abstractions for public consumption. Helen Maria Williams, an early British partisan of the Revolution, acted the part of Liberté in an emblematic tableau, shouting "Vive la nation!" Revolutionary leaders assumed that the great, unrepresented majority of the French would be swayed by the power of allegorical figures thus come to life.[12]

---

10 William Wordsworth, *The Prose Works of William Wordsworth*, ed. W. J. B. Owen and Jane W. Smyser, 3 vols. (Oxford: Clarendon Press, 1974), 2:31–32n.

11 Joanna Baillie, "Introductory Discourse," *A Series of Plays*, 2 vols. (London: T. Cadell and W. Davies, 1798), pp. 35, 39, 43.

12 Mona Ozouf, *Festivals and the French Revolution*, trans. Alan Sheridan (Cambridge, MA: Harvard University Press, 1988), pp. 211–12; Lynn Hunt, *Politics, Culture, and Class in the French Revolution* (Berkeley: University of California Press, 1992), pp. 62–66, 89–90; Robert Darnton and Daniel Roche, eds., *Revolution in Print* (Berkeley: University of

Yet this use of allegory for propangandist purposes also negotiated incompatible extremes. By using allegorical abstractions like Fanaticism, Monarchy, Abundance, Liberty and Justice in reenactments of revolutionary events, revolutionary leaders hoped to channel volatile popular opinion into safe, because safely abstract, enthusiasm for the revolutionary project. But because these allegorical figures often carried real weapons, it was always possible that they could be used for real, rather than allegorical, fighting. For this reason, organizers of revolutionary festivals increasingly proscribed their use. As the rhetoric of Robespierre and other architects of the Terror also makes clear, allegorical violence could be at least as damaging because it suggested that human lives could be subsumed by allegorical abstractions.

Coleridge argues that because allegory transforms persons into personifications and abstractions, it is antithetical to the transcendent imagination, which he allies with the symbol as the figure in which the particular and the universal are held to be "translucent" to each other. Whereas late antique Neoplatonic allegorists had made similar claims about symbols without distinguishing them from allegory, Coleridge and his German contemporaries, particularly F. W. J. Schelling and J. W. Goethe, centered such ideas on the symbol and opposed them to allegory.[13] This strategic move recentered figuration from Coleridge on: the synecdochic power of concrete-abstraction became the work of symbol, as distinct from the purely abstract allegory of Neoclassical poetry and critical theory.

In the *Biographia Literaria*, Coleridge's autobiography of the growth of his philosophical mind, he aligns *phantasia* or fancy with allegory, although the Greek term had long been translated as "imagination." He argues instead that the history of usage for the words *fancy* and *imagination* and their Latin and Greek cognates illustrates what he calls "desynonimization," a process in which once synonymous terms become distinct as concrete and abstract meanings separate. Wary of abstraction though he is, Coleridge here invokes it to show how *phantasia* is different from the imagination. His argument draws heavily on German philosophy of the period, particularly

California Press, 1989), plate 13, no. 188; Helen Maria Williams, *Letters Written in France, in the summer of 1790, vol. 1, Letters from France, by Helen Maria Williams*; facsimile reproductions with an introd. by Janet M. Todd, 8 vols. in 2 (Delmar, NY: Scholars Facsimiles & Reprints, 1975).

13 Samuel Taylor Coleridge, *Statesman's Manual, Lay Sermons*, ed. R. J. White (NJ: Princeton University Press, 1972), p. 30; F. W. J Schelling, *Philosophie der Kunst*, Part II, in *Sämtliche Werke* 5 (Stuttgart: Cottascher Verlag, 1859): 354ff., and for English translation, see F.W.J. Schelling, *Philosophy of Art*, trans. Douglas W. Stott (Minneapolis: University of Minnesota Press, 1989), pp. 45–50; J. W. von Goethe, "Über Laokóòn" and "Symbolik," in *Goethes Werke* 12, eds. Herbert von Einem et al. (Hamburg: Wegner Verlag, 1953): 56–66 and 322–23.

Jean Paul Richter's claim that imagination (*Einbildungskraft*) is inferior to fancy (*Phantasie*): "Fancy makes all parts whole . . . she totalizes everything, even the endless universe."[14] In the *Biographia*, Coleridge finally reassigns fancy's synthesizing power to imagination, but not until he has made several efforts, in his main text and in notes, to extricate the philosophical fortunes of the Platonic *idea* and the Romantic imagination from the clutches of *phantasia*.

The narrative path of Coleridgean allegory in the *Biographia* registers the aspect of allegory that Coleridge tends to suppress and his most formidable twentieth-century critic Paul de Man revives – the role of narrative and temporality in the work of allegory. De Man takes skeptical aim at the project Coleridge defends with every philosophical argument and seeming digression: his belief that persons can write and live authentic and coherent histories. From this vantage point, poet and critic are uncannily well-matched antagonists. For de Man, echoing Walter Benjamin's view of allegory and history, allegory is the necessary angel of ruin, historical fragmentation, and commodifying energies that turn persons into abstractions and things.[15] On similar grounds but for contrary reasons, allegory is the demon figure Coleridge hopes to cast aside lest it undermine the coherence of persons and the Scriptures as true revelations and histories. For this reason, the distinction between symbol and allegory matters more to Coleridge than it does to his German contemporaries, who eventually adopt one or the other term to describe qualities formerly assigned to the other.

Coleridge's resistance to allegory participates in a long-standing tradition which reads Aristotle's definition of *ideas* not as the experiential perception of the material and phenomenal world but as, following Plato, the transcendent reality that was for Coleridge the only possible ground for knowledge. In the *Logic* he insists that the *idea* is "anterior to all image" and thus has nothing in common with abstraction or generality, which extract principles from images and things. In the *Biographia*, he explicitly opposes this claim to Aristotle's discussion of how ideas that might follow from the perception of visual images or shapes. Coleridge's more immediate target is the empiricist

14 Coleridge, *Biographia Literaria*, ed. James Engell and W. Jackson Bate, 2 vols in 1 (NJ: Princeton University Press, 1983), 1:82. See the editors' comments, 1:lxxxvi–lxxxvii, xcvii–civ, 306n.; Jean Paul Richter, *Vorschule der Aesthetik* (Munich: C. Hauser, 1963), pp. 31–37. The English translation is mine.
15 Paul de Man, "The Rhetoric of Temporality," in *Blindness and Insight*, 2nd edn. (Minneapolis: University of Minnesota Press, 1983), pp. 190–96, 211; Walter Benjamin, "Theses on the Philosophy of History," in *Illuminations*, ed. Hannah Arendt, trans. Harry Zohn (New York: Schocken Books, 1969), pp. 257–58.

and skeptical use of Aristotle's *De Anima* to argue that sense impressions lead, albeit in complex ways, to ideas in the mind.[16]

Located on the opposite side of images and things from ideas in this scheme, abstractions look very much like the paintings of Milton's Death that Coleridge judges inadequate because they present that shadowy, shapeless allegory as "A Skeleton, perhaps the dryest image that could be discovered which reduced the mind to a mere state of inactivity & passivity & compared with which a Square or a triangle was a luxuriant fancy." Painted in oils (or on velvet), Death is a stand-in for what Coleridge elsewhere calls the "hollowness" of allegorical abstractions, that is, the way they extract from particular shapes and forms to produce concepts and, later, a second order of generalities about classes and species that are twice removed from particular images and things. The indirection of Coleridge's remarks in his lecture on Milton is remarkable. Neoclassical critics repeatedly chastised Milton for his allegory of Satan, Sin and Death on the grounds that it was not realistic. Coleridge defends this episode but never says that it is an allegory, yet Milton's description of Death as that "other shape, If shape it might be called that shape had none / Distinguishable in member, joint, or limb" is a brilliant poetic instance of Coleridge's hollowed out allegorical abstraction.[17]

In his 1818 lecture on the allegorical tradition, Coleridge is more vigilant about preserving what he admires in allegorical works from the contaminating effect of allegory:

> if the allegoric personage be strongly individualized so as to interest us, we cease to think of it as allegory – and if it does not interest us, it had better be away. – The dullest and most defective parts of Spenser are those in which we are compelled to think of his agents as allegories – and how far the Sin and Death of Milton are exceptions to this censure, is a delicate problem which I shall attempt to solve in another lecture. (*Lectures 1808–19*, 2:102–3)

Although he never mentions Milton's allegory again, Coleridge does return to the problem of allegorical narrative by way of Tasso, who had explained the allegorical significance of his epic *Gerusalemme liberata*. Tasso's explanation, writes Coleridge, has "the very opposite quality that Snakes have – they come out of their Hole into open view at the sound of sweet music,

16 Coleridge, *Logic*, ed. J. R. de J. Jackson (NJ: Princeton University Press, 1981), p. 63 and *Biographia Literaria*, 1:98.

17 Coleridge, *Lectures 1808–19: On Literature*, ed. R. A. Foakes, 2 vols. (NJ: Princeton University Press, 1987), 1:311–12, and *Statesman's Manual, Lay Sermons*, p. 28; John Milton, *Paradise Lost*, ed. Merritt Y. Hughes, rev. edn. (New York: Odyssey Press, 1962), 2:666–67, p. 63.

while the allegoric meaning slinks off at the very first notes – and lurks in murkiest oblivion – and utter invisibility" (*Lectures 1808–19*, 2:13). Like the muffled allegory of Hazlitt's assurance that *The Faerie Queene* won't bite if it is not disturbed, Coleridge's remark rather perversely offers an allegorical narrative to argue against paying attention to such narratives.

Much as Coleridge finds it difficult to extricate symbol and allegory from the figure of *phantasia*, so does G. F. W. Hegel (1770–1831) find it difficult to extricate the same figure from his presentation of the symbolic form of art, where he tries to oppose the good offices of imagination as *Bildungskraft* from its dark other *Phantasie*, the German form of the Greek term from which both imagination and fantasy derive. In Hegel's *Aesthetics*, where the symbolic form of art is presented as an unstable middle term in the development of art and consciousness, it looks more like allegory than symbol, and more like trouble. The Coleridgean cast of Hegel's thinking about the symbol is clear in his 1827 *Enzyklopädie der Philosophischen Wissenschaften*. There he argues that whereas the sign is arbitrarily related to what it signifies, the meaning of the symbol "more or less corresponds, essentially and conceptually, to the content it expresses as a symbol."[18]

But consider for a moment Hegel's famous criticism of allegory in his *Aesthetics*, where he insists that allegory is "frosty and cold" because it does not achieve "the concrete individuality of a Greek god," saint or "some other actual person."[19] At such moments, Hegel's treatment of unstable relations between abstraction, spirit and form or material shape dramatically revisits the abiding concern of his *Science of Logic* – how to ground the abstract idea in a particular form. In that work he argues that only subjective philosophical reflection can effect this critical relationship.[20] But in the *Aesthetics* two versions of allegory stand in the way of this achievement. The first of these he calls allegory. The second, which he calls *Phantasie*, governs the conflicted middle space between abstraction and sensuousness. Hegel assigns both to cultural forms whose allegorical strangeness and estrangement inevitably afflict Western eyes. He characterizes *Phantasie* as an activity of the imagination, but issues these cautions: "fine art cannot range in wild unfettered fancy" (*in wilder Fessellosigkeit der Phantasie*) and "an unknown block of

18 G. F. W. Hegel, *Enzyklopädie der Philosophischen Wissenschaften* (1827 edition), vol. 19, in *Sammelte Werke*, ed. Wolfgang Bonsiepen and Hans-Christian Lucas, 21 vols. (Hamburg: Felix Meiner Verlag, 1989), sec. 458, p. 333. Paul de Man offers this English translation in "Sign and Symbol in Hegel's *Aesthetics*," *Critical Inquiry* 8 (1982), 766.

19 Hegel, *Aesthetics: Lectures on Fine Art*, trans. T. M. Knox, 2 vols. (Oxford: Clarendon Press, 1975), 1:399.

20 Hegel, *Science of Logic*, trans. A. V. Miller (London: George Allen and Unwin, 1969), p. 44.

stone may symbolize the Divine, but it does not represent it . . . when shaping begins, the shapes produced are symbols, perhaps, but in themselves are fantastic and monstrous" (*Aesthetics*, 1:46, 76n).

Thus whereas Hegel supposes that one of the goals of art is to "let fancy [*Phantasie*] loose in the idle plays of imagination [*Einbildungskraft*] and plunge it into the seductive magic of sensuously bewitching visions [literally "intuitions," *Anschauungen*]," he presents *Phantasie* as an oriental despot whose proliferation of sensuous shapes to represent divinities works against the emergence of the spiritual in art (*Aesthetics*, 1:343–44). Hegel insists that to understand the form of the romantic as the repository of inner spirit, we must preserve that form from the predations of the sensuous, whose liabilities he assigns to foreign cultures, past and present, that exemplify the earliest, least evolved moments in his history of art. Under the sign of the symbolic, he orientalizes allegory so that it can, in hidden as well as exposed ways, perform the alienation his preference for the symbol requires. Whereas classical art displays a perfect, beautiful but fleeting match between spirit or ideality and external form, and the self-consciousness of romantic art imbues form with the subjectivity and spirit that for Hegel constitute fine art, the symbolic form of art unevenly defines the terrain between the classic and the romantic. In its most evolved stages, symbolic art like that of the Egyptians (here Hegel revives the older Neoplatonic association between symbol and Egypt) registers the immanent if as yet unrevealed authority of spirit over sensuous shape. In its least evolved forms, which he identifies with Indian art, the symbolic collapses into seductive, multiple forms that draw the eye and mind away from spirit and divinity. Thus the Romantic form of art is achieved when human self-consciousness learns or draws out the spirit that the sensuous shape can only approximate (*Aesthetics*, 1:76–89).[21]

Hegel's schematic interposes a safe distance between abstraction and sensuous shape, two equally if differently hazardous extremes. Tilted toward abstraction, art is emptied, hollowed out and thus unaffecting. Tilted toward sensuous shape, art fills mind and eye with seducing images and thereby leaves no mental space for spirit without which, Hegel insists, there can be no fine art (*Aesthetics*, 1:39). What Hegel fears in Indian art and Hindu mythology is what Neoclassical critics and some Romantics feared about allegory: a swift, unchartable movement between form and idea; abstraction, coupled with an unnerving attachment to pictorial and sensuous shape; the erotic implications of its semiotic proliferation; and an air of manic contingency

---

21 Hegel excludes Asia from "the process of historical development" in the *Philosophy of History*, ed. C. J. Friedrich, trans. J. Sibree (New York: Dover, 1956), pp. 87–88.

(if not this form, then some other), offset only (and with dubious rewards) by the fixed, self-evidently allegorical figures for which Hegel reserves the term *allegory*.

Whereas Hegel plots a solution to the dual problem of abstraction and sensuous shape by way of Romantic subjectivity – the Hegelian synthesis ever at work – Shelley and Keats are more interested in the conflict between idea or spirit on the one hand, and sensuous shape on the other. The poetic figures of this conflict are by turns grotesque, monstrous and rigidly abstract, and almost always identified, either distantly or at close range, with eroticism and female figures. Neither Keats nor Shelley frees allegorical female figures that are, like Milton's Lady in *Comus*, "in stony fetters fixt." But the poetic means they use to bind them specify a more expansive narrative desire.

Percy Shelley is the only English Romantic who declares that allegory can be an imaginative and moral agent, yet he is also wary of allegory's tendency to self-petrify. In *Prometheus Unbound*, the torturer turns out to be a Blakean reification of Prometheus himself, a psychic embodiment of rage whose name is Jupiter. In *The Triumph of Life*, it is the "Shape all light," who does to Rousseau's brain what the Medusa does to those who gaze on her.[22] In Shelley's political poems, where allegorical figures might be expected to serve a coded, but hardly veiled, agenda, some muster figural power in unexpected ways.

The most remarkable instances occur in *The Mask of Anarchy*, which Shelley wrote in September 1819, after learning about the August massacre of civilians who had gathered in St. Peter's Field near Manchester to hear speeches in favor of Parliamentary reform, only to be fired upon by drunken militia and cavalrymen who had misunderstood their orders. The poem begins with a parade of allegorical villains whose names and features make them particular as well as abstract. Walking in the "visions of Poesy," the speaker first meets "Murder" who pointedly has "a mask like Castlereagh." The seven "bloodhounds" that follow him at the ready to consume any human hearts thrown their way may represent the seven-nation agreement with Britain to postpone abolishing the slave trade or the pro-war "blood-hounds" of Pitt's administration. Such particulars, implied or explicit, have always been the stuff of political allegory. What makes Shelley's figures unusual is his insistence that Murder is a man who, like his bloodhounds, is fat with gore; that Fraud is Lord Eldon, whose tears turn to millstones; that Hypocrisy is Sidmouth, who rides by on a crocodile and an allegory. In an

---

22 Percy Bysshe Shelley, *Triumph of Life*, in *Shelley's Poetry and Prose*, ed. Donald H. Reiman and Neil Fraistat (New York: W. W. Norton, 2002), ll. 400–68, pp. 496–97. Subsequent citations from this edition are cited parenthetically as *SPP*.

era when allegory was so often charged with abstraction, this particularity humanizes abstraction with something like figural vengeance.

The rest of the poem, which Leigh Hunt did not dare to publish until 1832, puts aside similarly actionable particulars. Instead, "Anarchy" is a figure whose absolute power is supported by various agents of government oppression. Deliberately modeled on Benjamin West's famous painting of Death on a pale horse, Anarchy wears the crown of absolute monarchy and boasts of having been educated for "ten millions," at the expense of the nation. After more than a decade of political caricature in which the Prince Regent, late crowned George IV, was represented as a fat, self-indulgent royal nuisance and expense to the nation, no reader among Shelley's contemporaries could have missed the implied referent.[23] Once the "Shape" arrives, looking like the Lady of *The Sensitive Plant* and a Venus/Morning Star, Hope walks and Anarchy lies dead. The Shape's questions about the nature of Freedom direct the poem toward a surprising conclusion. After attacking "paper coin," the Shape forecasts the arrival of Justice, Wisdom, Peace, Love, Science, Poetry, Thought, Spirit, Patience, and Gentleness, then urges nonviolence and trust that the laws of the land will be fair "arbiters of the dispute." It is hard to know whose political argument this allegory serves. For although this is Shelley's vision for the future, it was intended for the English people at large, who would surely have been ill-advised to stand still with an eye on futurity while the militia took aim.

The reason for the oddly placed call for nonviolence and civil obedience in *The Mask of Anarchy* becomes clearer in Shelley's *Ode to Liberty* of the next year, which chronicles the history of the world, beginning with the reign of chaos when Liberty was not. After identifying the moment of Liberty's birth with ancient Greece, the speaker compares her nurture of infant Rome to that which a "Maenad" nurse-mother gives to her wolf-cub. This disquieting analogy forecasts Liberty's dubious nurture of the Roman republic's deeds of "terrible uprightness." In successive drafts of these lines, Shelley makes the figure of Liberty less particular and more abstract, yet his accompanying sketches make her more a "palpable, more physically present" image of a nursing mother even as she also becomes dangerously ambiguous. In the final draft, Shelley leaves all particularity behind, choosing instead a synecdochic representation of Liberty's "robe of vestal whiteness" that displaces the nursing mother with a vestal virgin who wisely quits Rome.[24]

23 *George Cruikshank, 1792–1878: Karikaturen zur englischen und europäischen Politik und Gesellschaft im ersten Viertel des 19. Jahrhunderts*, ed. Ursula Bode, et al. (G. Hatje: Stuttgart, 1983).
24 Nancy Goslee, "Pursuing Revision in Shelley's 'Ode to Liberty,'" *Texas Studies in Language and Literature* 36 (1994), 172–73.

After a thousand-year absence, Liberty reemerges in medieval Italy, only to succumb a few centuries later to Napoleon I, "Anarch of thine own bewildered powers" (*Ode to Liberty*, *SPP*, p. 312). This is the unspecified risk of the Shape's invocations to Freedom in *The Mask of Anarchy*, that Liberty bewildered can become anarchy. Like that of the older, more conservative Wordsworth, Shelley's backward glance at post-revolutionary France acknowledges this difficult truth and its unwelcome consequence – that the birth of English liberty might crumble into anarchy.

Prometheus Unbound is inhabited by, as Shelley puts it, "poetical abstractions" that witness an intra-psychic, then world-wide renewal of love and political liberty after Prometheus' long and, in Shelley's version of the myth, self-imposed incarceration and torture ("Preface," *PU*, in *SPP*, p. 208). These named abstractions talk, some may even walk, but few convey interior or psychological realism. Turning de Man's arguments concerning the rhetoricity of such figures back to Hegel, Rajan compares the poem's allegorical figures to mere signs, hollow abstractions like those that Hegel finds wanting in his *Aesthetics*.[25] Yet the materialist edge of Shelley's idealism presses against this outcome. Even in this idealist drama the term "shape" remains stunningly available to abstraction on the one side and material particularity on the other. As it does elsewhere in Shelley's writing, "shape" may refer to visible forms, including sketches he drew beside early drafts of the poem and even in the fair-copy transcription he sent to his publishers.[26] In the oxymoronic climate of this poem, the same term may be used to designate "unimaginable shapes" as well as figured abstractions. From our sublunary perspective as readers of this poem, this second usage is oxymoronic; for Shelley it is an index of how allegorical ideas and material forms share the same poetic space.

In Shelley's tragedy *The Cenci*, its female protagonist is the front woman for crimes committed in the name of allegorical abstraction – by poets as well as women. The highly marked pathos of Shelley's preface insists obliquely on this point. Asserting that the Cenci story is true and that he tells it in the "real language of men" instead of the language of a single class, he invokes Wordsworthian verisimilitude and human feeling and, continuing in a neo-Wordsworthian vein, insists that he (Shelley) has not created "cold impersonations of my own mind," but a real person named Beatrice Cenci whose involvement in "crimes and miseries" are "the mask and the mantle in which circumstances clothed her for her impersonation on the scene of

25 Tilottama Rajan, *The Supplement of Reading* (Ithaca: Cornell University Press, 1990), pp. 299–316.
26 Shelley, *The Prometheus Unbound Notebooks*, ed. Neil Fraistat, vol. 9 of *The Bodleian Shelley Manuscripts* (New York: Garland, 1991), pp. 82, 424, 480.

the world" ("Preface," *Cenci*, in *SPP*, pp. 142 and 144). This mix of pathos with theatricality makes her a stage impersonation. Beatrice likewise drifts from human particularity toward abstraction when she explains why she is justified in plotting to kill her incestuous father: "Like Parricide . . . / Misery has killed its father; yet its father / Never like mine . . . O, God! What thing am I?" (*Cenci* 3.1.37–39, *SPP*, p. 164). This syntactic disorder prefigures other, deeper ruptures. Beatrice proclaims (with ample provocation) that her father is "a spirit of hell" whom they must harry "out of a human form" (*Cenci* 4.2.7–8, *SPP*, p. 180). Shelley's Beatrice exposes the faultline where allegorical abstractions and pathos part company. As the figure who walks this faultline, Beatrice is forced to operate in an arena where abstract allegorical ideas have human names and exercise absolute power over her body and identity.

In Keats's understanding of what it means to have a "life of allegory," that life is stubbornly poised between an animated human (or, paradoxically, immortal) body and one that is cast in stone.[27] Endymion is the first Keatsian figure to be caught in this way. Swooning early in the poem, he goes into a "fixed trance" so deep that he looks "as dead-still as a marble man, / Frozen in that old tale Arabian."[28] That old tale in which a young man is a man to his waist but black marble below, is less extreme than Keats's, which deadens and freezes the entire body. In the *Hyperion* poems, questions about the fixity or mobility of its divine, quasi-allegorical figures take particular note of their material shape or form. In *Hyperion* Saturn calls his fellow Titans "the first-born of all shap'd and palpable Gods." The narrator compares Saturn and Thea to "natural sculpture in cathedral cavern;" Thea resembles "the bulk / Of Memnon's image at the set of sun;" and the other fallen Titans, with their "limbs / Lock'd up like veins of metal, crampt and screw'd," look like "a dismal cirque / Of Druid stones, upon a forlorn moor" (*Hyperion*, in *Poems*, 2:153 and 3:61, pp. 345 and 354; 1:86; p. 331; 2:373, p. 351; and 2:24–25 and 34–35, pp. 341–42).

By slightly abbreviating this presentation of the fallen Titans as sculptured personifications, *The Fall of Hyperion* edges closer to abstraction, a point Keats recognizes when he describes it to Fanny Brawne, with a whiff of condescension, as a "very abstract poem" (*Letters*, 2:132). In this version the punt toward abstraction puts the poet-narrator himself at risk. First

---

27 Keats, *The Letters of John Keats*, ed. Hyder Rollins, 2 vols. (Cambridge, MA: Harvard University Press, 1958), 2:67. Subsequent citations from this edition are cited parenthetically as *Letters*.

28 Keats, *Endymion*, in *The Poems of John Keats*, ed. Jack Stillinger (Cambridge, MA: Harvard University Press, 1978), ll. 405–06, p. 114. Subsequent citations from this edition are cited parenthetically as *Poems*.

Figure 15.1 J. M. W. Turner, *The Slave Ship, or Slavers throwing overboard the Dead and Dying – Typhoon coming on.*

he sinks down in a "cloudy swoon...Like a Silenus on an antique vase" (*Hyperion*, in *Poems*, ll. 55–56, p. 479). In a letter to George and Georgiana Keats written in early 1819, Keats explains that "heavy and spirituous" wines "transform a Man to a Silenus" (*Letters*, 2:64). Keats's poetic figure goes one step further by making the goal a fixed element in the relief design on a vase. Whether frozen, marble or like the "natural sculpture" of a limestone cavern, the Titans in both epics and the poet of *The Fall of Hyperion* mark the reification and abstraction that relegate the Titans, like the Egyptians, to their historical position as superannuated gods in what Keats elsewhere calls the "grand march of intellect" (*Letters*, 1:282). Yet in both *Hyperion* poems Keats turns away from this Hegelian program to emphasize how even the statuesque Titans have, to Saturn's utter surprise, human feelings. As the Titans mourn their new, unwanted resemblance to mortals who suffer and die, they painfully renegotiate the putative distance between abstract personification and human suffering (*Hyperion*, in *Poems*, 1:332–35, 2:97–100, pp. 339, 343).

Unlike many of his contemporaries, the painter J. M. W. Turner (1775–1851) was not at all queasy about allegory. Indeed, his choice of subject and medium frequently conveys an allegorical disposition that co-exists with realist surroundings and historical anecdote. One remarkable example from late in his career must suffice, the *The Slave Ship*, or *Slavers throwing overboard the Dead and Dying – Typhoon coming on*, first exhibited in 1840 (see Figure 15.1). The event and the widespread practice it depicts had long been a staple of arguments against slavery and the slave trade. To lighten the load and capture insurance money that wouldn't be available in port were slaves to die at sea, captains of ships carrying slaves to ports in the New World would throw weakened slaves overboard to drown. Turner's accompanying verse from his *Fallacies of Hope* pushes the scene away from the documentary toward the emblematic. Beginning with "hands," a common nautical synecdoche for sailors at work, the verse presses toward figured abstractions, among them the "angry" sun and "fierce-edged" cloud; the apostrophized "Hope;" and nominalized, hence generic phrases – "the dead" and "the dying" instead of dead and dying people. In this crowd, "Typhoon" looks like an angry god of wind and sea.[29]

The painting amplifies this allegorical reading. In the foreground iron chains float above the water as, in some cases, the only physical evidence that slaves have been thrown overboard. In realist terms this detail makes no sense, for iron chains would sink faster and lower than the arms or legs

---

29 Martin Butlin and Evelyn Joll, *The Paintings of J. M. W. Turner*, rev. edn., 2 vols. (New Haven: Yale University Press, 1984), 1:237.

to which they are attached. Read allegorically, this visual detail advertises a synecdochic gesture that sponsors an allegorical argument. By holding these human body parts aloft in a grotesque display, the chains reduce the dying slaves to their working appendages. Allied figurative dismemberments govern other visual details. The unseen slavers of Turner's title are known only by their actions: violently displaced images figure what they do to others and what the painter does to them. This metafigural logic suggests too that the murderous turbulence of the water as the typhoon moves is itself a figure for the human rapaciousness left on board ship. With emphatically painted mouths that are larger than they would be in nature, the fish are similarly hyperbolic visitors from the real world.

Conclusion

In Book 7 of *The Prelude*, Wordsworth's narrator describes an odd mix of shop signs, "allegoric shapes" and "real men" which suggests that allegory lives, or half-lives, in Romantic London:

> Shop after shop, with symbols, blazon'd names,
> And all the tradesman's honours overhead:
> Here, fronts of houses, like a title-page
> With letters huge inscribed from top to toe;
> Stationed above the door like guardian saints,
> There, allegoric shapes, female or male,
> Or physiognomies of real men.[30]

Like the superscripts and emblematic shop signs of Wordsworth's London, allegory is a bold "front" for what other, less declared Romantic figures do to and with particulars. As such, allegory specifies the necessary surplus or excess of figure writ large. The "excess of flesh and blood" that Hunt presents as a weakness of Spenser's *Faerie Queene* had long been implicit, hidden (more or less) in the folds of allegorical narratives. Its more insistent visibility in Romantic allegory, a visibility more often spectral than neatly iconographic, embodies the friction that signals allegory's modern reinvention in the time and place of Romanticism, where allegory is marked by a history that is one part figural but another part revolution and terror. Under these pressures, Romantic allegory persistently exceeds the measure of fixed abstractions and images as it moves on to be remade, recast or (since this too is always possible) cast in stone.

30 Wordsworth, *The Prelude 1799, 1805, 1850*, ed. Jonathan Wordsworth, M. H. Abrams, and Stephen Gill (New York: W. W. Norton, 1979), 7:173–80, p. 234.

16

DEBORAH L. MADSEN

American allegory to 1900

Throughout its history in the Old World and the New, allegory has functioned in two dominant forms: as a style of writing or rhetoric but also
as a way of reading, a hermeneutic. Literary allegory in America is bound
up with philosophy to the point that Olaf Hansen, in his book on late
nineteenth-century allegory, sees it as a substitute for America's failure to
develop a distinctive school of philosophy. But the transformations of American religion, as Puritan orthodoxy gave way to a diversity of Churches and
the emergence of a weak New England Unitarianism, also provide a forceful
context for the development of both American allegorical hermeneutics and
allegorical rhetoric.

The 1850s in American literature has famously been termed "the American Renaissance," following F. O. Matthiessen's 1941 book *American
Renaissance: Art and Expression in the Age of Emerson and Whitman*. That
Matthiessen referred to an American *renaissance*, a rebirth, to describe what
he saw as the coming to maturity of American literary culture, rather than
the birth of American literature, owes much to the colonial New England
legacy of allegorical expression. Matthiessen describes the period 1850 to
1855 as "one extraordinarily concentrated moment of expression,"[1] united
by a commonality of themes, and particularly by the desire of his designated
writers (Emerson, Thoreau, Hawthorne, Melville, Whitman, and Poe) to
discover rhetorical means by which the word and the thing might become
one. The course of this rhetorical discovery took them back in time, to Puritan models of allegory and symbolism, and specifically to the typological
style of rhetoric and interpretation that united object and referent, making
God's word a material or, to borrow Emerson's parlance, "natural" fact.
Together with typological rhetoric, the Puritan strain of Protestant theology,
brought to the New World in the early seventeenth century by those who

---

1 F. O. Matthiessen, *American Renaissance: Art and Expression in the Age of Emerson and
Whitman*, 1941, rpt. (Oxford: Oxford University Press, 1968), p. vii.

dissented from what they saw as the Anglican compromise of the Reformation's revolutionary potential, had a formative influence on the nature and practice of American allegorical expression. In Matthiessen's estimation, and the writer's own reflections on their work, this great renaissance happened when it did because of the emergence of Romanticism in Europe and the development of a nativist American form of Romantic thought, Transcendentalism. The Romantic emphasis upon nature at the expense of civilization, on the individual rather than society, appealed to intellectuals in the new American Republic who were painfully self-conscious about the lack of history, culture, and "civilization" in the New World. What the United States had in abundance was raw, unformed nature and the residue of a revolutionary ideology concerning the primacy of the common man, his self-reliance, and democratic commitment to independence. This was also a period of increasing materialism in American society as the economy expanded and industrialization took hold. Increasingly, American religion was perceived as becoming more secular as the older Puritan doctrine was supplanted by a diluted form of Unitarian Calvinism, especially in the period following and in reaction to the excesses of the Great Awakening. The cultural scene was then set for the emergence of an American strain of Romantic aesthetics, which we find in the thought of Ralph Waldo Emerson and the school of Transcendentalists in the shaping of which he was instrumental.

The impact of Romantic aesthetics on American allegory

Emerson's allegorical practice reflects not so much a break with late eighteenth-century American rhetorical styles as a shift in emphasis away from Enlightenment privileging of rational laws and processes. For example, much of Philip Freneau's poetry that does not address the political consequences of the Revolutionary War and subsequent Independence is concerned with characterizing a fundamentally Romantic vision of landscape, where God inheres in Nature. The 1815 poem, "On the Universality and Other Attributes of the God of Nature," for example, celebrates a God that no longer operates through the mechanism of Providence to guide natural life but is a part of that corporeal life. Natural laws are not simply the expression of divine causality but they incarnate, in earthly terms, that sacred intentionality. This view echoes the explanation given by Samuel Taylor Coleridge in *The Statesman's Manual* (1816), that the mysterious correspondence between the mind of man and the laws of nature can only be resolved in the understanding of God as: "the one before all, and of all, and through all."[2] It is in this context that Coleridge developed his well-known distinction between symbol and allegory. His suspicion that a literal interpretation of Scripture had undermined the power of the sacred text as the receptacle of inspired truths was shared by Romantics like Emerson, who saw the Bible being read as a historical allegory rather than as both historically real and also a symbolic vehicle of imagination, consubstantial with the divine truth to which it allows access. Coleridge criticizes allegory as working through similitude to express extrinsic meanings; symbolism, however, operates through a kind of incarnation to represent an intrinsic and potentially redemptive meaning.

> Now an Allegory is but a translation of abstract notions into a picture-language which is itself nothing but an abstraction from objects of the senses; the principal being more worthless even than its phantom proxy, both alike unsubstantial and the former shapeless to boot. On the other hand a Symbol ... is characterized by a translucence of the Eternal through and in the Temporal. It always partakes of the Reality which it renders intelligible; and while it enunciates the whole, abides itself as a living part in that Unity, of which it is the representative.   (*The Statesman's Manual*, pp. 30–31)

Cognitive access to this "Unity" is reserved for the individual who, through the power of imagination, is able to receive this inspired meaning. Consequently, we find in Romantic rhetorical practice a shift of emphasis from objective to subjective authority within the interpretive act. No longer was the Church to dictate the meaning of Scripture to the inspired individual. This separation was a development of post-Reformation theology; however, it found a renewed theoretical focus in the influence of the Higher Criticism upon nineteenth-century biblical studies.

Hans W. Frei, in his study of nineteenth-century biblical interpretation, distinguishes between "precritical" and modern methods of reading the biblical text. The precritical reader "was to see his disposition, his actions and passions, the shape of his own life as well as that of his era's events as figures of that storied world."[3] But the possibility of this reflection between self and biblical world was fractured by the emergence of modern techniques of reading to verify, rather than to access, the historicity of Scripture. This historicism reduced the Bible to one of many available forms of historical account (Frei, *Eclipse*, pp. 4–5). Philip Gura and Lawrence Buell have

2 Samuel Taylor Coleridge, *The Collected Works of Samuel Taylor Coleridge*, ed. R. J. White (Princeton: Princeton University Press, 1972), p. 79.
3 Hans W. Frei, *The Eclipse of Biblical Narrative* (New Haven: Yale University Press, 1974), p. 3.

both addressed the influence of the Higher Criticism upon biblical studies in America. Gura describes the debates of the early nineteenth century that centered on whether the Bible is figurative poetry as much as it is objective truth, and so should be read not only in the context of belief but also in historical and philological contexts as well.[4] Arising from this question of how the sacred text should be approached is the issue of how much authority should be attributed to the interpretive power of human reason, on the one hand, and the mystical authority of divine revelation, on the other. Basically, the question to be answered was whether the Bible constitutes a unique kind of text and so requires a unique method of interpretation.

At the same time that this question was subject to debate, as Lawrence Buell notes, not only was the Bible's privileged status under question but secular literature was increasingly seen to provide a legitimate expression of devotional experience.[5] Buell refers to the claims made by commentators such as William Blake in England and Ralph Waldo Emerson in America (echoing Boccaccio centuries earlier) that Scripture is essentially poetry produced by the inspired, mystical vision of the poet. Buell sees this trend as a response to changes in demands made by congregations, in the period after the disestablishment of the churches was completed in 1833 when churches were obliged to compete for members and the financial support which the congregation provided. Buell also argues that this trend toward a more literary approach to religion, and to the Bible specifically, was also a response to changes in perceptions of how faith or belief is to be understood: "Secular literature acquired greater spiritual legitimacy as the propagation of religion came to be seen as dependent upon verbal artistry and as the record of revelation was seen to be a verbal artifact" (*New England Literary Culture*, p. 168).

What an overly close relationship between religion and secular literature risks, as Buell sees it, is the tendency to promote subjectification. This can lead to the identification of spirituality not with religious doctrine but rather with the subjective perception of what Scripture means. An extreme subjectivism threatens the validity of any objective referent for devotional experience, or indeed any other kind of experience that demands interpretation in terms of semantic and spiritual absolutes. This history of devaluation of biblical authority, and the rise of subjectivism in its place, produces such responses as Emerson's revival of Neoplatonic allegorical cosmology, where

4 Philip Gura, *The Wisdom of Words: Language, Theology, and Literature in the New England Renaissance* (Middletown: Wesleyan University Press, 1981), p. 17.
5 Lawrence Buell, *New England Literary Culture: From Revolution Through Renaissance* (Cambridge: Cambridge University Press, 1986), p. 167.

the inspired individual assumes the privileged hermeneutic position previously held by Christ.

The revival of Neoplatonic allegorical cosmology in the thought of Emerson

The work of Emerson, the multifaceted New England scholar, essayist, poet, philosopher, and social commentator, is characterized by two kinds of rhetoric: what Coleridge would call either allegory or symbolism. The more conventional style of allegorical rhetoric that Emerson uses is derived from the traditional Christian homily, where an image stands for some abstract concept. This kind of figurative language marks the entire Christian tradition of preaching and in America this rhetorical style was perhaps made most famous by Benjamin Franklin's many published homilies. The second and more interesting style of rhetoric used by Emerson is a mystical Neoplatonic style of expression, where an image incarnates some ideal form of itself. In a journal entry dated October 5, 1835, for example, Emerson confesses that:

> [t]he deepest pleasure comes I think from the occult belief that an unknown meaning & consequence lurk in the common every day facts & as this panoramic or pictorial beauty can arise from it, so can a solid wisdom when the Idea shall be seen as such which binds these gay shadows together.[6]

Here Emerson is describing a Neoplatonic relationship between shadows and reality, or the ideal and the real, together with an understanding of knowledge as an incremental process that is motivated by beauty. The culmination of this process is "a solid wisdom" of the Ideal to which material signs point and with which they form correspondences. This journal entry can be seen as an early expression of the theory of symbolic correspondence that Emerson explores in his 1841 essay, "The Over-Soul." There he writes: "We live in succession, in division, in parts, in particles.... Meantime within man is the soul of the whole; the wise silence; the universal beauty, to which every part and particle is equally related; the eternal ONE."[7] Here, the perception of nature, including human nature, as an emblematic network of material signs is enhanced by the mystical understanding of the power of the soul to facilitate an absolute unification of creation: "the act of seeing

6 Ralph Waldo Emerson, *The Journals and Miscellaneous Notebooks of Ralph Waldo Emerson, vol. V, 1835–1838*, ed. Merton M. Sealts, Jr. (Cambridge, MA: Belknap Press, 1965), p. 212.
7 Ralph Waldo Emerson, *The Collected Works of Ralph Waldo Emerson, vol. II, Essays: First Series*, ed. Joseph Slater, Alfred R. Ferguson, and Jean Ferguson Carr (Cambridge, MA: Belknap Press, 1979), p. 160.

and the thing seen, the seer and the spectacle, the subject and the object, are one" ("The Over-Soul," p. 160). Emerson echoes Coleridge's understanding of the symbol as an inspired sign that "partakes of the Reality which it renders intelligible; and while it enunciates the whole, abides itself as a living part in that Unity." But the site of unity is the individual human soul, which functions through imagination as both receiver and revealer of Truth. Emerson places at the center of his network of rhetorical correspondences not the divine unity or godhead but the inspired human subject.

This is an inspired subject conceived in a particular way: in the essay "History" Emerson explains that because one divine mind is common to all individual men, human history is but the record of the works of the universal mind. This thought is not unfamiliar to anyone who understands the Calvinist doctrine of predestination that so shaped New England Puritanism. According to this idea of predestination, all of human history was brought into being at the Creation and, although history appears to us to unfold in a linear chronology, in God's view all of history occurs simultaneously. In each event of human history the divine mind expresses itself, but in human terms this history is experienced as human. Consequently, for Emerson all history is subjective and, as he famously asserts: there is no history, only biography. Emerson displaces the divine intelligence of Protestant providential history and in the place of God situates the inspired individual. In this way, Emerson revives the Platonic system of symbolic correspondences between the real and the ideal. The inspired individual perceives the human world of the real as an allegory of the realm of spirit, of the ideal: he is, as Emerson describes, "true to his better instincts or sentiments, and refuses the dominion of facts, as one that comes of a higher race, remains fast by the soul and sees the principle, then the facts fall aptly and supple into their places; they know their master, and the meanest of them glorifies him."[8] Facts are subsumed by imagination, as is the real by the ideal. History is governed by the human subject in its mystical dimension of imagination and the universal mind, together; and it is the divine mind that dictates the writing of history through the inspired medium of human imagination:

> The universal nature, too strong for the petty nature of the bard, sits on his neck and writes through his hand; so that when he seems to vent a mere caprice and wild romance, the issue is an exact allegory. Hence Plato said that "poets utter great and wise things which they do not themselves understand."
>
> ("History," p. 19)

8 Ralph Waldo Emerson, ibid., p. 19.

The inspired individual through whom the universal mind communicates is Emerson's privileged figure of the poet, who mediates among God, Scripture, natural history, and the human soul. The poet stands at the interpretive center of Emerson's system of mystical correspondences. Through his mediating power, the poet takes the place occupied by Christ in conventional Christian doctrine. This quasi-divine status is described by Emerson, within the context of a reconstituted Trinity, in the essay "The Poet" (1844):

> For the Universe has three children, born at one time, which reappear, under different names, in every system of thought, whether they be called cause, operation, and effect; or, more poetically, Jove, Pluto, Neptune; or, theologically, the Father, the Spirit, and the Son; but which we will call here, the Knower, the Doer, and the Sayer. These stand respectively for the love of truth, for the love of good, and for the love of beauty. These three are equal. Each is that which he is essentially, so that he cannot be surmounted or analyzed, and each of these three has the power of the others latent in him, and his own patent. The poet is the sayer, the namer, and represents beauty. He is a sovereign, and stands on the center.[9]

In Emerson's Romantic reworking of the concept of the divine Trinity, the poet as "the namer" takes over both Christ's function as the privileged interpreter of the divine will and also Christ's status as the normative meaning of sacred history. Emerson claims: "All that we call sacred history attests that the birth of the poet is the principal event in chronology" ("The Poet," p. 7). But it is the role of Christ as the mediator of meanings, from the divine to the human, rather than as the object of divine knowledge, that is assumed by Emerson's figure of the poet.

It is the poet's capacity to unite the real with the ideal that Emerson values as the poet's interpretation of the symbolic language of nature. Those individuals who are not gifted with the power of imagination, as is the poet, are unable to penetrate beyond the surface of nature, its appearance, to access the spiritual dimension of nature as a symbolic language: "We are symbols, and inhabit symbols ... [but] being infatuated with the economical uses of things, we do not know that they are thoughts" ("The Poet," p. 12). The cognitive dimensions of nature are inaccessible to all except the poet who is able to liberate them, through imaginative reinterpretation, into a new life. "The expression is organic, or, the new type which things themselves take when liberated" ("The Poet," pp. 14–15). What appears to the uninspired individual as a superficial appearance in nature is, by the poet,

---

9 Ralph Waldo Emerson, *The Collected Works of Ralph Waldo Emerson, vol. III, Essays: Second Series*, ed. Joseph Slater, et al., p. 5.

re-presented as an inspired poetic symbol and, more than this, a mystical access to a multiform world of symbolic Truth.

In Emerson's account, the exegetical function of Scripture is supplanted by poetic imagination. The poet has made available to human interpretation the symbolic language of nature as an effective substitute for the interpretive authority of scriptural revelation. The interpreting human subject is no longer brought to a condition of identity with the revelation of Scripture through the mediating power of Christ; rather, it is the poet-as-Christ who reveals this mystical identity by interpreting the nature as a Neoplatonic allegory, as a system of correspondences between the real and the ideal, each of which reveals metonymically the ideal of which it is a real part. Both nature and Scripture are characterized by this rhetorical structure of correspondence: natural and biblical figures both refer metonymically to a mystical ideal, or divine mind, that directs the movements of history from outside the realm of temporality. For instance, the "Language" chapter of "Nature" describes this metonymic relationship of correspondence between the human and the ideal worlds, where a secularized concept of God, embodied in language, enables this correspondence:

> Man is conscious of a universal soul within or behind his individual life, wherein, as in a firmament, the natures of Justice, Truth, Love, Freedom, arise and shine. This universal soul, he calls Reason: it is not mine or thine or his, but we are its; we are its property and men. And the blue sky in which the private earth is buried, the sky with its eternal calm, and full of everlasting orbs, is the type of Reason. That which, intellectually considered, we call Reason, considered in relation to nature, we call Spirit. Spirit is the Creator. Spirit hath life in itself. And man in all ages and countries, embodies it in his language, as the FATHER.[10]

Emerson is here proposing a radically intrinsic form of mystical reference that is found both in words and in things. Emerson asserts an intrinsic correspondence between nature and human thought, where it is in nature that the origin of all the spiritual significances possessed by words is to be found. But it is here that Emerson betrays a nostalgic impulse; he laments the loss of an original semantic unity, lost as secondary naming relationships come into the ascendant. All spiritual facts are represented by natural facts, which function as "emblems," Emerson asserts, in "Nature." But when the desire for riches, pleasure, power, and praise compromises the power of nature as the interpreter of the human will, words must be "perverted to stand for things which they are not" ("Nature," p. 20). Then, mechanistic form

10 Ralph Waldo Emerson, *The Collected Works of Ralph Waldo Emerson, vol. I*, ed. Joseph Slater, et al., pp. 18–19.

replaces organic form, and the power of metonymic referentiality is replaced by an arbitrary and metaphoric referentiality. Emerson opposes the crisis of modern reference to an understanding of language that owes much to the Puritan legacy of sacramental referentiality. In the New England mind, to borrow Perry Miller's phrase, divine providence operates directly through material signs such as nature and language to act upon the individual soul. The precise meaning of the providential intervention is determined by reference to Scripture and with the guidance of ministers, who perform a crucial mediating function. The divine will is made present to human understanding through the sacramental power of earthly signs. It is against this sacramental inheritance that Emerson stages the modern alienation of words, as names, from a divine origin. Emerson's ceaseless quest for a unitary point of meaning is symptomatic of his perception of nineteenth-century American culture as undergoing a referential crisis. The primary consequences of Emerson's Romantic quest for transcendental meaning were, first, the separation of symbolism from allegory within American literary culture and, second, the alienation of allegorical interpretation from the earlier biblical context of Puritan allegorical practice.

The afterlife of Protestant allegory in American literary culture

All allegories are characterized by a twofold function: allegory is simultaneously an interpretation (biblical, historical, natural, and so on) and also a metacritical statement that regulates interpretation. So in allegory two kinds of truth are compounded: the truth that is the meaning of the allegorical text and the truth that is formulated by the allegorical text as the interpretation of some external text. Consequently, allegory is marked by hermeneutic circularity. The Puritan understanding of Scripture as self-validating draws on this circularity in the idea that the truth of Scripture and the truth of one's reading of Scripture should be mutually validating. But if allegory is not to appear tautological then authority must be invested in a third interpretive factor. One of the primary shifts engendered by the Reformation was the redirection of interpretive authority away from the Church towards the individual soul. In Puritan New England, this legislative authority was located in the individual sanctified soul, supported by the ministry.

Protestant exegesis was motivated by the desire for a direct communion with God. The effect of grace on the individual soul could not be validated by the ecclesiastical institution. The site of validation shifts, in Protestant allegory, to the immediate relationship between soul and Scripture. This is exemplified in the changing attitude towards the crucial question arising from the doctrine of predestination: how can I know that I am a member of the elect? While for the early Calvinist Church the assurance of election was closely bound to the Church as well as to Scripture and the sacraments, through time the individual was increasingly driven to self-examination, in order to find assurance of grace in the events of their own life histories. So assurance of grace, like evidence of election, became a matter for the individual to ascertain. This shift away from the objective means of grace towards individual subjectivity wrought a fundamental change in the nature of allegory after the Reformation and, through the legacy of New England Puritan allegorical practices, shaped American literary rhetoric in very precise ways.

Protestant allegory valorizes uncertainty in interpretation. Human understanding cannot comprehend the pure reality of God, that vision of history occurring all at once, so no claim to absolute knowledge is possible. What is at stake in Protestant allegory is quite different from patristic interpretations of Scripture that involve gaining or losing salvation. Protestant interpretation questions the certitude of election, and seeks positive signs of the workings of grace in the soul. The search for such certainty is perhaps most explicitly sought in Puritan spiritual autobiography, and this search is most dramatically conducted in the genre of captivity narratives. These stories of abduction by Native American tribes were particularly popular in the later seventeenth century. Many were transcribed, edited, and promoted by Cotton Mather, the influential writer and minister of Boston's original North Church, as part of his campaign to restore the power and privilege of the New England Puritan ministry. These narratives are all written using the interpretive paradigm of typology. Historically, typology dates from the early exegetes of the New Testament who interpreted the relations between the Old and New Testaments as one of promise and fulfillment. The Old Testament was read as offering symbolic promises of the new Christian dispensation to come, and which would be fulfilled in the events set down in the New Testament. Thus, Jonah's time spent in the whale's belly was seen as the symbolic "type" of Christ's Harrowing of Hell, the rhetorical "antitype." The figure of Moses leading his people out of bondage and into the Promised Land was interpreted as Christ's liberation of the redeemed soul from the Law into a new dispensation of Grace. For colonial American Puritans, this style of allegorical rhetoric also offered a way of articulating their own escape from Anglican persecution and liberation into the Promised Land of New England. The typological parallel was interpreted not only as a repetition of biblical events but also as a part of the same divine providential scheme. By colonizing New England they were fulfilling the divine scheme of history. The relationship between lived events and a biblical precedent allowed Puritans to determine whether they were of the elect or preterite, though this knowledge was not static and had continually to be rediscovered.

In captivity narratives such as Mary Rowlandson's *Sovereignty and Goodness of God* (1682), an account of her experiences as the hostage of Narra-
gansett Indians during the winter of 1676, the first-person autobiographical
narrator continually searches for biblical models against which to measure
her experiences. In particular, she is concerned to discover whether her suffering is a form of punishment, meted out by God to one of his chosen people
in order to chastise Mary, or whether this life in the wilderness is an image
of her own lost, unredeemed spiritual condition. The narrative plays on the
double meaning of the word "redemption" – to signify both salvation and
the release of a hostage after the payment of a ransom – so that, even after
her return to her family and community in Boston, Mary remains unsure
whether she may be punished again in the future for sins she is unknowingly
committing. She never knows with certainty that she is a member of the
elect, though she confesses that before her captivity she had foolishly wished
that God would indeed single her out for suffering as a sign that she was
one of His chosen. This punitive style of allegorical rhetoric, like typology
more generally, shares with Protestant allegory the privileging of a direct
mystical relationship with Scripture. Alone in the wilderness, captives like
Mary Rowlandson would pore over their Bibles, searching for typological
clues to the meaning of their experience, which would also function as clues
to their spiritual destiny.

The emphasis placed upon subjectivity by Protestant (and especially Puritan) allegorists led, in the nineteenth century, to a radically subjective style
of interpretation. We have seen how Emerson shifted hermeneutic authority towards the gifted individual – the poet possessed of Romantic imagination. However, Emerson's vision of the poet is based upon a fundamentally
benevolent view of the universe. In the more skeptical allegorical practice of
Nathaniel Hawthorne and Herman Melville, this assumption that the power
of imagination must always be benign is challenged. The character of Roger
Chillingworth in Hawthorne's *The Scarlet Letter*, for example, is possessed
of the kind of imaginative capacity that Emerson attributes to the Poet.
Chillingworth is able to look into the visible signs of nature and read their
secrets, which endow him with almost mystical powers. He is able to read
the mystery of Hester's adulterous lover and identify him as the minister,
Dimmesdale. Further, Chillingworth uses his medicinal knowledge of nature
and his insight into the emotional history that surrounds him to torture the
young minister to death and so satisfy his desire for vengeance, as Hester's
cuckolded husband. While Chillingworth is able to penetrate the secrets of
nature and to harness what is seen by others as an almost supernatural
knowledge, this evil is set against the pervasive ambiguity that characterizes
all other attempts at interpretation in the narrative. This is dramatized in

the opening scene when Hester emerges from the prison, holding her illegitimate baby daughter, to confront the judgment of the crowd who have gathered to witness her public humiliation on the scaffold. Each of the voices that is transcribed by the narrator offers a different interpretation of Hester, her situation, and how she should be judged. This cacophony of voices is symptomatic of the attitude towards interpretation revealed throughout the narrative. Each individual subject interprets on his or her own terms; there is no consensus concerning truth, justice, or law. Indeed, where Hester believes that in her relationship with Dimmesdale she has conformed to the dictates of the law of nature, Dimmesdale condemns the relationship as violating the law of God. Nature and spirit, the real and the ideal, are incommensurate in Hawthorne's atomized world of individual subjective interpreters. Commentators have viewed this attempt to confront and move beyond the limitations imposed upon interpretation by the absence of some objective legislative authority as fundamental to the fiction written by Hawthorne and by Herman Melville. *Moby Dick* can be seen as Melville's response to Emerson's belief that through the power of sacramental rhetoric the exegete can access and reconcile a mystical dimension of meaning. Ahab, the crippled captain of the whaling ship that pursues the quasi-mythical white whale, seeks to break through what he calls the "pasteboard" masks of the visible world, to access and possess some mystical relationship with an absolute point of origin, some point of semantic unity that will redeem his world of superficial appearances.

Allegorical practice in nineteenth-century America developed in response to increasing skepticism toward institutional authorities such as the Churches and the mystical authority of the Bible itself. In the course of the century, this produced a new privileging of secular literature, as we have seen in Emerson's description of the figure of the poet. The poet, inspired by the artistic imagination, took the place of the divinely inspired interpreter in Romantic allegorical practice. The emphasis placed upon private and individual agency, rather than collective and structural prescriptions for interpretation, generated in large part the sense of a cultural crisis of meaning that is now identified as "modernity."

17

HOWARD CAYGILL

Walter Benjamin's concept
of allegory

The work of Walter Benjamin has made a fundamental contribution to the re-assessment of allegory during the twentieth century. It not only made a powerful case for the significance of allegory as a radical art practice but also extended its reach from the aesthetic to other realms of experience. However, the precise contours of the concept of allegory are hard to trace because Benjamin lends such broad significance to the allegorical. In so far as he possessed an integrated theory of allegory, it is one made up of the intersection of several discrete lines of inquiry whose precise relations were left deliberately undefined. For Benjamin, allegory is a concept with implications that are at once philosophical, religious, aesthetic, political and historical. In many ways it is emblematic of the internal complexity of Benjamin's work, which is rooted in the attempt to bring together the approaches of philosophy, aesthetics and cultural history. While the manifold senses of allegory are never bound unequivocally together into a general theory, it is clear that they depend upon each other, often in quite astonishing and illuminating ways. It is also evident that allegory is central not only to his understanding of modernism in art and literature, but also to the shifts of religious and political experience that for Benjamin constituted modernity.

Benjamin's two major projects of the 1920s and 1930s are both individually concerned with allegory and together propose a historical account of the role played by allegory in the origins of modernity and modernism and its centrality to the high modernism of the nineteenth century. *The Origin of German Tragic Drama* (1928) is widely acknowledged as a seminal discussion of allegory, with its second section "Trauerspiel and Allegory" dedicated explicitly to the theme. Much of its notorious difficulty is due to its subtle interweaving of a multi-layered discussion of allegory, an account of the dramatic genre of *Trauerspiel* or "mourning play," a study of baroque culture and its role in the transition to modernity as well as a vindication of expressionism. It is also a *summa* of radical discussions of allegory, providing the theoretical basis for the *Arcades Project* which immediately succeeded it and which describes the culture of the nineteenth century and its high modernism in terms of the allegorical. In notes for a never-to-be-completed book on Baudelaire, he explicitly linked Baudelaire's modernism to the baroque theory of allegory elaborated in *The Origin of German Tragic Drama*. Alongside the composition of the *Arcades Project* during the 1930s, Benjamin also published an influential series of critical essays on writers as diverse as the surrealists, Kafka, and Brecht; these essays were structured according to the concept of allegory, understood both as a condition of modern experience and as an aesthetic means for its artistic expression.

The very method of *The Origin of German Tragic Drama*, one that will finally disclose itself as "allegorical," resists definition. But fragments that he wrote in 1916 provide a clue to the conceptual process that informed the book (as suggested in the dedicatory note to his wife, "Conceived 1916 Written 1925"). These fragments do not mention the term "allegory," but their lines of philosophical and aesthetic reflection were to be united in the later book. The fragments may be distributed into three groups: those of explicit philosophical content such as "Socrates" and "On Language as Such and on the Language of Mankind"; those concerned with aesthetics, "Mourning-Play and Tragedy" and "The Role of Language in Mourning-Play and Tragedy"; and those on history and political theology, "On the Happiness of Ancient Man" and "The Middle Ages."

The philosophical foundations of Benjamin's concept of allegory are evident in the substantial fragment "On Language as Such and on the Language of Mankind." Here Benjamin employs an allegorical commentary on the book of Genesis to the end of analyzing the concept of communication (*Mitteilung*). The concept of allegory emerges from certain formal properties of communication which, broadly understood as language, spans expressive and communicative registers. Language expresses a human spiritual essence or *"geistiges Wesen"* and the areas of expression called upon to illustrate it are music, sculpture, justice and technology. Benjamin insists expression is intrinsically directed towards communication, but also maintains that communication in words is a particular, but not especially privileged case. The mutual implication of expression and communication is both epistemological – characteristic of a human *geistiges Wesen* – and ontological, described as co-extensive with "absolutely everything." The orders of expression and communication in turn communicate with each by means of translation: the expressive communication of a natural object is translated into the expressive communication of human language. The potential for mistranslation or the lack of fit between what is expressed and what is communicated provides the condition for a philosophical understanding of allegory.

Benjamin explores various ways in which expression and communication fall out of alignment with each other, each of which offers a perspective on the allegorical. The first case he mentions is that of the "Idea" which will return in the "Epistemo-Critical Prologue" to the *Origin of German Tragic Drama*. The "Idea" is an expression that is not dependent upon communication, and is presented as an extreme case of separation. As an incommunicable expression it stands as a limit case that cannot be directly translated. Another limit case of perhaps even greater significance for Benjamin is the dissolution of expression in communication, the view that "all language communicates itself *in* itself."[1] In this case, the medium of communication itself presents the message or the "expressed;" only what may be communicated in this language is expressible, a position Benjamin immediately identifies as paradoxical. For if there is no "outside" of language, no expressed contents to be communicated, there is also, by the same token, no addressee: language can only communicate with itself, leading to the conclusion that it does not communicate. If a language can express only itself to itself, then it is no longer communicative, no longer, by definition, a language. With this, Benjamin arrives artfully at the conclusion that a language of pure communication arrives at expressing only itself, that it is an "Idea."

Benjamin describes two limits to human language. The first is set by the language of nature, which, deprived of its expression by a violent translation into the human language of the name, nevertheless retains a reserve, a mute expression that is enough to trouble the absolute claim to meaning of the language of the "lords of nature" (what in the *Origin of German Tragic Drama* Benjamin will describe as "sovereignty"). The reserve is enough, potentially, to evacuate the entire world of any meaning, since it indicates a limit to the power of an expressive communication that imagines itself to be absolute. This limit, however, can be experienced ecstatically if the claim to a monopoly of expression and communication (sovereignty) is surrendered. With this, languages, through mutually recognized translation, "become *continua* of transformation, not abstract areas of identity and similarity"(*Origin*, p. 70). In this case, a language ceases to mark a territory of expression and communication and becomes instead a site of transformation of its own expression and communication, as well of that which it expresses and communicates. Setting an absolute system of expressive communication within a frame by determining its limits is another aspect of the allegorical that will become important for Benjamin.

---

[1] "On Language as Such and on the Language of Mankind," in *Walter Benjamin: Selected Writings Volume 1*, eds. Marcus Bullock and Michael W. Jennings (Cambridge, MA: Harvard University Press, 1996), p. 64.

A second limit to human language is posed not so much by its inability to effect a full translation of expressive communications issuing from beyond its borders, but by its ability to express and communicate objects which do not exist. Benjamin's example, to which he devotes a great deal of attention, is good and evil. He writes:

> Knowledge of good and evil abandons name; it is a knowledge from outside, the uncreated imitation of the creative word. Name steps outside itself in this knowledge: the Fall marks the birth of the *human word*, in which name no longer lives intact and which has stepped out of name language.
>
> (*Origin*, p. 71)

The myth of the Fall is emblematic of the surrender of the communicative vocation of human language. Instead of communicating through the translation of other expressive communications, human language becomes purely expressive, expressing objects – good and evil – that do not exist. Benjamin is here describing a transition to abstractive and evaluative language, a passage from the "naming" to the "judging" word to which he lends a "threefold significance." In the first, language becomes a means, and the name a "mere sign" resulting in "the plurality of languages" (*Origin*, p. 71); there is no longer an easy translation between expressive communications, but the situation described above, that of a reserve. In place of the "immediacy of name" that designates the translation of an object's expressive communication emerges "judgment" – and then thirdly, language is abstracted, since judgment depends upon a law founded in "the unnameable and nameless" (*Origin*, p. 72). Benjamin concludes his biblical commentary with a definition of what he will later describe as the allegorical condition: "The enslavement of language in prattle is joined by the enslavement of things in folly almost as its inevitable consequence. In this turning away from things, which was enslavement, the plan for the Tower of Babel comes into being, and linguistic confusion with it" (*Origin*, p. 72).

The abstract reflections of "On Language as Such and on the Language of Man" already point to a range of other considerations. The entire discussion is couched within the idiom of political theology, with reflections on the Fall and the origins of judgment and law. It is also related to aesthetics, in the view of artistic forms as sites of translation for "the language of things into an infinitely higher language" (*Origin*, p. 73) and the critique of the symbol towards the very end of the essay. The symbol marks for Benjamin the main threat to the communicative vocation of language, marking the presence within language "of the noncommunicable" (*Origin*, p. 74). This is the germ of the later critical distinction between allegory and symbol as two negotiations of the outside of language, with allegory looking to voice the "reserve" of objects silenced in the human name, and the symbol to the law according to which the legitimacy of human names is secured.

The contents of *The Origin of German Tragic Drama* are organized under three headings: a methodological introduction or "Epistemo-Criticial Prologue," and two large sections, "Trauerspiel and Tragedy" and "Allegory and Trauerspiel." One of the basic premises of the book is that the character of seventeenth-century German drama – above all the work of Andreas Gryphius, Johann Christian Hallmann, Daniel Caspar von Lohenstein and Martin Opitz – has been substantially misunderstood. The methodological basis for this misunderstanding is both philosophical and historical. In the "Epistemo-Critical Prologue" Benjamin argues that the aesthetic objectives of German baroque drama were confused with those of tragedy and its allegorical technique confused with that of symbolism. While the "Epistemo-Critical Prologue" ventures a philosophical revision of the concept of form that will accommodate *Trauerspiel*, the first part distinguishes *Trauerspiel* from tragedy and the second part aligns it with allegory.

The "Epistemo-Critical Prologue" begins with a justification for the philosophically informed criticism of works of art. Already in its opening lines, the "Prologue" proclaims itself as a manifesto protesting against the philosophical aesthetics of the nineteenth century. Against the dominant, authoritative form of the philosophical "system" which captures "the truth" through an act of symbolic representation, Benjamin advocates the "treatise" as a new form for the philosophical criticism of art. The latter, we shall see, pursues an allegorical method that assembles fragments, that "juxtaposes the distinct and the disparate" in pursuit of a fugitive truth.[2] The allegorical method of philosophizing pursues a strategy of representation quite different from that of the symbolic: it departs from a crisis of representation, seeking to construct constellations out of the material of the past. Benjamin proposes an approach that avoids the alternatives of an *a priori* philosophical notion of aesthetic form, in which works of art with varying degrees of success embody the aesthetic idea, and an *a posteriori* "literary historical analysis" in which form is derived inductively from existing works of art. The notion of the constellation, in which patterns connecting past objects and events are inseparable from the perspective of the present, assumes that form is never entirely present, nor completely absent from works of the past. The concept of "origin" derived from the philosophical work of Hermann Cohen and prominent in the title of the work – the *origin* of German tragic drama – is central to Benjamin's approach. He defines it as describing "that which

---

2 Walter Benjamin, *The Origin of German Tragic Drama*, trans. John Osborne (London: New Left Books, 2003), p. 28.

emerges from the process of becoming and disappearance" and relates it to a "dual insight" of the "restoration and re-establishment" of a work by the historian, but adds as a necessary premise of such insight the recognition that a work is "imperfect and incomplete."[3] The task of the philosophical critic is to contribute to the "restoration" of a work by recognizing the ways in which and the reasons why it is "imperfect and incomplete."

Having detailed the reasons why German baroque *Trauerspiel* had been denied historical resonance, Benjamin attempted to "restore and re-establish" its historical significance. This involved three methodological steps. The first, carried through in the closing pages of the "Epistemo-Critical Prologue," consisted in establishing a new historical constellation between the present and the past. Not only was the "authority of old prejudices beginning to wane"[4] in criticism and literary history, but, more significantly, contemporary expressionist drama pursued similar themes and used similar techniques to the baroque, allowing it to become recognizable as a form distinct from that of classical tragedy. The second step pursued in "Trauerspiel and Tragedy" consisted in freeing *Trauerspiel* from the shadow of tragedy, showing how it pursues artistic intentions and formal techniques generically distinct from those of tragedy. After the work of freeing the form of *Trauerspiel* from its subordination to that of tragedy, Benjamin then proceeds to analyze and isolate its distinct formal properties. These are then revealed – in "Allegory and Trauerspiel" – to consist in the pursuit of an "allegorical intention" by means of allegorical techniques. *The Origin of German Tragic Drama* then emerges as a vindication of allegory, as much in the aesthetic field of baroque and expressionist drama, as in the method of philosophical criticism itself.

The opening lines of "Trauerspiel and Tragedy" locate the three parts of this major section of the work within the methodological objectives stated in the "Epistemo-Critical Prologue." The aim of providing a "representation of the origin of German tragic drama"[5] will be achieved by means of attention to those extreme elements of the dramas that are taken to define the limits of its form. In the first part of this section the objective is pursued by "taking account of the baroque theory of drama"[6] and distinguishing it from the Aristotelian theory of tragedy. The grounds of distinction are introduced by means of a theoretical statement by the baroque dramatist Opitz, which for Benjamin locates the subject matter of *Trauerspiel* in history, rather than in myth. The dramatic action of tragedy is the mythical conflict of the hero with God and fate, while that of *Trauerspiel* consists in "the confirmation

3 *Origin of German Tragic Drama*, p. 43.   4 Ibid., p. 55.
5 Ibid., p. 57.   6 Ibid., p. 58.

of princely virtues, the depiction of princely vices, the insight into diplomacy and the manipulation of all the political schemes."[7] Benjamin places at the center of *Trauerspiel* the figure of the "sovereign" and the predicament of the "state of emergency" and identifies the action of *Trauerspiel* in the depiction of the responses of the sovereign to the state of emergency.

Benjamin's conception of the "sovereign" and the "state of emergency" is deeply indebted to the work of the philosopher of law Carl Schmitt, notably his *Political Theology* of 1922.[8] Benjamin situates the state of emergency against the terms of the medieval mystery play, which is seen to provide a story of redemption; the secularization of the mystery play in baroque drama leaves a state of emergency without redemption, resulting in the evacuation of eschatology. In the baroque drama, the state of emergency is expressed in the ambivalence of the character of the sovereign and sovereign action. The virtuous prince suffers stoically the state of emergency, giving rise to the genre of martyr drama, while the vicious prince responds tyrannically in the drama of tyranny. The *Trauerspiel* locates both responses within the character of the sovereign, with the character of the monarch in the state of emergency vacillating between passive martyrdom and tyrannical violence. Yet Benjamin considers this vacillation so characteristic of the *Trauerspiel* as to point to a more fundamental formal condition of the drama: "For no one will regard the stoic morality, to which the martyrdom of the hero leads, or the justice, which transforms the tyrant's rage to madness, as an adequate foundation for the tension of an independent dramatic structure."[9] The replacement of the tragic catastrophe and the mystery play's Christian narrative of redemption leaves the *Trauerspiel* in the dramatic predicament of the "hopelessness of the earthly condition."[10] The *Trauerspiel* combines tragedy and mystery play in its extension of catastrophe to Everyman, making catastrophe "typical" rather than extra-ordinary, an aspect of the "very estate of man as creature." In place of the catastrophic resolution of tragedy, Benjamin locates the formal principle of *Trauerspiel* in the mourning for a perpetual and irresolvable state of emergency.

7 Ibid., p. 62.
8 Schmitt's subsequent support of the National Socialist government made Benjamin's debt to his work controversial. However Schmitt's response to the crises of the early Weimar Republic in *Political Theology* and the *Concept of the Political* is analogous to, but distinct from, that of Benjamin in works such as the *Critique of Violence* and *Capitalism as Religion*. As will be seen below, Benjamin regards the secularization of theological concepts central to Schmitt's concept of sovereignty as the occasion for crisis or an extended period of emergency, as posing difficult questions rather than a solution. For a lucid discussion of this issue and the reproduction of Benjamin's correspondence with Schmitt, see Jacob Taubes, *Ad Carl Schmitt: Gegenstrebige Fügung* (Berlin: Merve Verlag, 1987).
9 *Origin of German Tragic Drama*, p. 78.   10 Ibid., p. 81.

If the presiding genius of the first two sections of "Tragedy and Trauer-spiel" was Carl Schmitt, his place is taken in the third part by Aby War-burg and his school. Benjamin shifts the emphasis of his inquiry from the absolutist court and state of emergency to the religious Reformation. His discussion develops themes intimated in an earlier fragment, "Capitalism as Religion" (1921), which comments critically on the debate provoked by Max Weber's 1906 "Protestant Ethic and the Spirit of Capitalism." In the *Trauerspiel* book, however, Benjamin takes an important step beyond Weber's diagnosis of a crisis of faith provoked by the Protestant doctrines of justification by faith and predestination, by drawing on the work of War-burg, especially his 1920 "Pagan-Antique Prophesy in Words and Images in the Age of Luther" and the studies that would emerge as *Saturn and Melancholy*.[11] Benjamin shows how the crisis of the meaning of life pro-voked by the Protestant doctrine has objective and subjective consequences in the draining of meaning of the world of objects and actions – the world is no longer a stage of salvation – and with this, the melancholy provoked in the sage or hero who experiences and contemplates the disenchantment of the world. The extended discussion of melancholy and the Saturnine brings together Weber and Warburg's understandings of the significance of the Reformation, and aligns both with the ineluctable crisis of meaning that is emerging as the essence of the allegorical.

In the second part of *The Origin of German Tragic Drama*, "Allegory and Baroque Drama," Benjamin again distances the allegorical from the symbolic while identifying a peculiar "antinomy" of the allegorical, one that introduces a dynamic into the concept that, as Benjamin suggests, admits of "dialectical analysis." The antinomy consists in the nihilistic devaluation of the meanings of the world of things and actions accompanied by their reevaluation in allegorical contexts. Meaning is first destroyed and then restored at a higher, allegorical level. The first movement of the allegorical is that of fragmentation – the destruction or ruination of contexts of meaning – with the ruin as an emblem of the destructive character of allegory. This destructive movement is associated with cruelty and intrigue and creates the state of emergency. For Benjamin, the classical trope of such fragmentation is the spatialization of time – temporal meanings are frozen, objects and actions either piled up or stratified according to structures that are indifferent to their natural meaning. It is as if they are words that have been translated into languages that are indifferent to their original meaning.

11 Aby Warburg, *The Renewal of Pagan Antiquity*, trans. David Britt (Los Angeles: Getty Research Institute for the History of Art and the Humanities, 1999), pp. 597–697; R. Klibansky, E. Panofsky, F. Saxl, *Saturn and Melancholy. Studies in the History of Natural Philosophy, Religion and Art* (London: Thomas Nelson, 1964).

The annihilation of natural meaning by the allegorical is then succeeded by an allegorical restitution, one in which the destructive impulse of allegory is applied to itself. In this way, the allegory of meaning is itself allegorized – the state of fragmentation is itself fragmented, allowing the possibility of putting into question the destruction of meaning.

In *The Origin of German Tragic Drama* the significance of Benjamin's concept of allegory for understanding modernism is obscured by the analysis of forgotten baroque dramatists. The method of his analysis of aesthetic allegory in the artwork of the Reformation and Counter-Reformation – the religious origin of modernity – becomes more explicit in the analysis of the culture of high capitalism in the *Arcades Project* and the reading of Baudelaire as an allegorist that formed an important, even freestanding part of that project. The *Arcades Project*, which occupied Benjamin from the late 1920s until his death, has survived as a vast card index of found materials and text that is organized into alphabetic "convolutes." The large Convolute J on Baudelaire collects materials and thoughts for a book on Baudelaire that was intended, between 1937 and 1939, as a "scale model" of the *Arcades Project*. The central and organizing concept of the Baudelaire studies is allegory, and its methodological application to a nineteenth-century poet is consistent with Benjamin's earlier statement in *The Origin of German Tragic Drama*.

Convolute J presents an intensification of early modern baroque allegory in the high capitalism of nineteenth-century Paris. The similarity and contrasts are marked throughout the Convolute, baroque and modern allegory being situated within a wider history of the allegorical. This takes two forms. The first, departing from an observation upon Baudelaire's esteem for late Latin poetry, parallels what may be described as the Warburg history of allegory, or the allegorization of the pagan Gods in late antique and Christian culture. At one point Benjamin refers to Hermann Usener's *Götternamen* (1896) as support for his view of the allegorization of the names of the gods in Latin literature. Yet, while pointing to classical and early Christian precedents, he also wishes to locate the sources of Baudelaire's "allegorical intuition" elsewhere, in the daily experience of life under high capitalism. While noting that "Antiquity and Christianity together determine the historical armature of the allegorical mode of perception, they provide the lasting rudiments of the first allegorical experience – that of the High Middle Ages,"[12] he distinguishes allegory as a vehicle for the rivalry of paganism

12 Walter Benjamin, *The Arcades Project*, trans. Howard Eiland and Kevin McLaughlin (Cambridge, MA: Harvard University Press, 1999), p. 324 (J53a, 1).

and Christianity from the "primordial experience – which had a substrate entirely sui generic" of Baudelaire's poetry.

Benjamin supports his reference to the rivalry of Antiquity and Christianity with a citation from his own *Origin of German Tragic Drama*, a practice he repeats in a parallel between the "threefold illusory nature" of allegory described in the *Origin of German Tragic Drama* and the structure of the *Fleurs du Mal*.[13] Benjamin more usually points to an intensification of the early modern experience of allegory in the period of high capitalism, an intensification summed up in the formula "Baroque allegory sees the corpse only from the outside, Baudelaire evokes it from within."[14] What Benjamin means by this may be gathered by looking at other descriptions he offered of the intensification of allegory. At one point he describes the difference in allegorical degree of the baroque and modern epochs in terms of the "fetish character of the commodity" identified by Marx in the early pages of *Capital*:

> In the Baroque age, the fetish character of the commodity was still relatively undeveloped. And the commodity had not yet so deeply engraved its stigma – the proletarianisation of the producers – on the process of production. Allegorical perception could thus constitute a style in the seventeenth century, in a way that it no longer could in the nineteenth.[15]

The distinction between an allegorical style and an allegorical predicament is specified later in the discussion of what Benjamin described as the extravagant and unprecedented role of the emblem in baroque allegory:

> Here may be found the key to the Baroque procedure whereby meanings are conferred on the set of fragments, on the pieces into which not so much the whole as the process of its production has disintegrated. Baroque emblems may be conceived as half-finished products which, from the phases of a production process, have been converted into monuments to the process of destruction.[16]

Focusing on the emblem of the "death's head," Benjamin regards it as "a half-finished product of the history of salvation, that process interrupted – so far as this is given him to realise – by Satan." The "death's head" or the "image of petrified unrest called up by allegory" "shows the forces of . . . Christianity suddenly arrested in their contest, turned to stone amid unallayed hostilities."[17] Yet, as is shown by the end of the *Trauerspiel*

---

13 See *Arcades*, p. 235, where the baroque allegorical illusions of freedom, independence, and infinity are mapped onto the cycles "Fleurs du Mal," "Révolte," and "Spleen et Idéal."
14 *Arcades*, p. 329 (J56, 2).   15 *Arcades*, p. 347 (J67, 2).
16 *Arcades*, p. 366 (J78, 4).   17 *Arcades*, p. 366 (J78, 4).

book, the interruption is temporary and the emblem of the "death's head" or Golgotha turns and recommences the history of salvation.

Benjamin did not see such an issue possible any longer in the nineteenth century. The commodity fetish is itself allegorical, modern culture is intrinsically allegorical, with the exchange value of the commodity devaluing all other traditional or use values, but being itself prone to crises of the inflation and deflation of values. Allegory is no longer a stylistic choice, but a predicament. The baroque redemptive solution of allegorizing allegory was no longer available to Baudelaire: "He sought to recall the experience of the commodity to an allegorical experience. In this, he was doomed to founder, and it became clear that the relentlessness of his initiative was exceeded by the relentlessness of reality."[18] The nature of the allegorical predicament – which it is the task of the entire *Arcades Project* to survey – may be seen from the use Benjamin makes of the phrase to describe allegory, namely "petrified unrest." In the baroque, this referred, as we have seen, to the interruption of the history of salvation, an interruption which may be infinitely extended or contracted by the intervention of God.[19] It constitutes the "state of emergency" to which the sovereign responds, but before which they are essentially powerless.

In the *Arcades Project* the history of salvation is perpetually interrupted, and the state of emergency is located in the crisis of value that is constitutive of the capitalist economy. The "Fetish Commodity," a term that Benjamin now uses for what he earlier described as "Capitalism as Religion," translates all values and meanings into its own terms – exchange value – and destabilizes them in the process. The condition of "petrified unrest" thus comes to stand for the stabilized instability of the capitalist economy in which values are perpetually being assigned and devalued. The political state of emergency and the possibility of a sovereign central to *The Origin of German Tragic Drama* have now been succeeded by an economic and cultural state of emergency or "crisis" for which the sovereign instance is the proletariat and the sovereign decision proletarian revolution. In Convolute J and the projected Baudelaire book, Benjamin analyzes this condition through the comparison of Baudelaire with the Revolutionary Louis-Auguste Blanqui.

Benjamin regards the poet and the revolutionary as complements. Blanqui's text on the eternal return of the stars is described as a projection of the allegorical onto the cosmos itself: "In Blanqui's view of the world,

---

18 *Arcades*, p. 347 (J67, 2).
19 See *Arcades*, p. 326 (J54, 5) "The image of petrified unrest, in the Baroque, is 'the bleak confusion of Golgotha...,'" citing from *The Origin of German Tragic Drama*.

petrified unrest becomes the status of the cosmos itself. The course of the world appears, accordingly, as 'one great allegory.' "[20] Baudelaire too is in the thrall of such petrified unrest, but locates it culturally and not cosmologically. Benjamin distinguishes very precisely between the two allegorists: "In Blanqui, the abyss has the historical index of mechanistic natural science. In Baudelaire doesn't it have the social index of *nouveauté*? Is not the arbitrariness of allegory a twin to that of fashion?"[21] The constant establishment and disestablishment of meaning and value in fashion, or petrified unrest of the repeatedly new, is the allegorical; or, as Benjamin comments, "The commodity form emerges in Baudelaire as the social content of the allegorical form of perception."[22] In the allegorical culture of high capitalism meaning is entirely destabilized, and the eternal return dreamt of by Blanqui is but the transformation of "the historical event into a mass produced article" subject to "an accelerated succession of crises." In this context "the idea of *eternal* recurrence derived its luster from the fact that it is no longer possible, in all circumstances, to expect a recurrence of conditions across any interval of time shorter than that provided by eternity."[23] The distension of the crisis of meaning to eternity threw the culture into a perpetual crisis of meaning, a petrified unrest in which novelty or the new eternally repeats and belies its own novelty.

In the closing pages of *The Origin of German Tragic Drama* Benjamin imagines the allegorization of allegory, the revelation that the allegorical destruction of meaning is itself an allegory. Such an about turn, however, is no longer available in the period of high capitalism. An allegorical art such as Baudelaire's seems little threat to an intensely allegorical culture. It would be difficult for such an art to resist being taken up as part of the broader process of the allegorization of meaning. In this respect, Benjamin considers Baudelaire's allegorical modernism to have "foundered" before the spectacle of an allegorical modernity. He sees it as seeking refuge and security in allegory-proof experiences such as those of the correspondences, *l'art pour l'art*, or the establishment of a "kingdom of art outside profane existence." However, a small chance does seem to survive, in that allegorical art can serve to threaten attempts to petrify or stabilize the innovative unrest of a capitalist economy, to mask its crises. Allegory is the "antidote"

---

20 *Arcades*, p. 329 (J55a, 4).
21 *Arcades*, p. 271 [J24, 2] or, as Benjamin noted later in the Convolute, "Thing and situation become obsolete for allegory more quickly than a new pattern for the milliner" (p. 336, J59a, 4).
22 *Arcades*, p. 335 (J59, 10).   23 *Arcades*, p. 340 (J62, a2).

to such myths,[24] the "politicized art" that would challenge an "aestheti-cized politics," that would uncover the unrest concealed in the stability of the *Volksgemeinschaft* (people's community). In this respect the work of Brecht becomes for Benjamin the site for the confluence of the accounts of allegory in *The Origin of German Tragic Drama* and the *Arcades Project*, the naming of the "proletariat" as such in the Third Reich, pointing, how-ever vainly, to the turnaround of the allegorical. Nevertheless, it is hard to avoid the conclusion that Benjamin's justification of allegory as a mod-ernist art practice was accomplished at the price of its increasing irrelevance as a site of critical social and political reflection, that it had its moment in the baroque, but that allegorical modernism paled before an allegorical modernity.

---

24 "Allegory should be shown as the antidote to myth. Myth was the comfortable route from which Baudelaire abstained" (*Origin*, p. 179). Benjamin will also contrast Baudelaire's allegory with Hugo's commitment to the comfort of the myth of the virtuous republican crowd.

18

STEVEN MAILLOUX

Hermeneutics, deconstruction, allegory

Allegory is narrative with a shadow story of corresponding characters, events, or ideas. Allegorical interpretation establishes the meaning of this figurative relation by tracing its correspondences of actions and concepts. Such working definitions will need revision as we consider the critical traditions of hermeneutics and deconstruction. In the second half of the twentieth century, these two ways of thinking offered unique perspectives on allegory as both a mode of writing and a strategy for reading. For the purposes of this essay, we can view hermeneutics generally as theories of interpretation, the establishment of textual meaning, especially those theories associated with the writings of Hans-Georg Gadamer and Paul Ricoeur. More provisionally, we can treat deconstruction as a radical form of poststructuralism and a certain way of interpreting against the grain of a text, developed within and against phenomenology and structuralism and often identified with the critical readings of Paul de Man and Jacques Derrida. Hermeneutics and deconstruction intersect and diverge on their shared topic of allegory in its relation to rhetoric, philosophy, and literature.

We begin with two very different figures who set the rhetorical stage for later developments in hermeneutics and poststructuralism. Early in the century, Martin Heidegger's ontological rereadings of Western theology and philosophy included suggestive comments on allegory in his 1930–31 lecture course on "The Essence of Truth." Preparing to interpret Plato's cave allegory (*Republic* book 7, 514a–20a) with all its shadows and light, Heidegger notes that allegory is presented through a "sensory image" that "is never intended to stand for itself alone, but indicates that something is to be understood, providing a clue as to what this is." But "what is to be understood is not a sense, but rather an occurrence." That occurrence is always a seeing, an understanding something "in the sense of" something else. "The presentation of an allegory, of a sensory image, is therefore nothing else than a clue for seeing (a provision of a clue through something which is presented sensuously). Such a clue leads us to what simple description, be it ever so accurate and rigorous, can never grasp."[1] We might take these admittedly schematic remarks as indicative of certain emphases to be found in the allegory theories of later hermeneutics and poststructuralism, both movements significantly indebted to Heidegger. For example, we will find in these traditions a focus on interpretation, not only as a process for making sense of allegorical clues but also as an occurrence to which allegory draws our attention, an occurrence that is either historically determinate through hermeneutic tradition or structurally troubled through self-deconstructing textuality.

At mid century, Northrop Frye's influential literary theories contributed to a formalist turn toward allegory as a topic in critical thinking. In *Anatomy of Criticism* (1957) Frye compares his project to that of Aristotelian poetics: a "theory of criticism whose principles apply to the whole of literature and account for every valid type of critical procedure."[2] Frye describes how literature and criticism actually work in formal terms but does not prescribe how they should work. He aims at producing "a coherent and comprehensive theory of literature, logically and scientifically organized" (*Anatomy*, p. 11). That is, he wishes systematically to describe "the organizing or containing forms" of literary criticism's "conceptual framework" (*Anatomy*, p. 16). His widely discussed taxonomy includes theories of modes, symbols, myths, and genres, which undergird complementary critical approaches, respectively, historical, ethical, archetypal, and rhetorical perspectives. Frye's theory of allegory finds its place under his theory of symbols, though, as we will see, allegorical commentary is, in one sense, the overarching category for all critical approaches not just a subset of ethical (character-related) criticism.

Frye's modernist theory of allegory attempts to stabilize distinctions at two discursive levels: distinctions between genuine allegories and narratives containing only some allegorical aspects and between allegorical interpretations that are indisputable (allegory is simply there) and those that are not (allegory is ambiguously present). However, as both hermeneutic and poststructuralist thinkers might point out, these distinctions cannot be so easily stabilized in theory. This very point is illustrated at times in the unfolding of Frye's own arguments. For example, in a 1965 encyclopedia entry, he writes: "Allegorical interpretation, as a method of criticism, begins with the fact that a[llegory] is a structural element in narrative: it has to be there, and is not added by critical interpretation alone." Here Frye tries to demarcate clearly the distinction between allegory in the text and allegory supplied

1 Martin Heidegger, *The Essence of Truth: On Plato's Cave Allegory and Theaetetus*, trans. Ted Sadler (London: Continuum, 2002), pp. 12–13.
2 Northrop Frye, *Anatomy of Criticism: Four Essays* (Princeton: Princeton University Press, 1957), p. 14.

by interpretation. Yet in the very next sentence this distinction becomes blurred: "In fact, all commentary, or the relating of the events of a narrative to conceptual terminology, is in one sense allegorical interpretation." After this admission, Frye tries to recuperate the distinction between true and partial allegories and between legitimate and illegitimate allegorical interpretation by claiming that "[s]trictly defined, allegorical interpretation is the specific form of commentary that deals with fictions which are structurally allegories" and that the "presence" of structural allegory "prescribes the direction in which commentary must go."[3]

In response to such foundationalist claims, a hermeneutical theorist might point out that for a prescription to prescribe effectively, it must first be interpreted as having a determinate content and force. That is, a prescription cannot control subsequent commentary prior to interpretation; rather a prescription's effects are the product of contextualized interpretations within an already existent tradition of commentary. Similarly, a deconstructionist might note that prescriptions often go awry and fail in their prescriptive efforts and, further, that "doubling commentary" once performed can never guarantee the proscription of a disruptive or contradictory "critical reading."[4] Both an argument for the hermeneutic circle and a poststructuralist rejection of permanently stable meaning call into question the reader/text, subject/object split assumed by Frye's modernist theory of allegorical interpretation. But this is not to say that hermeneutics and deconstruction are opposed to allegorical interpretation as such. Quite the contrary. They are simply suspicious of foundationalist theories attempting to ground interpretive practices, including allegorical interpretive practices (allegoresis).

Indeed, in the second half of the twentieth century, hermeneutics and deconstruction contributed significantly to the rehabilitation of allegory and allegoresis, a revaluation that included distinctively new interpretations of classical, medieval, and romantic theories. Hans-Georg Gadamer's monumental treatise on philosophical hermeneutics, *Wahrheit und Methode* (1960; English trans. *Truth and Method*) advanced this conceptual transformation through a historical critique of German Romanticism and its privileging of symbol over allegory. Gadamer's account formed part of his influential attempt to champion a mode of artistic truth that went beyond contemporary methodological reductions restricting knowledge to scientific objectivity.

3 Northrop Frye, "Allegory," in *Princeton Encyclopedia of Poetry and Poetics*, ed. Alex Preminger (Princeton: Princeton University Press, 1965), pp. 12–13. Cf. Frye, *Anatomy*, pp. 89–90.

4 Jacques Derrida, *Of Grammatology*, trans. Gayatri Chakravorty Spivak (Baltimore: Johns Hopkins University Press, 1976), p. 158.

Gadamer's overall goal in *Truth and Method* is to examine aesthetic and historical consciousness in order to establish the legitimacy of non-methodical, non-scientistic modes of truth and ways of knowing within the human sciences. He achieves this goal partly through a criticism of "aesthetic differentiation," the cultural process through which German Idealism advocated a subjective artistic autonomy grounded in the separation of aesthetic consciousness from mechanical rationalism and scientific procedure. "The shift in the ontological definition of the aesthetic toward the concept of aesthetic appearance has its theoretical basis in the fact that the domination of the scientific model of epistemology leads to discrediting all the possibilities of knowing that lie outside this new methodology."[5] Gadamer mounts his critique in the area of aesthetics through a detailed history of concepts in European poetic theory. He asserts that the Romantic cult of genius and its emphasis on subjective experience formed historical conditions of thought for an aesthetic differentiation that brought with it a claim for the superiority of symbol over allegory.

Gadamer argues that aesthetic non-differentiation is a more useful framework for understanding the experience of art than a one-sided focus on aesthetic consciousness:

> It should be admitted that, say, an ancient image of the gods that was not displayed in a temple as a work of art in order to give aesthetic, reflective pleasure, and is now on show in a museum, retains, even as it stands before us today, the world of religious experience from which it came; the important consequence is that its world still belongs to ours. What embraces both is the hermeneutic universe. (*Truth and Method*, p. xxxi)

Gadamer notes that "the vindication of allegory, which is pertinent here, began some years ago with Walter Benjamin's major work, *The Origin of German Tragic Drama*" (*Truth and Method*, p. xxxi, n. 8).

Gadamer extends that vindication in his criticism of the Kantian subjectivization of aesthetics and the subsequent Romantic celebration of symbol over allegory. He makes his case most effectively in the section of *Truth and Method* called "The Limits of Erlebniskunst [art based on experience] and the Rehabilitation of Allegory." He begins by noting that as late as the eighteenth century "poetry and rhetoric [were] side by side in a way that is surprising to modern consciousness." But the nineteenth century developed a different conception of art based on the "criteria of being experienced and of the inspired genius," a conception that "eliminates everything merely

---

5 Hans-Georg Gadamer, *Truth and Method*, 2nd edn., trans. Joel Weinsheimer and Donald G. Marshall (New York: Crossroad, 1989), p. 84.

occasional and banishes rhetoric entirely" (*Truth and Method*, p. 71). Ultimately, "the aesthetic opposition between allegory and symbol" follows from this "devaluation of rhetoric" and the embrace of "the doctrine that genius creates unconsciously" (*Truth and Method*, p. 72).

Gadamer traces the conceptual history of symbol and allegory, observing that in their classical use the two terms were initially associated with different fields of activity:

> "Allegory" originally belonged to the sphere of talk, of the logos, and is therefore a rhetorical or hermeneutic figure. Instead of what is actually meant, something else, more tangible, is said, but in such a way that the former is understood. "Symbol," however, is not limited to the sphere of the logos, for a symbol is not related by its meaning to another meaning, but its own sensory existence has "meaning." As something shown, it enables one to recognize something else. (*Truth and Method*, p. 72)

For example, a religious symbol or secular badge allows community members to recognize each other as members. Though from different spheres, allegory and symbol do have a basic structure in common: "Both words refer to something whose meaning does not consist in its external appearance or sound but in a significance that lies beyond it" (*Truth and Method*, p. 72).[6] Also, both terms find "their chief application in the religious sphere," though "the concept of symbol has a metaphysical background that is entirely lacking in the rhetorical use of allegory": through the symbolic coincidence of "visible appearance and invisible significance," it becomes "possible to be led beyond the sensible to the divine" (*Truth and Method*, pp. 73–74).

By the end of the eighteenth century, the symbol's presupposed "metaphysical connection between visible and invisible" (*Truth and Method*, p. 73) semantically fostered a contrast between "the symbolic (conceived as something inherently and essentially significant)" and "the allegorical, which has external and artificial significance." That is, the symbol was seen as "the coincidence of the sensible and the non-sensible" in contrast to allegory, "the meaningful relation of the sensible to the non-sensible" (*Truth and Method*, p. 74). Then, in the nineteenth century, "under the influence of the concept of genius and the subjectivization of 'expression,' this difference of meanings became a contrast of values." Gadamer summarizes the

---

6 Commenting briefly on Stoic and Neoplatonist writers, Gadamer anticipates recent classical scholarship in his claim about the common structure that symbol and allegory assumed in late antiquity; see Peter Struck's essay in this volume, "Allegory and ascent in Neoplatonism."

results of this conceptual history: "The symbol (which can be interpreted inexhaustibly because it is indeterminate) is opposed to allegory (understood as standing in a more exact relation to meaning and exhausted by it) as art is opposed to non-art" (*Truth and Method*, pp. 74–75). The nineteenth-century concept of the symbol becomes a basic justification for aesthetic autonomy as the concept "implies the inner unity of symbol and what is symbolized," thus establishing the coincidence of finite sensible appearance and suprasensible infinite meaning (*Truth and Method*, pp. 77–78). "For this is what is characteristic of the work of art, the creation of genius: that its meaning lies in the phenomenon itself and is not arbitrarily read into it" (*Truth and Method*, p. 77). In contrast to the symbol, allegory "is certainly not the product of genius alone. It rests on firm traditions and always has a fixed, statable meaning" (*Truth and Method*, p. 79).

Gadamer's history of concepts demonstrates how the contrast between symbol and allegory is shaped differently at different times, whereas the aesthetics of experience makes the contrast appear absolute rather than relative. Gadamer's concern here is not simply with changes in aesthetic taste, but with the very "concept of aesthetic consciousness itself," which now "becomes dubious, and thus also the standpoint of art to which it belongs." He asks rhetorically (in both senses): "Is the aesthetic approach to a work of art the appropriate one? Or is what we call 'aesthetic consciousness' an abstraction?" (*Truth and Method*, p. 81) compared to the actual hermeneutic experience of aesthetic non-differentiation, of refusing the "false dichotomy" of regarding art "either as originally contemporary with all times and outside history or as a way of attaining culture through the experience of history"? (*Truth and Method*, p. 573). He summarizes and concludes that "the revaluation of allegory that we have been describing indicates that there is a dogmatic element in aesthetic consciousness too. And if the difference between mythical and aesthetic consciousness is not absolute, does not the concept of [autonomous] art itself become questionable?" (*Truth and Method*, p. 81).

In his influential essay, "The Rhetoric of Temporality" (1969), Paul de Man folds Gadamer's account into his own poststructuralist deployment of allegory and its history.[7] In de Man's deconstructive rhetoric of reading, allegory becomes both a topic of historical consideration and, more crucially, a figure of interpretive exploitation. Indeed, probably more than any other

7 Paul de Man, "The Rhetoric of Temporality," in *Interpretation: Theory and Practice*, ed. Charles S. Singleton (Baltimore: Johns Hopkins University Press, 1969), rpt. Paul de Man, *Blindness and Insight: Essays in the Rhetoric of Contemporary Criticism*, 2nd edn. (Minneapolis: University of Minnesota Press, 1983), p. 191.

theorist of the late twentieth century, de Man extends and complicates (what Gadamer calls) the "rhetorical-hermeneutical" dimensions of the concept of allegory.[8]

Like Gadamer, de Man characterizes the fall and rise of allegory over the last two hundred years as parallel with and part of the fortunes of rhetoric more generally:

> Since the advent, in the course of the nineteenth century, of a subjectivistic critical vocabulary, the traditional forms of rhetoric have fallen into disrepute. It is becoming increasingly clear, however, that this was only a temporary eclipse: recent developments in criticism [and here his footnote citations include Walter Benjamin and Northrop Frye] reveal the possibility of a rhetoric that would no longer be normative or descriptive but that would more or less openly raise the question of the intentionality of rhetorical figures.
>
> ("Rhetoric of Temporality," pp. 187–88)

De Man encourages this possibility of a new rhetorical theory and criticism through a preliminary "historical clarification" of the Romantic period in European literature, a time when "the rhetorical key-terms undergo significant changes and are at the center of important tensions" ("Rhetoric of Temporality," p. 188). Central to these changes is the explicit opposition of symbol and allegory.

In his revisionist history, de Man argues for a more complicated account of debates over these two terms in the late eighteenth and nineteenth centuries. "[E]ven in the case of Goethe, the choice in favor of the symbol is accompanied by all kinds of reservations and qualifications. But, as one progresses into the nineteenth century, these qualifications tend to disappear" ("Rhetoric of Temporality," p. 189). In the work and influence of Coleridge, de Man finds a similar pattern in which "what appears to be, at first sight, an unqualified assertion of the superiority of the symbol over allegory" is actually accompanied by a striking ambiguity, an ambiguity that is then ignored by most British and American critics that followed. De Man summarizes Coleridge's view that "the symbol is the product of the organic growth of form; in the world of the symbol, life and form are identical.... Its structure

---

8 Gadamer refers to the "rhetorical-hermeneutical concept of allegory" in explaining: "Allegory arises from the theological need to eliminate offensive material from a religious text – originally from Homer – and to recognize valid truths behind it. It acquires a correlative function in rhetoric wherever circumlocution and indirect statement appear more appropriate" (*Truth and Method*, p. 73). On Gadamer and rhetorical hermeneutics more generally, see Steven Mailloux, *Disciplinary Identities: Rhetorical Paths of English, Speech, and Composition* (New York: MLA, 2006), pp. 20–21, 59–61, 73–82; and on de Man and Gadamer, see Rita Copeland and Stephen Melville, "Allegory and Allegoresis, Rhetoric and Hermeneutics," *Exemplaria* 3 (1991), 159–87.

is that of synecdoche, for the symbol is always a part of the totality it represents." This "symbolic imagination" contrasts with "allegorical form," which "appears purely mechanical, an abstraction whose original meaning is even more devoid of substance than its 'phantom proxy,' the allegorical representative, it is an immaterial shape that represents a sheer phantom devoid of shape and substance." However, de Man points out, later critics fail to notice that there is "a certain degree of ambiguity" in Coleridge's account ("Rhetoric of Temporality," pp. 191–92). Rather than stressing the symbol's "organic or material richness" ("Rhetoric of Temporality," p. 192) as one would expect, Coleridge characterizes the symbol as manifesting a "translucence of the eternal through and in the temporal."[9] In such a characterization, the "material substantiality" of the symbol "dissolves and becomes a mere reflection of a more original unity that does not exist in the material world." Thus, surprisingly, "the moment of material existence by which [the symbol] was originally defined has now become altogether unimportant; symbol and allegory alike now have a common origin beyond the world of matter." Coleridge ends up with "a description of figural language as translucence, a description in which the distinction between allegory and symbol has become of secondary importance" ("Rhetoric of Temporality," pp. 192–93).

Later British and American critics did not develop this ambiguity in Coleridge's account but instead focused on "the romantic image as a relationship between mind and nature, between subject and object," and they took the "ultimate intent of the image" to be, not translucence, but rather "synthesis ... defined as 'symbolic' by the priority conferred on the initial moment of sensory perception" ("Rhetoric of Temporality," p. 193). In contrast, de Man reads Romantic European literature against the grain of its usual interpretation as privileging organic symbolism over dogmatic allegory. De Man challenges the traditional focus on the Romantic image as a symbolic synthesis of subject and object and through a critical reading of Rousseau's *Julie ou la Nouvelle Héloïse* puts "to the test the nearly unanimous conviction that the origins of romanticism coincide with the beginnings of a predominantly symbolical diction" ("Rhetoric of Temporality," p. 200). The result: de Man's close reading demonstrates that the novel "could not exist without the simultaneous presence of both metaphorical modes [of symbol and allegory], nor could it reach its conclusion without the

---

9 "Rhetoric of Temporality," p. 192, quoting Samuel Taylor Coleridge, *The Statesman's Manual*, ed. W. G. T. Shedd (New York: Harper, 1875), pp. 437–38, quoted in Angus Fletcher, *Allegory: The Theory of a Symbolic Mode* (Ithaca: Cornell University Press, 1964), p. 16, n. 29.

implied choice in favor of allegory over symbol" ("Rhetoric of Temporality," p. 204).

Building on this reading, de Man argues that symbolism's "dialectic between subject and object does not designate the main romantic experience." Rather it is in Romanticism's "allegorizing tendencies" that "an authentic voice becomes audible" ("Rhetoric of Temporality," pp. 204–05). More exactly, "the prevalence of allegory always corresponds to the unveiling of an authentically temporal destiny" ("Rhetoric of Temporality," p. 206). Here is de Man's most important rethinking of allegory as a mode: "in the world of allegory, time is the originary constitutive category." By this he means that for allegory to exist, the allegorical sign refers to another, preceding sign; for it is not external dogma that decrees the relation of allegorical sign to its meaning. "The meaning constituted by the allegorical sign can then consist only in the repetition (in the Kierkegaardian sense of the term) of a previous sign with which it can never coincide, since it is of the essence of this previous sign to be pure anteriority" ("Rhetoric of Temporality," p. 207). De Man's readings illustrate this temporal relation in allegory when he describes Rousseau's literary allusions to the *Roman de la Rose* and Defoe's *Robinson Crusoe*, anterior texts with their own allegorical elements. In sum, "whereas the symbol postulates the possibility of an identity or identification, allegory designates primarily a distance in relation to its own origin, and, renouncing the nostalgia and the desire to coincide, it establishes its language in the void of this temporal difference" ("Rhetoric of Temporality," p. 207). For de Man, such a conclusion leads to a radical revision of "the customary picture": "The dialectical relationship between subject and object is no longer the central statement of romantic thought, but this dialectic is now located entirely in the temporal relationships that exist within a system of allegorical signs" ("Rhetoric of Temporality," p. 208). Thus, the nineteenth century's "asserted superiority of the symbol over allegory" turns out in the end to be simply a rhetorical form of "tenacious self-mystification" ("Rhetoric of Temporality," p. 208).

De Man goes on to theorize the allegorical discontinuity of sign and meaning by considering the relation of irony to allegory in some Romantic writers. The temporal noncoincidence of the allegorical sign and its antecedent is a structural discontinuity that allegory shares with irony: In both modes, "the sign points to something that differs from its literal meaning and has for its function the thematization of this difference." Noting that this "important structural aspect may well be a description of figural language in general" ("Rhetoric of Temporality," p. 209), de Man focuses on the distinguishing temporal dimension of irony and allegory and then identifies a distinction between allegorical and ironic discontinuity: allegory's fundamental structure stretches toward narrative duration, whereas irony "appears as an instantaneous process that takes place rapidly, in one single moment" ("Rhetoric of Temporality," p. 225). Irony approaches "the pattern of factual experience and recaptures some of the factitiousness of human existence as a succession of isolated moments lived by a divided self." In contrast, "allegory exists entirely within an ideal time that is never here and now but always a past or an endless future." In other words, "[i]rony is a synchronic structure, while allegory appears as a successive mode capable of engendering duration as the illusion of a continuity that it knows to be illusionary." Still, de Man temporarily concludes, despite their differences, irony and allegory "are the two faces of the same fundamental experience of time" ("Rhetoric of Temporality," p. 226).

De Man's rhetorical interpretation of allegory summarized above formed part of his early effort to write a history of Romanticism. But, as he describes in the preface to *Allegories of Reading* (1979), what "started out as a historical study... ended up as a theory of reading." Analyzing Rousseau in preparation for a historical consideration of Romanticism, de Man found himself "unable to progress beyond local difficulties of interpretation"; and in trying to deal with this problem, he shifted from "historical definition to the problematics of reading."[10] We might view de Man's brief introductory account as itself a little allegory, an allegory about the kind of rhetorical reading he thematizes throughout *Allegories of Reading*. Narratives are allegories of reading when they diachronically represent elements (characters, events, or ideas) as figurations of the reading act (an agent using an instrument or an inside merging with an outside, for example, figuring the act of reading as application or appropriation); or, conversely, when they represent temporal reading acts as allegories for theories of reading (say, hermeneutics or deconstruction).

De Man's own allegories of reading result from "a process of reading in which rhetoric is a disruptive intertwining of trope and persuasion" (*Allegories of Reading*, p. ix), a process he explains and illustrates in his famous essay, "Semiology and Rhetoric," chapter one of *Allegories of Reading*. Rejecting charges of radical negation or nihilistic destruction, de Man figures deconstruction as an analytical undermining, a systematic critique, through the close textual reading of, for example, inside/outside metaphors or literary and figurative meanings or figural praxis and metafigural theory, a rhetorical reading that puts in question those distinctions. In later chapters, de Man's rhetorical interpretations specify the allegories of reading in a

---

10 Paul de Man, *Allegories of Reading: Figural Language in Rousseau, Nietzsche, Rilke, and Proust* (New Haven: Yale University Press, 1979), p. ix.

range of texts, giving support to the claim that "any narrative is primarily the allegory of its own reading" (*Allegories of Reading*, p. 76). This claim is almost a tautology: any narrative when specifically read is an allegory of that specific reading in the sense that the narrative text (its literal sign) necessarily points to a second textual narrative (its own allegorical meaning) as a result of any interpretation. (We are reminded here of Frye's earlier point that all interpretation is allegorical interpretation.) What is distinctive about de Man's rhetorical interpretations is the allegory of unreadability he again and again uncovers. We might say that allegories of reading embody the product and process of deconstruction: they are its products insofar as texts are interpreted as allegories of reading that self-deconstruct; they constitute its process in that rhetorical interpretation allegorizes a text's unreadability.

In his interpretation of Proust's allegory of reading, de Man asserts that "the allegorical representation of Reading" is "the irreducible component of any text": "All that will be represented in such an allegory will deflect from the act of reading and block access to its understanding. The allegory of reading narrates the impossibility of reading" (*Allegories of Reading*, p. 77). Similarly (or is it?), de Man reads Rousseau's Second Preface to *Julie* in relation to the main text and notes that the model generated "cannot be closed off by a final reading" as "it engenders, in its turn, a supplementary figural superposition which narrates the unreadability of the prior narration." Such narratives we call allegories: "Allegorical narratives tell the story of the failure to read ... Allegories are always allegories of metaphor and, as such, they are always allegories of the impossibility of reading – a sentence in which the genitive 'of' has itself to be 'read' as a metaphor" (*Allegories of Reading*, p. 205). The temptation here is to conclude where we began in our account of de Man, with rhetoric as an allegorical emblem. In his reading of Nietzsche's history of rhetoric, de Man writes: "Considered as persuasion, rhetoric is performative but when considered as a system of tropes, it deconstructs its own performance. Rhetoric is a *text* in that it allows for two incompatible, mutually self-destructive points of view, and therefore puts an insurmountable obstacle in the way of any reading or understanding" (*Allegories of Reading*, p. 131).[11]

---

11 For commentaries on and elaborations of de Man's allegories of reading, see, for example, J. Hillis Miller, *The Ethics of Reading: Kant, de Man, Eliot, Trollope, James, and Benjamin* (New York: Columbia University Press, 1987); Andrzej Warminski, *Readings in Interpretation: Hölderlin, Hegel, Heidegger* (Minneapolis: University of Minnesota Press, 1987); Fredric Jameson, *Postmodernism, or, The Logic of Late Capitalism* (Durham, NC: Duke University Press, 1991); and Rodolphe Gasché, *The Wild Card of Reading: On Paul de Man* (Cambridge, MA: Harvard University Press, 1998).

In both Gadamerian hermeneutics and deManian deconstruction, allegory turns out to stand as a synecdoche for rhetoric itself. In Gadamer, allegory's historical fate is part and parcel of rhetoric's throughout the nineteenth century. In his account, the rise of aesthetic differentiation and the privileging of symbol entailed the decline of rhetoric and the devaluing of allegory. A similar historical narrative appears in de Man, but, additionally and more importantly for him, allegorical figuration is itself constitutive of rhetoric's destabilizing structure. Thus, whereas rhetoric and hermeneutics, language-use and interpretation, are inseparable and complementary for Gadamer, this is not the case for de Man, who sees linguistic figures as troubling interpretive reading and rhetorical and hermeneutic theories to be in a dynamic tension. Gadamer argues for a view of textual interpretation as the fusion of horizons within a tradition, a historically situated dialogue that at least temporarily stabilizes meaning and makes successful communication possible though not guaranteed. Rhetoric (as contextualized language use) is the medium for these exchanges. In contrast, de Man criticizes the "aesthetic restraint" of the hermeneutic tradition, which tends to "swerve" or "draw back" from the "rhetorical dimension of language" in both its interpretive practice and hermeneutic theory: in practice, it "pays little attention to the semantic play of the signifier," and in theory it presents a stabilizing mimetic model of reading rather than a destabilizing allegorical one.[12] Instead of literary interpretation mimetically imitating aesthetic perception, de Man sees such interpretation, which he calls reading, to be a form of allegoresis that separates aesthetics and hermeneutics from poetics and rhetoric: "Allegory names the rhetorical process by which the literary text moves from a phenomenal, world-oriented to a grammatical, language-oriented direction."[13] In spite and because of these significant rhetorical differences, hermeneutics and deconstruction continue to advance the contemporary rehabilitation of allegory.

12 Paul de Man, "Introduction" to *Toward an Aesthetic of Reception* by Hans Robert Jauss, trans. Timothy Bahti (Minneapolis: University of Minnesota Press, 1982), pp. xx–xxii. De Man is here discussing the work of Jauss, who in his aesthetics of reception depends on concepts from Gadamer's hermeneutics even while disagreeing with him at times, a point noted by de Man. Also see Hans Robert Jauss, "Response to Paul de Man," in *Reading de Man Reading*, ed. Lindsey Waters and Wlad Godzich (Minneapolis: University of Minnesota Press, 1989), pp. 202–08; and de Man, "Conclusions: Walter Benjamin's 'The Task of the Translator,'" in Paul de Man, *The Resistance to Theory* (Minneapolis: University of Minnesota Press, 1986), pp. 73–105.

13 De Man, "Introduction," p. xxiii. For additional discussions of the relation between deconstruction and hermeneutics, see *Dialogue and Deconstruction: The Gadamer-Derrida Encounter*, ed. Diane P. Michelfelder and Richard E. Palmer (Albany: State University of New York Press, 1989).

19

LYNETTE HUNTER

Allegory happens: allegory and the arts post-1960

Allegory, as others in this volume have explored, is derived from *allôs* and *agoreuein*, signifying "other speaking," other than what is said, or, what is not said. Because of the interest in "otherness" in the cultural, social and philosophical contexts of many Western academic disciplines, much of the recent discussion and development of allegory has been toward issues of difference and absence. Most of the critics turning their attention to the topic quickly cast aside the relationship of allegory to one-on-one emblem, or "naïve" allegory. Similarly, the connections with fable, a genre that plots the associations between A and B, and even with irony, which uses techniques similar to those found in allegory to convey the common grounds needed for ironic or satirical reflection, are not much pursued. Allegory fascinates those who want to explore the complexities and difficulties of speaking about the not-said, or more interesting, the not-yet-said.

Allegory has come to be perceived as a rhetorical stance, one that in literature includes the writer, the words and the reader into a reading event called "text" or textuality. It is not a thing but an event that happens. Any one piece of writing may be an allegory if the reading constitutes it as such, while at another time it may be read more generically as utopian or satirical or even realist. This does not mean that it is entirely up to the reader to make an allegorical event. At any particular time or in any particular place, a writer, artist, musician or whoever, will have available a range of strategies, techniques and devices that are more or less conducive to encouraging the allegorical event. In general an allegory rests on few *a priori* assumptions, but requires a negotiation of probable common grounds for interpretation and engagement. It uses strategies for insisting that the language human beings employ is limited: it can never fully or exactly describe the actual world, and in this enacts the impossibility of human control over the actual, and of human knowledge of spiritual absolutes or universal truth.

Allegory steps outside representative strategies and man-made [sic] definitions posing as facts or truths, to recognize otherness. It foregrounds these strategies as assumptions, conventions and habits. Words, devices and narrative worlds fossilize with historical accretions, which allegory chips away, often with non-referential techniques, and in doing so also chips away the accretions of the self. It allows us to see differently and with intensity the things other than ourselves that surround and place us, and which we can never fully know. Allegory insists on historical materiality, the separate contexts of the writer, the words and the reader that come together in the moment of the text. The topics of category, structure, person and act are set within socio-cultural and political specifics, which can be flexible or fixed. Allegory happens when they are flexible and responsive, when the words are read as devices that readers recognize as "making" or as "in process" – today such devices might include dream, paradox, pun, joke, aporia, catachresis, and many contemporary critics explore particular devices in some depth.

Allegory generates complexity often by way of contradictory rhetorical strategies and semiotic codes that generate new contradictions and further possibilities. The strategies may be linguistic, generic, discursive or semiotic, or semantic and rooted in recognized ideological codes for society, culture, politics, economics, religion and such like. The contradictions are focused through literary devices that are historically appropriate to the elements of the textuality. For example, George Orwell may well have thought that the use of the dream sequences in *Nineteen Eighty-Four* (1949) would defamiliarize as Freud's techniques had suggested. If readers today have no way of constituting a defamiliarization effect for dream, whether it's Freudian or not, that literary device will not work allegorically. On the other hand another device, say one brought from the environmental debate so current today, might well suddenly spring to allegorical life. Or, for example, the use of sexuality in John Barth's pre-AIDs *Giles Goat-Boy* (1966), defamiliarized in the 1960s in a different way than it does today.

The allegorical stance uses structures, strategies, techniques, that are more or less appropriate to instigating awareness of otherness, flexible interpretation, and contradiction, within particular reading environments. If the reading is situated within such an environment, allegory happens. Nevertheless it is possible to narrativize the late twentieth century as a period in which academic criticism, and to some extent literary writing, changes the focus on what constitutes allegorical work, and, as I will go on to suggest, various performance arts have to a large extent colonized the allegorical into what we now refer to as "performativity."

Critics in the Euro-American western academies of the second half of the twentieth century have tended to use allegory to deal with universals. The twentieth century saw the socio-political implications of universalist philosophies played out in totalitarianism and authoritarianism. Idealism, by definition never achievable, shifted that one degree to its other face, total power. Mid twentieth century commentaries on allegory suggest it is not a theory of knowledge, or a specific genre, but is, as Angus Fletcher, after Northrop Frye, defined it in *Allegory: The Theory of a Symbolic Mode* (1964), a "mode."[1] On the whole it is taken as a mode of writing about what is impossible to know or impossible to articulate: God, Love, Truth, the animal, the not-human. For example, Kafka used what has been called the "anagogic and allegoric anecdote" to communicate the impossible.[2] But if allegory can be used to indicate the impossible-to-say, it can also be used to undermine those universals. Walter Benjamin suggests that allegory collapses the beauty of totality by exposing the limitations of humanity, yet it achieves its own beauty in the grotesque ruin of subjective identity that it exposes.[3]

As part of the socio-political revolution in Western nation states that has accompanied the growth of the franchise, people have become more engaged in a critique of the idea of those human "limitations" as predetermined or fixed. Studies of ideologies, whether they be nation-state, religious, or domestic, and of the relations between ideology and the individual subject, led to allegory being used to critique systems of power. Systems of power that are perceived as all-pervasive and determining are impossible to describe, so allegory enables a critique by sidestepping a realist agenda and positioning writers to use strategies and techniques that foreground the assumptions of the system so they can be questioned and challenged. Certain devices are semiotically coded to do this, for example, the dystopian genre, use of which in the mid twentieth century temporarily gave "allegory" the characteristics of a genre. William Golding's *Lord of the Flies* (1960), Orwell's *Animal Farm* (1946), Anthony Burgess' *Clockwork Orange* (1962), have many generic features that disorient and generate contradiction, yet place the text within a particular temporal and social location that asked the then readers to re-think their own concurrent settings.

At the same time, allegorical flexibility has been used to investigate the impact of the new kinds of power on individuals, generating dense webs of significance that are still with us. The linguistic complexity of James Joyce's *Ulysses* (1922) or *Finnegan's Wake* (1939), the elusive absurdity of Samuel

---

1 Northrop Frye, *Anatomy of Criticism* (Princeton: Princeton University Press, 1957); Angus Fletcher, *Allegory: Theory of a Symbolic Mode* (Ithaca: Cornell University Press, 1964).
2 See George Steiner, *After Babel: Aspects of Language and Translation* (London: Oxford University Press, 1975), p. 66.
3 Walter Benjamin, *The Origin of German Tragic Drama*, trans John. Osborne, intro. George Steiner (London: New Left Books, 1977), p. 181.

Beckett's *Molloy* (1951), Jean-Paul Sartre's *La Nausée* (c. 1938), Albert Camus' *L'Etranger* (1953), or Alain Robbe-Grillet's *Les Gommes* (1953), engage the reader into allegorical aspects of the text stressing the experience of nothingness, of the arbitrary and the existential – those othernesses of mid twentieth century life that still trail us, even though they are today realized in different environments.

In 1981 two significant essay collections appeared, *Allegory, Myth and Symbol*, edited by Morton Bloomfield, and *Allegory and Representation*, edited by Stephen Greenblatt.[4] These collections presented work by critics from previous decades considering allegory as a mode that addressed the "other" as apprehended truth, approached truth, and unattainable truth.[5] The critics taking the role of allegory in apprehending truth focused on God, unity, matter, nothingness, goodness, and of course, truth. Those considering it in terms of its ability to approach truth generally separated into camps representing definitions of truth as polysemous, with multiple layers of discourse that could indicate it, or truth as contradictory and disruptive, indicating truth by oppositional tactics. Both approaches, however, assume that the value of allegory lies in getting you closer to "truth." Those considering it as a communicator of unattainable truth, or as communicating that truth is unattainable, resituated value *as* fact, combining means and ends. Nevertheless all three positions imply that allegory is a process by which we grow closer to knowing or representing.

Many of William Golding's novels have been critically received in this manner, the most well-known being *The Lord of the Flies*, which casts issues of untrammeled power into the isolated community of a group of boys who behave with the characteristics of English public school stereotypes. Other works, such as *The Inheritors* (1962), also appear to satisfy readers because "in the end" we can understand that the meaning of the book is a discussion about the paranoid barbarity and selfishness of human behavior. Interestingly, this book has considerable potential for reclamation by younger generations concerned with animal rights. John Barth's *Giles Goat-Boy* provides a set of clashing codes from a post-World War II America that many readers have mapped onto Cold War East–West relations and how we come to terms with a humanity that we now unavoidably recognize as corruptible. The novel uses strategies that allow specific topical registers such as "the university," "Cold War," "sexual freedom," to

4 Morton Bloomfield, ed., *Allegory, Myth, and Symbol* (Cambridge, MA: Harvard University Press, 1981); Stephen Greenblatt, ed., *Allegory and Representation: Selected Essays of the English Institute 1979–80* (Baltimore: Johns Hopkins University Press, 1981).
5 Lynette Hunter, *Modern Allegory and Fantasy: Rhetorical Stances of Contemporary Writing* (London: Macmillan, 1989), pp. 149–66.

crush each other with the weight of their linguistic nets, only to have one or another surface through the mix from time to time before it too is crushed and submerged, the apotheosis of the book arguably allowing all to surface into a pre-Baudrillardian simulacrum.

Similarly, Thomas Pynchon's *Gravity's Rainbow* (1973) constructs an enormous kaleidoscope of fantastic, realist, surrealist, and magic realist generic strategies, that subtly interpenetrate each other, so that readers suddenly find themselves reading in an inappropriate way. It's dislocating, nerve-wracking and curiously empathetic with the topical field of World War II warscapes, and increases in speed of dislocation as the novel progresses. In some ways it is ironic that critics who pin down the meaning of the novel are the most sympathetic toward it, when its strategies appear intended to engage the reader to the point that they give up on meaning altogether and meditate on the reading moment's significance. A book that offers critical strategies that could helpfully be employed with this and other Pynchon novels is Gordon Teskey's *Allegory and Violence*, in which he notes "we may define the material in allegory as that which gives meaning a place to occur but which does not become meaning itself."[6] A similar strategy is used by Robert Kroetsch from his earliest works such as *The Studhorse Man* (1969), which crosses Greek myth with cowboy myth, to the more sustaining allegorical opportunities of, for example, *The Puppeteer* (1992), which resist not only knowledge of the topics but also frustratingly/seductively resist an understanding of narrative voice.

The clearest exception to the critical positions in the two 1981 collections is found in an essay by Michael Holquist on allegory in the work of Mikhail Bakhtin.[7] Holquist focuses on language and the reader, emphasizing that the question is not just about *langue* and *parole*, but a continuum of activity that generates social meaning from the constant tension between canonization (or representation) and heteroglossia (other speech/the speech of others marginalized from power). The focus has the effect of acknowledging the material world around the event of the allegorical reading. It thinks of history as an interaction between human beings and their surroundings, and emphasizes the historical moment of the text, with the writer, the words and the reader, keeping truth flexible, and generating value in the moment that allegory happens.

The focus on the reader as a vital element in allegory became central to the development of ideas about the stance in the latter part of the century. The

---

6 Gordon Teskey, *Allegory and Violence* (Ithaca: Cornell University Press, 1996) p. 19.
7 Michael Holquist, M., "The Politics of Representation," in Greenblatt, ed., *Allegory and Representation*, pp. 163–83.

concept of readers and audiences as engaged in making the text had been introduced into criticism by Prague School aesthetics in the 1930s.[8] But it was not extensively taken up until the rhetorical methods of deconstruction fed into some versions of poststructuralism and found a different weighting for allegory, especially through reader-reception theory. Many reader-based theories of allegory emerge from Edwin Honig to Frank Kermode, Maureen Quilligan, and Paul de Man. They and others became involved in a distinctive attempt to distinguish allegory from naïve mimetic representation and reductive generic definitions, and to focus on it as something that reminds human beings of their limitations, their differences from the material world.

Honig's *Dark Conceit* speaks of an anagogic realization of an intrinsic presence evading explanation, but also introduces the concept of the "allegorical waver" between the external forces of ideology and the individual subject that indicates the "enigma of the material world."[9] The reader experiences the waver as a dialectical transfer, a constant interaction between word, object and human being. This idea is found again in J. Hillis Miller's commentary that allegory reveals the "eternal disjunction between the inscribed sign and its material embodiment."[10] Quilligan argues that allegory generates more open reader response by using a linguistic process of working against the accepted meaning of words; it opposes the literal (material) function of words to their referential (ideological) meaning.[11] Reading for the materiality of the text by engaging with the resistance of the world is allegory, while reading for referential functions is termed "allegoresis." The analysis is echoed in Kermode's understanding of the secrecy of allegory's allusion to something irreducible that works through texts of displacement. Allegory is enigmatic because life is enigmatic and encourages continual interpretation in an oppositional and agonistic mode.[12] Concurrent with this singling out of oppositional and agonistic modes in allegory, is the significant shift in continental critical theory from ideology to

8 See Michael L. Quinn, *The Semiotic Stage: Prague School Theatre Theory* (New York: Peter Lang, 1995).

9 Edwin Honig, *Dark Conceit: The Making of Allegory* (London: Faber and Faber, 1959), p. 141.

10 J. Hillis Miller, "The Two Allegories," in Bloomfield, ed., *Allegory, Myth, and Symbol*, p. 365.

11 Maureen Quilligan, *The Language of Allegory: Defining the Genre* (Ithaca: Cornell University Press, 1979), pp. 138, 145. See also Quilligan, "Allegory, Allegoresis, and the Deallegorization of Language: the *Roman de la Rose*, the *De planctu Naturae*, and the *Parlement of Foules*," in Bloomfield, ed., *Allegory, Myth, and Symbol*, pp. 163–86.

12 Frank Kermode, *The Genesis of Secrecy* (Cambridge, MA: Harvard University Press, 1979), pp. 146–47.

hegemony, and the discussion of oppositional and agonistic strategies by Ernesto Laclau and Chantal Mouffe.[13]

Possibly the most integrative exploration of allegory is Paul de Man's *Allegories of Reading*. De Man treats allegory as a stance in which the way writing is read, and reading is written, confuses the referent.[14] This prescient move heralds the recent shift in philosophy, especially political philosophy, toward the idea of a differentiated public, and a situated textuality, with their concomitant moves toward chaos theory, string theory and mess. There is no specific end or truth in the engagement of writer, text and reader, but there are distinct value systems that raise the distinction between the *allôs* in allegory as either an other that is impossible to say, or an other that is different, or as Derrida had already said, *différant*.[15]

It is difficult to know whether writers respond to readers' interpretations of earlier work, but the work of Angela Carter certainly grows in complexity, and her novels increasingly resist the reader's strategies for finding referentiality. *The Passion of New Eve* is a novel that mixes topical codes about sexuality and gender in an exploration of bisexuality, tranvestism, transgender and other sexualities. Readers in 1977, the year of its publication, were probably not as attuned to the multiplicitous possibilities of sexualities and genders as we are today. Reading it then it was a phantasmagoria of not-said states of being straining belief. Reading it in the early twenty-first century it feels a more straightforward political allegory. Carter's later work *Nights at the Circus* (1984) however, still resists attempts at meaning, possibly because it is also read as a metanarrative about fictionality. The possibility of making fictions is a strong feminist strategy, and part of a need to create alternative figurations for "woman" if they, and men, are to articulate their experiences in their own words – their experiences being the not said "other" of a literary world largely constructed by men. Carter's ability to enmesh topical questions of sexuality within a set of contradictory generic conventions appears to have the ability continually to re-engage readers. A similar generic mix with more pointed political aim is Margaret Atwood's *The Handmaid's Tale* (1985), which alternates realist narrative

---

13 Ernesto Laclau and Chantal Mouffe, *Hegemony and Socialist Strategy: Towards a Radical Democratic Politics*, trans. W. Moore and P. Cammack (London: Verso, 1985).

14 For further and more recent discussion, see Theresa Kelley, *Reinventing Allegory* (Cambridge: Cambridge University Press, 1997), pp. 12–13.

15 Paul de Man, *Allegories of Reading: Figural Language in Rousseau, Nietzsche, Rilke, and Proust* (London: Yale University Press, 1979), p. 148; Jacques Derrida, *Of Grammatology*, trans. Gayatri Spivak (Baltimore: Johns Hopkins University Press, 1976), pp. 113–122. See also Paul de Man, "Pascal's Allegory of Persuasion," in Greenblatt, ed., *Allegory and Representation*, pp. 1–25.

(albeit set in the future) with lyric prose, and concludes rather mischievously with a report. The elusive quality injected by the generic juxtapositions has helped to maintain the political commentary as a responsive site for readings. In contrast, Atwood's later *The Robber-Bride* (1993) is far more complex linguistically, structurally and topically, but the generic codes are not as obviously strategic, so it is difficult to know if future readers will be able to engage more with the topics, or less.

Michael Holquist's essay on Bahktin and allegory speaks about a concern with the impossibility of representation, and the anachronistic presence of universal/relativist dualities in a Western nation-state world of presumptively empowered citizens that had arisen under communist, socialist and liberal democracies. Suddenly, from the middle of the twentieth century, there were large and diverse populations all claiming cultural power and needing new modes of articulation such as magic realism, or needing to find new ways of valuing previously ignored aspects of their lives in different literary genres. There was a constant tension between these material needs of individuals, and ideological or hegemonic representations, which generated a discursive vision that parallels the shift from universalism to pluralism or relativism in the last two decades of the century. This parallel has been recognized by a number of critics, including Craig Owens and later Longxi Zhang.[16] Yet pluralist concepts often end up simply being the obverse face of universalism. Allegory, however, is uniquely suited to engage with the locations of partial knowledge that have resulted from concepts of *différance* in aesthetics coming together with the new political realities of an enfranchised population. The contradictions of allegory generate and carry the enigmatic experience of partial knowledge, in which we honestly recognize that others are radically different from our selves, and that our engagement with that *différance* generates difference that we can value.

Roland Barthes' 1967 essay on "The Death of the Author" replaced the author with the scriptor, the discursively structured individual who writes, and the birth of the reader. Michel Foucault's essay "What is an Author?" (originally published in 1969) positioned the writer as discursive, not uniquely in touch with universals, but socially constructed or constituted.[17] The shift in critical theory to historical particularity and to

16 Craig Owens, "The Allegorical Impulse: Toward a Theory of Postmodernism," *October* 12 (1980), 67–86; Zhang Longxi, "Historicizing the Postmodern Allegory," *Texas Studies in Language and Literature* 36 (1994), 212–31.

17 Roland Barthes "The Death of the Author," trans. Richard Howard, *Aspen*, Numbers 5+6 (1967) (unpaginated); Michel Foucault, "What is an Author?" trans. Donald Bouchard and Sherry Simon, in *Language, Counter-Memory, Practice: Selected Essays and Interviews by Michel Foucault* (Ithaca: Cornell University Press, 1977), pp. 113–38.

the needs of audiences and readers paralleled a semiotic turn: the recuperation of rhetoric and an insistence on audience and the context of the audience in any aesthetic or communicative event. Techniques such as intertextuality, metafiction, historiographical metafiction, magic realism, came into play. While no technique will necessarily enable allegory, these literary techniques of layering, of weaving, of knotting, with paratactic and juxtaposed devices, generated a strangeness or otherness that in their inceptions encouraged allegorical encounters with readers.

Some of the most remarkable opportunities for literary allegory in the late twentieth century and beginning of the twenty-first come from writers from countries that were once subject to direct European colonization. Salman Rushdie's *Midnight's Children* (1980) remains an engrossing experience through its ability to cross the domestic with the personal with the political, leaving a Euro-American reader unsure as to whether the dislocation is due to the cultural difference, the social difference, the political difference, or indeed the difference in focus between the personal and the political. His notorious *The Satanic Verses* (1988) is a good example of a work that can be read allegorically in the West as an unsettling account of the disruption and difficulty of being a Muslim in England in the 1980s, but has been read realistically if not literally by some Muslims elsewhere as blasphemous. Conversely, the work of Gabriel García Márquez, such as *One Hundred Years of Solitude* (1982), is often read in Euro-American contexts as "magic realism," a surreal extension of realistic device to the point where it can no longer bear the representational burden of bourgeois realism, while in his native Colombia the works are often considered pointed and immediate political allegories.

Ben Okri's writings, for example, the short stories *Incidents at the Shrine* (1986), have encountered a similar response. Those set in England, in which characters from Nigeria find themselves isolated and fractured, can be read through conventions of cultural displacement and psychoanalytical techniques. But those set in Nigeria highlight the additional difficulties that a non-Nigerian reader encounters when they read – are the literary strategies encouraging a reading of realism? magic realism? or allegory? They present moments of intense defamiliarization and contradiction for a Euro-American reader, and can generate allegorical responses about what is difficult to say, what is not said, or what is not-yet-said. But there is a political dimension to the reading: do "postcolonial" writers construct allegorical texts because their experiences are traditionally outside of ideological representation, or is the allegorical reading only available to Euro-American readers who do not understand their experience? When Métis writer Alice Lee says an old medicine woman "showed me / how to crawl inside him [her lover] / and make him love me // today he died / i was still inside him // Kohkom / never told me / how to get out,"[18] does she hope for literal or metaphorical or allegorical readings? One finds similar questions in different contexts: books such as Orhan Pamuk's *My Name is Red* (2001), a historical novel about Turkey at a time when it is centrally and powerfully positioned between East and West, can be read allegorically as an exploration of contesting cultural ideas about representation current today. A similar response occurs with the writing of Philip Pullman, whose *His Dark Materials* (1995–2000) trilogy is read relatively happily as a children's fantasy, despite the text making available philosophical principles from Daoism that completely undercut any promise of realism that fantasy makes.

Among the more subtle allegorists of the late twentieth and early twenty-first century are W. G. Sebald and Nicole Brossard. Sebald, a German émigré to England in the 1960s, wrote a series of novels in German, translated into English by others, exploring the post-war history of Europe, including *The Rings of Saturn* (1998). This novel is an unnerving palimpsest of the landscape of south-east England. It layers social, cultural, political, aesthetic, scientific, geographical and architectural moments from the last 400 years on top of each other, as if they were transparent layers superimposed by an alien eye that had little clue as to what was important to the inhabitants or not. One of its primary devices is the intermediality of printed writing and visual graphics, in which the written word does not always or often marry with the visual presentation.[19] The effect is to generate not an articulation of what is not said or even not-yet-said, but a distinct sense that we feel significance but have no idea of what the significance might be.

Nicole Brossard is a Québecoise writer also writing in her first language and being translated by others. Her novels *Mauve Desert* (1987) and *Baroque at Dawn* (1995) are clear examples of writing the not-yet-said, as she traverses a huge philosophical terrain exploding notions of conventional beauty, and sliding bodies, identities, strategies and moralities, through the surface oils of simulacra, inviting readers to sense the moment of linguistic skin that holds significance. Brossard's extensions of narrative, genre, language and poetics, pose substantial contradictions for the reader that may or may not be exacerbated by their translated status. But translation and allegory frequently go hand in hand, as the translator's art is the one where irreducible difference is most keenly felt. The point about allegory is that it asks the reader to choose to make a text with the writer's words. This

---

18 Alice Lee, "love medicine," in Jeanne Perreault and Sylvia Vance, eds., *Writing the Circle: Native Women of Western Canada* (Edmonton: NeWest Publishers, 1990), p. 161.
19 Jeffrey Orr, "Visuality, Genre, and Translation in Selected Works of Michael Ondaatje and W. G. Sebald," unpublished PhD thesis, University of Leeds, 2005.

happens to some extent or another with all readings, but with allegory it is foregrounded as part of the process. If allegory did not insist on history, readings could be delightfully pluralist. But it does, and so it requires a commitment to a particular cross-cultural, trans-individual collaboration that defines the difference of the reader as well as that of the writer.

Perhaps it is not so surprising, if allegory is perceived as a stance that includes the writer, the words and the reader into a reading event called "text" or textuality, that theater and performance studies have taken over the term since the 1980s. In many art media the aesthetics of making is separate from the aesthetics of the art object, but the performance of theater has them going on at the same time. Theatricality and performativity are about process, the audience is involved in the "making." Arguably, this is the opportunity offered by Beckett's *Waiting for Godot* (published in French, 1952; in English, 1954), a play in which he crosses not narrative convention but theatrical expectation, of character, plot and structure, bringing the audience into the event of waiting as an allegorical event of life. The advent of improvisation as the study of highly skilled makers and audiences interacting in the making of a performance "in the moment," has many similarities with allegory's rhetorical features. As the performance events known as "Happenings" in the 1960s coalesced into simultaneous political commentary, they took on many other elements of the stance as they included the social context on which allegory insists.

Some critics have indicated that theatre in itself is potentially allegorical in spirit. Not only is there a fully fledged theory of theater allegory in Bertolt Brecht's writing, but the coincidence of the new media with performative modes has intensified the relationship. Brecht, as Elin Diamond elegantly argues, develops his idea of gestus alongside Benjamin's work on allegory. Benjamin "drags the essence of what is depicted as art before the image, in writing, as a caption," while Brecht says that every gesture has a caption that is "set out and laid bare to the understanding of the audience." In Benjamin's allegorical case the sign of the caption is empty: allegory is transitoriness, decline, dissipation, death.[20] In contrast and elaborating on Diamond, Brecht's position can be read as a conflict of codes between the gesture and the caption that shatters notions of artistic unity, of representation and ideology. Brecht's gestus, Diamond says, invokes political will and the possibility of change. Specifically, Brecht's concepts of alienation, the not...but, historicization, and the gestus that combines them all, are

---

20 Elin Diamond, *Unmaking Mimesis: Essays on Feminism and Theater* (London: Routledge, 1997), p. 79; *Brecht on Theatre; The Development of an Aesthetic*, ed. and trans. John Willett (London: Methuen, 1964), p. 201.

directly parallel to allegory's combination of foregrounding and disruption, its construction of contradiction and conflicting codes, and its insistence on context and history.

Performance studies, working hand in hand with theatre studies, has developed "performativity" as largely a recognition of audience response, the conditions for its involvement and engagement. Allegory's insistence on context and historicity makes it an ideal stance for thinking about this process. For example, conceptual art is a way of passing a conventional meaning through a particular and socially immediate conceptual lens or coding, so that it becomes an allegorical gesture toward what has not yet been said. Martha Rosler's *Semiotics of the Kitchen* (1975) is a short video of a woman in a claustrophobically small kitchen talking one through kitchen objects in alphabetical order with a controlled rage that occasionally erupts into knives being stabbed into wooden boards as she disrupts the conventions of television cookery demonstrations, and simultaneously creates a new genre that will inspire, for example, work such as Bobby Baker's *Drawing on a Mother's Experience* (1988). Mierle Laderman Ukeles's *Maintenance Art Series* (1973–74 and later) at the Wadsworth Atheneum in Hartford, Connecticut, included a performance in which she washed the floor of a museum, crossing social codes to do with art and labor, with class and service, with gender and domestic identity, to leave audiences perplexed by their inability to work out their social relationship to this working figure, or indeed, if they should respond at all. More recent artists who focus on the allegorical include Ilya Noé, whose *The Return of the One Who's Always Been Around* uses bio-degradable paint pumped through specially made deer shoes to imprint the image of a deer in the Portuguese town of Vila Nova de Cerveira, where deer have been hunted out for nearly two centuries. This process leaves an indelibly enigmatic figuration which asks people to think about the environment, human occupation, and ecological responsibility.

At the same time the conjunction of new media in performance art, conceptual art and theater and dance, has meant that techniques of layering, of collage, hypertext, hologram and others, have been employed to make palimpsests[21] of experience, the imbrications of referential codes that create allegory's contradictions and enigmas. When used first, the effect of a new medium is often disconcerting, the conventional understanding of how communication works breaks down. This can leave us feeling shut out, or with a lack, or with a sense of relative position or plurality. But it may also leave us with an energy for engagement that is needed to recognize *différance* and

---

21 See Gérard Genette, *Palimpsests: Literature in the Second Degree*, trans. Channa Newman and Claude Doubinsky (Lincoln: University of Nebraska Press, 1997).

make social value. Cindy Sherman's 1980s' sequence of photographs of herself presents the female body in an often witty and always disruptive framing that dismantles notions of photographic realism in what has been called a "blasted allegory."[22] Bill Viola's work with video and projected image, for example, *The Crossing* (1996), backs a continuous video of a person walking who is then engulfed in flames, with a continuous video of a man walking who is engulfed in water. The two enormous screens on which these images are projected dwarf the viewer, and accompanying sound recordings and the darkness of the exhibition room play generic conventions of video across audience expectations of gallery exhibition, with conventions of larger-than-life sublime aspirations across the limited human body. In ways analogous to literary disruptions of generic and linguistic expectation, these artists play with the possibilities of media and socio-cultural reception to engage the audiences in the event of allegory.

On stage, some of the most profound changes in theater performance have grown from highly allegorical productions. In the mid twentieth century one finds several writers playing with allegorical devices, such as Jean Genet or Antonin Artaud or Tadeusz Kantor. Kantor's work, which includes *Dead Class* (1975) and *Wielopole, Wielopole* (1980), runs traditional notions of "liveness" on stage alongside concepts of the "dead actor;" it crosses the potential of the human body with the idea of puppetry, to call upon an audience engagement with concepts of human presence, automatons, bureaucracy, in an extended Kafkaesque landscape. In contrast, Ariane Mnouchkine's *Les Atrides* (1987) collapsed Greek myth into and onto present-day political discussions of colonialism and feminism through Kathkali acting techniques. The collocation of registers split apart traditional interpretations of the *Oresteia* and instantiated strategies with which the audience could engage to re-make the significance of this pervasive Western story from the perspective of those whom the Greeks themselves barred from society: strangers and women.

More recently the work of Tim Etchells with the company Forced Entertainment, in Sheffield, England, has been producing extraordinary allegorical work, continually reconstituting the textual moment they are producing. An example of their work is the bus tour production *Nights in This City* through Sheffield (1995) and later through Rotterdam (1997), which disturbingly re-mixed the histories of the cities as the audience travels through. Another performance group, Xplo, refined this technique with bus tours of New York (*Dencity*, 2000) and then London (*Found Wanting*, 2003), in which the bus audience listens to a fabricated sound score as the tour proceeds through

22 Karen L. Kleinfelder, "Ingres as a Blasted Allegory," *Art History*, 23:5 (2000), 800–17.

widely economically varied metroscapes, juxtaposing unpredictable social, cultural and political expectations through sound and sight. One of the most elusively alluring sites for political allegory has been Walid Raad's *The Atlas Group Archives* (2001), which construct a web-accessible hypertext with video material that has to be mail-ordered, to offer a place for potential insight into the recent crises in Lebanon. Playing openly with the fictional quality of newsmaking, Raad destabilizes accepted stereotypes of Middle Eastern events by generating an unsettling sense of "what is missing" in the traumatic event of war.

There are many examples of allegorical opportunities in the performing arts, especially since the growth of conceptual art. But one area in particular is of note: contemporary modern dance. Yvonne Rainer's *Lives of the Performers* (1972), a film of a production process, is in many ways an essay on allegory. It visually discusses the relation of image to meaning, process to significance, and of convention to time and space. For example, she literally writes over on the film and reads over in sound, a rehearsal process that is itself improvised; or, the final section of the video presents static melodramatic images whose temporal extension over several minutes deconstructs their clichéd force. The catalogue of other contemporary dancers who produce work filled with allegorical opportunity includes, to take just one specific grouping, the 1980–2007 San Francisco dance world, and productions such as Della Davidson's potent dance-theatre constructions of intimate trauma in her collaboration with Ellen Bromberg on *The Weight of Memory* (2006); or Keith Hennessey's explicit dismantling of physical images that re-engage audiences in social and political questioning in, for example, *How to Die* (2006); or Kim Epifano's work with community and disabled dancers, including her *Fears of Your Life* (2006–7), which materializes the world of autistic writer Michael Bernard Loggins, actively bringing the audience into a landscape that engenders allegorical interaction at the same time as realizing its literalness, foregrounding the choice of involvement that allegory makes possible.

It is possible that these performative areas, which are among the least supported, and least embedded in the capitalist world of entertainment, have been able to generate allegorical texts precisely because they are not seeking to offer the meanings and satisfactions of conventional entertainment. In other performing arts, especially in film, allegorical strategies that encourage disruption and contradiction, are not welcome. Only those practitioners with a long track record such as David Lynch, can afford to take the chance on a film such as *Mulholland Drive*, which is structured to resist translation into meaning, its narrative movement creating a Möbius strip of unending significance.[23] Otherwise, possibly unintentionally, the film world throws forward and underlines the frequency with which artistic works foreign to the audience are susceptible to producing allegorical moments and events, places where we read difference.

More difficult to locate than in events that are strange to the audience, are the possibilities for allegory in the situated environments of particular lives. This, however, is where allegory in the twenty-first century may flower. We are no longer able to read all that is written and supposed to be "good," nor are we able to experience all the artistic products of the many other media there are. Audiences are becoming more selective, creating their own circles of culture within larger capitalist systems of entertainment. Practices that are aimed at the more situated and acknowledgedly partial strategies for living that many people are building, may need to engage the allegorical to communicate with each other.

23 Alex Lichtenfels has written a number of essays on allegory in film, including the as-yet-unpublished "Self-Reflexivity in David Lynch's *Mulholland Drive*" (2005).

FURTHER READING

Works cited frequently in this volume

Benjamin, Walter. *The Origin of German Tragic Drama*. Trans. John Osborne. London, New Left Books, 2003

Bloomfield, Morton W., ed. *Allegory, Myth, and Symbol*. Cambridge, MA, Harvard University Press, 1981

De Man, Paul. *Allegories of Reading: Figural Language in Rousseau, Nietzsche, Rilke, and Proust*. New Haven, Yale University Press, 1979

Fletcher, Angus. *Allegory: The Theory of a Symbolic Mode*. Ithaca, Cornell University Press, 1964

Greenblatt, Stephen J., ed. *Allegory and Representation*. Baltimore, The Johns Hopkins University Press, 1981

Quilligan, Maureen. *The Language of Allegory: Defining the Genre*. Ithaca, Cornell University Press, 1979

Teskey, Gordon. *Allegory and Violence*. Ithaca, Cornell University Press, 1996

Whitman, Jon. *Allegory: The Dynamics of an Ancient and Medieval Technique*. Cambridge, MA, Harvard University Press, 1987

Further reading

General

Barney, Stephen A. *Allegories of History, Allegories of Love*. Hamden, CT, Archon, 1979

Bastida, Rebeca Sanmartín, and Rosa Vidal Doval, eds. *Las metamorfosis de la alegoría: discurso y sociedad en la Península Ibérica desde la Edad Media hasta la Edad Contemporánea*. Madrid, Iberoamericana; Frankfurt am Main, Vervuert, 2005

Bruns, Gerald L. *Hermeneutics Ancient and Modern*. New Haven, Yale University Press, 1992

Copeland, Rita, and Stephen Melville. "Allegory and Allegoresis, Rhetoric and Hermeneutics." *Exemplaria* 3 (1991), 159–87

Dawson, David. *Christian Figural Reading and the Fashioning of Identity*. Berkeley, University of California Press, 2002

Fineman, Joel. "The Structure of Allegorical Desire." In Greenblatt, ed., *Allegory and Representation*, pp. 26–60

Frye, Northrop. *The Great Code: The Bible and Literature.* New York, Harcourt Brace Jovanovich, 1982

Gadamer, Hans-Georg. *Truth and Method.* 2nd edn., trans. Joel Weinsheimer and Donald G. Marshall. New York, Crossroad, 1989

Haug, Walter, ed. *Formen und Funktionen der Allegorie.* Stuttgart, Metzler, 1979

Honig, Edwin. *Dark Conceit: The Making of Allegory.* London, Faber and Faber, 1959

Leeming, David A., and Kathleen M. Drowne, eds. *Encyclopedia of Allegorical Literature.* Santa Barbara, ABC-CLIO, 1996

Madsen, Deborah. *Rereading Allegory: A Narrative Approach to Genre.* Basingstoke, Macmillan, 1995

Todorov, Tzvetan. *Theories of The Symbol.* Trans. Catherine Porter. Ithaca, Cornell University Press, 1982

Whitman, Jon, ed. *Interpretation and Allegory: Antiquity to the Modern Period.* Leiden, Brill, 2000

Ancient

Le Boulluec, Alain. "L'allégorie chez les Stoïciens." *Poétique* 23 (1975), 301–21

Boyarin, Daniel. *Sparks of the Logos: Essays in Rabbinic Hermeneutics.* Leiden, Brill, 2003

Boys-Stones, G. R., ed. *Metaphor, Allegory, and the Classical Tradition: Ancient Thought and Modern Revisions.* Oxford, Oxford University Press, 2003

Brisson, Luc. *How Philosophers Saved Myths: Allegorical Interpretation and Classical Mythology.* Trans. C. Tihanyi. Chicago, University of Chicago Press, 2004

Buffière, Félix. *Les Mythes d'Homère et la pensée grecque.* Paris, Les Belles Lettres, 1956

Coulter, James A. *The Literary Microcosm: Theories of Interpretation of the Later Neoplatonists.* Leiden, Brill, 1976

Dawson, David. *Allegorical Readers and Cultural Revision in Ancient Alexandria.* Berkeley, University of California Press, 1992

Ford, Andrew. *The Origins of Criticism: Literary Culture and Poetic Theory in Classical Greece.* Princeton, Princeton University Press, 2002

Kirk, G. S., J. E. Raven, and M. Schofield. *The Presocratic Philosophers*, 2nd edn. Cambridge, Cambridge University Press, 1983 (chapter 1 "The Forerunners of Philosophical Cosmogony")

Lamberton, Robert. *Homer the Theologian: Neoplatonist Allegorical Reading and the Growth of the Epic Tradition.* Berkeley, University of California Press, 1986

Lamberton, Robert, and John J. Keaney, eds. *Homer's Ancient Readers. The Hermeneutics of Greek Epic's Earliest Exegetes.* Princeton, Princeton University Press, 1992

Olbricht, Thomas H. "Analogy and Allegory in Classical Rhetoric." In J. T. Fitzgerald, T. H. Olbricht, and L. M. White, eds., *Early Christianity and Classical Culture: Comparative Studies in Honor of Abraham J. Malherbe.* Leiden, Brill, 2003, pp. 371–90

Pépin, Jean. *Mythe et allégorie: les origines grecques et les contestations judéo-chrétiennes.* 2nd edn. Paris, Études Augustiniennes, 1976

Ramelli, Ilaria, and Giulio Luccheta. *Allegoria.* vol. I: *L'età classica.* Milano, Vita e Pensiero, 2004

Rappe, Sara. *Reading Neoplatonism.* New York, Cambridge University Press, 2000

Struck, Peter T. *Birth of the Symbol: Ancient Readers at the Limits of Their Texts.* Princeton, Princeton University Press, 2004

Ancient to renaissance (reception studies)

Auerbach, Erich. "Figura." Trans. Ralph Mannheim. In Auerbach, *Scenes from the Drama of European Literature,* ed. Wlad Godzich and Jochen Schulte-Sasse. Minneapolis: University of Minnesota Press, 1984, pp. 11–76

Dahan, Gilbert, and Goulet, R., eds. *Allégorie des poètes, allégorie des philosophes. Etudes sur la poétique et l'herméneutique de l'allégorie de l'Antiquité à la Réforme.* Paris, Vrin, 2005

Godwin, Joscelyn. *The Pagan Dream of the Renaissance.* London, Thames and Hudson, 2002.

Murrin, Michael. *The Allegorical Epic: Essays in Its Rise and Decline.* Chicago, University of Chicago Press, 1980

Pépin, Jean. *La Tradition de l'allégorie de Philon d'Alexandrie à Dante.* Paris, Études Historiques, 1987

Pérez-Jean, Brigitte, and Patricia Eichel-Lojkine, eds. *L'Allégorie de l'Antiquité à la Renaissance.* Paris, Champion, 2004

Seznec, Jean. *The Survival of the Pagan Gods: The Mythological Tradition and its Place in Renaissance Humanism.* Trans. Barbara F. Sessions. New York, Pantheon Books, 1953

Warburg, Aby. *The Renewal of Pagan Antiquity: Contributions to the Cultural History of the European Renaissance.* Trans. David Britt. Los Angeles, Getty Research Institute for the History of Art and the Humanities, 1999

Medieval and renaissance

Ascoli, Albert. *Dante and the Making of a Modern Author.* Cambridge, Cambridge University Press, 2008

Baswell, Christopher. *Virgil in Medieval England: Figuring the Aeneid from the Twelfth Century to Chaucer.* Cambridge, Cambridge University Press, 1995

Borris, Kenneth. *Allegory and Epic in English Renaissance Literature: Heroic Form in Sidney, Spenser, and Milton.* Cambridge, Cambridge University Press, 2000

Chance, Jane. *Medieval Mythography,* vol. 2, *From the School of Chartres to the Court at Avignon, 1177–1350.* Gainesville, FL, University Press of Florida, 2000

Copeland, Rita. "Rhetoric and the Politics of the Literal Sense in Medieval Literary Theory: Aquinas, Wyclif, and the Lollards." In Michael Hyde and Walter Jost, eds., *Rhetoric and Hermeneutics in Our Time.* New Haven, Yale University Press, 1997, pp. 335–57

Guynn, Noah. *Allegory and Sexual Ethics in the High Middle Ages.* New York, Palgrave Macmillan, 2007

Heath, Peter. *Allegory and Philosophy in Avicenna (Ibn Sīna), with a Translation of the Book of the Prophet Muḥammad's Ascent to Heaven.* Philadelphia, University of Pennsylvania Press, 1992

Kay, Sarah. *The Roman de la Rose.* London, Grant & Cutler, 1995

Kay, Sarah. *The Place of Thought: The Complexity of One in Late Medieval French Didactic Poetry.* Philadelphia, University of Pennsylvania Press, 2007

Matter, E. Ann. *The Voice of My Beloved: The Song of Songs in Western Medieval Christianity.* Philadelphia, University of Pennsylvania Press, 1990

Minnis, Alastair. *Magister Amoris. The Roman de la Rose and Vernacular Hermeneutics.* Cambridge, Cambridge University Press, 2001

Murrin, Michael. *The Veil of Allegory: Some Notes toward a Theory of Allegorical Rhetoric in the English Renaissance.* Chicago, University of Chicago Press, 1969

Paxson, James. *Poetics of Personification.* Cambridge, Cambridge University Press, 1994

Simpson, James. *Burning to Read: English Fundamentalism and its Reformation Opponents.* Cambridge, MA, Harvard University Press, 2007

Steiner, Emily. "Naming and Allegory in Late Medieval England." *Journal of English and Germanic Philology* 106 (2007), 248–75

Stock, Brian. *The Implications of Literacy: Written Language and Models of Interpretation in the Eleventh and Twelfth Centuries.* Princeton, Princeton University Press, 1983

Strubel, Armand. *"Grant senefiance a": Allégorie et littérature au Moyen Âge.* Paris, Champion, 2002

Treip, Mindele Ann. *Allegorical Poetics and the Epic: The Renaissance Tradition to Paradise Lost.* Lexington, The University Press of Kentucky, 1994

Trimpi, Wesley. *Muses of One Mind: The Literary Analysis of Experience and its Continuity.* Princeton, Princeton University Press, 1983

Tuve, Rosemond. *Allegorical Imagery: Some Mediaeval Books and their Posterity.* Princeton, Princeton University Press, 1966

Watkins, John. "The Allegorical Theatre: Moralities, Interludes, and Protestant Drama." In David Wallace, ed., *The Cambridge History of Medieval English Literature.* Cambridge, Cambridge University Press, 1999, pp. 767–92

Wetherbee, Winthrop. *Platonism and Poetry in the Twelfth Century: The Literary Influence of the School of Chartres.* Princeton, Princeton University Press, 1972

Neoclassical to modern

Bahti, Timothy. *Allegories of History.* Baltimore, Johns Hopkins University Press, 1992

Brown, Jane K. *The Persistence of Allegory: Drama and Neoclassicism from Shakespeare to Wagner.* Philadelphia, University of Pennsylvania Press, 2007

Christensen, Jerome C. "The Symbol's Errant Allegory: Coleridge and His Critics." *ELH* 45 (1978), 640–59

Cohen, Josh. *Spectacular Allegories: Postmodern American Writing and the Politics of Seeing.* London, Pluto Press, 1998

Cope, Kevin L., ed. *Enlightening Allegory: Theory, Practice, and Contexts of Allegory in the Late Seventeenth and Eighteenth Centuries.* New York, AMS Press, 1993

De Man, Paul. "The Rhetoric of Temporality." In *Blindness and Insight.* 2nd edn. Minneapolis, University of Minnesota Press, 1983, pp. 187–228

"Sign and Symbol in Hegel's *Aesthetics,*" *Critical Inquiry* 8 (1982), 761–76

Fried, Michael. *Absorption and Theatricality: Painting and Beholder in the Age of Diderot*. Berkeley, University of California Press, 1980

Hegel, G. W. F. *Aesthetics: Lectures on Fine Art*. Trans. T. M. Knox, 2 vols. Oxford, Clarendon, 1975

Hunter, Lynette. *Modern Allegory and Fantasy: Rhetorical Stances of Contemporary Writing*. London, Macmillan, 1989

Kelley, Theresa M. " 'Fantastic Shapes': From Classical Rhetoric to Romantic Allegory." *Texas Studies in Language and Literature* 33 (1991), 225–60

  Reinventing Allegory. Cambridge, Cambridge University Press, 1997

Knapp, Steven. *Personification and the Sublime: Milton to Coleridge*. Cambridge, MA, Harvard University Press, 1985

Madsen, Deborah. *Allegory in America: From Puritanism to Postmodernism*. London, Macmillan, 1996

Melville, Stephen. "Notes on the Reemergence of Allegory, the Forgetting of Modernism, the Necessity of Rhetoric, and the Condition of Publicity in Art and Criticism." *October* 19 (1981), 55–92

Owens, Craig. "The Allegorical Impulse: Toward a Theory of Postmodernism." *October* 12–13 (1980), 67–86; 59–80

Paulson, Ronald. *Emblem and Expression*. Cambridge, MA, Harvard University Press, 1975

Schlossman, Beryl. *The Orient of Style: Modernist Allegories of Conversion*. Durham, NC, Duke University Press, 1990

Wheeler, Kathleen, ed. *German Aesthetic and Literary Criticism: The Romantic Ironists and Goethe*. Cambridge, Cambridge University Press, 1984

Wolin, Richard. *Walter Benjamin: An Aesthetic of Redemption*. Berkeley, University of California Press, 1994

Zhang, Longxi. "Historicizing the Postmodern Allegory." *Texas Studies in Language and Literature* 36 (1994), 212–31

  Allegoresis: Reading Canonical Literature East and West. Ithaca, Cornell University Press, 2005

Abelard, Peter 106
Abraham ben Ezra (Ibn Ezra) xiii, 90
Abulafia, Abraham xiv
Achillini, Claudio 207
Acts, book of 69
Addison, Joseph 189
Aeneid (see Virgil)
aenigma (see allegory, and *aenigma*)
aesthetics 58, 241, 244, 245, 253, 257–59, 265, 271, 276
Akiva ben Joseph xi, 53
Al-Fārābī xii, 90
Al-Ghazālī xiii, 92
Alan of Lille xiii, 6, 105, 107, 110–15, 126, 142, 143, 144
Alcaeus ix, 16
Alciati, Andrea xviii
Alcidamas x, 15, 23, 24
Alcuin of York xii
Alexander the Great 139
Alexandria and allegory (see also Origen) 39–54
Alexandria and philology (see also Aristarchus) 31
Alfonse de la Torre xvii
allegoresis (see allegory, as interpretation)
allêgoria (see allegory, and *allêgoria*)
allegory
  and *aenigma* 2, 16, 20, 68, 175
  and *allêgoria* 2, 3, 4, 16, 37, 79, 128, 163, 180
  anagogical (see also contemplation; mysticism) 68, 71, 72, 73, 80, 92, 93, 131, 132, 134
  biblical (see Christianity, biblical hermeneutics)
  and commentary traditions 149

  as composition 2, 4, 5, 16, 33–37, 128, 129, 131, 150, 162, 193
  in cosmogony and in creation (see also Genesis, book of) 105–10, 128, 234
  cosmological 162
  and divination and prophecy 63–64, 88, 120
  eros in (see also Song of Songs) 87, 92, 97–99, 115, 119–27, 137–40, 144, 148, 153, 222
  four levels of (see also Cassian, John) 5, 8, 71–74, 128, 130–31, 132–35, 184
  and Hellenistic culture 28
  historical 162
  historical events as (see also Christianity, biblical hermeneutics) 80
  and *hyponoia* 2, 4, 16, 18, 19, 26, 37, 175
  as interpretation (allegoresis) 2–4, 10, 15–16, 17–22, 27, 68, 92, 120, 128, 129, 135, 136, 150, 162, 237, 254, 255, 256
  journey in 92–97, 143, 167
  vs. metaphor (see metaphor)
  moral 19, 23–24, 85–86, 130, 132, 134, 136, 139, 144, 145, 149, 151–54, 162–67, 174, 175, 222
  obscurity in 60, 75, 134, 141, 163, 192, 200
  and ontological connection 68, 197, 206, 234
  philology vs. 30–33
  philosophical (see philosophy)
  physical 162, 169
  of poets vs. of theologians (see allegory, sacred vs. secular)
  political 99–100, 136, 139, 140, 159, 162, 166, 175, 197, 200, 222, 241

in rhetoric (see rhetoric)
and ritual 3, 19, 21–22, 29, 30, 64–66,
   156, 192, 237
sacred vs. secular conceptions of 1, 5, 124,
   128–35, 163
secular 136–47
as screening device 17
spatial 203–06, 248
and symbol (*symbolon*) 2, 3, 4, 16, 65,
   67–70, 79, 163, 175, 206, 220–22, 234,
   235, 244, 248, 258–59
vs. symbol in Romanticism 217–18, 219,
   220, 231, 233, 234, 256, 257, 258–59,
   260–62
and synecdoche 10, 59, 66, 214, 217,
   228
theological, vs. literary trope (see also
   rhetoric) 78–81, 82, 164
three-fold theory of in Origen 46
and translation 242–43
and tripartite theology 28
and *Trauerspiel* (see Benjamin, Walter,
   and *Trauerspiel*)
typological 149, 163, 229, 238
as veil or integument 76–78, 105, 111,
   126, 153, 163, 167
and writing 24–25
Allen, Michael J. B. 171
Ambrose 76, 181
analogy vs. anomaly 31
Anaxagoras ix, 19, 20
anecdote 85
Antisthenes 27
Apocalypse, book of (see Revelation, book
   of)
Apollodorus of Athens 32
Apollonius Rhodius x, 35–36
Aquinas, Thomas xiv, 5, 69, 78–81, 82, 125,
   163, 165
Aratus 32, 35
Archilochus ix
Ariosto, Ludovico xviii
Aristarchus x, 31, 32, 35
Aristophanes x, 17, 18, 23
Aristophanes of Byzantium 31
Aristotle x, 15, 26–27, 33, 44, 59, 68, 92,
   130, 139, 154, 164, 175, 187, 196, 202,
   206, 207, 218, 246, 255
   On Interpretation 44
   Metaphysics 26
   Poetics 164, 207
Arminius, Jacobus 178

Armstrong, A. H. 58
Arnulf of Orléans xiv, 114, 145, 151
l'art pour l'art 252
Artaud, Antonin 278
Artemidorus of Daldis xi, 63
Arthur legends 150, 155–57
`Aṭṭār, Farīd al-Dīn xiv, 92, 93 94
Atwood, Margaret xxiii, 272–73
audience, control of 162, 173–76
Auerbach, Erich 84, 149
Augustine xii, 5, 28, 69, 71, 74, 76–78, 79,
   81, 102, 141, 149, 179, 181
authorial intention 61, 123, 131, 135, 152,
   164, 179
autobiography 238
autos sacramentales 8, 194–95
Avempace (Ibn Bājja) xiii, 90
Averroes (Ibn Rushd) xiii, 90
Avicenna (Ibn Sīna) xiii, 88–90, 91

Babel 244
Babylonia 63
Bacis 63
Baïf, Jean Antoine de 200
Baillie, Joanna 216
Baker, Bobby 277
Bakhtin, Mikhail xxii, 270, 273
Bale, John 193
Balet comique de la Royne xix, 192–93,
   200
ballet de cour 200–01
Bardi, Giovanni xviii, 201
baroque drama 241, 245, 246–49, 250,
   253
Barth, John xxii, 267, 269
Barthes, Roland 273
Baudelaire, Charles xxi, 242, 249–52
Baudrillard, Jean 270
beauty (see aesthetics)
Beckett, Samuel xxii, 268, 276
Bede xii, 5
Benjamin, Walter (and see *Trauerspiel*) xxii,
   8, 10, 141, 218, 241–53, 260, 276, 277
   The Origin of German Tragic Drama
   241–53, 257, 268
   Arcades Project 242, 249–52
Benvenuto da Imola 165
Bernard of Clairvaux xiii
Bernardus Silvestris xiii, 5, 6, 102, 107,
   108–10, 114
Bersuire, Pierre 145
Beza, Theodore 177

Bible (see also individual books) 40, 69, 75,
  101, 128, 130, 133, 163, 186, 218, 231,
  232, 237–40
  Hebrew Bible 39
  Old Testament 39, 40, 50, 73, 74, 75, 80,
    134, 179, 191, 238
  New Testament 74–75, 181, 238
Bidermann, Jakob xix, 194
Bien-Avisé, Mal-Avisé xvii, 192
Blake, William xx, 212–15, 232
  Visions of the Daughters of Albion 213
Blanqui, Louis-Auguste 251–52
Bloomfield, Morton 269
Boccaccio, Giovanni xv, 142, 144, 162,
  163–66, 167–68, 170, 173, 175, 232
Boethius xii, 7, 108, 125, 137, 140, 141,
  146, 197
Boiardo, Matteo Maria xvii, 162, 169–70,
  175
Boileau-Despréaux, Nicolas 176
Bonaventure xiv, 173
Brabant, Duke of 139
Bracciolini, Poggio xvi
Brecht, Bertolt xxii, 242, 253, 276–77
Brisson, Luc 58
Bromberg, Ellen 279
Brossard, Nicole xxiii, 275
Brown, Jane K. 5
Bruni, Leonardo 196
Bucer, Martin 177
Buell, Lawrence 231–33
Bunyan, John xix, 189–90
Burgess, Anthony xxii, 268
Burkert, Walter 22

Calcidius 4, 105
Calderón de la Barca, Pedro xix, 8, 191,
  194–95
Calixt, Georg 178
Calvin, John (see also Christianity,
  Calvinism) 177, 188
Cambridge Platonists (see Neoplatonism)
Camerarius, Joachim 177
Camões, Luís Vaz de xviii, 162, 168–69,
  170, 175
Camus, Albert xxii, 269
Canticles (see Song of Songs)
Cappadocian Church Fathers 69
captivity narratives 238
Carter, Angela xxiii, 272
Casaubon, Isaac 178
Caspar von Lohenstein, Daniel xx, 245
Cassian, John xii, 4, 72, 74–75, 79, 81

Castle of Perseverance xvii, 192, 204–06
Castor and Pollux 107
Cavalieri, Emilio de xviii, 194
cave of the nymphs 60–62, 213
Caxton, William xvii
Chaldean Oracles xi, 63, 65
Chamaeleon 27
Charles d'Orléans xvi
Chartier, Alain xvi
Chaucer, Geoffrey xvi, 6, 110, 140, 142,
  143, 144
Chemnitz, Martin 177
Chrétien de Troyes xiii
Christine de Pizan xvi, 145–46, 147
Christianity (see also religion; mysticism) 1,
  3, 4–5, 44, 51, 69, 106
  biblical hermeneutics 39–54, 71–82,
    128–35, 149, 163, 168, 178, 181, 192,
    249–50
  Calvinism 184, 188, 230, 234, 238
  Catholicism 193, 194
  Christ 40, 45, 73, 80, 126, 132, 134, 149,
    156, 158, 159, 160, 181, 183, 184, 185,
    190, 191, 233, 235, 236
  Church 75, 133, 134, 149, 160, 185, 193,
    231, 237
  crucifixion 49, 50, 155, 156, 159
  Eucharist 156, 185, 188, 194–95
  Great Awakening 230
  incarnation 46, 47, 48, 50, 51
  logos 39, 42, 44, 46, 47, 50–51
  literalism in (see literalism)
  Presbyterianism 186
  Protestantism 8, 9, 163, 174, 177–90,
    193, 197, 229, 234, 237–40, 248
  Puritans 183, 229, 234, 237
  Reformation 177, 184, 185, 230, 248,
    249
  Trinity 106, 126, 154, 203, 235
  Unitarianism 229
Chrysippus x, 30, 31
Cicero x, 27, 133, 142, 164
Cleanness xvi
Cleanthes x, 29, 30, 33–34
Clement 45
Cohen, Hermann 245
Coleridge, Samuel Taylor xxi, 9, 70, 190,
  208, 217–20, 230, 231, 233, 234,
  260–61
Colonna, Francesco
Commedia (see Dante Alighieri)
commodity 250, 251
conceptual art 276, 277

contemplation 45, 64, 166
Conti, Natale xviii, 200
Copeland, Rita 149, 153
Coppe, Abiezer 189
Corinthians 49
Corneille, Pierre xix
Cornutus x, 30, 33, 60
Council of Sens 107
Council of Trent 193, 206
Counter-Reformation 7, 8, 193, 194–95,
    249
Crates of Mallus x, 31–33
Cronius 60
Cudworth, Ralph 184

dance (see also drama) 196, 197, 201, 277,
    279
Daniel 185
Dante Alighieri xv, 5, 7, 82, 92, 108, 115,
    128–35, 142, 146, 164, 167, 170, 175,
    191, 214
    Commedia 7, 82, 92, 128–35, 141, 146,
        162, 164, 166, 191, 214
    Convivio 129–33, 163
    Epistle to Cangrande 82, 129–30,
        133–35
    Vita Nuova 173
d'Aubigné, Agrippa xix, 7
Davidson, Della 279
Dawson, David 19, 40–41, 45, 52
deconstruction 254–65
Defoe, Daniel 91, 262
Deguileville, Guillaume de xv, 148, 150,
    154
de Man, Paul xxii, 10, 141, 218, 224, 254,
    259–65, 271, 272
Demetrius xi, 37
Democritus x, 17
Denys the Carthusian xvii, 73, 81
Derrida, Jacques xxii, 254, 256, 272
Derveni Papyrus x, 2, 19–22, 25, 58, 63
Descartes, René 207
Deschamps, Eustache xvi, 140, 142
Dezir a las siete virtudes xvii
Diamond, Elin 276, 277
Diego de San Pedro xvii
Diogenes of Apollonia 22
Diogenes of Babylon 32
Diogenes Laertius 30
Dionysius the Areopagite, Pseudo- xii, 4, 69,
    181, 207
drama (see also Trauerspiel and baroque
    drama) 8, 191–208, 278–79

dreams 6, 63, 110, 121, 122, 123, 127, 136,
    138, 140, 141–43, 154, 158, 159–61,
    189, 190, 196, 267
Drusius, Johannes 178
Dryden, John xix
du Bellay, Joachim xviii, 200
Dubos, Jean-Baptiste

Eckhart, Meister xv, 69
Edwards, Mark 41, 45
Egypt 61, 63, 65, 208, 221
Elckerlijk 193
Elizabethan tragedgy (see also drama) 194
Emerson, Ralph Waldo xxi, 9, 229, 230,
    232, 233–37, 239, 240
Empedocles 61
Enlightenment 230
Enos, Richard 43
Enrique de Villena xvi
Epicurus 27, 30
Epifano, Kim 279
Episcopius, Simon 178
Epistle to Cangrande (see Dante Alighieri)
Epistles of the Brethren of Purity (Ikhwān
    al-Ṣafā') xiii, 87
Erasmus, Desiderius xvii, 179, 180–83
Eriugena, John Scotus xii, 4, 69, 104
eros (see allegory, eros in)
esotericism 3, 48, 49, 65, 66, 73, 88, 102,
    127, 141, 167, 197, 206
Etchells, Tim 278
etymology (as interpretive technique) 2, 18,
    20–21, 29, 30, 32, 37, 58, 61, 179
euhemerism 111, 115, 151, 162, 167–69
Euripides 29, 32
Everyman xviii, 193
Évrart de Conty xv
Exodus, book of 53, 182
expressionism 241
expressionist drama 246

fable 266
Fairie Queene (see Spenser, Edmund)
Fall, myth of 244
Farrar, Frederic 178
Fattāhī 97
Federigo of Arezzo 163, 164, 165
Fenner, Dudley 183
Ficino, Marsilio xvii, 70, 171, 173–74, 197
film 279
Il Fiore xv
first-person narration 120, 121, 122, 123,
    124, 136, 145, 147

Fletcher, Angus 8, 176, 268
Foucault, Michel 273
Franklin, Benjamin 233
Fraunce, Abraham 185
free will 181
Frei, Hans W. 231
French Revolution 216–17
Freneau, Philip xx, 230
Freud, Sigmund xxi, 267
Froissart, Jean xvi, 139–40, 142
Frye, Northrop xxii, 255–56, 260, 264, 268
Fulgentius xii, 3, 145
Fuzūlī xviii, 98

Gadamer, Hans-Georg xxii, 254, 256–59, 260, 265
Galatians 74
Gallus, Thomas xiv
García Márquez, Gabriel xxii, 274
Garcilaso de la Vega xviii
Garden of Eden 160
Genealogy of the Gentile Gods (see Boccaccio)
Genesis, book of 61, 74, 76, 81, 174, 179–80, 242
Genet, Jean 278
Gersonides xv
Gerusalemme conquistata (see Tasso, Torquato)
Gerusalemme liberata (see Tasso, Torquato)
Giovanni del Virgilio 145
Gnosticism 62
Goethe, J. W. xx, 9, 217, 260
Golding, William xxii, 268, 269
Góngora, Luis de xix
Gonzalo de Berceo xiv
Gorgias of Leontini ix, 15, 22–23, 42–44
Gower, John xv, 144–45, 154
Greenblatt, Stephen 269
Gregory the Great xii, 72, 74, 76–78, 149
Grotius, Hugo 178
Gryphius, Andreas xix, 245
Guillaume de Lorris (see Roman de la Rose)
Gura, Philip 231

Hallmann, Johann Christian xx, 245
Harsdörffer, Georg Philipp xix
Hawes, Stephen xviii
Hawthorne, Nathaniel xxi, 229, 239–40
Hazlitt, William xxi, 211, 220
Hegel, G. W. F. xx, 220–22, 224
Heidegger, Martin xxii, 35, 254–55
Heine, Heinrich xxi

Hennessey, Keith 279
Henry of Navarre 200
Heracleides Ponticus 27
Heraclitus ix, 18, 61
Heraclitus the Allegorist xi, 33, 37
Hermann of Carinthia 107
Hermann von Sachsenheim xvi
hermeneutics (see also interpretation; see also Christianity, hermeneutics) 1, 41, 59, 229, 254–65
Hermeticism 62, 109, 197
Hermias 33
Hesiod ix, 16, 17, 22, 24, 29, 30, 32, 36, 39, 66
hieroglyphs 208
Hilary of Poitiers 179, 181
Hildegard of Bingen xiii
Hobbes, Thomas xix, 178
Hoccleve, Thomas xvi, 146–47
Hoffmansthal, Hugo von xxi
Holquist, Michael 270, 273
Homer ix, 3, 16, 17, 18, 24, 26, 29, 30, 36, 39, 58, 63, 66, 176, 180, 192, 214
"Homer from Homer" 31, 61
L'Homme juste et l'homme mondain xviii, 192
Honig, Edwin 271
Horace 183
Hosea, book of 189
Hugh of St. Victor xiii, 78–79
Humanism 4, 164, 178, 183, 196
Hunt, Leigh 211, 223
hyponoia (see allegory, and hyponoia)

Iamblichus xi, 63, 64–66, 67, 197
Ibn al-Muqaffaʿ xii, 85
Ibn al-Nafis 90
Ibn ʿArabī, Muḥyī al-Din xiv, 93, 95–96
Ibn Bājja (see Avempace)
Ibn Ezra (see Abraham ben Ezra)
Ibn Sīna (see Avicenna)
Ibn Ṭufail xiii, 88, 90
imagination 215, 217, 220–22
imitation (see mimêsis)
India 221
Íñigo López de Mendoza xvi
intention (see authorial intention)
intermedio (see also dance) 201, 207
interpretation (see also allegory, as interpretation; Christianity, hermeneutics; hermeneutics) 1, 39, 42, 46, 48, 50, 52, 59, 66

irony (see rhetoric, irony)
Irvine, Martin 51
Isidore of Seville xii
Islam (see also Qur'an; religion) 1, 3, 7,
    83–100
    Muhammad 83, 84
Isocrates 24

Jāmī, 'Abd al-Raḥmān xvii, 98
Jean d'Hanville xiv, 114
Jean de Meun (see Roman de la Rose)
Jerome xi, 180, 181
Jerusalem 71, 75, 154, 157, 195, 203
Johannes von Tepl xvi
John, Gospel of 46, 185
John of Bohemia 139
John of Garland 145
John of Salisbury 107
Johnson, Samuel xx
Jonah 238
Jones, Inigo 201
Jonson, Ben xix, 201, 208
Joyce, James 268
journey (see allegory, journey in)
Juan de Mena xvii
Judah ha-Levi xiii
Judaism (see also religion) 1, 3, 42, 44, 46,
    51, 77, 90, 101, 192, 195, 197
    and midrash 52–54
    Rabbinic 52–54, 179

Kafka, Franz xxi, 242, 268, 278
Kalīla wa-Ḍimna, Book of 85
Kant, Immanuel xx, 257
Kantor, Tadeusz 278
Keats, John xxi, 222, 225–26
Kermode, Frank 271
khabar (see anecdote)
Kierkegaard, Søren 262
Kolve, V. A. 194
Koran (see Qur'an)
Kristeva, Julia 10
Kroetsch, Robert 270

Laclau, Ernesto 272
Lactantius xi
Lamberton, Robert 18
Landino, Christoforo xvii, 166
Langland, William (Piers Plowman) xv, 7,
    159–61
language, theories of 20–21, 28, 31, 34,
    42–46, 52–54, 66, 103–08, 180,
    235

Larson, R. P. 47
Lee, Alice 274
Letter to Anebo 65
Life of Homer (see Plutarch, Pseudo-)
Lightfoot, John 178
literalism 39, 72, 73, 78–81, 82, 129, 132,
    135, 149, 166, 177–90, 231
Llull, Ramón xiv
Locke, John xx, 9, 178, 207
Loggins, Michael Bernard 279
logos (see also Stoicism; Christianity; and
    Platonism) 51
London 228
Longinus 215
love (see allegory, eros in)
Lucretius 17, 27
Luke, Gospel of 49, 50
Luther, Martin xviii, 177–82, 188, 248
Lycurgus of Athens 23
Lydgate, John xvi, 147
Lynch, David 279

Machaut, Guillaume de xv, 142
Macrobius xii, 4, 6, 64, 104, 110, 119, 120,
    122, 123, 142, 197
macrocosm (see microcosm and macrocosm)
magic 44, 45, 64, 66, 68, 174, 221
Maimonides xiv, 90
Manilius 172
Marguerite de Valois 200
Marlowe, Christopher xix, 194
Martianus Capella xii, 7, 16, 107, 108,
    109
Marx, Karl 250
Masen, Jakob xix, 194
masquerade (see also drama) 196, 207
Mather, Cotton 238
Matthew, Gospel of 183, 195
Matthiessen, F. O. 229
Mechthild von Magdeburg xiv
Medici 196, 200
medicine 42, 239
Melanchthon, Philipp xviii, 177
Melville, Herman xxi, 229, 239, 240
metaphor 2, 4, 10, 15, 19, 29, 37, 68, 77,
    78–81, 82, 101, 112, 121, 141, 143,
    149, 178, 180, 185, 191, 192, 237
metonymy (see rhetoric, metonymy)
Metrodorus of Lampsacus ix, 18, 19
microcosm and macrocosm 88, 108–09, 171,
    197, 201
midrash (see Judaism)
Middle Platonism (see Platonism)

Miller, J. Hillis 271
Milton, John xix, 6, 169, 189, 190, 211,
    219, 222
mimêsis 23, 24, 57, 59, 66–68, 70, 121, 126,
    159, 207
Der Minne Lehre xv
Minnis, A. J. 129, 149
Mirrors for Princes 86
Mithraism 61
Mnouchkine, Ariane 278
modernism 241, 242, 253, 255, 256
Monteverdi, Claudio 207
morality plays (and see drama) 192–93, 195,
    200
More, Thomas xviii
Moses 42, 45, 46, 48, 50, 134, 139, 179,
    238
Moses Nahmanides xiv
Mouffe, Chantal 272
Mūsā ibn Maimūn (see Maimonides)
Musaeus 17, 29
music 137, 197, 200, 201
De mysteriis 65–66, 67
mystery plays 193, 247
mystery religions 1, 19–22, 26, 66, 68, 104,
    202
mysticism 7, 59, 63, 64, 73, 140, 149, 191,
    232, 233, 236
  apophatic 69, 207
  Christian 69, 73
  Islamic 83, 85, 86–87, 91, 92–97
myth and mythography 2, 3, 6, 22, 25, 26,
    28, 58, 66, 103, 105, 114, 125, 126,
    136, 138, 139, 140, 142, 143, 145, 150,
    152, 164, 171, 255

Nabokov, Vladimir xxii
Native American captivity narratives (see
    captivity narratives)
nature, Nature, natura (see also allegory,
    as cosmogony) 101, 104, 126, 137,
    143, 152, 206, 230, 233, 235, 236,
    239
negative theology (see mysticism, apophatic)
Nietzsche 35, 264
Neoclassicism 8, 211–12, 217, 219, 221
Neoplatonism
  Cambridge Platonists 184
  Late antique 3–4, 8, 9, 27, 33, 57–70, 92,
    104, 109, 120, 126, 143, 163, 166–67,
    170, 197, 214, 217, 221, 232, 233–37
  Renaissance 171, 173–74, 197–200, 202,
    206–07

Nicholas of Lyra xv, 71–74, 77, 78, 81, 168,
    173
Niẓām al-Mulk 86
Noé, Ilya 277
Notker the German (Notker Labeo) of
    St. Gall xiii
Novalis xxi
Numenius of Apamea xi, 57, 60, 62
numerology 158

Okri, Ben xxiii, 274
Opitz, Martin xix, 245, 246
Oresteia (Aeschylus) 278
Origen xi, 3, 39–54, 57, 71, 73, 74, 75–76,
    77, 81, 180, 181
Orpheus and Orphic poetry 2, 17, 19–22,
    29, 63, 107, 130, 132–33, 134, 163,
    174, 197
Orwell, George xxii, 267, 268
Osiander, Andreas 177
Ottoman Turkish literature 98–99
Ovid 114, 120, 121, 122, 124, 125, 130,
    132, 137, 139, 140, 142, 144, 146,
    151–54, 170, 172, 180
Ovide moralisé xv, 151–54, 155
Owens, Craig 273

painting (see also visual arts) 226–28
Pamuk, Orhan xxiii, 275
Paradise Lost (see Milton, John)
Paris, University of 125
Parmenides ix, 43, 44
pathos 216
Patience xvi
Paul 3, 39, 45, 48, 148, 180, 181
Peacham, Henry (the Elder) xviii, 183
Pearl xvi, 155, 157–59
Pelerinage de la vie humaine (see Guillaume
    de Deguileville)
Pépin, Jean 18, 130, 133
performance, performativity (see also visual
    arts) 267, 276–80
performance studies 276, 277
Perkins, William 184–85, 188
personification 6–8, 9, 16, 112, 121, 122,
    124–26, 138, 139, 140, 146, 147, 154,
    175–76, 189, 191, 200, 212, 215, 217
Peter 160
Petrarch, Francis xv, 142, 162, 163–66,
    167–68, 169, 173, 175, 191, 195
Pfeiffer, Rudolf 15
phantasia (see imagination)
phenomenology 254

Pherecydes of Syros ix
Philo x, 44–46, 48, 51
Philodemus x, 27, 32
philosophy and philosophical allegory (see
    also Presocratics, Platonism,
    Neoplatonism, Stoicism) 1, 3, 7, 17, 26,
    28, 29, 59, 61, 83, 85, 86, 87 92, 103,
    105, 107, 124, 130, 136, 141, 164, 241,
    242–43, 245–46, 254
Pico della Mirandola, Giovanni xviii, 171,
    174, 206
Pierre de Ronsard (see Ronsard)
Pilgrim's Progress (see Bunyan, John)
Pindar 23
Plato x, 3, 4, 17, 19, 22, 23, 24, 26, 33, 39,
    57, 61, 63, 67, 68, 70, 86, 101, 105–07,
    113, 173, 196, 197, 218, 254
  Euthyphro 22
  Hippias Minor 24
  Ion 19, 23
  Phaedrus 19, 26, 33, 173
  Protagoras 17
  Republic 3, 19, 24, 26, 66–68, 113, 254
  Symposium 24
  Theaetetus 17
  Timaeus 4, 26, 105–07
Platonism and Middle Platonism (see also
    Neoplatonism) 39, 41, 44–46, 51, 57,
    58, 62–64, 171
  logos 44
Pléiade 200
Plotinus (see also Neoplatonism) xi, 58–59,
    63, 208
Plutarch 2, 37
Plutarch, Pseudo- (*Life of Homer*) xi, 33
Poe, Edgar Allan xxi, 229
poet as philosopher 57–70, 133
poet as theologian 57–70, 130–31
Poliziano, Angelo xvii
Porete, Marguerite xv
Porphyry (see also Neoplatonism) xi, 3,
    60–62, 63, 64, 68, 214
poststructuralism 10, 254, 255
Prague School 271
Praxiphanes 27
Presocratics (see also Heraclitus,
    Anaxagoras, Democritus) 19
Prison of Love (*Cárcel de Amor*)
Proclus xii, 3, 59, 63, 66, 173, 197
Prodicus 15, 18
Protagoras 15, 18, 42
Protestantism (see Christianity)
Proust, Marcel 264

Proverbs, book of 74
Prudentius xii, 6–7, 16, 109, 191
Psalms, book of 80, 131, 134
psychoanalysis 10
Ptolemy 92
Pullman, Philip xxiii, 275
Puttenham, George xviii, 186
Pynchon, Thomas xxiii, 270
Pynotheüs 140
Pythagoreanism 66, 68, 197, 207

Qābūs ibn Vushmgīr 86
Querelle du Roman de la Rose xvi
Queste del saint graal xiv, 155–57
Quilligan, Maureen 150, 159, 271
Quintilian xi, 2, 4, 38, 182, 183
Qur'an 84–85, 92, 179

Raad, Walid 279
Rabbis (see Judaism)
Rainer, Yvonne 279
Rastell, John 193
Redford, John 193
Reformation (see Christianity)
religion (see also Christianity; Islam;
    Judaism; mysticism; mystery religions)
    8, 9, 19–22, 29, 32, 61, 203
Remigius of Auxerre xii
Renart, Jean 137
Reuchlin, Johannes xvii
Revelation, book of 150, 158, 168, 173,
    185, 188, 206
rhetoric 4, 9, 10, 16, 37–38, 42–44, 60, 79,
    84, 99, 112, 119, 124, 127, 137, 143,
    153, 163, 229, 233, 242–44, 254, 255,
    257, 266
  vs. allegory in Protestant hermeneutics
    177–86
  catachresis 267
  ekphrasis 149
  irony 4, 266
  metaphor (see metaphor)
  metonymy 10, 19, 112, 236, 237
  polyonymy 19
  simile 19
  synecdoche (see allegory, and synecdoche)
Rhetorica ad Herennium x
Richardson, N. J. 15, 18, 23, 24
Richter, Jean Paul 218
Ricoeur, Paul xxii, 84, 254
Ridewall, John 145
Rilke, Rainer Maria xxi
Ripa, Cesare xix, 206

Robbe-Grillet, Alain xxii, 269
Robertson, D. W. 141
Rolle, Richard xv
Roman de la Rose 6, 7, 110, 112, 115,
    119–27, 136–40, 148, 152, 154, 158,
    166, 191, 262
    Jean de Meun xv, 5, 115, 119, 124–27,
        130, 136, 137, 144, 154
    Guillaume de Lorris xiv, 5, 119–24, 126,
        136–39, 142
romance 115, 119–27, 151
Romanticism 8, 9, 70, 178, 208, 211–28,
    230, 256, 257, 260, 261, 262, 263
Ronsard, Pierre de xviii, 200
Rosler, Martha 277
Rousseau, Jean-Jacques xx, 222, 261, 262,
    263, 264
Rowlandson, Mary 239
Ruiz, Juan xv
Rūmī, Jalāl al-Dīn xiv, 92, 94–95
Rushdie, Salman 274
Ruskin, John xxi

Sachs, Hans xviii
Samuel ibn Tibbon xiv
Sanā'ī xiii, 92–93
Sartre, Jean-Paul xxii, 269
Satyrus 27
Scaliger, Julius Caesar 178
Schelling, F. W. J. 70, 217
Schiller, Friedrich von xx
Schlegel, A. W. xx
Schlegel, K. W. F. xxi
Schmitt, Carl 247, 248
Scholasticism 130, 163, 164, 171, 178,
    179
Scripture (see Bible)
Sebald, W. G. xxiii, 275
secrecy, see esotericism
Seneca 164
Servius xi, 3, 36, 37, 167, 173
Sextus Empiricus 42
Şeyh Galip xx, 99
Shakespeare, William xix
Shelley, Mary xxi, 214–15
Shelley, Percy Bysshe xxi, 222–25
Sherman, Cindy xxiii, 278
Sherry, Richard 182
Sibyl 146
Sibylline Oracles 63
Sidney, Sir Philip xix, 186
Simonides 17
Sir Gawain and the Green Knight xvi

Skelton, John xvii, 193
Solomon ibn Gabirol (Avicebron) xiii
Song of Songs, book of 40, 53, 73, 77, 80,
    81, 184
sophists 19, 24, 43
Spenser, Edmund xix, 6, 7–8, 102, 115, 162,
    166, 167, 171–73, 174–76, 186–88,
    190, 211, 219, 228
Speusippus 27
Sprat, Thomas 102
Stoicism (see also Zeno of Citium, Cleanthes,
    and Chrysippus) 3, 26–28, 34, 36, 58,
    61, 68, 109
    logos 28, 34, 37, 44
structuralism 254
Suhrawardī xiv, 89, 91
Susenbrotus, Johannes xviii
Suso, Heinrich xv
Swedenborg, Emanuel xx
Swift, Jonathan xx, 9
symbol (see also allegory, and symbolon) 9,
    244, 255
sympathy (see allegory, and ontological
    connection)
synecdoche (see rhetoric)

Le Tableau allégorique des moeurs xx,
    194
Tasso, Torquato xviii, 162, 166, 167,
    174–75, 196, 200, 219
Taylor, Thomas 214
Teatro Farnese 207
Teresa of Avila xviii
Teskey, Gordon 270
theatre studies 276, 277
theatricality (see performance; drama)
theurgy 64–66, 67, 79
Thierry of Chartres xiii, 104,
    107
Thoreau, Henry David xxi, 229
Todorov, Tzvetan 9
Torjesen, Karen 47, 50
tragedy 245, 246, 247
Transcendentalism 9, 230
Trauerspiel (see also Benjamin, Walter) 8,
    10, 207, 241–50
triumph 203
Turner, J. M. W. xxi, 226–28
Tyndale, William 184

Ukeles, Mierle Laderman 277
Usener, Hermann 249

Valla, Lorenzo xvii
Varro x, 29, 33
Vasari, Georgio 196
Vatican Mythographer I xii, 145
Vatican Mythographer II xii, 145
Vatican Mythographer III xiv, 114,
    145
vernacular literature 119, 136–47,
    149
via negativa (see mysticism, apophatic)
Vico, Giambattista xx
Viola, Bill xxiii, 278–79
Virgil x, 3, 36–37, 101, 107, 130, 132, 142,
    146, 162, 163, 165–68, 173, 183
visual arts 278
Vondel, Joost van den xix

Warburg, Aby 248, 249
Weber, Max 248
West, Benjamin 223
Wetherbee, Winthrop 105, 106
Whitman, Jon 150

Whitman, Walt xxi, 229
William of Conches xiii, 105
Williams, William Carlos 212
Wilson, Thomas 183
Wisdom xvii, 192
Wolfram von Eschenbach xiv
Wordsworth, William xx, 215–16, 224,
    228
Wyclif, John xv

Xenocrates 27
Xenophanes ix, 17
Xenophon x, 17
Χρlo 278

Ysengrimus xiv

Zeno of Citium x, 29, 30
Zenodotus 32
Zhang, Longxi 273
Zohar (Moses de Leon) xiv
Zwingli, Huldrych 177

Cambridge Companions to...

AUTHORS

Edward Albee edited by Stephen J. Bottoms

Margaret Atwood edited by
Coral Ann Howells

W. H. Auden edited by Stan Smith

Jane Austen edited by Edward Copeland and
Juliet McMaster

Beckett edited by John Pilling

Aphra Behn edited by Derek Hughes and
Janet Todd

Walter Benjamin edited by David S. Ferris

William Blake edited by Morris Eaves

Brecht edited by Peter Thomson and
Glendyr Sacks (second edition)

The Brontës edited by Heather Glen

Frances Burney edited by Peter Sabor

Byron edited by Drummond Bone

Albert Camus edited by Edward J. Hughes

Willa Cather edited by Marilee Lindemann

Cervantes edited by Anthony J. Cascardi

Chaucer edited by Piero Boitani and Jill Mann
(second edition)

Chekhov edited by Vera Gottlieb and
Paul Allain

Kate Chopin edited by Janet Beer

Coleridge edited by Lucy Newlyn

Wilkie Collins edited by Jenny Bourne Taylor

Joseph Conrad edited by J. H. Stape

Dante edited by Rachel Jacoff (second edition)

Daniel Defoe edited by John Richetti

Don DeLillo edited by John N. Duvall

Charles Dickens edited by John O. Jordan

Emily Dickinson edited by Wendy Martin

John Donne edited by Achsah Guibbory

Dostoevskii edited by W. J. Leatherbarrow

Theodore Dreiser edited by Leonard Cassuto
and Claire Virginia Eby

John Dryden edited by Steven N. Zwicker

W. E. B. Du Bois edited by Shamoon Zamir

George Eliot edited by George Levine

T. S. Eliot edited by A. David Moody

Ralph Ellison edited by Ross Posnock

Ralph Waldo Emerson edited by Joel Porte and
Saundra Morris

William Faulkner edited by
Philip M. Weinstein

Henry Fielding edited by Claude Rawson

F. Scott Fitzgerald edited by Ruth Prigozy

Flaubert edited by Timothy Unwin

E. M. Forster edited by David Bradshaw

Benjamin Franklin edited by Carla Mulford

Brian Friel edited by Anthony Roche

Robert Frost edited by Robert Faggen

Elizabeth Gaskell edited by Jill L. Matus

Goethe edited by Lesley Sharpe

Günter Grass edited by Stuart Taberner

Thomas Hardy edited by Dale Kramer

David Hare edited by Richard Boon

Nathaniel Hawthorne edited by
Richard Millington

Seamus Heaney edited by
Bernard O'Donoghue

Ernest Hemingway edited by Scott Donaldson

Homer edited by Robert Fowler

Horace edited by Stephen Harrison

Ibsen edited by James McFarlane

Henry James edited by Jonathan Freedman

Samuel Johnson edited by Greg Clingham

Ben Jonson edited by Richard Harp and
Stanley Stewart

James Joyce edited by Derek Attridge
(second edition)

Kafka edited by Julian Preece

Keats edited by Susan J. Wolfson

Lacan edited by Jean-Michel Rabaté

D. H. Lawrence edited by Anne Fernihough

Primo Levi edited by Robert Gordon

Lucretius edited by Stuart Gillespie and
Philip Hardie

David Mamet edited by Christopher Bigsby

Thomas Mann edited by Ritchie Robertson

Christopher Marlowe edited by Patrick Cheney

Herman Melville edited by Robert S. Levine

Arthur Miller edited by Christopher Bigsby

Milton edited by Dennis Danielson
(second edition)

Molière edited by David Bradby and
Andrew Calder

Toni Morrison edited by Justine Tally

Nabokov edited by Julian W. Connolly

Eugene O'Neill edited by Michael Manheim
George Orwell edited by John Rodden
Ovid edited by Philip Hardie
Harold Pinter edited by Peter Raby
(second edition)
Sylvia Plath edited by Jo Gill
Edgar Allan Poe edited by Kevin J. Hayes
Alexander Pope edited by Pat Rogers
Ezra Pound edited by Ira B. Nadel
Proust edited by Richard Bales
Pushkin edited by Andrew Kahn
Rilke edited by Karen Leeder and Robert Vilain
Philip Roth edited by Timothy Parrish
Salman Rushdie edited by Abdulrazak Gurnah
Shakespeare edited by Margareta de Grazia
and Stanley Wells
Shakespearean Comedy edited by
Alexander Leggatt
Shakespeare on Film edited by Russell Jackson
(second edition)
Shakespeare's History Plays edited by
Michael Hattaway
Shakespeare's Last Plays edited by
Catherine M. S. Alexander
Shakespeare's Poetry edited by Patrick Cheney
Shakespeare and Popular Culture edited by
Robert Shaughnessy
Shakespeare on Stage edited by Stanley Wells
and Sarah Stanton
Shakespearean Tragedy edited by
Claire McEachern
George Bernard Shaw edited by
Christopher Innes

Shelley edited by Timothy Morton
Mary Shelley edited by Esther Schor
Sam Shepard edited by Matthew C. Roudané
Spenser edited by Andrew Hadfield
Laurence Sterne edited by Thomas Keymer
Wallace Stevens edited by John N. Serio
Tom Stoppard edited by Katherine E. Kelly
Harriet Beecher Stowe edited by
Cindy Weinstein
August Strindberg edited by Michael Robinson
Jonathan Swift edited by Christopher Fox
J. M. Synge edited by P. J. Mathews
Tacitus edited by A. J. Woodman
Henry David Thoreau edited by Joel Myerson
Tolstoy edited by Donna Tussing Orwin
Mark Twain edited by Forrest G. Robinson
Virgil edited by Charles Martindale
Voltaire edited by Nicholas Cronk
Edith Wharton edited by Millicent Bell
Walt Whitman edited by Ezra Greenspan
Oscar Wilde edited by Peter Raby
Tennessee Williams edited by
Matthew C. Roudané
August Wilson edited by Christopher Bigsby
Mary Wollstonecraft edited by
Claudia L. Johnson
Virginia Woolf edited by Sue Roe and
Susan Sellers
Wordsworth edited by Stephen Gill
W. B. Yeats edited by Marjorie Howes and
John Kelly
Zola edited by Brian Nelson

TOPICS

The Actress edited by Maggie B. Gale and
John Stokes
The African American Novel edited by
Maryemma Graham
The African American Slave Narrative edited by
Audrey A. Fisch
Allegory edited by Rita Copeland and
Peter T. Struck
American Modernism edited by
Walter Kalaidjian
American Realism and Naturalism edited by
Donald Pizer
American Travel Writing edited by
Alfred Bendixen and Judith Hamera

American Women Playwrights edited by
Brenda Murphy
Arthurian Legend edited by Elizabeth Archibald
and Ad Putter
Australian Literature edited by Elizabeth Webby
British Romanticism edited by Stuart Curran
British Romantic Poetry edited by
James Chandler and Maureen N. McLane
British Theatre, 1730–1830 edited by
Jane Moody and Daniel O'Quinn
Canadian Literature edited by
Eva-Marie Kröller
Children's Literature edited by M. O. Grenby
and Andrea Immel

The Classic Russian Novel edited by Malcolm V. Jones and Robin Feuer Miller

Contemporary Irish Poetry edited by Matthew Campbell

Crime Fiction edited by Martin Priestman

Early Modern Women's Writing edited by Laura Lunger Knoppers

The Eighteenth-Century Novel edited by John Richetti

Eighteenth-Century Poetry edited by John Sitter

English Literature, 1500–1600 edited by Arthur F. Kinney

English Literature, 1650–1740 edited by Steven N. Zwicker

English Literature, 1740–1830 edited by Thomas Keymer and Jon Mee

English Novelists edited by Adrian Poole

English Poetry, Donne to Marvell edited by Thomas N. Corns

English Poets edited by Claude Rawson

English Renaissance Drama, second edition edited by A. R. Braunmuller and Michael Hattaway

English Restoration Theatre edited by Deborah C. Payne Fisk

Feminist Literary Theory edited by Ellen Rooney

Fiction in the Romantic Period edited by Richard Maxwell and Katie Trumpener

The Fin de Siècle edited by Gail Marshall

The French Novel: from 1800 to the Present edited by Timothy Unwin

German Romanticism edited by Nicholas Saul

Gothic Fiction edited by Jerrold E. Hogle

The Greek and Roman Novel edited by Tim Whitmarsh

Greek and Roman Theatre edited by Marianne McDonald and J. Michael Walton

Greek Mythology edited by Roger D. Woodard

Greek Tragedy edited by P. E. Easterling

The Harlem Renaissance edited by George Hutchinson

The Irish Novel edited by John Wilson Foster

The Italian Novel edited by Peter Bondanella and Andrea Ciccarelli

Jewish American Literature edited by Hana Wirth-Nesher and Michael P. Kramer

The Latin American Novel edited by Efraín Kristal

The Literature of the First World War edited by Vincent Sherry

The Literature of World War II edited by Marina MacKay

Literature on Screen edited by Deborah Cartmell and Imelda Whelehan

Medieval English Literature edited by Larry Scanlon

Medieval English Theatre edited by Richard Beadle and Alan J. Fletcher (second edition)

Medieval French Literature edited by Simon Gaunt and Sarah Kay

Medieval Romance edited by Roberta L. Krueger

Medieval Women's Writing edited by Carolyn Dinshaw and David Wallace

Modern American Culture edited by Christopher Bigsby

Modern British Women Playwrights edited by Elaine Aston and Janelle Reinelt

Modern French Culture edited by Nicholas Hewitt

Modern German Culture edited by Eva Kolinsky and Wilfried van der Will

The Modern German Novel edited by Graham Bartram

Modern Irish Culture edited by Joe Cleary and Claire Connolly

Modern Italian Culture edited by Zygmunt G. Barański and Rebecca J. West

Modern Latin American Culture edited by John King

Modern Russian Culture edited by Nicholas Rzhevsky

Modern Spanish Culture edited by David T. Gies

Modernism edited by Michael Levenson

The Modernist Novel edited by Morag Shiach

Modernist Poetry edited by Alex Davis and Lee M. Jenkins

Narrative edited by David Herman

Native American Literature edited by Joy Porter and Kenneth M. Roemer

Nineteenth-Century American Women's Writing edited by Dale M. Bauer and Philip Gould

Old English Literature edited by Malcolm Godden and Michael Lapidge

Performance Studies edited by Tracy C. Davis

Postcolonial Literary Studies edited by Neil Lazarus

Postmodernism edited by Steven Connor

Renaissance Humanism edited by Jill Kraye

Roman Satire edited by Kirk Freudenburg

The Roman Historians edited by Andrew Feldherr

The Spanish Novel. from 1600 to the Present edited by Harriet Turner and Adelaida López de Martínez

Travel Writing edited by Peter Hulme and Tim Youngs

Twentieth-Century Irish Drama edited by Shaun Richards

The Twentieth-Century English Novel edited by Robert L. Caserio

Twentieth-Century English Poetry edited by Neil Corcoran

Victorian and Edwardian Theatre edited by Kerry Powell

The Victorian Novel edited by Deirdre David

Victorian Poetry edited by Joseph Bristow

War Writing edited by Kate McLoughlin

Writing of the English Revolution edited by N. H. Keeble